Applied Language Studies

Edited by David Crystal

Linguistic Minorities, Policies and Pluralism

Edited by

John Edwards

Department of Psychology
St Francis Xavier University
Antigonish, Nova Scotia, Canada

1984

Academic Press

(Harcourt Brace Jovanovich, Publishers)

London · Orlando · San Diego · San Francisco · New York
Toronto · Montreal · Sydney · Tokyo · São Paulo

ACADEMIC PRESS INC. (LONDON) LTD.
24/28 Oval Road
London NW1

United States Edition published by
ACADEMIC PRESS INC.
(Harcourt Brace Jovanovich, Inc.)
Orlando, Florida 32887

British Library Cataloguing in Publication Data
Linguistic minorities, policies and pluralism.
—(Applied language studies)
1. Linguistic minorities
I. Edwards, J.   II. Series
305.7   P119.315

ISBN 0-12-232760-8
LCCCN 83-73316

Photoset by Paston Press, Norwich
Printed in Great Britain by St Edmundsbury Press, Bury St Edmunds, Suffolk

Contributors

BRIAN M. BULLIVANT, *Monash University, Clayton, Victoria, Australia 3168*

JIM CUMMINS, *Modern Language Centre, Ontario Institute for Studies in Education, 252 Bloor Street West, Toronto, Ontario M5S 1V6, Canada*

GLENDON F. DRAKE, *California State University, Long Beach, California 90840, USA*

CAROL M. EASTMAN, *University of Washington, Seattle, Washington 98195, USA*

JOHN EDWARDS, *Department of Psychology, St Francis Xavier University, Antigonish, Nova Scotia B2G 1C0, Canada*

VIV EDWARDS, *18 Morgan Road, Reading, Berks, UK*

PHILIP GLEASON, *University of Notre Dame, Notre Dame, Indiana 46556, USA*

WILLIAM F. MACKEY, *Centre International de Recherche sur le Bilinguisme, Université Laval, Quebéc, P.Q. G1K 7P4, Canada*

TOVE SKUTNABB-KANGAS, *Nyvej 17, DK 4050 Skibby, Denmark*

COLIN H. WILLIAMS, *Department of Geography, North Staffordshire Polytechnic, Stoke-on-Trent ST4 2DE, UK*

Biographical Notes

BRIAN BULLIVANT is Reader in Education, Monash University. He was chairman of the university's Centre for Migrant Studies for 1977–78, and director of the cross-national Survey of Teacher Education for Pluralist Societies (STEPS) during 1978–79. His major fields of interest are the anthropology of education and ethnographic research methodology. His publications include *The Way of Tradition: Life in an Orthodox Jewish School* (1978), *The Pluralist Dilemma in Education* (1981) and *Race, Ethnicity and Curriculum* (1981).

JIM CUMMINS is Assistant Professor, Modern Language Centre, Ontario Institute for Studies in Education. He received his PhD from the University of Alberta in 1974. His research interests include minority group achievement, bilingualism and reading disability. He was the recipient (with J. P. Das) of the International Reading Association's Albert J. Harris Award (1979), for the best paper on detection and remediation of reading disability.

GLENDON DRAKE is Vice President for Academic Affairs, California State University. Previous positions include Dean of Arts and Science, University of Michigan (Flint) and Chairman, Linguistics Department, San Diego State University. He is the author of *The Role of Prescriptivism in American Linguistics, 1820–1975* (1977), and of "Ethnicity, values and language policy in the United States".

CAROL EASTMAN is Professor of Anthropology and Adjunct Professor of Linguistics, University of Washington. Her major interests include anthropological linguistics and sociolinguistics; she has studied Swahili-speaking areas in East Africa and the Haida language in North America. She has written *Aspects of Language and Culture* (1975), *Linguistic Theory and Language Description* (1978) and *Language Planning: An Introduction* (1982).

JOHN EDWARDS is Associate Professor, Department of Psychology, St Francis Xavier University. His research interests include language and educational disadvantage, bilingual education and the language/identity relationship. He is the author of *Language and Disadvantage* (1979), *The Social Psychology of Reading* (1981) and *The Irish Language* (1983). Another work, *Language and Identity*, is currently in preparation. Dr Edwards is the review editor of the *Journal of Language and Social Psychology*.

VIV EDWARDS is the author of *The West Indian Language Issue in British Schools* (1979) and *Language in Multicultural Classrooms* (1983). She has taught socio-linguistics and worked widely in pre-service and in-service teacher training. She currently co-directs the SSRC project "Patterns of Language Use in the British Black Community" in Reading.

PHILIP GLEASON is Professor of History, University of Notre Dame. His interests include American intellectual and social history, with emphasis on ethnic history and that of Catholicism. He is the author of "American identity and Americaniza-tion" in the *Harvard Encyclopedia of American Ethnic Groups* and of "Americans all: World War II and the shaping of American identity".

WILLIAM MACKEY is Professor in the Centre International de Recherche sur le Bilinguisme, Université Laval. He is a fellow of the Royal Academy of Belgium and of the Royal Society of Canada. He studied at Laval, Manitoba, Harvard and Geneva, and has taught in several universities in Europe and America. He has served on national language commissions in Australia, Canada and Ireland, and is the author of more than two dozen books and two hundred articles on bilingual education, language policy and language teaching.

TOVE SKUTNABB-KANGAS was raised and educated in both Finnish and Swedish. Currently guest researcher at the University of Roskilde, she has been associated with Helsinki, Lund and Harvard University. Her major interest is the way in which the powerless status of minorities is reproduced in different countries; this is the subject of a forthcoming book, *Bilingualism or Not: The Education of Minorities*.

COLIN WILLIAMS is Senior Lecturer, Department of Geography, North Stafford-shire Polytechnic. Educated at the University of Wales and the University of Western Ontario, he was a Visiting Professor and Fulbright Scholar at Pennsyl-vania State University during 1982–83. He is interested in political geography and comparative ethnic relations, and has written *National Separatism* (1982). He is the founder editor of *Discussion Papers in Geolinguistics*.

Preface

Linguistic minority groups are much in the news nowadays. Of clear intrinsic interest, they also provide a useful perspective on group relations and can tell us much about the aims, purposes and values held by the societies in which they exist. The existence and the study of minority groups raise questions about the structure of society—about perceptions of pluralism and assimilation—which might otherwise not be discussed. Within the general area of minority group studies, language matters play a particularly important part. This is because language is one of the most salient group markers; indeed, some regard a distinctive group language as an essential component of a unique identity.

The aim of this book is to examine the current position of some linguistic minority groups, and the policies (particularly educational) which affect them. Of special concern is the relationship between language and identity which, for some at least, is the essence of the pluralism-assimilation question. While it has obviously been impossible to deal exhaustively with the subject, the reader will find here both specific illustrations of minority status and policy and general discussions of important and recurring features of minority matters. Although there is a large literature, both popular and academic, dealing with linguistic minority groups, treatment has not always been unbiased. As one might expect in an area in which academic interest and social policy can intersect, there has been a considerable amount of advocatory and polemical writing. It has been an aim in the present collection, therefore, to try and avoid this pitfall and to attempt an objective account of minority history, status and policy.

At the most general level, the book attempts to assemble information bearing upon rationales and policies for linguistic and cultural pluralism. In fact, it is the hope of the contributors that readers will find in this collection a balanced and reasonable account of assimilation and pluralism—an account which has so far been lacking in the literature. At the very least, the chapters here demonstrate that there is not a simple opposition between pluralism and assimilation, that there are difficulties with educational programmes intended to support minority group language and identity, that minority views are not themselves homogeneous, and that advocates of cultural pluralism often hold over-simplified and unrealistic ideas. At the same time, it will be seen that pluralism has strong attractions for certain groups and that, as a philosophical position, it is not without merit. The task confronting the serious student of minority issues is the separation of fact from wish, of objective assessment from subjective polemic. I hope this book will be useful in this effort.

February 1984   JOHN EDWARDS

Contents

Introduction

John Edwards

I think it is fair to say that, in recent years, there has been a great resurgence of interest, among the academic community, in minority languages and linguistic groups. Furthermore, there has been a considerable swing from the espousal of an assimilationist point of view to one which embraces some form of pluralism. The possibility of an enduring, linguistically plural society has animated many writers, some of whom have been apologists for the position, departing from the disinterested and objective stance which we usually associate with scientific treatment. This has led to an increasing confusion in the area of facts and values, of dispassionate assessment and provocative polemic. Drake (1979, chapter 5) has referred to this as a reflection of "Mannheim's Paradox", in which personal values colour perceptions of issues and of data bearing upon them. This is certainly not a problem unique to sociolinguistics, or to social science generally, but its effect is perhaps most pronounced in these areas, which so often deal with matters of immediate and ongoing concern. The naive reader, attempting to grasp modern thinking on such issues as language maintenance, assimilation/pluralism and linguistic identity, will find a confusing mixture of controversy, claim and counterclaim. Often one can faintly hear the grinding of particular axes and, occasionally, these are brought out into full view. It is regrettably true that much special pleading is hidden behind what looks to be objective social science argument—jargon-ridden, illiterate and pretentious though this so often is.

It is important to be able to consider the matters under study here with some historical awareness. While linguistic minorities and the fate of "small"

LINGUISTIC MINORITIES
ISBN 0-12-232760-8

languages are experiencing a renewed attention, questions of linguistic identity, of language shift, of the "new ethnicity" or the "Roots phenomenon", and so on extend back at least to the times of the European linguistic nationalists of the early nineteenth century. Fichte and Herder, Schleiermacher and Humboldt all had pronounced views on the language-identity link (and many of these views can be examined in the works of contemporary writers). To cite an example of their influence, we could consider the Celtic revival movements of the late nineteenth century. Romantic, nationalistic and idealistic in nature, they clearly endorsed sentiments which had gained currency a century and more before. Consider the following:

> Absolutely nothing is so important for a nation's culture as its language.
>
> Humboldt, 1797: see Grafton, 1981

> [By forsaking language], a *Volk* destroys its "self" for language and the national consciousness to which it gives rise are inseparably joined.
>
> Herder, 1772: See Barnard, 1965

> Has a nation anything more precious than the language of its fathers?
>
> Herder: see Berlin, 1976

> The German speaks a language which has been alive ever since it first issued from the force of nature, whereas the other Teutonic races speak a language which has movement on the surface only but is dead at the root.
>
> Fichte, 1807

> A people without a language of its own is only half a nation . . . to lose your native tongue . . . is the worst badge of conquest.
>
> Davis, 1945

The last expression here, made by Davis in 1843, would stand as a motto for the Irish revival movement. Indeed, de Valera (cited in Dwyer, 1980) noted: "If I had to make a choice between political freedom without the language, and the language without political freedom . . . I would choose the latter." Douglas Hyde, first president of the revivalist Gaelic League, summarized much of the pro-Irish sentiment in his famous address on the de-anglicization of Ireland, the essence of which is the necessity for Irish for a true Irish identity (1894). The Irish movement, like others, flourished for about twenty-five years or so, between 1890 and 1915, and presents an instructive example for students of the area (see Edwards, in press (a)). Interest waned, for a number of reasons, but has recently resurfaced and, in this resurgence, it joins with the new wave of linguistic nationalism. A crude documentation of this cycle is given by the number of publications dealing with the sociolinguistics (broadly defined) of Irish (Edwards, 1983). In the five-year periods 1880–1884, 1885–1889 and 1890–1894, less than ten publications per period appeared. In 1895–1899, however, the number rises to 19, in 1900–1904 to 59, in 1905–1909 it is 29 and, in 1910-1914, publications number 47. From this time until the mid-sixties, the average production per five-year period is between 20 and 25. But, between 1965 and 1969, 77 publications were traced, 81 in 1970–1974, 139 between 1975 and 1979, and 82 for the shorter 1980–1982 period. These figures are, of course, not completely accurate, but the trend they reveal is unmistakable. The point is twofold: there is a fairly broad modern interest in Irish, and this interest is not without historical precedent (for more on the Irish situation, see Chapter 10).

Why should this be of concern to the student of linguistic shift among the *Gastarbeiter*, the Chicanos or the Bretons? Can the situation of indigenous linguistic minorities (like the Irish) be profitably compared with that of immigrant populations? There are, of course, important differences among minority populations which may render exact comparisons impossible. However, there are often important similarities, too, which unite the indigenous and immigrant groups. These most often have to do with perceptions of group identity and the role of language therein. An historical awareness and a contemporary cross-cultural perspective are useful if one wishes to avoid reinventing the wheel.

As I have suggested, the "new ethnicity" is not new, but is rather the latest manifestation of concern for immigrant minority groups. Similarly, interest in indigenous minority situations has appeared before. Generally, the modern trend reflects a twentieth-century conception of nationalism which bears considerable resemblance to the form of the last century, with one apparent exception. Nineteenth-century concern for minorities and for the links between language and identity was essentially prescriptive and philosophical. In an area now dominated by social science, early pronounce-ments (such as those I have reproduced above) seem decidedly dated— although they are trotted out whenever it is thought useful. The early views had strong moral overtones, the writers were clearly committed to them and, for ease of consumption, they were often summarized in terse, motto-like statements.

An observer of the modern scene might think all this has changed. Now, writings on the same matters emanate largely from social scientists of various stripes, are backed by elaborate theoretical structures and are supported by empirical data ranging from extensive surveys to reductionist experiments. Yet, as I suggested in the beginning, things have not changed that much. Although modes of expression and acceptable styles have altered, much modern work is *still* essentially polemical and moralistic. This is itself disturbing, for it means that subjectivity is masked by apparent objectivity. How, one might ask, can all the social scientific apparatus now brought to bear on the topic lead to anything other than disinterested assessment? Surely the views of the writer, however impassioned, must give way to the data, however they fall? The answer is that all the apparatus, all the methodology, focusses an inordinate amount of attention upon only one-third of the scientific endeavour. Before it comes the selection and delineation of topics to be addressed, and after it comes interpretation of results. Both of these elements are subjective and no statistical formula exists to guide the researcher.

In the area of linguistic minority research, the first element suffers mainly from selective historical awareness, or none at all. It is easy to select writers from the past who will bolster one's feelings that linguistic nationalism is essentially a social good; but, it is equally easy to ignore others who have been more critical. Toynbee (1956), for example, had rather scathing comments upon the "archaism" of the "nationalistic craze for distinctiveness". Kedourie (1961) expressed at least cautionary remarks on nationalism. These writers are not over-cited. How many, under the guise of a general regard for cultural pluralism, are really interested only in the one group they are writing about? Too often the focus is narrow, lacking an international perspective (or even a broadly national one, for multicultural societies) and exhibiting an historical tunnel vision. In a recent review, Abramson (1983) has suggested that sociological enquiry in America has not come to grips with ethnicity. In particular, he remarks upon a lack of concern for historical developments and for cross-cultural comparison. Indeed, he speculates that this reflects the American interest—in research and in life—for the "here and now". Thus, "there is a kind of unconscious ethnocentrism in the parochiality and culture-bound quality" of work in the area, and "the ahistorical character of most of our research is only too clear" (p. 135). Given the overwhelming American influence on current social science, Abramson's comments are relevant and worrying. If the allegedly objective academic approach is deficient, and if the subject itself is a highly-charged one, and if writers in the area are personally committed to a particular group or position, then it is easy to see how the whole enterprise rests upon unsteady foundations.

The second element has to do with the interpretation of results, and I need hardly say that social science data are usually almost infinitely malleable. An instructive example is found in the recent report from the Committee on Irish Language Attitudes Research (1975). Voluminous, detailed and conforming to all the modern statistical requirements, it was nevertheless hailed by *both* pro- and anti-Irish groups as vindicating their longstanding arguments.

The thrust of all this is simply that, when considering linguistic minorities, policies and pluralism, we enter an emotionally charged arena in which exists a confusing mélange of subjectivity and objectivity, of research and speculation, of *a priori* and *ad hoc* judgements. This is disturbing because if social scientists cannot, to some extent at least, overcome "Mannheim's Paradox", they will have forfeited their claim to be reckoned with in matters of social policy. To remain in the groves of academe is to attract accusations of irrelevance; but, if the excursions into the real world taken by some modern writers on linguistic minority issues are anything to go by, we should value irrelevance.

It is against this background that the present collection has been assembled, and it is my hope that, in reading the contributions here, one will rediscover an objectivity of approach. I do not claim, of course, that the writers of this book are without their preferences and prejudices, nor do I think that these are always absent from their statements. However, the authors have been selected carefully on the basis of their ability to maintain a sense of perspective in a hot climate. I hope, at least, that where personal values intrude, these are made clear to the reader. Such is my own impression, at any rate.

The present collection

The ten chapters here have been assembled for two major purposes. The first of these is to provide an up-to-date assessment of the situation of linguistic minorities. With the exception of the first chapter, coverage is largely restricted to English-speaking contexts. However, given the importance of the minority situations in Canada, Britain, Australia and the United States, and given that they may provide useful generalizations for other settings, perhaps no great apology is called for. I would not wish, however, to create the impression that situations elsewhere are seen as relatively less interesting, or perhaps carbon copies of those treated here. Quite the contrary: it would be useful if this collection could prompt further works dealing with other contexts. The second purpose of this book is to present arguments concerning the fundamental issues which underlie linguistic minority matters (and here generalizability will surely be evident). Pluralism, assimilation, identity, bilingual and multilingual education—all of these are relevant *across* contexts.

Roughly speaking, the first five chapters relate primarily to the descriptive purpose of this book, and the last five deal more with general issues. The reader will appreciate, however, that it is neither possible nor desirable that these two sections be independent of one another. A discussion of, say, West Indian children in Britain must of necessity consider questions of assimilation and pluralism. Nevertheless, in the first half of the book, treatments of such questions are generally limited to specific contexts; the last five contributions attempt more wide-ranging discussion.

In Chapter 1, Skutnabb-Kangas analyses the position of the so-called "guestworkers" and immigrants of Europe, concentrating mainly on the Swedish and West German contexts. I use the word "so-called" here because these workers (and their children) now constitute permanent blocks in many parts of Europe (see Widgren, 1975; Willke, 1975). Skutnabb-Kangas notes that educational problems abound for these two groups, that children are in fact mis-educated, and that socio-political goals lie behind educational policies. Because of this, she implies a more active role for researchers in which they would broaden their scope to include important extra-educational variables. Skutnabb-Kangas claims that the benefits involved in migration are more than countered by disadvantages, and that the guestworker/immigrant situation is a reflection of capitalist need. First brought in to provide cheap labour, the migrants serve a new function when industrial progress slows—they become a buffer, absorbing the most upsetting shocks which economic stagnation entails. Schools abet social aims by ensuring generational continuity of low-status employees. I think that the author is right to emphasize that policies of migration are not erected on altruistic bases, but she neglects to consider the motivations of those migrating. Since, as we have seen above, the matter now has some historical dimension, and since conditions in the new society are reported back to those still in the "sending" countries, we might ask why migrants remain willing to move. At a general level, of course, the answer is economic—employment in the countries of origin is less available and/or remunerative than it is in the host states. This might lead us to pay some attention to conditions existing in the former contexts as well as (as Skutnabb-Kangas does) to those in the receiving countries. While this, of course, does not mean we should be any easier in our criticisms of malpractices in countries like Sweden and West Germany, it does mean taking a broader perspective. While ideological imperatives may make criticizing northern European capitalist and industrialized societies more attractive, they must not be allowed to blinker our vision.

Skutnabb-Kangas distinguishes between guestworker and immigrant policies in a useful way. Perhaps the most interesting note here is the extension of the sending countries' educational, and even policing policies to the host society, so far as guestworkers are concerned. Turning to education specifically, the author notes that in West Germany a number of types of schooling are possible. It would be useful to know *how* guestworker and immigrant children are actually assigned to, or choose, different types. It is clear, however, that the thrust of German policy is German-only or transitional education. In Sweden, on the other hand, there are assimilationist, transitional and maintenance classes in existence; as Ekstrand (1982) has suggested, the usual debate between pluralism and assimilation is, in Sweden, replaced by conflict over pluralism and a radical mother-tongue ideology. Incomplete education appears to be a serious problem in Germany, but is less so in Sweden where, Skutnabb-Kangas implies, a more enlightened policy exists. It is not made clear, however, exactly how we should interpret the educational difficulties of guestworker and immigrant children. Do they leave formal education early because of the system alone? Perhaps there are other factors, relating to personal and family attitudes and values, which operate here. While Skutnabb-Kangas clearly wishes to establish a model in which powerless and uneducated status is intentionally produced (and reproduced), it has not been demonstrated that official policy is the only important operative factor.

Skutnabb-Kangas provides a useful summary of theoretically possible linguistic policies in education, and makes her own preferences clear. She supports immersion and language maintenance programmes. There may be some practical difficulties, however, relating to the provision of services across what may be, in some situations, a wide range of languages. As well, insufficient attention is given to *needs* and *outcomes*. To say, for example, that children in Britain, Germany, France, etc. could all receive early education through a minority language (i.e. via immersion) without disadvantage may or may not be true; what end would it serve? How many would want such a service, and what long-term use would it have. Skutnabb-Kangas does note that existence of such a policy would prove that European minorities had strengthened to the point where their language was "instrumentally attractive", but available evidence (e.g. from Quebec immersion programmes) indicates that such attraction may well be limited to a small segment of the majority population. As to outcomes, Mackey (1981) has recently adverted to the lack of *use* of a second language acquired in immersion programmes (see also Genesee, 1981). It would be anti-climactic, to say the least, if we were so zealous in our purely educational objectives that we lost sight of the larger society into which the products of education are released.

Chapter 2, by Viv Edwards, presents an overview of linguistic policy in Britain. Treatment of indigenous minorities was, for a long time, based upon an English-only policy. At school, Welsh youngsters found using their mother tongue were beaten and stigmatized by the wearing of the "Welsh Not" (Jones, 1973; Ellis, 1974). MacKinnon (1974) reports that a similar Scottish device, the *maide-crochaidhe*, survived until the 1930s. It is important to note, however, that in Wales and Scotland (and in Ireland, too) parents often acquiesced in this process. Now, as Edwards notes, there are new grounds for optimism about the future of Welsh and Scots Gaelic (see

Williams, Chapter 7). A public tolerance for linguistic diversity, a resurgence of ethnolinguistic identity and a more enlightened bureaucracy make the status of these languages somewhat more secure. We must not forget, however, that for real language maintenance a regular set of domains is necessary and these must not, in the long term at least, depend upon specific or artificial support (see Chapter 10). The Gaeltacht in Ireland—"Wild West reservations for the native Irish", in the bitter words of Weir (1973, p. 91)—is in danger of turning completely into an enclave.

As Edwards points out, it is with the post-war influx of immigrants that changes were set in motion in linguistic policies, although these changes were (and continue to be) slow. Her documentation of this process is perhaps the most important part of the chapter. In the process, Edwards mentions the differences between self-initiated and government-supported mother-tongue programmes. An inability to see that public tolerance for diversity does not necessarily equate with public support (via government involvement) confuses the issue here for many cultural pluralists and proponents of enduring linguistic diversity. Edwards pays special attention to the West Indian population, a group she has previously dealt with at length (Edwards, 1979). Children here seem at special risk because they do not speak a foreign language, but rather an extreme form of non-standard English (Bailey, 1966; Trudgill, 1975). Thus, while West Indian speakers insist their language is English, teachers often consider it, at best, as substandard English. Differences can thus be marked, in terms of linguistic and educational adaptation, between West Indian children and, say, Asian youngsters (and these differences are now receiving further attention; see Scarr in *Sunday Times*, 6 March 1983).

In Chapter 3, Cummins considers multicultural policy in Canada, and reviews types of educational provision made for speakers of "third" or "heritage" languages (i.e. neither French nor English). One observes here a general similarity with the British context (and with the Australian; see Chapter 4), but the special piquancy in the Canadian setting derives from the fact of *two* official (charter) languages. When Prime Minister Trudeau proclaimed the multicultural policy in 1971, it was for aid to all ethnic groups, within a bilingual framework. As can be imagined, this has left supporters of ethnic *languages* confused and/or annoyed. The policy can be interpreted as sustaining a difference between the status of English/French and that of the others. And, in fact, French Canadians have been less than completely enthusiastic about the multicultural policy, fearing a reduction in status to the level of the "other" groups; this, of course, reflects the unequal power distribution between French and English in Canada—the French, although nominally on a par with English, feel less secure. Even within

Quebec itself, recent moves to buttress French in education have been rejected by the courts (see Chapter 7).

Cummins outlines in some detail the traditional policy of "anglo-conformity" and how this has come under increasing attack, especially in large centres with concentrations of "ethnics". He describes the ground-breaking work of O'Bryan *et al.* (1976) and Berry *et al.* (1977), which shows complicated patterns of language shift, maintenance and attitudes. Cummins concludes with a case study of the Toronto debate, and obviously intends this to represent the points of general importance throughout the Canadian context; however, students of minority situations elsewhere will also find much of value here. The scope and cost of the Canadian Heritage Language programme has inevitably led to criticism. While ethnic populations, in the main, have supported it, the anglophone community has been wary of possible social fragmentation. Cummins notes that the preference of the latter group is either for minorities to assimilate completely, or for them to undertake any cultural–linguistic maintenance on a private (i.e. not underwritten by government) basis. Matters are confused by the fact that minorities form majorities in certain areas and, as well, are in many cases Canadian citizens (i.e. the issue cannot be posed along citizen versus immigrant lines).

Bullivant extends our awareness of such matters to Australia (Chapter 4). He provides a well-organized and detailed account of the development of multicultural policy in that country. Showing that the Australian context bears similarities to those of Canada, Britain and the United States, Bullivant notes that the importation of policies and systems from overseas has been a feature of Australian education; this certainly has attendant difficulties, including "vacillations and ambiguities" and faddism. However, these problems are not markedly more pronounced in Australia than in other settings. The change from a "White Australia" policy to a multicultural one has been built around schools and media, and this reflects practice elsewhere. Bullivant notes, as well, that the change has involved the reorganization of government priorities and, indeed, the creation of new institutions. Most controversial here is the Australian Institute of Multicultural Affairs (established 1979). Having the look of an independent or semi-state body, it has been suspect from its inception and a case can be made that it is essentially an arm of the government. Bullivant's brief "inside" glance (see his second footnote) is a worrying indication that this may be so. Bullivant refers to the body's first major publication, *Review of Multicultural and Migrant Education* (1980), as badly prepared and politically motivated. This would not be immediately apparent to the average reader who, judging by the book's title, its introductory preface and the very name of the Institute itself, might well see it as an objective, if pedestrian report. Yet one notes, on further inspection, that none of those mentioned in Bullivant's chapter as critics of Australian multicultural policy (Atchison, Martin, and Bullivant himself) figure as consultants in the report's list of thirty contributors, nor are any of their works referenced there. *Caveat emptor*.

Bullivant clearly documents the pluralist dilemma which exists in Australia (and elsewhere). He claims that a danger arises if multicultural programmes sidestep the important socioeconomic and political disadvantages of ethnic groups. In fact, programmes may maintain groups' subordinate positions while appearing to help them, in linguistic and cultural matters. The extreme scenario here is one in which governments placate the "ethnics" while sustaining existing power relations (see Edwards, 1981a). Bullivant supports diversity but feels that its maintenance is a "private-domain lifestyle" concern. The fact that Bullivant arrives at this position after much study, while Cummins (Chapter 3) suggests this is one of the preferred "ethnic options" voiced by mainstream populations, is food for thought. Drawing upon the work of Higham (1975) and others, Bullivant notes that the dilemma, in education, is to assist the maintenance of cultural diversity at a private level while preparing *all* children for survival in the larger society.

In Chapter 5, Drake deals with language planning in the United States specifically but, because he focusses on bilingual education, his contribution also relates to more general themes. His chapter is short and to the point. Like Bullivant and others (and *unlike* many apologists for pluralism and maintenance bilingual education), Drake supports diversity only after careful thought, and with some reservations. He calls for detachment in evaluations of bilingual education, and refers to the particular problem for social science posed by "Mannheim's Paradox" (see above). Bilingual education is an area plagued by difficulties of definition, ideology and selective historical awareness and it is not surprising, therefore, that much of the literature is polemical (see Edwards 1981b, 1982). Is it good that researchers, as Drake claims, are tolerant of linguistic diversity "to the point of celebrating it"?

Drake also refers to the emphasis on *ethnicity* which neglects the explanatory power of *social class*. Some recent writers (Mann, 1979; Steinberg, 1981; see also Chapter 10) who are critical of the "new ethnicity" in the United States have touched upon this neglect. In a recent comment (Edwards, in press (b)), I drew attention to Steinberg's assertion that, while ethnic groups espouse pluralism to protect their interests, ethnic boundaries are readily crossed and ignored if this becomes socioeconomically advantageous. Indeed, should we expect otherwise? The obvious rejoinder to this will be that we should seek a society in which aspects of ethnicity do not have to be jettisoned in the quest for material advancement. This is a reasonable objective, perhaps, but it is not likely to be served by those who argue while wearing historical, ideological and subjective blinkers. Drake's view is that it is wrong to see the greater current tolerance for ethnicity as necessarily reflecting a pro-pluralistic attitude. Until realistic assessments are provided, it is unlikely that a widespread bilingual education can evolve, and Drake's concluding sentiments echo Bullivant's remarks on the educational dilemma.

Mackey (Chapter 6) provides further details on bilingual education. He notes the problems associated with the compartmentalized study of the topic—by psychologists, linguists, educators and others—and these obviously add to the difficulties I have referred to already (lack of historical awareness, of objectivity and of ideological neutrality). Mackey gives us, in straightforward fashion, an outline of important features of language education and national policy. The degree of linguistic heterogeneity, the relative status of different varieties, questions of standardization and literacy—all of these affect (or should) any policy decisions. As well, there are aspects of greater generality still, including the social structure of the population, its facilities and its priorities. We can see that the differences outlined by Skutnabb-Kangas (Chapter 1) between German and Swedish policy for immigrants and guestworkers will be fully analysable only within a very broad sociocultural framework. Mackey also deals with national and regional control over educational priorities; this is an important matter in all of the contexts surveyed in this book.

Having outlined some aspects, Mackey turns to an illustrative case study of the linguistic situation in Montreal (see also Williams, Chapter 7). The dynamics of the French, English and immigrant communities are particularly interesting. For English speakers, French immersion programmes became increasingly popular in the quest for bilingualism. For French-speaking children, a shift for a year or two to English-only schools seemed a useful undertaking (although frowned upon by a nationalistic provincial government). And, for immigrants, the linguistic solution was often to learn French in the community while enrolling in English schools (again, viewed with disfavour by the government). With regard to immersion education, Mackey has noted elsewhere (1981) that it does not necessarily promote societal bilingualism since it may involve a "somewhat artificial French" and, of course, does not represent children's home language situations. Genesee (1981) has also pointed out that while immersion programmes may provide more French *competence* than do traditional language instruction classes, subsequent *use* of this ability may not be great. It is as well to remember that we should always consider the uses or functions of educational programmes, and not concentrate solely upon psychological or statistical differences between forms of instruction within the context of that instruction only. Mackey's final statement relevant to this is that social implications of bilingual education affect the application of "isolated linguistic or psychological criteria".

In Chapter 7, Williams provides a theoretical discussion of separatism, or autonomist nationalism, supplementing this with studies of Wales, Euskadi (Basque region) and Quebec. In so doing, he gives an historical and cross-cultural perspective within which other linguistic minority settings can usefully be evaluated. Noting that the watchwords of separatism are identity, authenticity and diversity, Williams outlines three basic preconditions for the development of autonomist sentiment: there must be a core territory; there must exist group markers—language and religion being the most important here; there must be "opposition" groups, concentrated regionally or in power. It is interesting to note that these three conditions often exist not only for indigenous minorities, but also for immigrant populations (newly-arrived ones, especially). It is also interesting to consider that, in some circumstances (the American "new ethnicity" scene today, for example) these conditions no longer exist, and cultural pluralists and group leaders often try to re-establish them—largely by re-invoking the idea of a common past/homeland, attempting to reinvigorate group markers (like communicative language) and re-establishing a "we–them" context (which is sometimes quite difficult, if group members have successfully penetrated mainstream corridors of power).

When Williams turns to consider the Welsh situation (see also Chapter 2), he notes that the language has made gains, notably in education, but that the messages conveyed through Welsh tend to be "middle class and statist". This leads him to reason that the legitimation of Welsh culture through language may perhaps have come too late. One cannot be certain, of course, about future directions but it is indeed serious for a language when it reaches the point where it is a conveyer for another culture. Williams' remarks on the Basque situation will be enlightening for those familiar only with violent headlines. Interestingly, the Basque area (unlike many other linguistic minority regions) is *not* one of economic underdevelopment. Indeed, it is an area into which Spaniards immigrate. Consequently, we see that a language can be weakened if its core area is economically viable (and if "foreigners" move in, diluting native homogeneity), just as it can suffer if the area is weak, and out-migration occurs (e.g. the Irish Gaeltacht). The fact that these two different conditions can produce similarly dangerous sapping of minority language is a reflection of the core-within-a-state scenario which is common to both. Finally, Williams discusses the Quebec setting (see also Chapters 3 and 6). One of the most interesting aspects here is the view of the Parti Québécois that, within Quebec, decisions should reflect the will, not of the majority *per se*, but of the majority of the dominant cultural group. This, while understandable from a nationalistic standpoint, has obvious difficulties, as Williams notes. If nothing else, it demonstrates that, in multi-ethnic societies where group concentrations exist, there may be bitter differences over the ways in which terms like "majority" are seen to be valid.

Gleason's Chapter 8 considers in some detail the terms "pluralism" and "assimilation". While drawing upon the American example, Gleason's remarks clearly have generalizable utility. The obvious contribution here is the demonstration of the dangers of historical naïveté. As an historian himself, Gleason is able to show clearly that pluralism and assimilation are not simple opposites, and that pluralism can mean, in fact, a sort of assimilation (and has often done so). He touches upon a vital point when noting that those who see an inherent opposition between these terms often do so from a moral as well as a theoretical perspective. Pluralism is good; assimilation is bad. Therefore, the rendered "ethnics" must be unmelted. Could anything be more simple or, as Gleason's chapter shows, more oversimplified (see also Chapter 10)?

Gleason shows how proponents of the "new ethnicity" have misunderstood recent work, as well as neglecting historical data. Glazer and Moynihan's *Beyond the Melting Pot* (1963) is, for example, often taken as an endorsement of the cultural pluralist position, whereas the authors' analysis showed the symbiotic relationship of pluralism and assimilation. It also demonstrated that ethnic groups in America today are not at all the same ones they once were—they have been, as Gleason says, "reshaped by the assimilative forces of American society". Thus, modern pluralists are actually attempting to sustain the products of assimilation. Misunderstanding has also occurred with Gordon's *Assimilation in American Life* (1964), particularly concerning his distinction between cultural and structural pluralism. Gordon argued that cultural pluralism (including linguistic aspects) was increasingly rare in American life; however, structural pluralism—indicating that groups have not fully penetrated institutions of the mainstream—remains somewhat more evident. Gleason implies that advocates of the ethnic revival were too quick or too incautious to see this important distinction.

Gleason notes that, in the early stages of the "new ethnicity", pluralism largely signified a "participationist" model (see Higham, 1975; Chapter 4). However, there has now developed a more militant, separatist variety too, which rejects all traces of assimilation (see also Chapter 7). Gleason points out that while militant pluralists advocate the elimination of racism, they themselves uphold group classifications based primarily on ancestry. Gleason concludes, therefore, that the area is a muddled one, that cultural pluralism does not mean the same thing for all people, and that militant pluralism can be expected to arouse a reaffirmation of traditional assimilationist values.

Eastman examines the link between ethnic identity and language in Chapter 9. Her point is a straightforward one: a language we associate with our group identity need not be one we use regularly (or even one we know at all). In this sense, Italian could be the "associated" language for Americans of Italian descent who are monolingual English speakers. This is a point I have made earlier (Edwards, 1977; see also Chapter 10)—language possesses both communicative and symbolic significance. For mainstream-group speakers these two aspects coexist, but they are separable and a symbolic value can persist long after communicative use has gone. In Ireland, for example, there exists a strong national identity which is not expressed through Irish, a language which nevertheless retains other values. To suggest that the Irish abandoned an identity with the shift to English is simplistic. This is not to suggest that the Irish identity today is the same as it was when the masses spoke Irish, nor would I wish to imply that the language shift itself caused no changes; however, identities change regardless of language used (see Edwards, 1981a, 1981b, 1982, in press(a)). As Eastman notes, the relationship of identity change to language change is more complicated than might be supposed. If the only shift is in the language we *use*, then ethnic identity need not change markedly. The reader may like to contrast this with the Welsh situation (Chapter 7), in which the language (medium) is preserved, but where the culture (message) has shifted.

In my own Chapter (10), I attempt to synthesize information bearing upon ethnic diversity, language and identity. Perhaps the single most important point here has to do with the confusion surrounding cultural pluralism and assimilation. These do not exist as polar opposites, nor can we characterize societies as either one or the other. The linguistic and educational policies to which cultural pluralism gives rise are, therefore, complicated. We know, however, that communicative language retention is *not* a feature of most settled minorities, and there is not much evidence that things could or should be otherwise. The symbolic value of language remains, however (as do other "private" elements of ethnicity). Educational programmes aimed at sustaining ethnic identity through communicative language maintenance are misguided, therefore, and may even damage those private aspects of ethnicity which are essentially out of the reach of external intervention. Pluralistic policies are more likely to be supported by atypical spokesmen for ethnic groups, and there are reasons to think that pluralism does not have widespread active support. It can be seen that there is increased public tolerance for ethnic diversity nowadays, but it is an error to equate this with desire for promotion (especially via government agencies). Identity, finally, is personal and does not respond well to attempts, however well-intentioned, to support or guide it. Thus, a policy of cultural pluralism—with its often warped assumptions about language and education—is not likely to create real alterations in identity formation, maintenance or change where it exists in isolation from large-scale sociopolitical forces.

Throughout this introduction I have been intentionally critical, and have drawn attention to the most controversial areas dealt with by the contributors. I hope that the reader will not interpret a critical stance as a hostile one. I am concerned with the topics of pluralism, assimilation, language maintenance/shift and ethnolinguistic identity, but also with the treatment these have received in the literature. My own views are laid out in Chapter 10. I hope that the reader will find that the contributors to this book have exercised, in the main, a disinterested view of the subject matter. If this sometimes seems critical, it is because an imbalance has crept into the area which needs to be corrected. If this volume, incomplete though it necessarily must be, is seen to contribute something to an objective consideration of the important matters under discussion, then it will have had the desired effect.

References

Abramson, H. J. (1983). On the passionate study of ethnicity (Review of A. D. Smith's *The Ethnic Revival*). *Contemporary Sociology* **12**, 134–136.

Australian Institute of Multicultural Affairs (1980). *Review of Multicultural and Migrant Education*. A.I.M.A., Melbourne.

Bailey, B. L. (1966). *Jamaican Creole Syntax*. Cambridge University Press, London.

Barnard, F. M. (1965). *Herder's Social and Political Thought*. Clarendon, Oxford.

Berlin, I. (1976). *Vico and Herder: Two Studies in the History of Ideas*. Hogarth, London.

Berry, J., Kalin, R. and Taylor, D. (1977). *Multiculturalism and Ethnic Attitudes in Canada*. Supply & Services Canada, Ottawa.

Bullivant, B. (1981). *The Pluralist Dilemma in Education*. George Allen & Unwin, Sydney.

Committee on Irish Language Attitudes Research (1975). *Report*. Government Stationery Office, Dublin.

Davis, T. (1945). *Essays and Poems with a Centenary Memoir*. Gill & Son, Dublin.

Drake, G. (1979). Ethnicity, values and language policy in the United States. In *Language and Ethnic Relations* (Eds H. Giles and B. Saint-Jacques). Pergamon, Oxford.

Dwyer, T. R. (1980). *Eamon de Valera*. Gill & Macmillan, Dublin.

Edwards, J. (1977). Ethnic identity and bilingual education. In *Language, Ethnicity and Intergroup Relations* (Ed. H. Giles). Academic Press, London, Orlando and New York.

Edwards, J. (1981a). The social and political context of bilingual education. Paper presented to the Invitational Symposium on Multiculturalism in Education, Queen's University (Kingston).

Edwards, J. (1981b). The context of bilingual education. *Journal of Multilingual and Multicultural Development* **2**, 25–44.

Edwards, J. (1982). Bilingual education revisited: A reply to Donahue. *Journal of Multilingual and Multicultural Development* **3**, 89–101.

Edwards, J. (1983). *The Irish Language: An Annotated Bibliography of Sociolinguistic Publications, 1772–1982*. Garland, New York.

Edwards, J. (in press(a)). Irish and English in Ireland. In *Language in the British Isles* (Ed. P. Trudgill). Cambridge University Press, Cambridge.

Edwards, J. (in press(b)). Further remarks on bilingual education. *Harvard Educational Review*.

Edwards, V. K. (1979). *The West Indian Language Issue in British Schools*. Routledge & Kegan Paul, London.

Ekstrand, L. H. (1982). Maintenance or transition—or both? A review of Swedish ideologies and empirical research. Paper presented to the Wenner-Gren Symposium on Multiculturalism, Stockholm.

Ellis, P. B. (1974). *The Cornish Language and its Literature*. Routledge & Kegan Paul, London.

Fichte, J. G. (1922). *Addresses to the German Nation* (Translated by R. F. Jones and G. H. Turnbull). Open Court (Original, 1807), London.

Genesee, F. (1981). Bilingualism and biliteracy: A study of cross-cultural contact in a bilingual community. In *The Social Psychology of Reading* (Ed. J. Edwards). Institute of Modern Languages, Silver Spring, Maryland.

Glazer, N. and Moynihan, D. (1963). *Beyond the Melting Pot*. M.I.T. Press and Harvard University Press, Cambridge, Massachusetts.

Gordon, M. M. (1964). *Assimilation in American Life*. Oxford University Press, New York.

Grafton, A. (1981). Wilhelm von Humboldt. *American Scholar* **50**, 371–381.

Higham, J. (1975). *Send These to Me*. Atheneum, New York.

Hyde. D. (1894). The necessity for de-anglicising Ireland. In *The Revival of Irish Literature* (Eds C. Duffy, G. Sigerson and D. Hyde). T. Fisher Unwin, London.

Jones, D. G. (1973). The Welsh language movement. In *The Welsh Language Today* (Ed. M. Stephens). Gomer Press, Llandysul.

Kedourie, E. (1961). *Nationalism*. Praeger, New York.

Mackey, W. F. (1981). Safeguarding language in schools. *Language and Society* **4**, 10–14.

MacKinnon, K. (1974). *The Lion's Tongue*. Club Leabhar, Inverness.

Mann, A. (1979). *The One and the Many*. University Press, Chicago.

O'Bryan, K. G., Reitz, J. G. and Kuplowska, O. M. (1976). *Non-official Languages: A Study in Canadian Multiculturalism*. Supply & Services Canada, Ottawa.

Steinberg, S. (1981). *The Ethnic Myth*. Atheneum, New York.

Toynbee, A. (1956). *A Study of History* (Abridgement by D. C. Somervell). Oxford University Press, London.

Trudgill, P. (1975). *Accent, Dialect and the School*. Edward Arnold, London.

Weir, A. (1973). Irish newspeak. In *Education in Great Britain and Ireland: A Source Book* (Eds R. Bell, G. Fowler and K. Little). Routledge & Kegan Paul, London (with the Open University Press).

Widgren, J. (1975). Recent trends in European migration policies. *International Review of Education* **21**, 275–285.

Willke, I. (1975). Schooling of immigrant children in West Germany–Sweden–England: The educationally disadvantaged. *International Review of Education* **21**, 357–382.

1
Children of guest workers and immigrants: linguistic and educational issues[1]

Tove Skutnabb-Kangas

In all industrialized Western countries the educational level is higher than ever: children get more education than their parents, and illiteracy has been more or less eradicated. Education is still seen as an instrument for social mobility, even if the evidence suggests that schools play an important role "in reproducing a stratified social order that remains strikingly unequal by class, gender and race" (Apple, 1980, p. 2). But now the general trend of more and more education is changing, notably because of one specific group which, in the year 2000, will account for a third of the young population in Europe—the children of the so-called guest workers, of seasonal workers, of "illegal" migrants and, to a certain extent, the children of immigrants. The industrialized countries non-educate these youngsters to illiteracy or semi-literacy, future unemployment and no hope.

In this chapter I shall give a short description of the situation of migrants, mainly in two European countries, both in general and in schools. I will use several different typologies of bilingual education in order to discuss some of the important variables which explain why some children are "made" to fail. I will also relate differing linguistic and educational outcomes to some of the economic and political goals behind educational programmes, to see how different programmes succeed in reproducing the functions migrants have (and will have) in capitalist societies.

LINGUISTIC MINORITIES
ISBN 0-12-232760-8

When one discusses outcomes of education, linguistic or otherwise, for migrant and other minority children, it is imperative to look at those societies which produce the bad results. It would seem natural that no societies *consciously* and cynically try to make children fail in schools—still they do fail. If one wants to understand some of the particular mechanisms and rationales behind the massive failure of migrant children in schools in Western European countries, it is not enough to look at narrow linguistic goals and outcomes only. It would be naive to think that schools or those who control schools would like to make children bilingual or prevent them from becoming bilingual just because they think that bilingualism is good or bad for the individual child. Even if we show with convincing research results that high levels of bilingualism are both possible to attain and linguistically and cognitively beneficial for a child (and that has in fact been done), that would not be enough to convince those in power that they should implement programs which make *all* children bilingual. Even if we show that not knowing any language at the level of monolingual norms is linguistically, cognitively or socially bad for the child (and that has also been shown), that would not be enough to convince the decision-makers to abandon programmes which prevent children from getting native command in any language. Behind the choice of programmes which are said to be bilingual or to lead to bilingualism (or not) there are not only linguistic, psychological, pedagogical or sociological reasons and goals, but always very substantial economic–political rationales and goals, regardless of whether those who choose the programmes admit it or not.

It is important for researchers to analyse those economic–political goals too, instead of leaving this to the politicians. Since the recommendations that researchers make for the education of migrant children can be absolute opposites (as, to a large extent, they are in Scandinavia and West Germany), analysing these goals is the only way to understand how conflicting recommendations are both realistic and necessary. Unless researchers themselves are fully aware of the role of research in politically important questions (like the education of migrant children), they can contribute to the reproduction of the exploitation of the very groups they may be trying to understand and help. At the same time it may become difficult for them to see in what ways their recommendations should be changed when political changes occur (like the ones at the end of 1981 and in 1982 in West German migration policy). A recommendation which is perfectly sound in one situation may be bad for children in another situation. This may be true even if the recommendation is firmly grounded in what we consider best for an individual child from a psychological, linguistic or pedagogical point of view.

Also, we cannot examine and compare *outcomes* of programmes unless we first analyse and compare the goals, both explicit and implicit. Outcomes of using the "same" methods (e.g. the same language of instruction) can be different if the goals are different. And, since every programme should be evaluated in relation to its implicit (and explicit) goals, we might be led to think that a programme producing students with very poor academic achievement is a bad programme if we only evaluate it in relation to its officially stated goals. But if we compare the outcomes with the implicit goals a programme may have, we might have to conclude that the results were exactly in accordance with the implicit goals. This means, in my opinion, that we cannot do good research in the field of minority education without putting our work in a broader societal framework (Skutnabb-Kangas, 1982a, b).

Migration as developmental aid from exploited countries to industrialized countries

One hopes that nobody believes any longer in the positive justifications of the immigrant, seasonal worker, guest worker or "undocumented alien" systems. Still, at the end of the sixties and even the beginning of the seventies, there were splendid claims that these systems were good for everybody, especially for the migrant workers themselves and their countries of origin. The claims stated that the system was good for the countries of origin because: it helped to give work to the unemployed; migrants would get an industrial training which they would be able to apply on their return and which would help to make their own countries less dependent on foreign "expertise"; the remittances which the migrants sent home would be invested so that there would be jobs waiting for them on their return. In addition the remittances would benefit the balance of payments by bringing in foreign currency.

While it must be admitted that there were some material benefits for the migrants themselves, and their families, the effects of these benefits have been counteracted by many negative aspects. Migrants were mostly drawn from the young, productive, best qualified part of the population (Horst, 1980). Their leaving affected both the age structure and the economic basis of the communities they left. Most of them got no training whatsoever in the countries of production—rather, there has been a process of dequalification going on, because most migrants with a training could not find jobs where they could use it. A large part of the remittances has been used in a non-productive way (investment in property) or in consumer goods which have often been imported, negatively affecting balance of payments.

The official views represented by many of the international organizations and the countries of production (Swetland, 1978) did admit that the system was also good for the receiving countries, because it was a convenient way of obtaining temporary labour during a phase of expansion. But it was above all presented as a generous aid to "developing countries", with guest workers as the winners.

But there were other types of analyses, too, mainly from two sources. Many of the liberal economists analysed the economic importance of migrant labour for industries in Western countries and concluded that it was profitable for them during certain expansive periods. Many of them saw access to migrant labour as one of the decisive causes for growth, while others saw the economic growth as the independent variable, causing among other things a demand for more labour (Horst, 1980).

Those economists, especially, who saw a permanent infrastructure for migrants as either unnecessary or of minor economic importance calculated from early on that migration was in the best interest of capital, both in the countries of production and internationally. These analyses were often amazingly cynical compared to the humanistic phrases about mutual benefit which the international organizations produced. The liberal economists usually looked at the economic factors from the point of view of capital, and not from the point of view of the sending countries or the migrants themselves. This was done instead by economists working in a marxist or neo-marxist framework. My discussion about the function of guest workers is mainly based on their thinking, especially that of Castles (1980; see also Castles and Kosack, 1973; Horst, 1980; Nikolinakos, 1973, 1982).

According to Castles, immigration after the Second World War had two main functions for capitalism. On the one hand, during a phase of rapid industrial and capital expansion, imported cheap labour was flexible, un-educated, unorganized and unable to demand rights for itself. On the other hand, the presence of migrants gave rise to a social, economic and political gulf within the working class: the domestic working class became more bourgeois as a section of it moved up one rung to such jobs as clerks, and away from the hardest and dirtiest industrial and service jobs. Because of this trend, and language difficulties, the indigenous working class could not even start to develop any solidarity with guest workers/immigrants. And this, along with the fact that migrants were deprived of most political rights, weakened the working class as a whole.

Ekberg investigated the extent to which immigrants and Swedes in the council of Växjö used and paid taxes for various local services, and argued that immigrants were "cheaper" for the municipality than Swedes (1979). In a new investigation he has tried to make the same type of calculation for the whole of Sweden. He summarizes (1980, p. 1; my translation):

> Over the years considerable sums have via the public sector been transferred *from* immigrants *to* the Swedish population. This can also be expressed such

that the available income of the Swedish population is greater or that the Swedish population has access to public services at a lower price (with lower taxation) because of the immigrants.

The same conclusion is reached in a new Swedish report, published by the National Board of Immigration and Naturalization (1982). The social security of immigrants as a whole is better in Sweden than in any other country in the world (see Hammar, in press). So is the information given to immigrants (in many languages) about their rights to social security and other services. If, regardless of this, the Swedes profit from the immigrants (and here we discuss the regular taxpayers, not the industries), we have reason to believe that all other countries profit even more.

During the seventies, however, the function of migrants changed. The labour-intensive expansion which, partly through exploiting the labour of migrants, made possible the accumulation of capital, could not progress at the same speed any longer in the industrialized countries (Castles, 1980; Nikolinakos, 1982). The most advanced sectors of capital found it more rewarding to begin to export capital to underdeveloped countries, rather than to continue to import labour. Despite loud public calls, particularly from (extreme) right-wing parties, for all immigrants/guest workers to be sent home when unemployment rates continue to rise, this has not happened to any real extent (even if the latest trends in West Germany seem to point in that direction—selective attempts to get rid of uneducated, unemployed youngsters, unprofitable children, etc.). According to Castles, migrants have not been sent home because that population now has a new function. It is used as a buffer at the lowest layer of society: migrants, by being at the receiving end of the worst shocks caused by the restructuring process of the capitalist world economy, protect the higher layers from experiencing them so directly. This is one way of helping prevent the working class becoming revolutionary. The US situation with the cut-backs hitting minorities, both migrant and indigenous, harder than other groups (Fendrich, 1982) fits all too well with this, and so does the recent decision to let great numbers of "undocumented aliens" from Mexico stay—they are also needed as a buffer.

But in order to get immigrants and guest workers to fulfil both these functions (a cheap, flexible, badly organized labour force and a buffer), the second and third generation of migrants must also be kept in the same weak position which the first had—educationally, socially, economically and politically—and made to think that it is their own fault. Also, they must be prevented from building up solidarity among themselves and with the domestic working class, and from canalizing any protest in a successful way. This is where school comes in, to assure that the second and third generation conform. In the following sections I will try to show that the ways in which the education of immigrant and guest worker children is organized are logical consequences and reflections of goals of continued exploitation of immigrants and guest workers; and to show that these goals are achieved, despite different methods used.

Before looking at schools and the different patterns of organizing them we will have to look at some of the main differences between a guest worker policy and an immigrant policy in general. School policy is part of a more general societal policy towards parents, and the way schools are organized and planned is or should be a reflection of children's futures. It is also necessary to place any recommendations in a broader societal framework, so as to understand their causes and functions.

Societal policy—guest worker or immigrant?

The crucial distinction between a guest worker policy and an immigrant policy is the question of permanency of stay. In a guest worker policy a rotation is hoped for. It is ideally hoped that fresh, young, healthy and single male workers will come alone to the country of production, work there a few years while living in barracks and go back, to be replaced by others exactly according to the needs of the labour market. In an immigrant policy, on the contrary, the idea is that those who come have a right to stay, and that most of them probably will make use of this right.

An insecure legal status characterizes a guest worker policy (GWP), compared to the much more secure one in an immigrant policy (IP). This is true in relation to a number of conditions which will be mentioned here (for an elaboration see Skutnabb-Kangas, 1981b): right to stay/right to residence; security of work permit; unemployment; the right to social security benefits; distinctions between civil and police administration of guest worker (GW) affairs; legal appeal rights.

Naturalization, the right to change nationality, is difficult, arbitrarily regulated or impossible for a GW (Franz, cited in Rieck and Senft, 1978). *The legal and educational system of the sending country is, in a GWP, often applied also in the receiving country*; in an IP, the system of the receiving country applies. Thus, the country of origin may send and train teachers, and decide on the syllabus and teaching materials. A GWP can also mean "cooperation" between the legal systems of both countries so that, for instance, the Turkish police can operate more or less freely in West Germany (Skutnabb-Kangas, 1981b). *Reuniting the family* is not encouraged in a GWP. On the contrary, there are often attempts to prevent families from coming or to make this difficult. In an IP, family reunion is considered natural, even if there are certain restrictions (and a family is given the western nuclear family definition). In GWP there is often severe *segregation in housing*, and there are demands for upper limits on GWs in certain areas. The segregation in an IP operates more subtly and invisibly. The most important feature, however, in a GWP is that GWs have *very few political rights*. Even their right to organize themselves is restricted, in different ways, in all GWP countries (see Hammar, in press) and there is no question of voting rights. Together with the attempts of certain sending countries to extend their legal system to the receiving country (and thereby control the political movement among the GWs) this leaves the GWs almost without any parliamentary channels to influence their own situation.

Demographic aspects

Since there exist already descriptions of migrant policies and regulations for several European countries as well as an overview comparing France, Great Britain, Holland, Sweden, Switzerland, West Germany and the United States (Hammar, in press), I shall not try to give any summary of policies here but rather some basic statistics. I shall then go on to a description of a typical GWP and IP from an educational point of view.

To give even an approximate picture of the number of migrants in Western European countries is an extremely difficult task. The statistics are often impossible to compare, sometimes inaccessible, and the definitions of migrant/guest worker/immigrant/seasonal worker are unclear (see Reinans, 1981; Rahbek Pedersen and Skutnabb-Kangas, 1982). Estimations of migrants vary between 14 and 18 million, not counting naturalized immigrants. The last figure contains an estimate of illegal migrants too—a recent Council of Europe meeting estimated their number to be about 2 million. The EEC commission also says that an additional 20% should be added to the official figures in the EEC countries (SIV-Dokumentation, October 1980).

Table 1 is based on information from several recent sources, but the figures are, of course, constantly changing.

Since my intention in this chapter is to discuss principles and patterns, rather than details in specific countries, I have chosen to discuss two "extremes"—West Germany with a typical GWP (Switzerland might be an even more polarized example), and Sweden with a typical IP (either Canada and Australia could be chosen here too).

West Germany

There are approximately 4·63 million foreigners in West Germany (Statistisches Jahrbuch, 1981), plus an additional number of illegal migrants,

TABLE 1
Foreigners in different European countries

Country	Number	Population (%)
Denmark	102 000	2·0
Finland	13 000	0·3
Belgium	851 000	8·7
France	4 124 000	7·8
Great Britain	(around 4 million?)	
Holland	441 000	3·2
Iceland	3 000	1·4
Luxembourg	100 000	30·0
Norway	80 000	2·0
Sweden	411 000	5·2
Switzerland	898 000	14·2
West Germany	4 630 000	7·5

estimated to comprise about 20% of the legal ones. Foreigners make up 7·5% of the population but 10% of the labour force. More than 25% of them have lived over 10 years in the country, and approximately two thirds of the rest more than 8 years. About 1 million of them are under 16 years of age (Kühn, 1979). Turkish nationals form the largest group (in mid-1981, 33·4%), and the six most represented countries of origin (Turkey, Yugoslavia, Italy, Greece, Spain and Portugal) account for three-quarters of all foreigners (TIP, 1/82).

The number of foreigners is increasing rapidly, regardless of the halt to migration, particularly because of the high birth rate and the fact that most migrants are young. Of all children born in 1978, 13% had foreign parents (Schmitt, 1981). In West Berlin the foreigners account for 10% of the population but 31% of all births (Spiess, 1979). This is, of course, not a specifically West German phenomenon: in the Greater London area the corresponding figures were 6·4% and 34% (CRE, 1978).

Sweden

At the end of 1981 Sweden had 411 000 foreigners, 5·2% of the population. Roughly 114 000 of them were under 15 years of age. Whereas 4·5% of Swedes are aged from 0–3 years, 6·9% of the foreigners belong to this group. In some groups (e.g. Turks, Greeks, Chileans), the percentage of children is even higher. On the other hand, there are extremely few old people: while 17·3% of the Swedes were over the age of 65, only 2·4% of the foreigners were over 65 (SIV-Dokumentation, 29 March 1982). Granted that around

401 000 foreigners have been naturalized between 1948–1981 (SIV-Dokumentation, 25 August 1980) and that their birth rate has probably been higher than that of Swedes, the following publicly available figures are probably reliable: there are 1·1 million people in Sweden with an immigrant background now, there will be one in four in the year 2000, and every other child born in the year 2000 will have an immigrant background.

Schools and migrant children—organization and results

There are many different ways to organize the education of minority children, and every attempt to summarize them must necessarily be a generalization—those who want to have detailed information are therefore requested to consult more specific sources. Minority education can be classified according to a variety of criteria (see, e.g. typologies by Mackey, 1972; Gonzáles, 1975; Fishman, 1976; see also Kjolseth, 1972).

As a first way of characterizing the education of GW and immigrant children I shall use three criteria: the language of instruction; the extent of educational integration/segregation (physically and ideologically); and the goal of the classroom (assimilation, maintenance or transition—the latter also leading to assimilation; see Kjolseth, 1972; Hernández-Chávez, 1978).

West Germany

GW children in West Germany can get their education in six different types of classes (Reich, 1979):

1. German "regular classes" (*Regelklassen*): classes planned for German children, with minimal or no consideration given to the fact that all the children are not German-speaking German children.
2. "Special classes" (*besondere Klassen*): GW pupils only, but with German as the medium of instruction and with German teachers, ideology and syllabuses. The results in these types of class should ideally be the same as in German classes. There are many such classes in West Berlin.
3. International preparatory classes: classes where the pupils represent several different nationalities and where their different mother tongues are not considered. The official goal is transitional—i.e. the pupils are supposed to get instruction, including German as a second language, which prepares them to transfer to "regular" German classes. There are many classes of this type in Baden-Württemberg.
4. 1–2-year national preparatory classes: all the pupils have the same nationality (but not necessarily the same mother tongue). The children

are often instructed both by a German teacher and by a teacher from the same country as the children. The official goal is that after 1–2 years they should know enough German and have a sufficient subject matter knowledge to be transferred to German classes.

5. National classes of several years' duration (mainly in Hamburg and Nordrhein-Westfalen): in these classes the largest part of the instruction is given by a teacher with the same nationality as the children, and German is supposed to be taught as a second language. Some of the classes have an optional transition to German classes (which means that most of the children are not being transferred), while others have an obligatory transition (for instance in Nordrhein-Westfalen after grade 6), which very often means that the children simply drop out of school completely after grade 6 because they cannot cope with the transfer and all-German instruction.

6. Complete national classes: here, syllabuses and teaching materials are from the country of origin, and teachers (often almost monolingual in their own language, newly arrived) are sent by the embassies of the countries of origin. These classes are also supposed to offer instruction in German as a second language, but this is often not lived up to. This type of class is mainly represented in Bavaria.

The language of instruction in the first three types is German only, a language which many of the children do not master, at least in the beginning. In the last two types it is mostly the mother tongue of the children or the official language in the countries where they come from. In alternative 4 it is a combination of both languages, with German as the dominant language. The first type, a German class, is clearly *integrative/assimilationist*[2] (as opposed to segregationist), because the goal is assimilation, the GW children are mixed both with German children and other GW children from other nationalities, and the instruction follows completely the German pattern. The second alternative, the special classes, is integrative with regard to the content and ideology of the instruction, and also physically with regard to other groups of GW children but not with regard to German children. This holds true to a large extent for the third alternative too, the international preparatory classes, but the content in the instruction is of course not the same in these classes as in German classes, even if it is completely German-oriented ideologically. The last three alternatives are all physically segregated, because the children in these classes are neither mixed with other GW children nor with German children. With regard to the content and ideology the complete national classes, alternative 6, are the most segregated, compared with the content and ideology in German classes, while the German orientation increases in alternatives 5 and 4.

Officially the class types 3–5 have a pronounced *transitional* goal: their main task is to prepare children for education through the medium of German in German classes. In the special classes this goal is self-evident and is not specifically underlined. Only the last alternative, national classes, has the *maintenance* of the language and culture of the children as one of its explicit goals (see Table 2).

If, rather than using things German as a point of reference we consider the possibilities the school gives for the children to go back to the country of origin, the characteristics of the classes are reversed. The national classes give the children the best possibilities for integration in the school system in the home country (even if these possibilities are far from good), with regard to both the physical organization of the classes and the content and ideology. The German classes segregate/alienate them most, by assimilating them into German values/ideology and by preventing them from learning their own language.

Of course, the official goals need not correspond to what happens in the reality of the classrooms. Stölting (1978) argues that, even in classes where the official goal is to prepare children for a transfer to German classes, instruction in German as a second language has been reduced and these classes are now developing into segregated national classes too; the so-called integrative model has ultimate assimilation as its goal and the children are not even encouraged to attend the voluntary mother-tongue lessons.

Sweden

In Sweden the instruction can roughly be divided into three groups according to the language of instruction.

First, there is instruction mainly through the medium of Swedish, in Swedish-speaking classes, together with Swedish children (and other immigrant children), with Swedish teachers, teaching materials and syllabuses. This instruction can be preceded by a shorter or longer period of instruction in a preparatory class (there were 141 of them at the end of 1981), or special lessons with intensive instruction in Swedish as a second language. It can be supported by auxiliary tuition, either in Swedish (language instruction) or in other subjects, through the medium of either Swedish or the mother tongue or both. This auxiliary tuition is obligatory for the child, if the school thinks that the child needs it. And it can also be accompanied by voluntary mother-tongue lessons inside school hours, usually no more than a couple of hours per week. This is still the most prevalent model of instruction for immigrant children in Sweden, affecting almost 80% of all pupils with another mother tongue.

Second, there is instruction in classes with two teachers, one Swedish and one from an immigrant group, and both Swedish children and immigrant

TABLE 2
West German classes

Type of class	Language of instruction	Goal	Integration/assimilation (yes/no) Physical vis-à-vis		Content (C)	Ideology (I)
			German children	other GW children		
1. "regular classes"	L2	Assimilation	+	+	C++	I++
2. "special classes"	L2	Transition and assimilation	–	+	C+	I++
3. International preparatory classes	L2	Transition(?)	–	+	C–	I+
4. 1–2-year national preparatory classes	L2 + L1	Transition(?)	–	–	C–	I±
5. National classes of several years' duration	L1	Transition(?)	–	–	C–	I–
6. Complete national classes	L1	Maintenance	–	–	C––	I––

TABLE 3
Swedish classes

| Type of class | Language of instruction | Goal | Integration/assimilation (yes/no) Physical *vis-à-vis* | | Content (C) | Ideology (I) |
			Swedish children	Other Immigrant children		
1. Swedish classes	L2	Assimilation	+	+	C++	I++
2. Compound classes	L2 + L1	Transition	+	−	C+	I++
3. Mother-tongue classes	L1	Maintenance + bilingualism	−	−	C+	I+

children from one nationality only, so-called *compound* or *composite* classes, or cooperation classes as the Swedish authorities also call them to make them more attractive to the immigrant organizations who prefer mother-tongue classes. As a principle the groups are instructed separately by their own teachers through the medium of their respective mother tongues part of the time, and together through the medium of Swedish during the rest of the time. In fact, the amount of instruction which the immigrant children get through the medium of their mother tongue is often quite small. The amount of Swedish-medium instruction increases rapidly, and usually the goal is that the children should be able to participate in exclusively Swedish-medium instruction at the latest after grade 3 (except for the voluntary mother-tongue lessons—all the auxiliary measures already mentioned also apply to these classes and mother-tongue classes, the third alternative). It is, accordingly, a typical transitional model (and it is clear that only the immigrant children, not the Swedish children, are to become bilingual). There were 284 classes of this type at the end of 1981.

Third, there exists instruction mainly through the medium of the mother tongue, with Swedish as a second language, in *mother-tongue* classes (the Swedish authorities often call them "monolingual classes" to make them sound segregatory, even if they in fact produce the most bilingual pupils in the Swedish school system—the only classes deserving the name "monolingual classes" are of course the Swedish-only-medium classes). These classes run for at least the first three years, but preferably at least through the first six grades, with an increasing number of lessons in Swedish, and later also through the medium of Swedish. This is the model which the immigrant organizations want and most researchers recommend (even if there are very strong and emotional debates about it—see Skutnabb-Kangas, 1982a, b), because it seems to produce the best results with relation to bilingualism, school achievement and the happiness of the children (see Hanson, 1982). At the end of 1981 there were 600 classes of this type, covering 10.6% of the immigrant pupils in comprehensive school, and their numbers have been rapidly increasing, despite opposition on the part of the Swedish local school authorities in many municipalities. Even if most of the existing classes are Finnish (468), many other languages are also represented, and the immigrant organizations are unanimous in demanding them. In 1981 there were 5 Arabic-medium classes, 2 Assyrian, 6 Chinese, 1 English, 2 German, 29 Greek, 1 Polish, 23 Spanish, 26 Turkish, 34 Yugoslav language (mostly Serbocroatian-medium) and 3 for other languages (see Table 3).

The first type is clearly *assimilationist*, the second *transitional*, and the third *maintenance* (including further development of the immigrant language and culture, *and* providing competence in Swedish language and culture). The last model is thus mainly geared towards a bilingual, bicultural life in Sweden, also because it makes use of the Swedish syllabus (added with new syllabuses, developed in Sweden, for mother-tongue and Swedish-as-a-second-language teaching), and teachers should preferably have a teacher training given in Sweden (or at least Swedish in-service training). The first two class types are integrative in relation to both content and ideology; the first is completely integrative physically, the second as far as Swedish children are concerned, but not with regard to other immigrant children. Mother-tongue classes physically segregate the immigrant children in the beginning, but *not* in relation to content or ideology (as the German national classes do).

Results: West Germany and Sweden

Let us first look at school attendance itself. In West Germany it is officially estimated (Kühn, 1979) that around 25% of the GW children of obligatory school age, living legally in the country, do not go to school. The Federal Government admits that the figure can be around 20% (Weiterentwicklung, 1980). Probably very few of the children whose parents are in West Germany illegally go to school. Widgren's estimate, made for Unesco in 1975, of the number of school-aged migrant children not attending school in the industrialized countries in western Europe was 300 000 to 500 000. Estimates by different researchers and migrant organizations now talk about figures of around 800 000.

In Scandinavia there are no official figures for immigrant children not going to school. There are certainly not as many children in Scandinavia, proportionally, not going to school as in West Germany, France or Switzerland, but it is reasonable to assume that there are more immigrant children than native children not attending school. We found out for instance, when comparing the school statistics with the census, that less than a third of young Turks in the last years of the obligatory school age-period residing in Denmark actually attended school (Rahbek Pedersen and Skutnabb-Kangas, 1982).

Kühn estimates in his report that more than 50% of all GW children leave school without a leaving certificate—and here he is, of course, only talking about those children who *do* go to school. The government report says that around 50% of the GW children do not attend any vocational school, more than 50% do not get any kind of leaving certificate from any kind of school, and more than two-thirds of the roughly 45 000 foreigners who leave school every year get no form of vocational training (Weiterentwicklung, 1980). The official figure for GW children leaving the obligatory school without a certificate in Nordrhein-Westfalen was 65% in 1977, compared with 20% of the German children, mostly working-class children (according to FIDEF,

1978). Of all German children around 30% continued to study either in Gymnasium or in Realschule, according to FIDEF (1978), but only 4% of the Turkish children did so; or, if one takes only Gymnasium and the latest figures, 23% of German but only 3% of GW children (Statistisches Bundesamt, 1981; Schmitt, 1981).

Even if the Scandinavian figures are not as alarming as the West German ones, the results for immigrant children do not seem to be as good as those for the majority children. According to immigrant school psychologist Sunil Loona, only 1% of the immigrant children finish an education after comprehensive school (see Viten, 1982). In Sweden, 69% of pupils with other mother tongues than Swedish, compared to 80% of those with Swedish, went straight on to upper secondary school from grade 9 of comprehensive school, according to a study of all compulsory school leavers in 1979. The immigrant pupils are admitted to a lesser extent than the Swedish pupils to the 3- and 4-year theoretical lines and more to the vocationally oriented 2-year lines and shorter courses (SÖ, 1981). It is also well known that drop-out rates for immigrant pupils in upper secondary schools are higher than for Swedish pupils. In Denmark, of all immigrant children from the two largest immigrant groups (from Turkey and Pakistan) who left the obligatory school between 1975 and 1978, only 1.8% had finished a further education by October 1978, while 11% underwent some kind of further education, and 87% got no further education whatsoever. Not a single child from Turkey or Pakistan finished Gymnasium during that time in Denmark. Many children dropped out before the 8th grade, or didn't come to school at all, and should therefore be added to the figure of 87% not getting any further education (Rahbek Pedersen and Skutnabb-Kangas, 1982).

There is also sometimes a tendency in all Scandinavian countries, on the part of the authorities (especially in Denmark) and even a few researchers (mainly in Sweden), to deny the bad results. The Danish Minister of Education, Dorte Bennedsen, tells us that "the present measures seem to function perfectly well" (1980, p. 341; my translation).

There exists abundant evidence for the bad results in schools, of overrepresentation of phenomena which reflect psychological, social and academic difficulties among migrant children and youth both in schools and outside. I have (among many others) written extensively about these manifestations of social injustice elsewhere (e.g. Skutnabb-Kangas, 1975, 1978, 1979) and will, consequently, not discuss them here. The future chances of immigrant and GW youth on the labour market also look grim—and this is a more important indicator of success of the school system than school marks or results on language tests. According to Kühn (1979) even those GW youngsters who *do* have a leaving certificate from

Hauptschule (less than half of those who attend) are without chances of getting qualified jobs with possibilities of advancement. His opinion is that almost all foreign children and youngsters in West Germany are in a situation where they are about to assume the role of complete outcasts, pariahs in society, if very drastic measures are not taken. And, it seems that the latest measures in West Germany increase rather than decrease these negative possibilities. In all Western European countries we are forcing part of the migrant youth to become a new type of bitter, physically violent "lumpenproletariat".

Again, even in Scandinavia where the results in schools, especially in Sweden, are better than in West Germany, the same type of figures exist, showing overrepresentation in unemployment statistics etc. SIV-Dokumentation (23 April 1982) notes that foreigners are twice as unemployed as Swedes. Unemployment has risen for both groups, but the relationship remains the same. And the situation is much worse in Denmark and Norway.

This becomes more understandable when we look at different rates of development in different countries. Minority children simply fail earlier (and more brutally) in typical GW countries, while immigrant countries may give the children an (illusionary?) better start, a better chance in the beginning. In GW countries the school already tells the foreign children what their future place is. In immigrant countries other societal forces like discrimination on the labour market, guarantee that they don't get good jobs anyway to the same extent as native youngsters, even if they succeed in getting the same training. In an American book, *Who gets ahead*, Jencks and others "document the fact that not only are economic returns from schooling twice as great for individuals who are economically advantaged to begin with, but for, say, black students, even finishing high school will probably not bring any significant benefits. Thus, even if we could alter the school to equalize achievement [and that is one of the goals in mother-tongue classes] the evidence suggests that it might not make a significant difference in the larger framework in which schools exist" (Apple, 1980, p. 3). So, even if minority children did get as much as majority children out of the school (and they don't) that might not help them in getting a good job. And this is clearly shown in the Scandinavian unemployment statistics, while in West Germany the failure comes even earlier. It seems that the powerless status of the parents is reproduced in both Scandinavia and West Germany, even if the results are much more disastrous (and show earlier) in West Germany, quite regardless of different methods and programmes. Before I come back to how the different programmes in Sweden and West Germany serve the goal of preparing the children to fulfil the functions Castles outlined (see earlier section), I shall compare the programmes with other educational programmes in other parts of the world.

Monolingual/bilingual: the relationship between method and goal

When one looks at different programmes and notices that some programmes teach children through their first language (L1), some through a second language (L2), and that some programmes succeed in making the children very bilingual while others don't, quite regardless of whether the children have been taught through the medium of one language or two, or through the medium of L1 or L2, confusion is unavoidable unless one tries to single out a few factors and understand some of the principles. Therefore, I will here distinguish between the *linguistic organization* of the programme (monolingual or bilingual) and the *goal* of the education (monolingualism or bilingualism). When speaking about goals, I will first look at the linguistic goals only, and then try to see what societal purposes the linguistic goals serve (i.e. treat them first as independent and then as mediating variables).

There are four theoretical possibilities:

1. *Monolingual* education leading to *monolingualism*
2. *Bilingual* education leading to *monolingualism*
3. *Monolingual* education leading to *bilingualism*
4. *Bilingual* education leading to *bilingualism*.

I will discuss all of them briefly and also distinguish, where appropriate, between majority and minority (defined in terms of power relationships, not numbers).

1A. *Monolingual education the goal of which is monolingualism for majority children* is the most common way of educating majority children in most countries with a large so-called international language as the majority language (e.g. West Germany, the United States, Britain, the Soviet Union, France, China, Spain, etc.). Canada is one of the most notable exceptions here. The method is likewise used in many smaller countries which are, or pretend to be, linguistically homogeneous, like all Scandinavian countries. In all these countries children often have some foreign languages in their curriculum as subjects, but they seldom approximate to anything resembling bilingual competence.

1B. *Monolingual education the goal of which is monolingualism for minority children* varies according to whether the goal is monolingualism in the majority language or monolingualism in the minority language. When the goal is (i) *monolingualism in the majority language*, a *submersion* programme is used.[3] Here there is often a very strong cultural assimilationist goal at the societal–political level. Often structural incorporation of the minority is not allowed on an equal footing with the majority members—i.e. the minority members do not have equal rights in the educational, social and political fields and on the labour market (but often they *do* have the same duties, for instance as far as paying taxes is concerned—see Ekberg, 1980). The mother tongue of the minority children is not even taught as a subject for them (let alone taught to majority children) in countries where cultural pluralism is not supported, and where it is seen as a threat to the unity of the country.

One of the more implicit goals in this type of programme is that those minority children who succeed in the programme are at the same time socialized into accepting those majority values which control the schools. In that way those minority children who succeed are pacified; they are alienated from their own group, and they don't feel solidarity with those minority children who do not succeed (see, e.g. Hernández-Chávez, 1978). It is the "we-made-it-and-they-can-do-it-too-if-they-work-hard-enough" syndrome. Those minority children, on the other hand, who don't succeed are pacified by shame; they are made to feel that it is their own fault—the "blame-the-victim" technique (Skutnabb-Kangas, 1980).

This is the most common model still for most minority children throughout the world. These programmes, which show bad results all over the world (see, e.g. Bhatnagar, 1976), assimilate the children at the same time as they prevent them from getting a good education. This model is used with almost almost all minority children in Australia and in Canada (though there are exceptions, notably the French but also, for instance, some of the Ukrainians in Canada). It was the model in the United States before the bilingual education programmes came into existence, and it is the model that the conclusions in the new "evaluation" of bilingual education research would lead to again if implemented (even if the new programmes are called "structured immersion" instead of submersion, to sell them better—Baker and de Kanter, 1981). This model is used almost exclusively in Denmark, Norway, France, Great Britain, Holland, etc., and to a great extent in Sweden (Table 3, Class 1) and West Germany (Table 2, Classes 1–3).

These programmes educate future assembly line workers and future unemployed, future losers. One of their perhaps unintended results is also the type of violent physical reactions which we have seen (and certainly will see more of) in riots in many cities during the last decade or two—and in the crisis climate now and the many racist attacks, more or less silently approved of by the establishment, in a way which would have been unthinkable ten years ago. These reactions are going to increase very rapidly.

If the goal is (ii) *monolingualism in the minority language*, there is often a situation with different types of segregational or apartheid programmes; see, for instance, the education for different African groups in different "home lands" (Bantustans) in South Africa, or typically for Turkish but also for other guest worker children, especially in Bavaria but also in other parts of West Germany (Table 2, Class 6 and, to a certain extent, Class 5). In this type of programme the implicit social goal is to try to prevent a minority (in a *power* sense, if not numerically) from getting their share of power and of the goods and services of the mainstream majority society. This is done, among other things, by limiting their linguistic capacity to influence the society: they do not learn the power language (or don't learn it well enough because, of course, they don't become completely monolingual). Subordinated groups are also prevented from cooperating with each other, because they are prevented from acquiring a common language, a shared medium of communication and analysis, a prerequisite for solidarity and common action.

These programmes also educate future assembly line workers, but these youngsters may have a better chance of uniting, developing solidarity and protesting than the youngsters coming from submersion programmes. These youngsters, or at least an élite among them, may have a constructive, articulate rage as a motive, and they may succeed in canalizing it, whereas the only motive forces many submersion youngsters may have are shame, rootlessness, an unanalysed destructive rage without direction and goal. This more positive perspective for segregation than for submersion may apply more to indigenous than to migrant minorities.

2. *Bilingual education the goal of which is monolingualism for minority children* may sound a bit harsh, because a complete monolingualism is not the goal here either. But characteristic of this type of programme is the goal of assimilation, too. It is said, often even officially, that children need not be taught bilingually (or even have instruction in their mother tongue as a subject in many cases) once they have learned enough of the majority language to be able to follow instruction through the medium of the majority language—this is typically the case, for instance, in the United States. The criteria for when children can be transferred to majority-medium instruction are often based on loose evaluations of when the children can manage orally in simple face-to-face interaction discussing concrete everyday things, situations where contextual cues help the child to understand (i.e. when they master basic interpersonal communicative skills (BICS)—see Cummins, 1980—superficial linguistic fluency in context-embedded and cognitively less demanding situations; see Cicourel, 1982, and Skutnabb-Kangas, 1982c). Often children at this stage still don't have any chance to succeed on a par with majority children in cognitively and linguistically more demanding de-contextualized tasks (see the discussion of cognitive/academic language proficiency (CALP) in Cummins, 1980). The result often is that they fail miserably at school, regardless of superficial oral fluency (see Cummins, 1981). All the transitional bilingual programmes belong to this type (see Table 2, Class 4; Table 3, Class 2).

Even if it is sometimes said officially that the goal in this type of programme is bilingualism (as is done in Sweden for instance, especially about the compound classes—see Skutnabb-Kangas, 1982a), the most important value being stressed is that the children learn the majority language (as early and as fast as possible). Often no real efforts are made to give the children a fair chance to reach native competence in their L1 even if lip service is paid to the importance of maintaining and sometimes even developing the mother tongue and the cultural ties of the minority children (and in many countries even this lip service is now disappearing and the harsh assimilationist demands are accompanied by close to fascist attitudes towards other cultures—see, for example, the interview with Storm Rasmussen, the person responsible for the Danish Social Democratic Party's immigrant policy, in *Information*, 4–5 September 1982.) This can easily be checked by looking at the measures which are taken to give equal status to both languages involved in the schools. If in such a comparison one finds several ponts where the languages have *not* been made equal (granted that the language which has a weaker status outside school should be "compensated for" inside the school), that shows that the real goal probably is closer to monolingualism than bilingualism, regardless of all the pious phrases.

3A. *Monolingual education the goal of which is bilingualism for majority children* is the Canadian speciality—immersion programmes[4] in the early grades, before the instruction through the medium of the mother tongue of the children has started. These types of programmes are likely to arise in situations where a linguistic majority needs to become bilingual for instrumental (not integrative) reasons, in order not to lose old privileges or in order to get new benefits or privileges guaranteed to bilinguals. This is a situation where the minority has become strong enough to get through demands for bilingualism and benefits for bilinguals (e.g. on the job market). But because, previously, the minority members were the ones who were bilingual, they were the ones who would now get all these new benefits, unless majority members also become bilingual. These types of programmes are supported by the powerful majority community, and that helps the L1 of the children in its development, even if it is not the language of instruction in the early years. In Canada and the United States there are many such programmes, in French, German, Spanish, Hebrew, Ukrainian, etc. (see Lambert and Taylor, 1982), but curiously enough they have not yet spread to Europe. From all the existing evidence we can predict that we would get very good results. Just to be a bit provocative we could, with good scientific backing, say: *not a single child* in West Germany, France, Great Britain, Holland, Sweden, Denmark and Norway needs *any* instruction in school through the medium of (respectively) German, French, English, Dutch,

Swedish, Danish and Norwegian, during the first 6 years of education. Everybody in these countries could be taught through the medium of minority languages (which, for minorities, should be their own mother tongue). When we get the first European immersion programmes, it will show that some of the minorities are approaching the strength needed for making their language instrumentally attractive to majorities—and I would like to predict that Finns in Sweden will soon be able to do that, to get Sweden to guarantee the Finnish language a special official or semiofficial status in Sweden.

3B. *Monolingual education the goal of which is bilingualism for minority children* is a maintenance or language shelter programme, where the L1 of the children is the medium of instruction for the first several years, possibly through the obligatory school, with the majority language as a second language. These programmes seem to function well (see, e.g. Cummins, 1981; Hanson, 1982; Skutnabb-Kangas, 1981b). Good examples are the Swedish-medium schools for the Swedish-speaking indigenous minority in Finland, the mother-tongue classes for immigrant children in Sweden (Table 3, Class 3), or the Francophone schools in English Canada. Maintenance programmes have arisen as a protest against suppression of minorities, and often their existence shows that the minority community has started a dynamic struggle to get their share of the goods and services of the majority society. A very good example of this is the programme declaration of the newly founded National Hispanic University in California, presented at the California Association for Bilingual Education conference in San Francisco in January 1982. Often these programmes also reflect a revitalization situation, like that of the Ukrainians in Canada. Sometimes they also reflect a situation where the minority had more power when the programmes came into existence, but even in these situations (like the one for the Swedish-speaking minority, a former power-majority) the programmes now seem to fulfil the same purpose for the children as "regular" maintenance programmes.

The above mentioned model, monolingual education leading to bilingualism, seems to lead to very good results for both minority and majority children, especially in situations where there are great status differences between the minority and majority languages and groups, but also in situations with smaller differences. One of the prerequisites for the model to function is that the other language, the language which is not the language of instruction, is taught as a subject. *The main principle for achieving high levels of bilingualism in general, namely, support via instruction in the language which otherwise is less likely to develop*, also applies to these programmes. The monolingual instruction in these programmes is always conducted in that language which the children otherwise would be less likely to learn properly (especially in its more formal aspects) in the society outside school. And that is, for both the majority children and the minority children, the minority language (i.e. for the majority children it is a foreign (or second) language; for the minority children, their mother tongue).

4. The last case is *bilingual education the goal of which is bilingualism*. It is a type of education where great concern is placed on trying to reach high levels in *both* languages, and where a realistic evaluation is made of how much support each language needs. It should be clear here, too, that if one of the languages would not otherwise develop, it should get most of the resources and time inside school. Even if the status differences are not terribly big, one or the other of the languages mostly needs compensation inside school, often because it is less used in that particular society or in the environment where the children live.

But it also seems that this type of model functions best in situations with fairly small status differences between the languages and speakers (regardless of the reasons why the differences are small), often (but not always) with children from privileged backgrounds, and often for students above the elementary level. The previous model, monolingual education leading to bilingualism could, at a later stage (e.g. after 6–9 years), develop to bilingual education leading to bilingualism (and it often does). But then the development of the minority language should get special attention.

If there are both majority and minority children in bilingual programmes (as, for instance, in the compound classes in Sweden), mutuality is absolutely essential. *Both groups should learn both languages* (for a good case study description of how that can be done see Curtis' article in Cummins and Skutnabb-Kangas, in preparation). More time should be spent with the minority language. If the minority children are the only ones to become bilingual, and the majority children learn but a few songs and phrases of the minority language (as in Sweden: Table 3, Class 2), then it is closer to the situation described earlier as bilingual education leading to monolingualism.

The four models presented could also be seen as forming a progression, where the first two models do not respond to the needs of individual children and do not give them the advantages that high levels of bilingualism can lead to—quite the opposite, they can be disastrous, at least for individual minority children—whereas the last two give them good chances. And, of course, in an ideal society of equality, peace and mutual understanding, all children should be educated bilingually (see Gonzáles, 1975).

One can also look at the monolingually organized programmes inside another type of framework. here I leave out the transitional programmes (because they later function in the same way as submersion programmes, even if they are more human in the beginning) and the bilingual programmes leading to bilingualism (because they are not (yet?) a realistic large-scale alternative). If we cross-tabulate the language used (IL) or not used (NIL) as the medium of instruction, with whether it is (L1) or is not (L2) the mother tongue of the children—and suppose at first that the IL always develops to a native-like level (+)—we obtain four logical possibilities, where we assume that the NIL either *does have* (+) a chance to develop (through society support, language arts instruction, positive peer contact, etc.), or that it does *not* have (−) this chance (it does not develop, starts to deteriorate, or is replaced by the IL). Thus:

	1	2	3	4
IL	L2 +	L2 +	L1 +	L1 +
NIL	L1 +	L1 −	L2 −	L2 +

According to this scheme, children in the first and last case would become bilingual, while those in the two middle cases would become either monolingual or dominant in one of the languages, in each case the language of instruction.

When we compare these four completely theoretical cases with the distinctions made earlier, we can see that they correpond to them. The *first* case, where L2 is the language of instruction and where L1 does develop, is the situation in *immersion* programmes. The *second* case, where L2 is also the IL, but where L1 does not develop or starts to deteriorate, characterizes *submersion* programmes. The *third* case, where L1 is the IL and where L2 does not develop, is the situation in *segregation or apartheid* programmes. And the *fourth* case, where L1 is again the IL but where L2 *does* develop, is the situation in *maintenance* or *language shelter* programmes, *mother-tongue* classes.

Now if it really were the case that the language of instruction would develop to a native-like level in all situations, we could stop screaming about minority education. We might think that it is a pity that a potential for bilingualism, biculturalism and international understanding is lost in the two middle cases, but we known that a lot of children in the world are monolingual and happy with that, and do well in school. But it is quite clearly the case, contrary to the common belief which has guided minority education, that using a language as a medium of instruction does not guarantee that that language develops to a native-like level in all aspects of linguistic competence. Some programmes produce deficits in that language too, and these deficits vary both quantitatively and qualitatively.

These deficits, if any, seem to be absolutely minor in immersion and maintenance programmes, and if they exist, they can be "cured" so to say inside the system, by the individual, with the help of school: better teacher training, better teaching materials (L1–IL in maintenance); increased peer contact in situations where there are no societal status-obstacles (L2–IL in immersion); or where the self-confidence, pride and strength given by the school organization gives children the means to cope with and increase peer contact even if there is some discrimination (L2–NIL in maintenance). It also seems that any deficits produced in these programmes have to do with aspects of language which don't necessarily affect school achievement (i.e. they are BICS-related factors, which in both cases may affect the L2 of the children but they can easily be coped with later, with increased peer contact with speakers of the children's L2).

The isolationist segregatory apartheid programmes may sometimes show deficits in the language of instruction, even if it is the children's L1, especially in GW-situations with poor teaching conditions and materials. But they show especially big deficits in the NIL because of poor teaching (which mostly is not the teachers' fault) and lack of contact with NIL and NIL speakers due to physical segregation, psychological discrimination or, mostly, a combination of both. As long as the goal of these programmes is segregation, it would be naive to think that the instruction of the second language could be improved so as to produce native competence in it, because native competence in the majority language is precisely what these programmes want to *prevent*. Here part of the solution of the problem quite clearly lies outside the school system and outside the families and individuals themselves. What is needed is not language treatment but social treatment.

The greatest deficits seem to be produced in the submersion programmes for minority children, both indigenous and immigrant—here they can affect both languages. The deficits in the mastery of the foreign language of instruction often seem to manifest themselves in the more cognitive/academic aspects of language proficiency (CALP), and since this is the aspect that instruction in the higher grades draws on, many children who in the beginning did well (because of well developed BICS) start to fail (Cicourel, 1982). More and better second-language teaching doesn't seem to help here either; the deficit needs social rather than linguistic remedies.

To sum up, it seems that an instruction in a second language which at the same time prevents the CALP of the L1 (which is part of the common underlying proficiency for cognitive/academic ability *across* languages; see Cummins, 1981) from developing, or doesn't support it, produces poor results in both languages and, accordingly, in school in general (Cummins, 1981). A life (and school) situation which develops the common underlying proficiency produces good results, quite regardless of which is the language of instruction. It is *not* axiomatic (as Unesco says, 1953) that the child's first language is always the best possible medium of instruction. The question is under which circumstances common CALP can be developed. It seems that programmes of immersion and maintenance succeed in developing CALP and making the children bilingual (already or, in some cases, with minor educational improvements; see Dutscher, 1982; also articles in Cummins and Skutnabb-Kangas, in preparation). Those programmes, on the other hand, which in the earlier scheme were characterized as monolingual programmes with the goal of monolingualism seem to produce (a risk of) deficits of a major character, deficits which pertain to the more cognitive/academic decontextualized aspects of language proficiency (in one or both languages) and, accordingly, school achievement; these cannot be coped with inside the school, regardless of how good, liberal and well-intentioned the teachers are (Stone, 1981). These programmes produce bad results because the bad results serve certain social, economic and political functions.

Concluding remarks

How then does school reflect the changing function of migrants, where a GW policy can be seen as mainly an answer to the earlier policy phase (exploitation of cheap flexible labour) and an immigrant policy as an additional answer to the new phase (development and retention of a new native underclass to function as a buffer)?

Since, according to Castles (1980), the old function of guest workers presupposes that they are mobile, even the children must be educated to be mobile, ready to be sent back whenever their parents' (or their own) labour is no longer needed. They should be prevented from being educated to stay and to be integrated. According to the new function as a buffer, the children of immigrants, on the other hand, must be *made* to stay and must be prevented from going back. Even if both groups are trained to be used as cheap labour (because they, as non-educated or badly educated, cannot choose their jobs), this conflict in function explains why the goal is monolingualism in different languages for the two groups: monolingualism in the minority language in *segregation* programmes makes the children linguistically "equal" (in the same weak position, unable to demand any rights, or better jobs, or more education) to their minority-language-monolingual mobile parents, and easy to send back. Monolingualism in the majority language in *submersion* programmes prevents the immigrant children from going back, at the same time as, by assimilating them to the values of (parts of) the majority society, it prevents the development of solidarity with others with the same low status.

In Germany, the GW children are kept unintegrated by preventing, both organizationally and linguistically, a real integration in German classes and in the German society. This is aided by the use of syllabi, teachers (sent and controlled by the embassies) and teaching materials from the country of origin. The immigrant children are prevented from wanting to return (because they are not taught enough of their own language and culture to know anything about the country of origin, of which they are made to feel ashamed) and from being able to return (mainly because they don't know the language well enough). Because of the different functions GWs and immigrants fulfil, different countries use different methods to make children fulfil them. Therefore, researchers in West Germany and Scandinavia must also provide different recommendations, if they want these to be scientifically sound. In West Germany enemy number one for the GW in the educational context is *forced segregation*. In that situation the *only way to ensure non-segregation is to put the children into German classes* (i.e. into submersion programmes, which we know don't work), and eventually force the German classes to change, so that the needs of GW children are better met. That should, in time, lead to a new "segregation" of the children (cf. Greeks in Germany) but with a completely different goal. But, for the time being, putting the children into German classes is the only way to ensure (especially for Turkish children) that they: (a) learn at least some German; (b) get instruction which is not directly, at least, undemocratic and strongly authoritarian; (c) get instruction which can give them the same qualifying content which German children get; (d) can become familiar with both other GW children and German children; (e) get access to the same economic resources as German children. In Scandinavia, especially Sweden, the worst enemy is not segregation, but *forced assimilation*. There is a minimal risk that those recommendations which suggest a physical segregation of limited duration could be misused to promote a negative segregation of a Gastarbeiter-type.

German researchers have to balance between different demands. By using what, from my point of view, is a defensive strategy—namely, recommending "integration" of GW children into German classes (something they know is not the best possible alternative from the individual child's point of view)—they try to prevent even worse things from happening, from the whole GW group's point of view. They also have to make their recommendations so that, on the one hand, they don't argue against what they know is good for the child (mother-tongue classes) when trying to push for "integration" while, on the other hand, they don't offer the authorities a chance of using research results and recommendations which have been achieved and are useful relative to an assimilationist immigrant policy to legitimize and even strengthen a segregatory GW policy. Some of the Scandinavian research is, for instance, sometimes presented by German authorities as a support for the segregatory Bavarian model, which it does *not* support, regardless of the superficial similarity of using the first language as the medium of instruction in both Bavarian Turkish classes and, say, Finnish mother-tongue classes in Sweden.

Although the climate for analyzing this type of problem has become harsher, even in Scandinavia, during the last couple of years (especially in Sweden) and the level of the debate is extremely low (especially in Denmark), it still seems to me that many of us Scandinavian researchers use a more offensive strategy in tackling the questions of minority education. Having more clear-cut lines in one aspect should give us better chances to deepen the analysis in other respects—and differentiation is badly needed. It would be naive of researchers or school authorities or immigrant organizations to believe in one global model, generalizable to minority education in all countries, for all minority groups and during different phases of economic and political development. Nice global theories are not worth much. But it is even more dangerous to say: let's be liberal and offer a lot of models. Random choice and repetition of the same old mistakes which many other countries have made is something other than differentiated choice preceded by thorough analysis.

Notes

1. I would like to thank Ingeborg Gutfleisch, Bert-Olaf Rieck, Hartmut Haberland and Wilfried Stölting for help with obtaining the latest materials and for discussions about the German situation; Jim Cummins, Merrill Swain and Pertti Toukomaa for our many discussions about the general theoretical framework; and Mahmut Erdem, Christian Horst, Marios Nikolinakos, Markku Peura and Sunil Loona for discussions and comments about connections between minority education, economy and politics and the role of research and researchers.

2. I use the double term *integrative/assimilationist* to reflect the terminological confusion: for me integration (when defined culturally, not structurally) means a voluntary learning of the language and cultural traits of the other group, without giving up one's own, whereas assimilation means giving up one's own. Integration, which is the only goal giving a possibility of choice to the minority member, should be the goal in societal minority policy although it may not always be possible.

3. A *submersion* (sink-or-swim) programme is a programme where minority children with a low-status mother tongue are forced to accept instruction through the medium of a foreign majority language with high status, in classes where some children are native speakers of the language of instruction, where the teacher doesn't understand the first language of the minority children and where the majority language constitutes a threat to their mother tongue—a subtractive language learning situation.

4. An *immersion* programme is a programme where majority children with a high-status mother tongue voluntarily choose (among existing alternatives) to be

instructed through the medium of a foreign (minority) language, in classes with majority children only, where the teacher is bilingual so that the children in the beginning can use their own language, and where their own mother tongue is in no danger of not developing or of being replaced by the language of instruction—an additive language learning situation (for an account of these programmes see Swain and Lapkin, 1981).

References

Apple, M. W. (1980). *Reproduction, Contestation and Curriculum*. SUNY, Buffalo. Department of Social Foundations and Comparative Education Center Occasional Paper No. 8.

Baker, K. and de Kanter, A. (1981). *Effectiveness of Bilingual Education: A Review of the Literature* (Final Draft). US Department of Education, Washington.

Bennedsen, D. (1980). Problemerne omkring de fremmedsprogede børn. *Uddanelse* **5/6**, 337–343.

Bericht zur Lage der Ausländer in Berlin (1978). Regierende Bürgermeister von Berlin, Senatskanzlei, Planungsleitstelle, Berlin.

Bhatnagar, J. (1976). Education of immigrant children. *Canadian Ethnic Studies* **8**, 52–70.

Castles, S. (1980). The social time-bomb: Education of an under-class in West Germany. *Race and Class,* **21**, 369–387.

Castles, S. and Kosack, G. (1973). *Immigrant Workers and Class Structure in Western Europe*. Oxford University Press, London.

Cicourel, A. (1982). *Living in Two Cultures: The Socio-Cultural Situation of Migrant Workers and their Families*. Gower (UNESCO Press), Paris.

Commission for Racial Equality (1978). *Ethnic Minorities in Britain: Statistical Background*. CRE, London.

Cummins, J. (1980). The entry and exit fallacy in bilingual education. *NABE Journal* **4**(3), 25–59.

Cummins, J. (1981). The role of primary language development in promoting educational success for language minority students. In *Schooling and Language Minority Students: A Theoretical Framework* (Ed. Evaluation, Dissemination and Assessment Center). EDAC (California University), Los Angeles.

Cummins, J. and Skutnabb-Kangas, T. (in preparation). *Education of Linguistic Minority Children*. Multilingual Matters, Clevedon.

Dutcher, N. (1982). *The Use of First and Second Languages in Primary Education: Selected Case Studies*. World Bank Staff Working Paper No. 504, Washington.

Dittmar, N., Haberland, H., Skutnabb-Kangas, T. and Teleman, U. (1978). *Papers from the First Scandinavian–German Symposium on the Language of Immigrant Workers and their Children*. Universitetscenter, Lingvistgruppen, Roskilde. Paper No. 12.

Ekberg, J. (1979). *Invandrarna i Växjö*. Högskolan i Växjö, Växjö.

Ekberg, J. (1980). *Inkomstfördelning Mellan Invandrare och Svenskar via Offentlig Sektor*. Högskolan i Växjö, Växjö.

Fendrich, J. M. (1982). The elite policy response to race and ethnic relations in capitalist societies. Paper presented to the World Congress of Sociology, Mexico City.

Fishman, J. A. (1976). *Bilingual Education: An International Sociological Perspective*. Newbury, Rowley, Massachusetts.

Föderation der Arbeitervereine der Türkei in der BRD e.V. (FIDEF) (1978). *Bericht zur Bildungssituation Türkischer Kinder in der BRD*. FIDEF, Gelsenkirchen.

Gonzáles, J. M. (1975). Coming of age in bilingual/bicultural education: A historical perspective. *Inequality in Education*, **19**, 5–17.

Hammar, T. (in press). *European Immigration Policy: A Comparative Study*. Routledge & Kegan Paul, London.

Hanson, G. (1982). Integration and participation. Paper presented to the Fifth International School Psychology Colloquium, Stockholm.

Hernández-Chávez, E. (1978). Language maintenance, bilingual education and philosophies of bilingualism in the United States. In *International Dimensions of Bilingual Education* (Ed. J. Alatis). Georgetown University Press, Washington.

Hill, J. (1981). Paper presented to the Sixth International Congress of Applied Linguistics, Lund.

Horst, C. (1980). *Arbejdskraft: Vare eller menneske? Migration og Vesteuropaeisk Kapitalisme*. Adademisk Forlag, København.

Information (1982). (København: daily newspaper). 4–5 September.

Kjolseth, R. (1972). Bilingual education in the United States: For assimilation or pluralism? In *The Language Education of Minority Children* (Ed. B. Spolsky). Newbury, Rowley, Massachusetts.

Kühn, H. (1979). Memorandum zur Integration der Arbeitsimmigranten in der BRD. Stand und Weiterentwicklung der Integration der ausländischen Arbeitnehmer under ihrer Familien in der Bundesrepublik Deutschland. *Deutsch Lernen* **3**, 82–99.

Lambert, W. and Taylor, D. (1982). Language in the education of ethnic minority immigrants: Issues, problems and methods. Paper presented to conference on Education of Ethnic Minority Immigrants, Miami.

Mackey, W. F. (1972). A typology of bilingual education. In *Advances in the Sociology of Language* (Ed. J. Fishman). Mouton, The Hague.

National Board of Immigration and Naturalization (1982). *Invandring och Kommunal Ekonomi*. Statens Invandrarverk, Norrköping.

Mot Rasismen (1982). *Temanummer Fremmedspråklige Barn og Skolen. Mot Rasismen*, 2.

Nikolinakos, M. (1973). *Politische Ökonomie der Gastarbeiterfrage*. Rowolt Taschenbuchverlag, Hamburg.

Nikolinakos, M. (1982). Research on migrant workers and the crisis of western capitalism. In *Invandrarminoriteter och Demokratisk Forskning* (Ed. M. Peura). Riksförbundet Finska Föreningar i Sverige, Stockholm.

Rahbek Pedersen, B. and Skutnabb-Kangas, T. (1982). *God, Bedre, Dansk?* Børn og Unge, København.

Reich, H. H. (1979). Deutschlehrer für Gastarbeiterkinder: Einer Übersicht über Ausbildungsmöglichkeiten in der Bundesrepublik. *Deutsch Lernen* 3, 3–14.

Reinans, S. (1981). Om den Andra Generationen. In *Invandringen och Framtiden* (Eds E. Hamberg and T. Hammar). Publica Liber Förlag, Stockholm.

Rieck, B-O. and Senft, I. (1978). Situation of foreign workers in the Federal Republic of Germany. In *Papers from the First Scandinavian-German Symposium on the Language of Immigrant Workers and their Children* (Eds N. Dittmar, H. Haberland, T. Skutnabb-Kangas and U. Teleman). Universitetscenter, Lingvistgruppen, Roskilde. Paper No. 12.

Schmitt, G. (1981). Auslandische Schuler in deutschen Klassen, in Die Unterrichtspraxis. *Beilage zur Lehrerzeitung Baden-Württemberg*, 14(3), 17–22.

SIV (Statens Invandrarverk) (1980, 1982). *Dokumentation*. SIV, Norrköping.

Skutnabb-Kangas, T. (1975). *Om Tvåspråkighet och Skolframgång*. Svenska Litteratursällskapets Nämnd för Samhällsforskning, Åbo, Forskningsrapporter No. 20.

Skutnabb-Kangas, T. (1978). Semilingualism and the education of migrant children as a means of reproducing the caste of assembly line workers. In *Papers from the First Scandinavian-German Symposium on the Language of Immigrant Workers and their Children* (Eds N. Dittmar, H. Haberland, T. Skutnabb-Kangas and U. Teleman). Universitetscenter, Lingvistgruppen, Roskilde. Paper No. 12.

Skutnabb-Kangas, T. (1979). Invandrarbarnens utbildning—forskning och politik. *Papers from the Second Nordic Conference on Bilingualism* (Stockholm: Akademilitteratur), pp. 158–178.

Skutnabb-Kangas, T. (1980). Violence as a method and outcome in the non-education of minority children. *ROLIG-papir*, 20 (Roskilde Universitetscenter).

Skutnabb-Kangas, T. (1981a). Bilingualism as an unrealistic goal in minority education. In *Bilingualism, Models of Education and Migration Policies* (Ed. I. Municio). Liber Förlag, Stockholm. (Commission for Immigration Research Report 1.)

Skutnabb-Kangas, T. (1981b). *Tvåspråkighet*. Liber Läromedel, Lund.

Skutnabb-Kangas, T. (1982a). Om metodologier, paradigm och ideologier i minoritetsutbildningsforskningen. In *Invandrarminoriteter och Demokratisk Forskning* (Ed. M. Peura). Riksförbundet Finska Föreningar i Sverige, Stockholm.

Skutnabb-Kangas, T. (1982b). Research and its implications for the Swedish setting—An immigrant point of view. Paper presented to Wenner-Gren Symposium on Multicultural and Multilingual Education, Stockholm.

Skutnabb-Kangas, T. (1982c). Arguments for teaching and consequences of not teaching minority children through the medium of their mother tongue, or, Rise and decline of the "typical" migrant child. Paper presented to conference on The Practice of Intercultural Education, Breukelen (Netherlands).

Spiess, U. (1979). Problemwandel in der Ausländerpolitik: Zur Entwicklung der ausländischen Bevölkerung in Berlin (West) 1972–78. *Deutsch Lernen*, 2, 43–66.

Statistisches Bundesamt (1981). *Statistisches Jahrbuch 1981 für die Bundesrepublik Deutschland*. SB, Stuttgart/Mainz.

Statistiska Meddelanden U. (1981). *Comprehensive Schools and Integrated Upper Secondary Schools 1980/81: Pupils with another Home Language than Swedish.* Statistical Reports, Stockholm.

Stone, M. (1981). *The Education of the Black Child in Britain: The Myth of Multiracial Education.* Fontana, London.

Stölting, W. (1978). Teaching German to immigrant children. In *Papers from the First Scandinavian-German Symposium on the Language of Immigrant Workers and their Children* (Eds N. Dittmar, H. Haberland, T. Skutnabb-Kangas and U. Teleman). Universitetscenter, Lingvistgruppen, Roskilde. Paper No. 12.

Swain, M. and Lapkin, S. (1981). *Bilingual Education in Ontario: A Decade of Research.* Ministry of Education, Toronto.

Swetland, C. (1978). *The Ghetto of the Soul.* UNESCO, Paris.

SÖ (Skolöverstyrelsen) (National Swedish Board of Education) (1981). Compulsory School Leavers in 1979 with Home Languages other than Swedish (Interim Report 1). SÖ, Stockholm.

TIP (Themen, Impulse, Projekte) (1982). *Informationen für die Arbeit mit Ausländischen Arbeitnehmern.* Bayerische Staatsministerium für Arbeit und Sozialordnung, München.

Türkei-Informationen. Föderation der Arbeitervereine der Türkei in der BRD e.V. (FIDEF), Düsseldorf.

UNESCO (1953). *The Use of Vernacular Languages in Education.* UNESCO, Paris.

Viten, G. (1982). Norsk skole—Ulike muligheter for norsk og utenlandske barn. *Mot Rasismen,* **2,** 4–8.

Weiterentwicklung der Ausländerpolitik: Beschlüsse der Bundesregierung vom 19. März (1980). *Deutsch Lernen,* **1,** 65–79.

Widgren, J. (1975). *Migration to Western Europe: The Social Situation of Migrant Workers and their Families.* UN/SOA/SEM/60/WP 2.

2
Language policy in multicultural Britain[1]

Viv Edwards

Inasmuch as a language policy existed in Britain in the first half of the twentieth century, it focussed on the unacceptability of Celtic languages and non-standard dialects of English in education, and the importance of teaching the standard. British schools were monolingual, monocultural institutions, one of whose functions was to enlighten those who departed from received linguistic and cultural norms. Dramatic population changes during the 1950s and 1960s, however, gave rise to important challenges to accepted values and practices. From the mid 1950s, settlers from Commonwealth countries in the Caribbean and the Indian sub-continent began arriving in Britain in response to the labour demand created by the post-war industrial boom. Though initial migration was associated mainly with these two areas, later there was settlement from East Africa and Hong Kong, and new waves of Cypriots and Italians arrived to join already established communities. Polish, Ukrainian, Hungarian, Vietnamese and other refugees, expelled or in voluntary exile, have also swelled the ranks of ethnic and linguistic minorities in Britain over the past three decades (Rosen and Burgess, 1980).

The presence of children from widely differing linguistic and cultural backgrounds in British schools made enormous organizational and pedagogical demands which were met only slowly by an education system remarkably resistant to change. Innovations were made on a piecemeal basis and for a very considerable period of time teachers and local education authorities

LINGUISTIC MINORITIES
ISBN 0-12-232760-8

(LEAs) received no political and little practical leadership from central government. The recognition of a need for language policies at national, local and school levels did not come until at least fifteen years after the first arrivals in the schools of the children of immigrants and the implementation of consistent policies is still at a very early stage.

At about the same time as non-English speaking children were arriving in England, language was also to prove a burning issue in Wales and Scotland. Growing ethnic consciousness and a sense of urgency about the need to halt the process of language decline have led to growing public pressure for the improved status of Welsh and Gaelic in education. Language policies in Scotland and, more particularly, in Wales have received considerably more thought, support and action than in England, and the results achieved are an impressive testimony to the importance of coherent policy. The lessons learnt in these areas, however, have not been applied elsewhere. Overseas migration to Wales and Scotland has been extremely limited and the Celtic developments as such have taken place quite independently of those in England.

The acceptance of ideas about linguistic and cultural diversity in some British schools has led to a questioning of traditional assumptions. It has produced demands for new pedagogies and a call for change in attitudes towards the learning and social needs of all children, not just ethnic minorities. This chapter attempts to trace developments over the last two decades, identifying issues that have been important in the formulation of policy and drawing attention to the unfortunate consequences of imprecise teaching strategies and general inaction.

Language policies for non-English-speaking pupils

Immigration to and settlement in Britain in the mid and late 1950s were almost exclusively adult affairs. It was not until the 1960s that heads of families were sufficiently settled to consider sending for dependants who had been left behind in the care of relatives. Housing shortages ensured that the only supply of low-price accommodation was in decaying inner city areas where schools were often under-staffed and had insufficient resources (Newsom, 1963; Plowden 1976). The arrival, throughout the school year, of considerable numbers of children of all ages, many of whom did not speak English, placed acute strain on teachers who were already working under difficult circumstances.

By the early 1960s it had become clear that the *laissez-faire* attitude frequently expressed in the comment "They'll pick up English in the playground" was untenable. The first official advice came in the Ministry of

Education pamphlet *English for Immigrants* (1963), which advocated the bringing together of non-English-speaking children in one school for English classes and stressed the need for a "carefully planned, intensive course making full use of modern methods of language teaching" (p. 15). Such a recommendation depended, of course, on the availability of teachers of English as a Second Language. There were, however, few trained teachers in this field and no attempt was made to attract those working abroad to return or, until the late sixties, to train new teachers. Even today there is a shortage of specialist staff (Bakhsh and Walker, 1980; CRE, 1980).

Throughout this period, one of the main obstacles to the development of a coherent national language policy was the marked degree of local autonomy in the education systems of England and Wales. In the absence of advice from central government, each LEA evolved its own system for meeting immediate needs. Little information was available on developments in other schools and authorities and the overall result was, in the words of one government report, "haphazard" (HMSO, 1973). The extent of diversity in provision is clearly illustrated by an extract from this report:

> Bristol has a large centre for secondary pupils and peripatetic teachers for primary ones; Haringey has no reception centre and no peripatetic teachers, but withdraws pupils within their own schools, with the backing of a resource centre, and, because of lack of space in schools, teaches some of them at home; Brent has a language centre for junior and secondary pupils, language classes at one high school and peripatetic teachers in infant schools; Ealing has immigrant reception classes in infant, junior and secondary schools and further withdrawal classes in a language centre for infants; Leicester has withdrawal classes in schools and no peripatetic teachers, but is thinking of setting up a reception centre; Liverpool appears to do little but has a small language centre in one school and intends to set up a language development centre; Bolton has a language centre to which primary pupils are withdrawn for half a day each day, peripatetic teachers in primary schools and a sophisticated system of help in secondary schools.
>
> p. 11

Dispersal policies

During the early 1960s discussion was marked by a preoccupation, among public and politicians alike, with the disruption of the normal class routine which could be caused by the presence of non-English-speaking pupils. There was a similar concern about the concentration within any one school or class. At the election of March 1966 it became clear that opposition to immigration was not the vote catching issue that some had feared but, nevertheless, official policy at this time "gave the accurate impression of having been devised under the pressure of circumstances and based on received ideas" (Rose *et al.,* 1969, p. 289).

The first public protest about the presence of immigrant children in schools was staged by parents at two primary schools in Southall in 1963. Sir Edward Boyle, as Minister of Education, attended a meeting organized by the parents. Although he totally rejected the idea of separate education for immigrant children, he later referred in Parliament to one school which had become "irretrievably immigrant" and, in order to prevent this happening elsewhere, suggested that LEAs should introduce zoning schemes which would limit the proportion of immigrant children within any one school to about 30%.

The Second Report of the Commonwealth Immigrants Advisory Council (CIAC, 1964), a body set up by the Conservative government, was published the following year, but had been drafted at the time of the Southall troubles. Significantly it stressed "the dangers of the creation of immigrant schools" and suggested the possibility of "arrangements to send children to some alternative school in order to preserve a reasonable balance" (p. 11). The official policy was first set out, however, in the HMSO White Paper of 1965, *Immigration from the Commonwealth,* and the Department of Education and Science (DES) Circular 7/65 which was incorporated in summary form in part (iii) of the White Paper. The need for dispersal in areas of high immigrant population was a keynote of these documents:

> In order to maintain the standards of education in schools attended by large numbers of immigrant children with language difficulties, special arrangements must be made to teach them English . . . Such arrangements can more easily be made, and the integration of the immigrants more easily achieved, if the proportion of immigrant children in a school is not allowed to rise too high.
>
> HMSO, 1965, paras 41–2

In accordance with Circular 7/65, the maximum proportion of immigrant children normally acceptable in a school was felt to be "about one third". This attempt at formulation of policy was, however, beset with difficulties. No statistics were available in 1965 for either the number of immigrant children in schools, or the proportion of these children experiencing language difficulties. Equally worrying, it has never been made clear whether the dispersal policy was to apply to all immigrant children or only to those who could not speak English. In the final analysis, government worries appear to have been completely unfounded. The publication of an Inner London Education Authority (ILEA) report in 1967, on 52 primary schools where immigrant children formed more than one third of the pupils, showed that non-immigrants in these schools achieved the same as the average for all pupils in ILEA schools on tests of English, verbal reasoning and mathematics. The formulation of the dispersal policy also represented a basic contradiction of earlier policy, since the pamphlet, *English for Immigrants,* had stated quite clearly that the most satisfactory arrangement for the teaching of English involved bringing children together for classes in one school (Ministry of Education, 1963).

Local reaction to the dispersal scheme varied a great deal (cf. Rose *et al.,* pp. 272–3). Some LEAs were already operating their own schemes; others found the practical difficulties of implementing dispersal too great; still others rejected the notion, either on the grounds that it violated the principal of the neighbourhood school, or because it could be perceived as discriminatory. The Plowden Report which appeared in 1967 also expressed strong reservations about dispersal and stressed that the only criteria for moving children to other schools should be language and other difficulties, and not simply their ethnic background. Yet, whatever the weakness of the policy which Power (1967, p. 6) described as "one of the unexplained administrative curiosities of the decade", the White Paper did stimulate discussion and formulation of more constructive policies.

Language policy after 1965

Undoubtedly one of the most important influences on the formulation of policy in the post-1965 period was the work undertaken by June Derrick and her colleagues as part of "The Leeds Project" (Derrick, 1967). Following proposals put forward by Derrick, the Schools Council, a government funded body, agreed to sponsor a feasibility study on LEA and classroom practices. On the basis of this study a three-year project was commissioned and set up at the University of Leeds Institute of Education from September 1966. The Leeds Project aimed to develop an introductory two-term course in English as a Second Language for children aged 8–13 years, a more advanced course for the same age group, and a course for newly arrived teenagers, as well as continuing research into the possibilities for 5–7 year olds. The extremely practical nature of the project gave rise to a set of policy imperatives quite different from those which had informed the pre-1965 dispersal schemes. It showed that the most urgent need was for books and materials; that initial teacher training should be extended to include language teaching for immigrants and that in-service training in this area should also be provided; and that nursery schools should be set up in areas of immigrant settlement. The teaching of English as a second language emerged as a priority irrespective of the proportion of immigrants in a school, since these children would be unable either to participate fully in school life or compete on equal terms for jobs without an adequate command of English. The project also served a useful teacher training function since approximately 150 teachers in 38 LEAs were involved in the trial of materials.

Another policy imperative which emerged in the wake of the 1965 White Paper was the need to collect accurate information on the distribution and language teaching needs of immigrant children. The collection of statistics in the early years of immigration had been avoided on the grounds that this action might be perceived as being discriminatory. It was not until January 1966 that Form 7 (i) (Schools) was issued by the DES as a supplement to the annual return of all pupils completed by head teachers. In Form 7 (i) "immigrants" were defined as

(1) Children born outside the British Isles who have come to this country with or to join parents whose country of origin was abroad.

(2) Children born in the United Kingdom to parents whose country of origin was abroad and who came to the United Kingdom on or after 1st January 19—. (Ten years before the date of the collection of statistics.)

DES, 1966–73

This definition, however, soon gave rise to a number of anomalies. The transition from "immigrant" to "non-immigrant" status for British-born children was apparently to be determined by the parents' length of stay and unrelated to educational needs. Thus the reduction of children "unable to follow a normal school curriculum with profit to themselves" (Townsend, 1971, p. 36) from 25 to 16% between 1967 and 1970 was likely to be a function, in part at least, of the smaller number of children classified as "immigrant" at the later date. It soon became clear that the definition did not provide a means of measuring the needs of schools for language teaching and the collection of statistics ceased in 1972. Margaret Thatcher's statement as Secretary of State for Education and Science that her department had "made no use of them whatsoever except to publish them" in June 1973 appeared to confirm that no attempt had been made to draw upon or use the statistics to inform official policy (Runnymede Trust and Radical Statistics Group, 1980, p. 93).

Nevertheless the need for accurate statistical information remained urgent. The 1965 feasibility study undertaken for the Schools Council by June Derrick of local authority policy and teaching practice in individual schools was never published. However, Hawkes (1966) had attempted a survey of local and national policy based on local press, correspondence, and personal contacts and, also in 1966, *Education* journal had undertaken a survey of local practices with the help of some 36 education officers in various parts of the country (see Power, 1967). The climate of opinion created by these independent initiatives may well have been highly instrumental in the DES decision to fund a series of projects based at the National Foundation for Educational Research (NFER). The first survey resulted in the publication of *Immigrants in England: the LEA Response* (Townsend,

1971) which concentrated on the administrative provisions of local education authorities to meet the needs of schools with immigrant pupils. This was followed by *Organisation in Multiracial Schools* (Townsend and Brittan, 1972) which dealt with the organizational measures appearing in a sample of multiracial schools, and *Multiracial Education: Need and Innovation* (Townsend and Brittan, 1973) which was designed to investigate teachers' views on syllabuses, and the need to identify development and innovation in this aspect of education. The findings of these three surveys have had important implications for the formulation of language and other policies relating to the education of non-English-speaking children.

Townsend and Brittan (1972), for instance, confirmed the special difficulties that had been created for both non-English-speaking children and schools by the acute shortage of specialist teachers of English as a second language. The comment of one headmaster drew attention to the extremely unsatisfactory arrangements at which some schools arrived:

> There seems little doubt that many immigrant pupils are placed with less able pupils because of language difficulties. There is a danger that at this stage the progress of the immigrants will be unduly retarded because of the effects of pupil and teacher expectations on pupils' performance.
>
> Townsend and Brittan, 1972, p. 29

The situation which the NFER reports outlined clearly pointed to the need for further and more accurate information than was currently available. Predictably, the decision in 1972 to cease the collection of educational statistics relating to children's ethnic origin caused considerable controversy for a number of years. It was felt that valuable opportunities were being lost both for informing government policy and for quantifying and locating particular needs (Bullock, 1975; HMSO, 1977). Rampton (1981) recommended that from 1st September 1982 all schools should record the ethnic origin of a child's family on school entry and that the DES should reincorporate the collection of information on ethnic origin of pupils in its annual statistical exercise and introduce ethnic classification into its school leavers' survey.

In the meantime the most significant initiative in this area has been undertaken by the ILEA who decided in 1978 to provide a linguistic map of schools in their authority. Prior to the collection of statistics they had expressed anxiety that the volume of specialist teaching had been determined "by overt demand rather than need, some of which may be latent" (ILEA, 1977, p. 10). The first census largely confirmed this suspicion, revealing that both the number and proportion of pupils not fully competent in English were found to vary considerably between divisions. The ILEA has also demonstrated the importance of updating information. Between 1978 and 1981, for instance, the number of Bengali-speaking children in London increased by at least 50% and Bengali overtook Greek as the language (apart from English) with most speakers. It has now been decided to institute a biennial language census to monitor the changing school population and its varying needs.

Second-stage language teaching

Three surveys were published by the DES in the early 1970s. The first, *Potential and Progress in a Second Culture* (DES, 1971a) dealt with the attainment and assessment of intelligence in immigrant pupils. The second, *The Education of Immigrants: Education Survey 13* (1971b), was concerned with general policies and practices in the education of immigrant children and made it clear that the official views on dispersal had undergone some modification since the 1965 White Paper. The third, *The Continuing Needs of Immigrants* (1972) concentrated on the need for special help beyond the initial stage of English teaching and drew attention to the fact that only one LEA had consciously evolved a policy on the continuing linguistic needs of immigrants. Stress was laid on the importance of "much more positive thinking and constructive action in matters relating to the linguistic, intellectual and social needs of second-phase immigrant pupils" (p. 27).

The whole area of progression from initial to second stage language teaching was extremely problematic. For many years there was an absence of any objective way of assessing the level of proficiency after which schools could decide that no special arrangements were necessary. The first battery of tests of proficiency in English, for instance, were not available from the NFER until 1973. The most lucid exposition of this general area is contained in the chapter on "Children from families of overseas origin" in the 1975 Bullock Report, *A Language for Life*. The expressed aim of initial language teaching which recurred in LEA policy statements at this time was to bring the child to a level at which "he could profit from the normal school curriculum" (Bullock, 1975, p. 290). In practice the time scale considered necessary to achieve this end varied between twelve and eighteen months. There was a growing recognition, however, that such a short period was inadequate and that some form of continuing support for second-stage learners was necessary.

> Although after a year he may seem able to follow the normal school curriculum, especially where oral work is concerned, the limitations to his English may be disguised; they become immediately apparent when he reads and writes. He reads slowly and often without a full understanding of vocabulary and syntax, let alone the nuances of expression. His writing betrays his lack of grasp of the subject and a very unsteady control of syntax and style. . . .

We regard it as a grave disservice to such children to deprive them of sustained language teaching after they have been learning English for only a comparatively short time. In our view they need far more intensive help with language in English lessons. This should be the task of a specialist language teacher, whose aim should be to help them achieve fluency in all the language skills.

Bullock, 1975, p. 290

The ILEA has further recognized a third stage of language learning in which pupils show few signs of non-native use in spoken and written language, but none the less lack the full range of skills utilized by native speakers of the same age and ability. No survey has been undertaken to date of second- or third-stage provision. Its extent and kind is likely to vary considerably from one authority to another, and detailed policy statements would appear to be something of a rarity. It is difficult to estimate, therefore, the response to the Bullock Report's recommendation that language teachers in multiracial schools should be consultants and advisors across the curriculum rather than confined to a single room:

As a matter of urgency teachers able to work in this way should be appointed extra to complement wherever secondary schools have on roll a significant number of children who are no longer classed as initial learners but need linguistic help.

Bullock, 1975, p. 291

Section 11 of the Local Government Act

The main source of funding for both first- and second-stage English teaching was Section 11 of the Local Government Act (HMSO, 1966). This Act initially allowed local authorities with "substantial numbers of immigrants from the Commonwealth whose language or customs differ from those of the community" to claim a grant of 50% of the total expenditure incurred in the employment of extra staff to meet the specific needs of the immigrant population. The rate of this grant was later increased to 75%. In practical terms, it was considered that a local authority qualified for a grant if 2% or more of children in their total school population were children of Commonwealth immigrants.

Section 11, however, has been the object of a great deal of criticism. The take-up by the authorities of the funding has been extremely uneven from area to area. A NUT Report in 1978 showed that Ealing claimed twice as much per immigrant as Brent, and only a third as much as Coventry. A further problem relates to the fact that under Section 11 authorities may provide extra staff without necessarily allocating them a specific task. One unfortunate consequence is that in some authorities Section 11 teachers are included in the establishment of schools, rather than being counted as extra to "establishment" (Bakhsh and Walker 1980). A working party of Chief Education Officers convened by the Community Relations Commission summed up the situation thus:

> As far as education services are concerned, the DES as the central department concerned has not been directly associated with LEAs to the extent necessary to achieve the identification of needs, desirable levels of provision and objectives. Perhaps for this reason no national policy on ethnic minority education has emerged during the period of nearly ten years in which the Section 11 fund has been administered.
>
> CRC, 1976b, p. 4

In February 1979 the Labour Government introduced the Local Government (Ethnic Groups) Bill (HMSO, 1979) in an attempt to remedy the defects of Section 11, but it had progressed only as far as a Second Reading before the Conservative Government took office, and it had to lapse as legislation.

Non-governmental initiatives

The initial response of central government to the presence of immigrant children and their needs in the schools was both negative and slow. Rose *et al.* (1969) comment on this situation thus:

> They (the teachers) received no leadership from the DES, practical or political, in a situation in which there was a need for in-service training, for liaison between teachers, and for teachers' centres. Above all, there was a need for an interpretation of events which would attract teachers into schools with immigrant pupils, rather than repel them from the situation. This was not provided.
>
> p. 290

Inevitably, initiatives in providing much needed teaching materials and background information came from teachers rather than politicians. The most notable development concerns the formation of an Association of Teachers of English to Pupils from Overseas (ATEPO). The first branch was established in Birmingham in 1962. Other branches grew up in various parts of the country over the next few years and were eventually federated. They organized conferences and workshops, compiled and circulated bibliographies and commissioned pamphlets on subjects of special interest. They have also worked as pressure groups to obtain more resources and adequate training facilities. The emphasis on teaching English as a second language broadened over the years, however, to include the educational needs of all children in present-day multiracial Britain, a development which is reflected in the change of title from ATEPO to the National Association for Multiracial Education (NAME).

Mother Tongue Teaching (MTT)

Minority community initiatives

The exclusive thrust of the educational establishment until very recently has been to provide non-English speakers with the necessary linguistic skills to benefit from the normal school curriculum. This task was conceived only in terms of teaching English as a second language and it was generally felt that children's mother tongues should play no part in this process (Townsend, 1971; CRC, 1977). During the first stages of settlement, minority communities shared the teaching profession's concern that their children should learn English and supported their methodology. But as time went on and families became more settled, there was a growing awareness of the considerable inroads which English was making on patterns of language use and of the pressures of the dominant society on cultural and religious values. By the late 1960s and early 1970s the number of voluntary "supplementary" schools teaching minority languages outside school hours had rapidly increased, but still could not meet the community demand (Saifullah-Khan, 1976, 1980).

The variation in the supplementary schools was considerable. Italian, Spanish and Portuguese embassies organized networks of classes centrally, while Gujarati, Chinese, Bengali and many other minority groups made uncoordinated locally based provision (Saifullah-Khan, 1980). Some classes placed exclusive or main emphasis on religious teaching; others attached importance only to the maintenance of oral skills; still others also aimed to make children literate in the mother tongue. Most mainstream school teachers and many LEAs know very little about the extent and organization of this community provision and even today are not necessarily fully informed (Tosi, 1979). By 1976 the demand for MTT was so great and the voluntary classes were sufficiently well organized for the National Committee on Mother Tongue Teaching (NCMTT) to be formed as a channel through which the information on the educational and cultural benefit of mother tongues other than English can be disseminated in Britain.

Government initiatives

The suggestion that the mother tongues of ethnic minority children should be incorporated into the normal school curriculum was at first met with widespread incredulity in the teaching profession. This is not simply because of the central place occupied by English teaching, but also because of the tendency to undervalue bilingualism in children of South Asian origin. One head teacher consulted by Townsend (1971), for instance, commented:

> The Community Relations Officer thinks we should be teaching Gujarati but we couldn't start that caper. I've thought of starting French but we haven't enough space.
>
> p. 60

A perceptible change of attitude towards minority languages on the part of the educational establishment, however, was to be observed in Bullock (1975):

> When bilingualism in Britain is discussed it is seldom if ever with reference to the inner city populations, yet over half the immigrant pupils in our schools have a mother tongue which is not English. . . . These children are genuine bilinguals, but this fact is often ignored or unrecognised by the schools. . . . In a linguistically conscious nation in the modern world we should see it as an asset, as something to be nurtured, and one of the agencies which should nurture it is the school. Certainly the school should adopt a positive attitude to its pupils' bilingualism and wherever possible should help maintain and deepen their knowledge of their mother tongues.
>
> pp. 293–4

No indication was given in the Bullock report, however, as to precisely how bilingualism should be promoted in the school.

The Council of the European Community's (EC) Directive on the Education of the Children of Migrant Workers

Strong pressure in relation to MTT has also resulted from the attention which has been paid in Europe since the mid 1970s to the linguistic education of migrants' children (Council of Europe, 1975a, b; European Communities Commission, 1976). This led to the circulation of the draft of the EC Directive to interested bodies in the United Kingdom in 1976. The response to proposals which had received little or no prior discussion in a British context was predictably hostile. Teacher organizations objected on the grounds that expansion in the area of MTT was unacceptable in the face of educational cut-backs and teacher unemployment. The Government objected on the grounds of cost, difficulty in providing teachers and the inability of a decentralized education system to implement the Directive.

When the EC Directive finally appeared in July 1977, important modifications had been made. Article 2, which referred to the need for member states to offer free tuition in the national language, and Article 3 which referred to the teaching of the mother tongue and culture of migrants' children, had both been qualified with "in accordance with their national circumstances and legal systems" (Council of Europe, 1977). Further, although it had originally been envisaged that the mother tongue and culture should form part of the curriculum for full-time education, with classes up to the normal standard for member states, the revised Directive simply called for member states to "promote" MTT. The Directive thus does not confer any entitlement on individuals to tuition in school and stands in marked contrast to the North American Acts which instituted bilingual education.

There were also very real problems posed by the definition of "migrant workers". The strict interpretation of the Directive would in fact have constituted a violation of the Race Relations Act (1976), since MTT would have been provided for children of workers from EEC member states but not for those from other linguistic minorities. However, a subsequent Council statement, public declarations from the Secretary of State for Education (CRE, 1980) and the DES circular 5/81 (July 31st, 1981) have all made it clear that the Directive will be applied to member state nationals and British ethnic minorities alike. It is unfortunate that the term "migrant worker" has been retained, since a primary motive of the Directive in the European continental context is to facilitate children's "possible reintegration into the Member State of origin" (Council of Europe, 1977). There have been calls for the retitling of the Directive and for the DES to state clearly and publicly that the reintegration of minority groups is not one of the aims of MTT.

While the EC Directive is legally binding on member states, considerable scepticism has been expressed about government willingness or ability to achieve even the modest aims set out in the revised version. As Bellin (1980) points out:

> There are so many ways in which a member state government can be let off the hook. It is possible to plead difficulties with national circumstances, problems with conforming to the legal system, and there is always the excuse that, however little is being done, almost anything can count as "promoting mother tongue teaching".

The extent of the DES commitment to date has been limited to the funding of three projects related directly or indirectly to MTT. The first was a study of linguistic diversity in a sample of London secondary schools (Rosen and Burgess, 1980). The second concerned Punjabi children entering two schools in Bradford in the term before their fifth birthday with little or no English: one group was taught equally in both English and Punjabi, the other almost exclusively in English. Children's progress and school and community attitudes were monitored. Thirdly, the Linguistic Minorities Project (1978–82) aims to establish the range of linguistic diversity in all schools in a small number of LEAs, to collect information on all forms of mother tongue provision in a few areas and to undertake more limited studies of language use by adults.

Two projects sponsored by the European Community can also be conveniently mentioned at this point. The Bedford Mother Tongue Pilot took place in Bedford in 1976–80 and was designed to investigate the educational implications of teaching children of Italian and Punjabi background the language, history, geography, music, games and social studies of their families' country of origin. There is also the Schools Council Mother Tongue Project which aims to develop materials for bilingual teachers of Greek and Bengali speaking pupils in the 7–11 age range, to develop a strategy for producing materials which may be applicable to other languages, and to produce guidelines for monolingual teachers working in linguistically diverse classrooms across the whole primary age range.

MTT as a current issue

Whatever the weaknesses of the EC directive, it has stimulated a great deal of discussion. Teacher organizations such as NAME have published policy statements on MTT. Local authorities, too, are beginning to look closely at the MTT requirements of ethnic minority children within their schools. Since 1978, the ILEA has funded ten schemes teaching mother tongue languages to children outside normal school hours. Within the ILEA, authorities such as Hackney have formulated detailed policies on MTT and the CRE (forthcoming) has recently completed a national survey of LEA policies on MTT.

The importance of close consultation with minority communities is also receiving growing recognition. It is widely accepted, for instance, that MTT does not always apply to the first language acquired by minority group children. Many Italian parents in Britain do not consider themselves as permanent residents and would be likely to show a strong preference for their children to be taught standard Italian, a variety very different from the Southern dialect which most of them speak, so as to equip them for reintegration into schools at home. By the same token, Punjabi-speaking Pakistani parents prefer their children to learn Urdu, the language of religion and "high culture". As Tosi (1979, p. 226) points out:

> Involving minority groups in policy decisions is not only a due recognition of their "adulthood" but also a guarantee of correctly interpreting the social and linguistic orientation of their neighbourhood.

Children of West Indian origin

West Indian Creole-speaking children arriving from the Caribbean posed a number of important questions which schools identified only slowly and on which central government provided little or no guidance for a disturbing period of time. The precise form of the West Indian Creole differed from island to island. However, all varieties drew on a predominantly English vocabulary and differed systematically from British standard and regional varieties in a number of important ways (Bailey, 1966; Edwards, 1979). Unfortunately, departures from the standard tended to be perceived as deficiencies rather than differences and ignorance about the rule-governed nature of West Indian speech was widespread. A report by the National Association of School Masters (NAS, 1969), for instance, considered: "The West Indian child usually arrives speaking a kind of 'plantation English' which is socially unacceptable and inadequate for communication" (p. 5.) An ATEPO (1970) report describes West Indian language as "babyish", "careless and slovenly" and "very relaxed like the way they walk". Even Townsend (1971), who acknowledges the validity of West Indian children's language, talks of their "abbreviated sentence structure, different pronoun values and restricted vocabulary".

West Indians, for their part, had grown up in a society where the institutions, including education, were closely modelled on the British system. They had been indoctrinated into believing that West Indian Creoles were "bad talk" and "broken". When they came to what many people regarded as "the mother country", it was therefore understandable that they should insist that they spoke English, since to have admitted otherwise would have been tantamount to an acceptance of the low status attached to Creole speech. Problems concerning mutual intelligibility between West Indian parents and children on the one side and teachers on the other were common throughout the early years of settlement (cf. Rose *et al.*, 1969; Edwards, 1979).

Any official recognition of the language needs of West Indian children was extremely slow, and DES statistics served to conceal rather than to draw attention to the true situation. Section Two of Form 7 (i) (DES 1966–73) required teachers to classify "immigrant" children according to their knowledge of English as follows:

i. No problem.
ii. Reasonably good spoken English but weak in written English.
iii. Some English, but needing further intensive teaching.
iv. No English.

It seems reasonable to assume that if teachers were required to choose between either group (ii) or group (iii) when classifying West Indian children, they would come out in favour of group (ii) (Power, 1967). Yet the following year the DES amalgamated groups (i) and (ii) and groups (iii) and (iv) on the assumption that only those children in groups (iii) and (iv) would require specialized language teaching. Such a move effectively excluded the possibility that West Indian children might need specialist help, albeit of a different nature from second language learners.

The actual arrangements for teaching West Indians reflect the unfortunate consequences of a lack of policy on either a national or a local level. Comments reported by Townsend and Brittan (1972), for instance, reveal the bewilderment and confusion which must have been experienced by teachers and pupils alike:

> We once arranged special coaching for West Indians whose English was very poor, but they tended to resent this, not accepting that there was anything wrong with their English, so little progress was made and the project abandoned.
>
> p. 26

All too often the solution adopted with West Indian pupils (as with non-English-speaking children) was to place them in classes with remedial indigenous children:

> Boys of West Indian origin: In each year we have a class for retarded pupils. Although not designed as such, all of these classes have about 90 per cent West Indians or pupils of West Indian origin.
>
> p. 26

Only in a very few cases did schools or LEAs make any serious attempt to meet the language teaching needs of West Indian pupils (cf. Rose *et al.*, 1969, p. 281).

Large-scale West Indian immigration predated migration from South Asia by several years. Yet it was not until 1967 that the Schools Council commissioned a project with aims similar to the Leeds project but whose brief was to develop teaching materials specifically for West Indian pupils. Although the number of children who might benefit from such materials was probably no smaller than the number of non-English-speaking children, the budget for this project was less than a third of that made available to the Leeds team.

The report and other publications produced by researchers for the project "Teaching English to Children of West Indian Origin" (Wight, 1969, 1970; Wight and Norris, 1970) can be seen to some extent as weak re-statements of the verbal deprivation hypothesis. Originally the materials were envisaged as a language course for West Indian children, but later the emphasis was changed and it was decided that many of the language skills that could be usefully developed with West Indian children would also be beneficial to a good number of native British children. The authors of the material maintained that the language of West Indian children (and, presumably, working-class white children) was perfectly logical and regular and that attempts to teach the standard should be reserved for children's writing and not their speech. However, they did feel that non-standard speakers needed to develop a whole range of verbal strategies which would enable them to take part more successfully in the education process. This stance has since been criticized (Sutcliffe, 1977; Edwards, 1979) on the grounds that the strategies which the materials were designed to encourage can in fact be found in the language which children use in non-school settings, and that the most plausible explanation for children's avoidance of particular verbal strategies in the classroom—if indeed this is the case—would seem to be in terms of situational constraints rather than an inability to do so.

The underachievement of West Indian children, first officially recognized with the publication of the DES *Statistics of Education* for 1970, was a major concern throughout the decade (Townsend, 1971; HMSO, 1977; CRC, 1977; Rampton, 1981). A particular bone of contention in the early 1970s was the question of the assessment of the ability of West Indian pupils. Although intelligence tests were waived in the case of non-English-speaking pupils, they were a normal part of the evaluation of West Indian children until 1974, despite strong evidence that intelligence tests have little validity because of their cultural and linguistic bias (Haynes, 1971). The possibility that language played a part in the underperformance of West Indian children was finally acknowledged in 1973 with the publication of the Select Committee on Race Relations and Immigration report on Education:

> More familiarity with the problems of West Indian children has shown that many of them also need special attention in the teaching of English. . . . There is little doubt that neglect of special attention in the past has handicapped many children. It may partly account for the disproportionately large numbers of West Indian children in ESN schools in London . . . and for the generally lower standards of achievement of West Indian pupils in some schools. It is not, of course, the only reason, but it is one which is now recognised and can be dealt with.
>
> HMSO, 1973, p. 13

Following the report, a DES memorandum to Chief Education Officers on 1st November 1973 drew attention to the fact that West Indian children as well as non-English speakers may have language difficulties. The only recommendation made by the Select Committee as to how the problem could be "dealt with", however, was that LEAs should consider how best "with tact and discretion" they could convince West Indian parents that some of their children might need special English teaching. The Bullock

Report (1975) offers only slightly more guidance. It stresses the need for a positive attitude towards the language and culture of West Indian children which should be encouraged by initial and in-service training. It also suggests that work relating both to dialect and to improving the ability to use standard English should be encouraged on a much larger scale. Yet it gives no indication of the most suitable materials and approach for this task. Nor does it set out criteria for selecting those children in need of special teaching and it ignores the possible resistance which British-born children and their parents might offer.

Many of the difficulties in formulating a coherent policy on the language needs of children of West Indian origin can be traced to the extensive delays in recognizing their special situation within the British education system. Although some West Indian children continue even today to show the influence of Creole in their most formal speech, reading and writing, by the mid-1970s the majority had been born in Britain and could produce speech indistinguishable or at least close to the local white norm. The CRE sums up the situation thus:

> It is ironical that at a time when Creole dialect did cause problems of communication and comprehension in schools, the question was ignored. However, by the time Creole had been identified as an educational issue, the majority of West Indian children were no longer speaking it in schools. It is often pointed out to us that sometime during the early years at secondary school many West Indian pupils who up till then have used the language of the neighbourhood, begin to use Creole dialect. But its use is a deliberate social and psychological protest, an assertion of identity, not a language teaching problem.
>
> CRE, 1976a, p. 5

Current practice would still seem to be little influenced by a coherent language policy. Little and Willey's (1981) survey of 70 LEAs shows that no more than a handful have made serious attempts to evaluate the needs of West Indian pupils. They point to the importance of clarifying the extent to which, and the ways in which, these children have "special" language needs, and of providing guidance and support to teachers. The Rampton Report (1981) on *West Indian Children in Our Schools* goes at least some of the way towards clarifying these needs. It stresses the importance of promoting positive teacher attitudes towards the language of West Indian children through initial and in-service training. It also follows the ILEA (1977) policy statement in encouraging schools to give West Indian pupils every opportunity to make full use of their linguistic repertoire through creative work in English, drama and discussion. It recognizes the possible ambivalence of West Indian parents to the use of an essentially low status language variety in the classroom, but argues that imaginative and creative use of a child's home language assists in developing awareness of different forms of language—including standard English—and their appropriateness for different situations.

Such an approach is radical and represents a significant departure from the practices of the 1960s and the greater part of the 1970s. Inevitably, it has attracted vituperative comment. The ILEA statement encouraging the use of Creole in poetry and drama drove one head teacher to announce that he would allow Creole in his school only "over his dead body" (*Sunday Times*, 16th October, 1977). It remains to be seen whether this headteacher and many of his conservative colleagues in the teaching profession will be persuaded of the wisdom of the current policy lead, or resist it to the end.

English as a Mother Tongue: policy and practice

The presence of ethnic minority children in British schools has contributed to important modifications in approaches not only to minority children but also to indigenous English children. There is increasing recognition of the language and learning needs shared by all children and moves are being made to see how these needs can best be accommodated within the multilingual classroom. There has also been a growing awareness of the educational potential of linguistic diversity and an exploration of how children's language—including working-class children's non-standard dialects—can be exploited in a classroom setting.

This represents a radical departure from the traditionally negative attitudes and prescriptivism prevalent in educational circles on the subject of non-standard English since the introduction of compulsory schooling and before. The Newbolt Report of 1921 on the *Teaching of English in England* had no doubt, for instance, that

> It is emphatically the business of the Elementary School to teach all its pupils who either speak a definite dialect or whose speech is disfigured by vulgarisms, to speak standard English, and to speak it clearly, and with expression.
>
> p. 65

The Spens Report of 1939 on *Secondary Education* refers in a similar vein to the "slovenly, ungrammatical and often incomprehensible" nature of the "English of common usage". The general consensus, then, for a considerable period of time was that dialect speech was educationally unacceptable and that teachers' main weapons of attack should be grammatical drills and parsing. By the 1960s, however, an important distinction had been made between descriptive and prescriptive approaches to English and the usefulness of grammatical exercises was being called into question (Plowden,

1967). There was also a growing concern about the relationship among school language, working-class language and educational failure (e.g. Newsom, 1963), and the work of Bernstein on speech codes played an extremely important part in informing teacher opinion during this period.

Bernstein postulated two codes: an elaborated code which allowed speakers access to "universalistic" context-free orders of meaning; and a restricted code which gave access to "particularistic", context-bound orders of meaning. Acquisition of these codes depended on different patterns of socialization and their use determined the ways in which speakers thought, remembered, perceived and learned. An ability to manipulate the elaborated code was said to be a prerequisite for educational success. Although it has been argued that the distribution of these codes was never intended to mirror divisions between working-class and middle-class speakers (Trudgill, 1975), this interpretation was common in educational circles, and was even extended to include ethnic minority pupils:

> English children who are culturally deprived suffer the limitations of a restricted code in the one language—their own; immigrant children may suffer this also but with the complication of attempting to learn a second language.
>
> ILEA, 1967; reprinted in CRC, 1970, p. 20

> With only a limited command of English . . . [non-English speakers and West Indians] are unable to derive much benefit from normal educational methods which make great demands on ability and facility in the use of language. . . . They are at the same disadvantage as the less fortunate native English children with whom they are mainly associated. Both Newsom and Plowden drew attention to those children who never achieve any real command of English and are unable to develop any intellectual interest.
>
> NAS, 1969, p. 5

By the mid 1970s, however, a counterforce to the theories of linguistic deprivation was emerging. It was very much embodied in the Nuffield Programme on Linguistics in Language Teaching established in 1964 under the auspices of the Schools Council. *Language in Use* (Doughty *et al.*, 1971), lesson plans designed to increase children's understanding of the nature and function of language, was published in 1971. It was also the keynote of the 1975 Bullock Report, *A Language for Life,* which made strong pleas for schools to respect the linguistic and cultural diversity of the pupils:

> No child should be expected to cast off the language and culture of the home as he crosses the school threshold and the curriculum should reflect those aspects of his life.
>
> p. 543

Language across the curriculum

Another important force which gained momentum during the 1970s was the suggestion that all teachers, and not simply English teachers, should be involved in language teaching. A document called "A Language Policy Across the Curriculum" emerged from a London Association for the Teaching of English (LATE) conference in 1968 and was later published with related papers as *Language, the Learner and the School* (Barnes *et al.*, 1969). The philosophy contained in this very influential collection of papers is mirrored in the DES survey, *The Continuing Needs of Immigrants* (DES, 1972) and also in the Bullock Report which made the following recommendations:

> In the primary school the individual teacher is in a position to devise a language policy across the various aspects of the curriculum, but there remains the need for a general school policy to give expression to the aim and ensure consistency throughout the years of primary schooling. In the secondary school, all subject teachers need to be aware of:
> (i) The linguistic processes by which their pupils acquire information and understanding, and the implications for the teacher's own use of language.
> (ii) The reading demands of their own subjects, and ways in which pupils can be helped to meet them. To bring about this understanding every secondary school should develop a policy for language across the curriculum. The responsibility for this policy should be embodied in the organisational structure of the school.
>
> 1975, pp. 528–9

No attempt has been made to evaluate the impact of the Bullock Report and many schools undoubtedly remain unaffected by its recommendations. It did, however, provide a framework for those schools which were already beginning to formulate language policies and serve as a stimulus for others who were broadly sympathetic to its aims. Some progress has clearly been made. Welch (1979, p. 33), for instance, asserts confidently:

> There is now sufficient information available for the ILEA to provide an adequate advisory service for those schools which have not yet developed language policies and for those who may wish to amend their original ideas.

Awareness of the importance of language and a move from traditional prescriptivism have grown considerably throughout the 1970s and have been reflected indirectly in government initiatives such as the setting up of the Assessment of Performance Unit, Educational Priority Areas and the Educational Disadvantage Unit which itself established the Centre for Information and Advice on Educational Disadvantage until its disbanding in

1980 as part of education cuts. This atmosphere of linguistic awareness has had a number of important educational repercussions. There is an increasing appreciation, for instance, of the common language needs of all children irrespective of their backgrounds. But whereas in the 1960s and early 1970s discussion centred on the linguistic deficiencies of non-English and dialect-speaking children, there is now more open recognition of the validity of dialect and the advantages of bilingualism, and initiatives which bring children's language into the classroom are multiplying at an impressive rate (cf. Edwards, 1979; Levine, 1982). There is also a growing understanding of the benefits of including second language learners wherever possible in mainstream classes rather than isolating them in special classes and centres (Wiles, 1981). As Levine remarks:

> More and more specialist teachers want to work in "ordinary" classes alongside children doing "ordinary" work, and "ordinary" class teachers want to know how to work with "second language learners" in their classes.
>
> pp. 25–6

Important strides have been made on a theoretical level in identifying language issues which demand consistent treatment throughout the child's school career—such as limited intervention in children's oral reading (Moon and Raban, 1980); the counterproductive nature of correcting dialect features (Edwards, 1979; Richmond, 1979; Rampton, 1981) and the importance of creating situations where the use of dialect is valued (Rampton, 1981). These remain to be translated into policy at a school level.

National language policy in Wales

Arguably the Welsh language began its decline with the 1536 Act of Union which gave official status only to English. The fall in the proportion of Welsh speakers during the twentieth century, linked very closely with economic developments, from 49.9% in 1901 to 20.8% in 1971 has been more rapid than in any other period. Many factors have contributed to this decline, including depopulation of the Welsh speaking strongholds in the North and West, the decreasing importance of the Chapel in community life, and the increasing inroads made by English mass media. Nor should the role of education in this process be minimized. In the nineteenth and early twentieth centuries, Welsh was consistently undervalued in an education system predicated almost exclusively on the use of English. In the post-war period, however, there has been a slow but very marked improvement in the status of Welsh, and the achievements of Welsh medium education, particularly during the 1970s, have been impressive. These achievements are due in large part to the formulation of coherent national and local language policies.

Clearly, many valuable lessons are to be learned from the Welsh experience.

Four different kinds of school are to be found in Wales today (Evans, 1978). The first, traditionally Welsh medium schools, are sited mainly in rural areas. The second, Welsh schools (Ysgolion Cymraeg), are found mainly in anglicized areas and concentrate exclusively on Welsh during the infants' stage, gradually increasing the use of English thereafter. The first such school was established in Llanelli in 1947 and demand for this kind of education has been so great that today there are some 53 "Welsh" primary schools and 13 secondary schools. The majority and, in some cases, all of the children attending these schools come from English-speaking homes. The rapid development of Mudiad Ysgolion Meithrin (the Welsh Nursery School Movement) during the 1970s would suggest that if adequate administrative arrangements are made, the numbers of fluent Welsh speakers will increase by 50% in Welsh primary schools and 100% in secondary schools within the next ten years. The third kind of provision is based on some 300 schools which have taken part in the Schools Council Bilingual Education Project since it began in 1969. Here Welsh is introduced gradually as the medium of instruction with the aim of producing fluency by the end of the primary stage. Testing undertaken as part of this project shows that not only do many children achieve a high level of performance in Welsh, but also that their performance in English and other subjects compares very favourably with children in matched schools who had not taken part in the project. Finally, traditionally English medium schools exist all over Wales, in some of which Welsh is taught as a subject.

Changes in language provision have succeeded in raising the percentage of children fluent in Welsh in the primary schools from 10.6% in 1975 to 13.7% in 1979. Although the future of Welsh is by no means certain, there are grounds for some optimism. As Bellin (forthcoming) points out:

> What has been shown in the changed education systems in Wales is that there is no inevitability about the decline of the language. If school and community could exert a combined influence, future language decline could be arrested if not reversed.

The formulation of coherent language policies and strategies for their implementation have undoubtedly played a major part in the achievements of the last decade. Although cynics would argue that active support for the teaching of and through Welsh has come extremely late, the government stance on the role of Welsh in education is unequivocal:

> The Government has a clear commitment to (the future of Welsh) based upon the belief that it is the wish of the majority of the people of Wales that Welsh should survive as a living tongue.
>
> Welsh Office, 1981a, p. 9

On a practical level recognition has been given to the additional financial burden placed on LEAs by Welsh language and Welsh medium education and Section 21 of the Education Act (1980) enables the Secretary of State to grant aid to LEAs and other bodies for Welsh language education, giving priority to the production of teaching materials and in-service training. The Government has also given a clear lead concerning the formulation of language policies by LEAs:

> The Secretary of State believes that each authority should have a clear policy for Welsh language teaching and Welsh medium work in its schools and make it known to all concerned; be aware of the extent to which its schools are able, within the resources available to them, to make curricular provision which is consistent with that policy; and plan future developments accordingly, in consultation with the teachers and others concerned in their area.
>
> Welsh Office, 1981a, p. 10

An important start in implementing this approach was made with the introduction of the Education (School Information) Regulations 1981 which requires that LEAs and individual schools publish policies regarding the use of Welsh from the school year 1982–3 onwards.

Local Education Authority language policies

The legal responsibility for the curriculum in schools, including provision for Welsh, lies with LEAs and not central government. Considerable strides in the formulation and implementation of language policy have in fact been taking place independently of central government for a number of years and the coordinating role played by the Welsh Joint Education Committee (WJEC), a body formed from all the LEAs in Wales, has been extremely important in this respect. *Towards a National Language Policy* (WJEC, 1976) reviewed policies and practices throughout Wales and made proposals for prioritizing and formulating bilingual objectives, and developing educational programmes which would allow LEAs to achieve these objectives. The main proposals have been accepted by all LEAs, most of which have also since published their own policy statements reflecting variation in local circumstances. The WJEC has also served a vital practical function in operating the Welsh Books Scheme which ensures a sufficiently large market that any publisher will at least break even. It has also been responsible for the establishment of the National Language Unit which produces a wide range of materials for the teaching of Welsh as a second language and runs an extensive in-service training programme.

School language policies

Policies within individual schools are equally important. The Welsh Office (1981b), report of Her Majesty's Inspectors' observations of Welsh medium work in secondary schools, identifies the following basic questions being tackled in schools by many heads, governors and teachers:

> What range of the curriculum is it reasonable or necessary to offer through the medium of Welsh? To what extent should the influence of Welsh side by side with English permeate the whole curriculum? What are pupil's needs for development of linguistic skills in English?
>
> What is the place of English as a subject and as a medium?
>
> Are the needs of pupils in bilingual schools of the more anglicised areas different in these respects from those of pupils in the Welsh heartlands?
>
> How may the development of interest of Welsh learners be encouraged, in relation to Welsh as either subject or medium, so that the secondary school may build on work commenced at the primary stage?
>
> In what ways could Welsh be associated, through organised social activity, with the interest and culture of the community which the school serves? How can easy communication in the language be safeguarded in a community which is linguistically mixed or predominantly English?

p. 9

Bilingual policy in Scotland

The history of the decline of Gaelic in Scotland follows a remarkably similar pattern to that of Welsh in Wales, though today Welsh is in a much stronger position in terms of both numbers of speakers and status. Like Welsh, Gaelic was either totally ignored in education until very recently, or merely paid lip service. It was not, for instance, until 1956 that the Schools (Scotland) Code (HMSO, 1956) conceded that

> In Gaelic speaking areas reasonable provision shall be made in schemes of work for the instruction of Gaelic speaking pupils in the Gaelic language and literature, and the Gaelic language shall be used where appropriate for instructing Gaelic speaking pupils in other subjects.

The Education (Scotland) Act (HMSO, 1962) reiterates this position, as, too, does the memorandum on Primary Education in Scotland (HMSO, 1965b). The legacy of low status conferred upon Gaelic by its almost complete exclusion from Scottish education over many years has, however, resulted in a widespread reluctance in accepting its validity, even for teaching Gaelic-speaking children. LEAs and individual schools have chosen to interpret the Code very narrowly, concentrating much more on the teaching of Gaelic as a subject than on using it as a medium of education (Macleod, 1978).

At a primary level the efforts of small groups of Gaelic and Gaelic-speaking advisors have led to a gradual recognition of the need for increased provision. But, by far the most significant development in this area arose indirectly from local government reorganization in 1975 which brought into being a new authority, the Western Isles, in which over 80% of the population speak Gaelic. A Gaelic–English Bilingual Education Project (Proisect Foghlum Da-Chananach, 1977), sponsored jointly by the Scottish Education Department and the Western Isles Islands Council, was set up in the same year and operates in some twenty schools with a team of three researchers. On completion of the second three-year phase of the Bilingual Education Project in 1982, the Western Isles Authority decided to continue the development of bilingual education in primary schools with their own resources. The project team continues as a unit with the education department and has been redesignated as the "bilingual education curriculum development unit". The principal tasks of the project team, in cooperation with teachers, advisory staff and others, are:

(a) to devise situations and activities which will stimulate children to use Gaelic as a natural language for exploration and description of experience;
(b) to devise and evaluate a wide range of materials—printed and audiovisual—which will facilitate the development of a bilingual curriculum;
(c) to provide in-service courses for teachers engaged in the project;
(d) to make materials and findings emanating from the project available to all schools in the Western Isles;
(e) to inform parents and the community and seek to involve them in the project;
(f) to develop and maintain connections with similar projects elsewhere and with other interested agencies.

                                                                    Murray, undated

The problems and priorities of bilingual education in Scotland thus closely resemble those of bilingual education in Wales. The extent and variety of provision for Gaelic teaching, however, compares extremely unfavourably with developments in Wales. It is notable, for instance, that the Bilingual Education Project operates only in primary schools. At the secondary level Gaelic is taught as a subject in some 34 schools but is not used as the medium of education for other areas. Useful work on the curriculum is, however, being undertaken by a joint working party on a syllabus for Gaelic Studies, at present being selectively piloted in the Highland Region and Western

Isles. The Central Committee on Gaelic of the Conservative Committee on the Curriculum is also actively engaged on a general evaluation of the position of Gaelic in education and in the study of specific aspects such as the publishing of materials (Macleod, personal communication).

In spite of these recent developments, the considerably smaller number of bilingual children in Scotland than in Wales, and the apparent lack of community and LEA demand for Gaelic to be taught as a second language, provide a very tenuous base from which to attempt the halting of the process of language decline. It would be wrong, however, to underestimate the considerable degree of support from teachers, parents and children in the Western Isles for the Bilingual Education Project and it will be interesting to monitor the community's response to the heightened status conferred on Gaelic by the Western Isles Council's commitment to bilingualism.

Conclusions

Language policy viewed as a whole for the United Kingdom reveals many striking contrasts. Developments in the role of the older mother tongues, Welsh and Gaelic, in education have been well orchestrated and remarkably successful. Strategies towards linguistic minorities in England, on the other hand, have been uncoordinated, contradictory, and, in some cases, inappropriate. Differences in treatment of mother tongue teaching and teaching English as a second language are also noteworthy. English teaching has generally been conceived as a route to assimilation and as a means of alleviating classroom pressures. Until recently it has been a very strong specialist domain characterized by considerable diversity in organization and practice. MTT, in contrast, represents a challenge to received monocultural values and has given rise to a number of clear policy statements on the part of both national bodies and local authorities. The very different patterns of response to diversity over the past twenty or so years do, however, make it possible to identify certain prerequisites for workable language policies and suggest a number of possible ways forward.

The British experience shows clearly the importance of accurate information about the linguistic composition of a local authority, and the distribution of that population within the authority and even within individual schools. Many of the administrative blunders of the past two decades can be traced to inaccurate information on the degree and kind of linguistic need which existed within an authority, and, in some cases, on no information at all. It is also important that information should be regularly updated in order to monitor the changing needs and the allocation of resources.

Equally important is the need for broad based discussion with parents and community leaders as to their desire for a given course of action and the form that action should take. Government or LEA initiatives in teaching Welsh or Gaelic, for instance, are doomed without community support. Similarly, in multilingual situations, guidance should be sought on the language or dialect to be taught, and for what purposes, if the social and linguistic orientation of a community is to be accurately gauged. The Education (School Information) Regulations 1981 offer all schools important opportunities for both the formulation of policy and for consultation with parents. The moves by an increasing number of LEAs such as ILEA and Berkshire to develop broad policies for multicultural education also serve as a useful stimulus for careful thought about language in schools.

The development of new resources and pedagogies is another priority. The considerable success, for instance, of the Welsh Books Scheme demonstrates the usefulness of interested parties joining forces to ensure a market for new materials, and points to the important role which coordinating bodies like the WJEC in Wales is currently playing. It also points to the potential of organizations like the NCMTT on a national basis both in the production of materials and the dissemination of ideas, if such a body were officially recognized and funded.

Finally, it is very important to have a clear understanding of the different levels at which successful language policies must operate. At a national level, a broad commitment to a given course of action is necessary, together with the financial backing which will enable those at a grass roots level to achieve their aims. At a local authority level, it is necessary to adapt the general statements of intent in accordance with local conditions, and to monitor needs and developments closely. At a school level, in particular, broad policies must be translated into educational programmes. Commitment at all three levels is essential for success. The decentralized nature of British education is not necessarily a disadvantage in this context. Government is required to give a clear lead but there remains considerable latitude for individual LEAs and schools to interpret and develop policy according to local need.

Language policies cannot and should not be definitive statements. Their value lies in the fact that they focus attention on important issues and demand that aims should be based on sound information rather than on impressions. They provoke discussion and stimulate educators to seek solutions to carefully defined problems. Inevitably the solutions change as situations themselves change. The recognition of the importance of language policies in Britain has been extremely slow, and, in England, at least, has largely arisen as a result of the presence in fairly recent times of ethnic minority children. Although this recognition has been slow, important initiatives have been taken in Wales, the Western Isles and in education authorities like the ILEA which will hopefully encourage others to follow in their wake.

Note

1. I would like to acknowledge the help of Wyn Bellin and Howard Williams who commented on earlier drafts on this chapter, and of Catherine Morrison and Murdo MacLeod who provided me with extra unpublished information.

References

Association of Teachers of English to Pupils from Overseas (ATEPO) (Birmingham Branch) (1970). *Work Group on West Indian Pupils Report.*

Boyle, Sir E. (1963). *Hansard,* Vol. 685, Cols 433–444.

Bailey, B. L. (1966). *A Transformational Grammar of Jamaican Creole.* Cambridge University Press, Cambridge.

Bakhsh, Q. and Walker, N. (1980). *Unrealised Potential. Gravesend Study: A Case for Additional Resources Under Section 11.* Gravesend and District Community Relations Council, Gravesend.

Barnes, D., Britton, J. and Rosen, H. (1969). *Language, the Learner and the School.* Penguin Books, Harmondsworth.

Bellin, W. (1980). The EEC directive on the education of the children of migrant workers: A comparison of the commission's proposed directive and the council directive together with a parallel text. *Polyglot,* **2**, Fiche 2.

Bellin, W. (forthcoming). Welsh and English in Wales. In *Language in the British Isles* (Ed. P. Trudgill). Cambridge University Press, Cambridge.

Bullock, Sir A. (1975). *A Language for Life.* HMSO, London.

Commission for Racial Equality (1980). *The EEC's Directive on the Education of Children of Migrant Workers. Its Implications for the Education of Children from Ethnic Minority Groups in the UK.* HMSO, London.

Commission for Racial Equality (forthcoming). *Survey of Local Education Authority Policies on Mother Tongue Teaching.* (Working title; prepared by Ming Tsow).

Commonwealth Immigrants Advisory Council (1964). *Second Report of the Commonwealth Immigrants Advisory Council.* (Cmnd. 2266). HMSO, London.

Community Relations Commission (1970). *Practical Suggestions for Teachers of Immigrant Children.* 3rd edition. CRC, London.

Community Relations Commission (1976a). *The Select Committee on Race Relations and Immigration Enquiry on the West Indian Community. Evidence on Education from the Community Relations Commission.* CRC, London.

Community Relations Commission (1976b). *Funding Multi-Racial Education: A National Strategy.* CRC, London.

Community Relations Commission (1977). *The Education of Ethnic Minority Children.* CRC, London.

Council of Europe (1975a). Meeting of experts on curricula for children of migrant workers. 26–27 June, Strasbourg.

Council of Europe (1975b). Meeting of experts on the teaching of the language of the host country to children of migrant workers. 30–31 October, Strasbourg.

Council of Europe (1976). Resolution on the education of migrant workers and their families (Ref. NOC. 38(2), IV), 9 February.

Council of Europe (1977). Council directive on the education of the children of migrant workers (77/486/EEC), 25 July.

Department of Education and Science (1965). *The Education of Immigrants.* Circular 7.

Department of Education and Science (1966–73). *Form 7i (Schools).*

Department of Education and Science (1971a). *Potential and Progress in a Second Culture.* HMSO, London.

Department of Education and Science (1971b). *The Education of Immigrants: Education Survey 13.* HMSO, London.

Department of Education and Science (1972). *The Continuing Needs of Immigrants.* HMSO, London.

Department of Education and Science (1981). Directive of the Council of Europe on the Education of the Children of Migrant Workers. Circular No. 5/81, 31 July (Welsh Office Circular No. 36/81).

Derrick, J. (1967). *English for the Children of Immigrants.* HMSO, London.

Doughty, P., Pierce, J. and Thornton, G. (1971). *Language in Use.* Edward Arnold, London, for the Schools Council.

Edwards, V. (1979). *The West Indian Language Issue in British Schools: Challenges and Responses.* Routledge and Kegan Paul, London.

European Communities Commission (1976). An education policy for the Community. Resolution of the Council and of the Ministers of Education. Meeting within the Council of 9 February. Background note published 26 March 1976.

Evans, E. (1978). Welsh. In *The Older Mother Tongues of the United Kingdom* (Ed. C. James). Centre for Information on Language Teaching and Research, London.

Hawkes, N. (1966). *Immigrant Children in British Schools.* Pall Mall Press, London, for Institute of Race Relations.

Haynes, J. (1971). *Educational Assessment of Immigrant Pupils.* National Foundation for Educational Research, Windsor.

HMSO (1956). *Schools (Scotland) Code.* HMSO, London.

HMSO (1962). *Education (Scotland) Act.* HMSO, London.

HMSO (1965a). *Immigration from the Commonwealth* (Cmnd. 2739). HMSO, London.

HMSO (1965b). *Primary Education in Scotland.* HMSO, Edinburgh.

HMSO (1966). *Local Government Act.* HMSO, London.

HMSO (1973). *Select Committee on Race Relations and Immigration, Session 1972–3, Education* (Vol. 1. Report). HMSO, London.

HMSO (1977). *Select Committee on Race Relations and Immigration, Session 1976–77. The West Indian Community* (Vol. 1. Report). HMSO, London.

HMSO (1979). *Local Government (Ethnic Groups) Bill.* HMSO, London.

HMSO (1981). *Education (School Information) Regulations.* HMSO, London.

Inner London Education Authority (1967). *The Education of Immigrant Pupils in Primary Schools: Report of a Working Party of the Inspectorate and the School Psychological Service.* ILEA, London.

Inner London Education Authority (1977). *Multi-ethnic Education. Joint report of the Schools Sub-committee presented to the Education Committee on 8 November.*

Inner London Education Authority (1979). *Report on the 1978 Census of those ILEA Pupils for whom English was not a First Language* (ILEA 9484).

Levine, J. (1982). Developing pedagogies for multilingual classes. *English in Education* **15**(3), 25–33.

Little, A. and Willey, R. (1981). *Multi-ethnic Education: The Way Forward.* Schools Council, London.

MacLeod, M. (1978). Scottish Gaelic. In *The Older Mother Tongues of the United Kingdom* (Ed. C. James). Centre for Information on Language Teaching and Research, London.

Ministry of Education (1963). *English for Immigrants* (Pamphlet No. 43). HMSO, London.

Moon, C. and Raban, B. (1980). *A Question of Reading.* Macmillan, London.

Murray, J. (undated). Bilingual education project in the Western Isles. Available from Proisect Foghlum Da-Chananach, Rosebank Stornaway, Isle of Lewis, Scotland.

National Association of Schoolmasters (1969). *Education and the Immigrants.* Educare, Hemel Hempstead, Herts.

National Foundation for Educational Research (1973). *Tests for Proficiency in English.* Ginn, London.

National Union of Teachers (1978). *Section 11: An NUT Report.* NUT, London.

Newbolt, H. (1921). *The Teaching of English in England.* HMSO, London.

Newsom, J. (1963). *Half Our Future.* HMSO, London.

Plowden, B. (1967). *Children and their Primary Schools.* HMSO, London.

Power, J. (1967). *Immigrants in School. A Survey of Administrative Policies.* Council and Education Press, London.

Proisect Foghlum Da-Chananach (1977). Interim report on the *Bilingual Education Project.*

Rampton, A. (1981). *West Indian Children in Our Schools* (Interim Report of the Committee of Inquiry into the Education of Children from Ethnic Minority Groups). HMSO, London.

Richmond, J. (1979). Dialect features in mainstream school writing. *New Approaches to Multiracial Education* **8**(1), 9–15.

Rose, E. J. B. *et al.* (1969). *Colour and Citizenship. A Report on British Race Relations.* Oxford University Press, London.

Rosen, H. and Burgess, T. (1980). *Languages and Dialects of London School Children.* Ward Lock Educational, London.

The Runnymede Trust and the Radical Statistics Race Group (1980). *Britain's Black Population.* Heinemann Educational, London.

Saifullah-Khan, V. (1976). Provision by minorities for language maintenance. In

Bilingualism and British Education (Ed. G. Perren). Centre for Information on Language Teaching and Research, London.

Saifullah-Khan, V. (1980). The mother-tongue of linguistic minorities in multilingual England. *Journal of Multilingual and Multicultural Development* 1(1), 71–88.

Spens, W. (1939). *Secondary Education.* HMSO, London.

Sutcliffe, D. (1977). The language of first and second generation West Indian children in Bedfordshire. M.Ed. Thesis, University of Leicester.

Tosi, A. (1979). Mother tongue teaching for children of migrants. *Language Teaching and Linguistics Abstracts* 213–231.

Townsend, H. E. R. (1971). *Immigrants in England: The LEA Response.* National Foundation for Educational Research, Windsor.

Townsend, H. E. R. and Brittan, E. M. (1972). *Organisation in Multiracial Schools.* National Foundation for Educational Research, Windsor.

Townsend, H. E. R. and Brittan, E. M. (1973). *Multiracial Education: Need and Innovation.* Methuen Educational, London.

Trudgill, P. (1975). *Accent, Dialect and the School.* Edward Arnold, London.

Welch, J. (1979). *Language Policy Statements in the ILEA. A Consideration of the Response from Secondary Schools.* ILEA, London.

Welsh Joint Education Committee (1976). *Towards a National Language Policy.* WJEC, Cardiff.

Welsh Office (1981a). *Welsh in Schools. Statement by the Secretary of State for Wales.* HMSO, London.

Welsh Office (1981b). *Welsh Medium Work in Secondary Schools. Gwaith cyfrwng-Cymraeg mewn Ysgolion Uwchradd* (Education Survey 9). HMSO, London.

Wight, J. (1969). Teaching English to West Indian children. *English for Immigrants* 2(2).

Wight, J. (1970). Language deprivation and remedial teaching techniques. In *Work Group on West Indian Pupils Report.* ATEPO (Birmingham Branch).

Wight, J. and Norris, R. (1970). *Teaching English to West Indian Children: The Research Stage of the Project.* Evans/Methuen Educational, London.

Wiles, S. (1981). Language issues in the multi-cultural classroom. In *Language in School and Community* (Ed. N. Mercer). Edward Arnold, London.

3
Linguistic minorities and multicultural policy in Canada

Jim Cummins

I Introduction

During the past 15 years in Canada as in many of the other western industrialized countries, there has been a dramatic increase in the number of students whose mother tongue (L1) is other than that of the school (L2). More than 50% of the school population in several Metropolitan Toronto school systems do not have English as an L1 (see for example, Deosaran *et al.*, 1976) while in the Vancouver school system the figure is around 40% (Yeung, 1982). This rapid increase in the number of minority language students has given rise to considerable debate about how Canadian school systems should respond to the cultural and linguistic diversity of their students. Attempts to improve the teaching of English-as-a-second-language (ESL) or French-as-a-second-language (FSL) in Quebec and to increase the sensitivity of school personnel to children's cultural background have been relatively uncontroversial. However, issues related to the teaching of languages other than English and French within the public school system have been extremely contentious.

The present paper focusses on this debate as a means of examining the limits and inherent ambiguities of multicultural policy in Canadian education. Languages other than English and French are usually referred to as "heritage" languages although the terms "ethnic minority", "ancestral",

LINGUISTIC MINORITIES
ISBN 0-12-232760-8

"third", and "non-official" languages have also been used. The latter two terms are intended to distinguish heritage languages from the two "official" languages of Canada—English and French. The term "heritage languages" will be employed throughout this chapter.

Although the official status of English and French in Canada makes the Canadian situation unique in certain respects, the opposing arguments for and against heritage language teaching in the public schools follow similar lines to those in other western countries. Advocates see promotion of heritage languages as academically advantageous for minority students and as a means of reducing ethnocentricism and expanding the social and cultural horizons of all students. Endorsement of heritage language teaching is seen as a rejection of the monocultural, monolingual ideal which dominated Canadian public policy until recently (see, for example, Harney and Troper, 1975) in favour of a pluralist ideal in which linguistic and cultural diversity is respected and fostered. Opponents, on the other hand, see heritage language teaching as socially divisive, excessively costly and educationally retrograde in view of minority students' need to learn English.

The sociohistorical context of this debate will be outlined first, followed by a description of the present provision for teaching heritage languages in different Canadian provinces. The research basis for social and educational policy will then be considered and, finally, the evolution of the public debate in Metropolitan Toronto during the past decade will be analysed.

II Sociohistorical context

The prevailing attitude towards ethnic diversity in Canada in the first half of this century has been termed "Anglo-conformity". It was assumed that all ethnic groups should give up their own languages and cultures and become assimilated into the dominant British culture. Harney and Troper quote a speaker at the 1913 Pre-Assembly Congress of the Presbyterian Church in Toronto:

> The problem is simply this: take all the different nationalities, German, French, Italian, Russian and all the others that are sending their surplus into Canada; mix them with the Anglo-Saxon stock and produce a uniform race wherein the Anglo-Saxon peculiarities shall prevail.
>
> 1975, p. 110

Education was naturally regarded as a major means of Canadianizing "foreign" students. As Harney and Troper (1975) point out, Canadianization was not a hidden curriculum but permeated every facet of the school's programme. Any traces of foreign values were eradicated in the process of impressing on students the Canadian values of "punctuality, regularity, obedience, industry, cleanliness, decency of appearance and behaviour, regard for the rights of others and respect for law and order" (p. 110).

Surveys of the views of Canadian educators in the early part of the century (Black, 1913; Sissons, 1917; Anderson, 1918) emphasized the desirability of rapid assimilation and the necessity to eradicate students' L1 in order to facilitate the learning of English and acquisition of "Canadian" values (see Lenskyj, 1981, for a review). Black, for example, concluded that:

> Generally speaking . . . it is evident that the wisest method of teaching English will aim at eliminating for the time being from the learner's consciousness all memory or thought of his vernacular tongue.
>
> 1913, p. 106

Overtly racist attitudes about the superiority of certain groups (specifically, Northern European) over others (for example, Southern European and Asian) were evident among many North American educators during this period (Kamin, 1974; Lenskyj, 1981). Lenskyj points out that educators tended to associate "low" social or racial origins with "low" morals and habits and to prescribe hard work as an effective antidote:

> Translated to the classroom, this belief was expressed by several of Black's respondents, who were totally opposed to the use of the mother tongue in schools on the grounds that it made the learning of English *too easy*. They claimed that immigrant students would not put forth sufficient "mental effort" if teachers knew and used their mother tongue. However, this danger of mental sloth apparently did not threaten students who already understood English and were spared the task of mastering a new language.
>
> 1981, pp. 3–4

The racist orientation in Canadian society found expression in the systematic exclusion of Jewish refugees during and after the second world war (Abella and Troper, 1982) as well as in the treatment of Japanese Canadians in the war years (confinement and confiscation of property). Immigration policy reflected this orientation. Bhatnagar (1981), for example, points out that the strict quotas for the least desirable immigrants, namely, Jews, Blacks, and Asiatics, in the 1952 immigration act, were justified on the grounds that it had been "scientifically proven" that these groups were unassimilable.

During the 1960s, the more liberal social climate, together with the fact that the "preferred" countries could not supply the labour required for a rapidly expanding economy, led to the 1967 immigration policy which abandoned the 1952 policy's discrimination on the basis of nationality, ethnic origin, "peculiar cultural traits" and inability to assimilate (Bhatnagar, 1981, pp. 74–75). However, despite the egalitarian immigration policies and the strong emphasis on multi-culturalism during the 1970s, there is considerable evidence that racial intolerance is still prominent among the Canadian public. For example, a study carried out by anthropologist Frances Henry in Toronto (see *Globe and Mail,* 18 September, 1982) revealed racist tendencies in more than half the sample (16% were described as "very racist" and another 35% as "somewhat racist"). The same article ("The Road to Racism") goes on to point out that several public opinion polls showed that more than half of Canadians were opposed to the Canadian Government's acceptance of 50 000 Indo-Chinese "boat people" in 1979.

I shall suggest that this sociohistorical pattern of racism in Canadian society and its contemporary ethnocentric residue is important for understanding the vehement debate regarding heritage language teaching. Although racism has been virtually eradicated from public policy and multiculturalism in its inoffensive manifestations (e.g. "ethnic" food, dance etc.) is supported by most Canadians (Berry *et al.,* 1977), the implicit expectations of the majority anglophone group are violated by "ethnic demands" for heritage language teaching. These implicit expectations are that ethnic groups should either assimilate and "disappear" socially and politically or, alternatively, withdraw and pursue their linguistic and cultural goals "quietly" outside the mainstream.

III Present policy context

A The policy of multiculturalism

During the 1960s the French-speaking population in Quebec became increasingly conscious of the fact that the small English-speaking minority controlled most of the business and industry of the province. Fluency in English was a prerequisite for social and economic advancement whereas fluency in French was not. The social changes brought about by Quebecers' increasing realization that their language and culture were threatened and that they occupied a near-colonial status within Canada became known as "the quiet revolution".

At around the same time the Federal Government recognized the need to develop a national cultural and language policy and instituted in 1963 the Royal Commission on Bilingualism and Biculturalism. The mandate of what is commonly referred to as the "B and B Commission" was to:

> Inquire into and report upon the existing state of bilingualism in Canada and to recommend what steps should be taken to develop the Canadian Confederation on the basis of an equal partnership between the two founding races, taking into account the contribution made by the other ethnic groups to the

cultural enrichment of Canada and the measures that should be taken to safeguard that contribution.

Royal Commission on Bilingualism and Biculturalism, 1970, p. 235

The early volumes of the B and B Commission resulted in the passage of the Official Languages Act, establishing English and French as the "official" Canadian languages. Book IV of the B and B Commission was subsequently published (1970) and dealt specifically with *The Cultural Contribution of the Other Ethnic Groups*. The recommendations of Book IV were accepted in their entirety by the Federal Government and led to the policy of "multiculturalism within a bilingual framework" announced by Prime Minister Trudeau in October 1971. The rationale for this policy was that:

National unity, if it is to mean anything in the deeply personal sense, must be founded on confidence in one's own individual identity; out of this can grow respect for that of others and a willingness to share ideas, attitudes and assumptions. A vigorous policy of multiculturalism will help to create this initial confidence.

Canada Parliament, 8 October, 1971, *Debates* 8

Within this policy Canada has two official languages but no official culture and all ethnic groups are encouraged to enrich Canadian society by continuing to develop their unique cultures. The policy has led many commentators to favourably contrast the Canadian "mosaic" with the American "melting pot".

Although multiculturalism has been much vaunted as "a policy of cultural democracy as opposed to a policy of cultural imperialism" (Bhatnagar, 1981, p. 81), it has also been severely criticized by francophones (e.g. Rocher, 1973) and by some members of ethnocultural groups. Lupul (1981), for example, describes the policy as "ambitious, experimental, vague and carefully qualified, largely due to the problem of reconciling the concepts of anglophone—francophone dualism and ethnocultural pluralism" (p. 5). He describes the policy as "a piece of political pragmatism" which

pleased no one who considered the policy seriously. The failure to provide multiculturalism with a linguistic base especially displeased the Ukrainians; the loosening of the ties between language and culture angered the francophones who disliked any suggestion that the status of their culture was on a par with that of other ethnic groups.

1981, pp. 12–13

Although the multiculturalism policy clearly represents a shift away from anglo-conformity, its political implementation, according to Lupul (1981), has been greatly impeded by the "persistent ambiguities" in the policy and by the indifference of Prime Minister Trudeau and other top government

officials. The most relevant "persistent ambiguity" for present purposes is
the uncertain status of heritage *language* promotion *vis-à-vis* French—English bilingualism. The rhetoric about the desirability of heritage language
teaching has usually been positive, but qualified with respect to issues of
feasibility, cost and the primacy of French as a second language for "English
Canada" outside Quebec. For example, Book IV of the B and B Commission
recommended that "the teaching of languages other than English and
French, and cultural subjects related to them, be incorporated as options in
the public elementary school programme, where there is sufficient demand
for such classes" (§378, p. 141). However, the Report also pointed out the
practical difficulties which could arise in providing instruction in heritage
languages at the elementary level and cautioned that these languages should
not be taught at the expense of the second official language, i.e. English or
French.

B Multicultural attitude surveys

Following the establishment of the multiculturalism policy, the federal
government commissioned two national surveys to explore attitudes of
Canadians to various aspects of multiculturalism and ethnic language
maintenance. The first study, known as the Non-Official Languages Study
(O'Bryan *et al.*, 1976), investigated the attitudes of "ethnic" (i.e. "non-official") language groups, whereas the second (Berry *et al.*, 1977) investigated
attitudes towards multiculturalism among English and French groups.

In the study by O'Bryan *et al.* and in the partial replication by Gregg (1980)
wide variation among ethnic groups was found in attitudes towards multiculturalism. In general, there was strong support for language retention and for
the teaching of heritage languages in public elementary schools among
Greeks, Italians, Chinese and Ukrainians and considerably less support
among Dutch and Scandinavian groups. However, less than 10% of those
surveyed by O'Bryan *et al.* found the concept of support for language
retention either somewhat or very undesirable. Respondents recognized
that parents had the primary responsibility for retaining the heritage language and culture; however, because many respondents were aware of the
rapidity of language loss, they felt that strong institutional support was
needed. Specifically, 57% of respondents considered primary and secondary
schools the most suitable institutions for ethnic language and cultural
promotion while only 20% nominated supplementary language schools as
the primary means of supporting language and culture retention.

The Non-Official Language Study also documented the basis for respondents' support for language and culture maintenance, namely, the reality of
rapid language shift across generations. The authors summarize their results
as follows:

We have provided clear evidence that by the third generation the question is not one of retention but of reacquisition and primary acquisition. That is to say, despite the vast reservoir of language knowledge held in Canada by first generation settlers—without direct and possibly substantial assistance—the non-official language skills will evaporate quickly in their children, and their grandchildren will know little if anything of their linguistic heritage.

1976, p. 165

The rate of language loss varied considerably across groups. For example, 60% of Greek respondents used L1 exclusively with family members compared to 20% of Dutch respondents (p. 165).

The policy impact of the Non-Official Languages Study was considerable insofar as it documented the need and the strong support among ethnocultural groups for heritage language promotion in the public schools as well as in supplementary schools. Its findings paved the way for the introduction of the Cultural Enrichment Program by the federal government in June 1977, whereby support is provided to community groups for heritage language teaching and curriculum development.

Among those of French and British backgrounds, the results of several studies (Berry et al., 1977; Lambert and Curtis, 1980) show that French-Canadians are less accepting both of the multiculturalism policy and of other ethnic groups than are English-Canadians. Among the latter, there was mild support for multiculturalism but much less for heritage language promotion; for some respondents, immigration was perceived as a threat to jobs. Lambert and Curtis (1980), however, have argued that it is important to distinguish between "cultural" and "racial" attitudes. English Canadians appeared less tolerant of other *racial* groups (e.g. native peoples, East Indians) than French Canadians, although more generally tolerant of other *cultural* groups (see Berry, 1981, for a review).

In general, all ethnic groups in Canada tended to evaluate their own groups highly and most other groups less highly (Berry and Kalin, 1979). English and French Canadians were found to share the most positive regard for each other while Ukrainians and French shared the most negative regard (Berry and Kalin, 1979). Berry (1981) suggests that degree of "cultural insecurity" is an important factor in accounting for the negative multicultural attitudes found among French Canadians.

In summary, multicultural policy receives mild support among the majority Anglo-Celtic Canadian group as long as it remains non-threatening in terms of perceived job availability or allocation of scarce resources (e.g. for heritage language promotion). An apparent policy implication is that "radical" multicultural policies (e.g. high levels of resource allocation for heritage language teaching, acceptance of large numbers of refugees, e.g. "boat people") are likely to evoke a strong negative backlash whereas more moderate (or symbolic) support would be tolerated.

IV Present provision for heritage language teaching

Since education is within the jurisdiction of the provinces, the provincial educational authorities must decide what constitutes "sufficient demand" for heritage language instruction in the public school system. In recent years programmes of heritage language instruction have been instituted in the public elementary school systems of several provinces. The principal aims of these programmes are to promote the continued vitality of ethnic cultures and to enrich children's educational experience. In other words, unlike most bilingual programmes in the United States, they are not compensatory in nature (see Cummins, 1982, for discussion of Canadian heritage language programmes).

In 1971 Alberta became the first province to legalize languages other than English or French as mediums of instruction in the public school system, largely as a result of pressure from the Ukrainian community (Lupul, 1976). Currently, bilingual programmes involving Ukrainian, German, and Hebrew respectively exist in several elementary schools in Edmonton. In these programmes the heritage language is used as the language of instruction for 50% of the school day throughout the elementary school. In 1979–80 a total of 1271 students were enrolled in these bilingual heritage language programmes, the Ukrainian programme being the largest with close to 800 students enrolled between kindergarten and grade 6 in seven Edmonton schools.

In 1979 Manitoba passed enabling legislation permitting the use of heritage languages as languages of instruction for up to 50% of the school day. In 1980–81 320 students were enrolled in the English–Ukrainian bilingual programme. Saskatchewan has similar enabling legislation and an English–Ukrainian bilingual programme has also been recently instituted.

In Ontario it is still not legal to use languages other than English and French as mediums of instruction in the public school system except on a temporary basis to help children acquire English skills. However, in 1977, the Ontario Ministry of Education instituted the Heritage Languages Program under which funding is provided to school boards for the teaching of heritage languages for up to 2 hours per week outside of the regular 5-hour school day. In 1981–82 there were 81 993 students representing more than 50 language groups enrolled in the Heritage Languages Program. This figure represents an increase of more than 25 000 students since the first year of the programme.

In Quebec, until recently English could be legally used as the language of instruction in the public school system only for children whose parents were English-speaking and who had themselves been educated in English schools in Quebec. French was the legal language of instruction for all others. This Provincial Law has recently (August, 1982) been declared unconstitutional by the Quebec courts but that ruling is currently under appeal. In 1978 the

Programme de l'Enseignement des Langues d'Origine (PELO) was started by the Quebec provincial government. The PELO involves teaching Italian, Portuguese, Greek and Spanish to children of these backgrounds for 30 minutes per day during regular school hours. Approximately 600 students are currently enrolled under this programme.

It is clear that both the numbers of students receiving heritage language instruction in the public elementary school and the types of programmes vary widely across provinces. By contrast, there is relative uniformity of programmes for minority francophones in all Canadian provinces. These programmes usually vary from between 50 and 100% of the day through French from kindergarten through grade 12. For Native peoples, there has been a revival in teaching native languages across Canada and some bilingual programmes have been started; however, none of these has been systematically evaluated. In addition to these programmes operating within the public school system there are many heritage language classes operated by the linguistic communities themselves on Saturday mornings or after school hours. These classes are eligible for financial assistance from the Federal Government under its Cultural Enrichment Program. During the 1979–80 fiscal year 532 grants were made under this programme to 42 linguistic community groups for a total of more than a million dollars.

There are two principal rationales for these Canadian programmes: first, cultural maintenance, and second, educational enrichment. For the most part, those enrolled in the bilingual programmes in western Canada are third-generation students who are not fluent in the heritage language on entry to the programme. Thus, the principal aims of the programmes are to revive the language and help students appreciate their cultural heritage. As in French immersion programmes,[1] however, parents view the acquisition of a second language as an educationally enriching experience, provided of course this can be achieved at no cost to students' English language skills.

The same rationales apply to the Ontario and Quebec programmes, although there is a much greater proportion of first and second generation students in these programmes than in their western Canadian counterparts. The Ontario and Quebec programmes also involve what can be termed a "survival" rationale, i.e. one of the aims of incorporating L1 into the school curriculum is to help minority students to "survive" educationally. It is argued that teaching heritage languages in the public school will help students overcome emotional and academic adjustment difficulties by improving their self-concept and developing some concepts through L1.

V Educational effects of heritage language programmes

Evaluations of four different types of heritage language programmes have been carried out in Canada; specifically, "enrichment" (Fishman, 1976) bilingual programmes involving Ukrainian students in Alberta and Manitoba, transitional bilingual programmes for Italian students in Toronto and Ottawa, enrichment trilingual Hebrew, French, and English programmes in Montreal and a large-scale questionnaire survey of the Metropolitan Separate School Board's heritage language programme in Toronto. In addition, evaluations of bilingual programmes for minority francophone students have been carried out (see Cummins, 1979–80, for a review).

A Enrichment bilingual programs

1 English–Ukrainian (Edmonton Public School Board)

In September 1973 the Edmonton Public School Board (EPSB) introduced the English–Ukrainian bilingual programme at the kindergarten level. In kindergarten 100% of instructional time was in Ukranian after which instructional time was divided equally between English and Ukrainian. Mathematics, English language arts and science were taught in English while social studies, physical education, Ukrainian language arts, art and music were taught in Ukrainian.

More than three-quarters of the students came from homes in which one or both parents could speak Ukrainian and only about 10% of the students had no Ukrainian ancestry. However, only about 15% of the students were fluent in Ukrainian on entry to school. Unlike typical students in French immersion programmes, the bilingual students were representative of the EPSB system both in terms of ability level and parental socioeconomic status. For example, their grade 1 score (averaged over five years from 1974 to 1978) on the Metropolitan Readiness Test was only one point above the EPSB mean and less than 50% of parents had post-secondary education (Edmonton Public Schools, 1980).

In the first year of the evaluation, control students were chosen from among students in regular unilingual English programme classes across the EPSB system whose parents had the same socioeconomic level and knowledge of Ukrainian as the programme parents. In subsequent years control students were randomly chosen from the same schools as the bilingual programme. The selection was stratified on the basis of sex, school and ability level.

No consistent pattern of differences emerged in comparisons of English and mathematics skills between programme and comparison students in the early grades. However, at the grade 5 level the first cohort bilingual programme students performed significantly better than comparison students on Mathematics and on both decoding and comprehension subtests of the standardized reading test that was administered. The evaluation was discontinued at this point so that it is impossible to say whether or not subsequent cohorts also outperformed the unilingual comparison group.

The evaluation carried out by the EPSB also examined the issue of whether the programme was equally appropriate for students of different ability levels. This was done by dividing students into high, medium and low ability levels and testing for programme-by-ability interaction effects in a two-way analysis of variance design. No evidence of interaction effects was found indicating that low ability students had no more difficulty in the bilingual programme than they would have had in the regular programme.

A study was carried out with grades 1 and 3 students in order to investigate bilingual children's metalinguistic development. The study (Cummins and Mulcahy, 1978) revealed that students who were relatively fluent in Ukrainian as a result of parents using it consistently in the home were significantly better able to detect ambiguities in *English* sentence structure than either equivalent unilingual English-speaking children not in the programme or children in the programme from predominantly English-speaking homes.

The EPSB evaluation also reported that students' Ukrainian skills developed in accord with programme expectations and they also developed an appreciation for and knowledge about the Ukrainian culture. In addition, a large majority of the parents and programme personnel were pleased with the programme, felt the students were happy and wished the programme to be continued to higher grade levels.

2 English–Ukrainian (Edmonton Catholic School Board)
The Edmonton Catholic School Board's (ECSB) bilingual programme was instituted at the same time as the EPSB programme. The programme itself was similar to that in the EPSB with the exception that religious instruction in the Ukrainian Catholic Rite was carried out in the ECSB programme but not in the EPSB.

As the programme progressed through the grades, students were matched with comparison students from the same schools on the basis of grade, socioeconomic status, sex, age and Primary Mental Ability score; performance of matched groups on a variety of achievement tests was compared. The 1977–78 and 1978–79 evaluations (Ewanyshyn, 1979, 1980) will be considered here since they involve comparisons of students between grades 1 and 5. Approximately 380 students were involved in the evaluation in each of these years.

The comparisons indicated that bilingual programme students progressed academically at least as well as students in the regular English-only programme. The 1977–78 evaluation reported seven significant group differences in achievement, six of which favoured the bilingual programme students; in 1978–79 three out of four significant differences favoured the bilingual programme. The most frequent group differences in achievement were on measures of Comprehension and Spelling. In addition, parents, teachers and principals all showed high levels of satisfaction with the programme.

3 English–Ukrainian (Manitoba)

In September, 1979, an English–Ukrainian bilingual programme was implemented in one grade 1 class in each of three school divisions in Manitoba. In subsequent years the programme spread rapidly to other school divisions with kindergarten as the starting grade. The programme was based on the Edmonton model. The evaluation is being carried out by the Manitoba Department of Education (Chapman, 1981).

The evaluation of the first two years of the programme involved 262 programme students in grades kindergarten, 1 and 2. The scores of these students were compared to those of regular programme students in the same schools. Comparison of the Metropolitan Readiness Test scores of kindergarten students who subsequently entered either the bilingual or regular grade 1 programme showed no significant differences, suggesting that the programme students are representative of the general school population.

Eighty-eight per cent of the parental respondents ($N = 203$) reported that their child was of Ukrainian descent. Ukrainian was spoken at least half of the time in 23% of the respondents' homes while 76% of the respondents' children regularly interacted with Ukrainian-speaking people. Thus, the Manitoba programme students appear very similar in background to students in the Edmonton programmes.

Comparison of students who attended regular and Ukrainian kindergartens revealed no group differences on English "readiness" skills, despite the fact that the Ukrainian kindergarten was conducted for about 70% of the time in Ukrainian. Although possible preprogramme differences are not controlled in these kindergarten comparisons, the acquisition of adequate English readiness skills despite no English instruction is consistent with the findings of other bilingual programmes (see Cummins, 1979).

No differences in English or subject matter achievement were found between programme and comparison students at either the grade 1 or 2 levels despite the fact that comparison students had spent about twice as much instructional time through the medium of English.

Almost all parents and teachers felt that students had developed a greater awareness of the Ukrainian cultural heritage as a result of the programme. In addition, some parents reported that their child had become more enthusiastic about learning other languages (60%) and other cultures (45%). In general, the bilingual programme teachers felt integrated with other teachers in the school (12 of 13) and all were satisfied with their level of integration with other teachers. Also, almost all (7 of 8) of the principals stated that they were "very satisfied" with the programme.

In summary, the evaluations of these enrichment bilingual programmes show that students acquire satisfactory levels of Ukrainian skills and appreciation of Ukrainian culture at no cost to achievement in English and other academic subjects. Student affective outcomes, as viewed by parents, teachers and principals also appear to be positive.

B Transitional bilingual programs

1 Italian kindergarten transition programme in Toronto (Shapson and Purbhoo, 1977)

In the early 1970s the Toronto Board of Education implemented an experimental transition programme which allowed the curriculum to be presented in the child's L1 (Italian) during the two introductory kindergarten years of schooling (i.e. ages 4–5, 5–6). Originally the proposal had recommended that literacy skills be introduced in L1 but this was rejected by the Board because the Ontario Education Act required that English or French be the language of instruction except on a temporary basis to ease students' integration into the school system. Because of this legal requirement, promotion of Italian skills was not an objective of the programme.

Almost all students in the programme were born in Canada and had learned some dialect of Italian as their first language. Seventy-nine per cent of the parents spoke Italian extensively with their children but only 53% of the children still spoke Italian as the main language at home. Only 7% of students who had older siblings were spoken to in Italian by these siblings. Thus, at the start of the programme some children used more English than Italian whereas others spoke no English at all.

In the classroom standard Italian, dialect, and English were all used quite freely with frequent spontaneous switching of languages by students and teacher. The proportion of English used increased consistently during the Junior Kindergarten year and by the Senior Kindergarten year "Italian was used only occasionally in activities involving the whole class, but more often with a few individuals who still used their mother tongue" (Shapson and Purbhoo, 1977, p. 489).

The evaluation of the transition programme involved observations of verbal participation in the classroom, tests of language comprehension, teacher assessments of student progress, and parent questionnaires. Comparisons were made with students in regular kindergarten classes from two other schools whose students had similar language backgrounds as the programme school. There is little reason to suspect initial pre-treatment difference between programme and comparison students since virtually all parents offered the transition option in the programme school accepted it and the enrolment justified two transition classes.

Classroom observations showed that a significantly larger proportion of the transition classes participated in class discussions ($\cdot$59 v. $\cdot$43), and contributed both spontaneously ($\cdot$45 v. $\cdot$28) and in response to questions ($\cdot$41 v. $\cdot$28). Shapson and Purbhoo suggest:

Increased participation in class discussions may be considered a signal that the child feels comfortable and important in school. It might be viewed as an indicator of self-concept.

1977, p. 490

No group differences in English (or Italian) language comprehension as measured by the Peabody Picture Vocabulary Test were found either in Junior or Senior Kindergarten. Teachers' ratings of overall academic performance revealed more positive comments for the transition students in the Senior Kindergarten year. Shapson and Purbhoo caution, however, that this result may be due to differences in teachers' styles of reporting.

The evaluation also found that direct contact of parents with the teacher and involvement with school events and their child's classroom were significantly greater for the bilingual programme. It was also reported that "while parents from the comparison group expressed as great an interest in their children's education, the transition group parents attended more school functions, participated more in classroom events and talked regularly with the teacher" (1977, p. 493). Shapson and Purbhoo attribute this greater involvement to the obvious fact that a common language makes communication easier.

In summary, the programme objectives were clearly met insofar as participation by students and their parents in the educational process was facilitated by the incorporation of Italian as a medium of instruction. Other evaluations of transition programmes in Toronto involving Portuguese and Italian (Henderson *et al.*, 1973; Henderson, 1977) have also reported better student integration and increased parental involvement at no academic cost as a result of the programme.

2 English–Italian kindergarten programme in Ottawa (Egyed, 1973)
Egyed (1973) compared the academic progress in Senior Kindergarten of three groups of Italian-background students randomly assigned to (1) a full-day English kindergarten, (2) half-day English, half-day Italian kindergarten, (3) half-day English, half-day French kindergarten. Using a pre- and post-test design, Egyed reported no significant differences in English academic progress between students in the bilingual Italian–English kindergarten compared to those in the full-day English programme. Thus, spending half the school day through Italian did not interfere with students' progress in English.

However, Italian-background students in the French–English bilingual kindergarten programme obtained significantly lower scores in English academic skills than students in either of the other two programmes. The French–English bilingual students were reported to have made "relatively low gains in auditory psycholinguistic development" (Edwards and Casserly, 1976, p. 248).

In summary, this study is consistent with the others reviewed in showing that spending instructional time through students' L1 involves no academic costs to their progress in English (L2).

C Trilingual programmes

1 Montreal Hebrew–English programmes (Genesee and Lambert, 1980)

Trilingual programmes involving Hebrew exist in most of the major Canadian cities and usually, but not always, operate outside the regular public school system. Other isolated examples of trilingual education exist; for example, in one predominantly Italian-background school (St Gaspar) in the Toronto Metropolitan Separate School Board (MSSB), students from grades 5–8 are enrolled in the Board's French–English bilingual programme (starting in grade 5) and also take Italian for half an hour a day during regular school hours (Feuerverger, 1982).

However, only the Montreal trilingual programmes have been systematically evaluated. Because the programme variations compared by Genesee and Lambert are complex, only the general pattern of findings is reported here. The complete evaluation data are available in Genesee et al. (1978a, 1978b), as well as in Genesee and Lambert (1980). The basic design involved comparing groups of students who participated in two slightly different "early Double Immersion" (EDI) programmes (i.e. Hebrew, French, English trilingual programmes) with students who attended a more traditional Hebrew day school (most initial instruction through English and Hebrew but with increasing amounts of French-medium instruction in the intermediate grades of elementary school). The Hebrew time allocation and curriculum was similar in all three schools. In one of the EDI schools English language arts was introduced in grade 3, and in grade 4 in the other school. The academic performance of students in these schools was also compared to that of students in regular French immersion and French-as-a-second-language (20–30 minutes per day of French taught as a subject) programmes.

It was found at the grade 4 and 5 levels that both EDI groups achieved as well in English as all other groups, despite considerably less instructional time through English than the traditional Hebrew day school or French-as-a-second-language groups. No group differences were evident in mathematics despite the fact that the EDI groups had received all initial mathematics instruction through French whereas the traditional Hebrew day school students received all initial mathematics instruction through English. The EDI students scored almost as well as the regular French immersion students on measures of French proficiency. On measures of Hebrew, the EDI students tended to score higher than students in the regular Hebrew day school despite the similarity of programme and time allocation.

Genesee and Lambert (1980) conclude that programmes of bi- and trilingualism are feasible and effective ways of enriching students' education insofar as:

> The Hebrew day schools were able (1) to achieve the goals of regular school programs with regard to native language development and academic achievement, (2) to maintain important religious, cultural and linguistic traditions, and (3) at the same time, to develop the children's competence in a language of local importance.
>
> 1980, p. 25

The authors acknowledge that the students in the trilingual programmes were highly capable and motivated youngsters but point out that the existing evidence (e.g. Cziko, 1975) pertaining to the suitability of single French immersion programmes for students who are less economically and intellectually advantaged suggests that these students would also benefit academically and linguistically from programmes of double immersion.

D Ontario Heritage Language Program (Keyser and Brown, 1981)

The only large-scale research to be conducted on the Ontario Heritage Language Program (HLP) since its inception in 1977 was the survey of parental and teacher perceptions carried out by the Metropolitan Separate School Board (MSSB). In 1982, the MSSB had about 35 000 students enrolled in the HLP out of a total student population of 94 000. Of these, 27 000 took Italian, Portuguese or Ukrainian courses integrated into an extended school day.

Almost 11 000 parents representing more than 18 000 students completed the questionnaire. It was found that the vast majority of students enrolled in the HLP were born in Canada. Elevent per cent of students in the programme were learning a language other than their parents' L1; in fact, nearly a thousand (15.6% of total Italian enrolment) students studying Italian were not of Italian heritage.

Parents were highly satisfied with their children's progress in learning the heritage language. In speaking and understanding, for example, 88 and 90% of respondents respectively thought their children's facility had improved "a great deal" or "some". More than 80% thought that the programme had contributed either some or a great deal to their child's confidence and sense of self-worth. Respondents also felt that the programme had increased communication between family members (80%), provided a deeper appreciation of family heritage (81%) and improved performance in other subject areas in the regular programme (59%).

Principals were similarly positive about the impact of the HLP in their schools, 61% indicating that it had had a positive impact (6% were negative). When principals were asked to break down the effects by principal, teachers, parents, and students, it became apparent that the over-all effect was perceived as most positive for principals (78%) and parents (82%) and somewhat less positive for students (57% positive, 4% negative) and teachers (55% positive, 18% negative). It is clear from this pattern and from other data in the survey that a small minority of regular teachers perceive the HLP as disruptive and time-consuming. However, the over-all trends in the survey data indicate a generally high level of satisfaction among all constituents with the HLP.

In summary, the available research data from several different models of heritage language programme indicate that benefits in terms of students' language acquisition or increased parental involvement are obtained at no cost to students' progress in English or in other core curriculum subjects. These data are consistent with findings from evaluations of programmes for minority francophone students in Canada (e.g. Hébert *et al.*, 1976) which show that instruction through French benefits students' French language skills at no cost to their achievement in the majority language (English).

Analysis of the public debate on heritage language teaching during the past decade in cities such as Metropolitan Toronto reveals that research evidence on the feasibility and educational potential of heritage language teaching has begun to play an increasingly prominent role in the political process. The evolution of this debate is outlined in the next section.

VI Heritage language teaching and Canadian identity: the Toronto debate

In the early 1970s, prompted by the federal policy of multiculturalism and the increasingly obvious presence of large numbers of non-English background (ESL) students, educators in several Metropolitan Toronto boards of education began to re-examine the assumptions underlying school curricula and policies. This awakening by the school boards was stimulated by the fact that immigrant organizations were becoming increasingly vocal in expressing concerns about their children's education. For example in the late 1960s the Dante Society, a cultural organization for Metropolitan Toronto Italians, pointed out that about 70% of students in vocational and technical schools were from immigrant families, and they accused the Toronto Board of streaming immigrant students out of academically oriented classes. The focus of ethnic group concerns in the early 1970s turned increasingly towards heritage language teaching and this debate has gone through several phases.

A Phase I. Initial skirmishes

The first shot in what has subsequently turned into Toronto's ten-year heritage language battle was fired in April 1972 with Anthony Grande's proposal for an Italian–English bilingual programme (see Lind, 1974; Grande, 1975). The Board heard a modified version of the plan one year later[2] and after considerable negotiation with the Ministry of Education about what was permissible under the Schools Administration Act, the kindergarten Italian transition programme (described earlier—Shapson and Purbhoo, 1977) emerged. At the same time the Board approved "bicultural/ bilingual immersion" programmes for Chinese and Greek students. These programmes involved 30 minutes a day of Chinese or Greek culture with some language, taught by volunteers. In the case of Chinese, the programme was on a withdrawal basis during the school day in two schools, while the Greek programme was taught after hours (see Deosaran and Gershman, 1976, for an evaluation of the Chinese programme).

Lind (1974) describes the Ministry of Education during these debates as "without clear policy, except to unbend as little as necessary to avoid confrontation" (p. 50). He also points to the "false advertising" implied by the label "bicultural/bilingual immersion" given the vast difference between the way the term "immersion" is used in these programmes as compared to French "immersion" programmes. Lind points to the politics of terminology stating:

> The euphemism was nothing but a gimmick for getting a bureaucratically acceptable program past the parents on the one hand and the Ministry on the other.
>
> 1974, p. 53

B Phase II. The Work Group on Multicultural Programs

In May 1974 the Toronto Board set up the Work Group on Multicultural Programs to investigate the philosophy and programmes related to the city's multicultural population. As stated in the Work Group's Draft Report issued in May, 1975, drastic rethinking of these programmes was necessary in view of the fact that:

> The shocking recognition for the Board of Education for the City of Toronto is that within the space of a decade its CULTURAL BASE HAS BECOME INCOMPATIBLE [emphasis original] with the cultural base of the society which supports its endeavour.
>
> Toronto Board of Education, 1975, p. 5

The Draft Report recommended, among other things, that the Ministry of Education be requested by the Board to amend the Ontario Education Act to allow languages other than English or French to be used both as medium and subjects of instruction at the primary level. The Report also recommended that existing "bicultural–bilingual" and transition programmes be continued and expanded and that the Board continue to be responsive to requests for the institution of "third" or "heritage" language subject credit programmes at the secondary school level.

These recommendations were based on the strong community (usually ethnic community) support in the briefs and consultations for proposals related to maintenance of original culture and language and the teaching of and through third languages (see Masemann, 1978–79). In the Work Group's Final Report (Toronto Board of Education, 1976) it is pointed out that publication of the Draft Report evoked a response from "newly participating groups in opposition to certain "ideas" contained in the report" (pp. 23–24). Concerns with ghettoization and cost were prominent as well as expectations regarding the appropriateness of "ethnic demands"; specifically, it was felt by many that immigrants chose to come to this country and they should therefore accept the existing educational and social system. If they chose to maintain the home language, it should be done in the home. The view was also expressed that maintenance of L1, whether in the home or school, was educationally ill-advised because it would impede students' acquisition of English. The strength of this "significant minority opinion" together with the Ministry's unwillingness to change the Education Act led the Work Group to withdraw its recommendations relating to third language teaching.

C Phase III. The Heritage Language Program (HLP)

The HLP was announced in the spring of 1977 and represented a carefully considered attempt to accommodate the persistent "ethnic demands" while minimizing the backlash from those opposed to publicly supported heritage language teaching. Under the HLP, the Ministry provides virtually 100% of the operating costs, based on a per-pupil formula for $2\frac{1}{2}$ hours of instruction per week, to school boards who agree to implement a programme at the request of community groups. Thus, the initiative must come from the community and school boards are under no obligation to accede to community requests. In several cases boards have resisted implementing a programme despite strong ethnic community pressure.

There are three basic options for when classes may be held: (1) on weekends; (2) after the regular 5-hour school day; and (3) integrated into a school day extended by half-an-hour. This last option is the predominant one in the Metropolitan Separate Board which operates by far the largest HLP (see evaluation results above).

Because the HLP is funded under the Continuing Education Program, instructors need not have Ontario certification and can be paid at a lower rate than regular certified teachers. Also, no major changes were required in the Education Act since the programme was being offered outside regular school hours. Thus, the programme appeared to represent a reasonable compromise whereby the concerns of the ethnic communities could be accommodated without excessively alienating other community sectors. However, the initial reaction of those opposed to the programme was vehemently hostile. In the words of a Ministry official, the phone rang constantly for three weeks with people voicing their disapproval.

The Ministry appears to have been caught off-guard by the demand for the programme. Costs for 1977–78 had been estimated at 1–$1\frac{1}{2}$ million dollars but actually totalled about 5 million and have risen appreciably every year since then as enrolment has continued to rise (Burke, 1982). The size of the HLP can be seen in the fact that its enrolment (1982–83) is approximately the same as that of all types of French immersion programmes across Canada (almost 80 000 students).

In short, it can be assumed that, as a result of implementing the HLP, the Ontario Ministry is acutely aware of the costs, both financial and political, of accommodating any further to "ethnic demands".

D Phase IV. The Third Language Workgroup Report (Toronto Board of Education, 1982)

As a result of dissatisfaction with certain aspects of the HLP, most notably its implication that heritage language teaching was not a legitimate part of students' "regular" education, the Ukrainian and Armenian communities placed proposals before the Toronto Board in the Spring of 1980 for the establishment of "Alternative Language Schools", essentially magnet schools (i.e. open to students from outside the immediate school area) in which the heritage language would be taught for half-an-hour during an extended school day (but school announcements and incidental "non-instructional" conversation could also be in the heritage language as a means of providing students with a greater amount of meaningful input in the language). These proposals evoked a public outcry of "ghettoization" and "balkanization" and were savaged by the press.

In June 1980, the Toronto Board referred the entire question of third language instruction to a Work Group. After extensive community consultation and visits to the Ukrainian–English bilingual programmes in western Canada, the Work Group issued its final report in March 1982. Its major recommendations were that the heritage language programme should be gradually integrated into a regular extended school day in situations where this was feasible and also that, as a long-term strategy, the Board work towards the implementation of bilingual and trilingual programmes involving heritage languages. An implication of this long-term strategy is that the

Board exert pressure on the Ministry to adopt permissive legislation with respect to language of instruction.

The ensuing debate was divisive and bitter. A large proportion of the ethnocultural communities strongly supported the Work Group proposals whereas much of the opposition came from anglophone communities. However, some individuals from minority backgrounds also vocally opposed the proposals. Almost 200 oral submissions were made to the Board which approved the Report on May 5, 1982. The style of the debate is summed up in a *Toronto Star* article on May 4:

> In essence it [the debate] seems to be a battle over the Canadian identity: are we stronger because of our cultural diversity, or weakened by institutionalizing it?
>
> It's been marred at times by charges of racism on one side and misrepresentation on the other, invective, catcalls and telephoned threats to trustees. Callers also have harassed board staff.
>
> 1982, A16

The basic arguments in the debate were not very different from those in previous Toronto debates on the issue, although the pitch and the level of community involvement on both sides was undoubtedly higher. Those arguing for the Work Group Report stressed the reality of language and culture loss among their children and were able to cite the research findings documented in the Work Group Report which supported both heritage language teaching in general, and bilingual and trilingual programmes in particular. The validity of bilingualism and trilingualism as *educational* goals for their children was stressed. Thus, the 1982 Work Group proposals appeared to have both a stronger empirical and community experiential (e.g. language loss) basis than those contained in the 1975 Draft Report.

Opponents tended to focus on the presumed financial and social consequences of implementing the Report. A letter to the *Globe and Mail* on April 17, 1982, by Trustee Michael Walker made these consequences explicit:

> If this report is passed, it would probably result in the segregation of children along linguistic and cultural lines, the busing of children on a major scale across the city, using linguistic and cultural quota to staff schools with teachers and very large additional costs to the taxpayer . . .
>
> The recommendations of this report will guarantee second-class status to any student attending a third language school and be of great disservice to the community at large. I also believe it will ultimately tear the public school system apart in Toronto.

A correspondent (Joan Lynn) in a May issue of the *Toronto Star* pointed out that many immigrants "are *quietly* [my emphasis] preserving their own

language in their homes and circles of friendship" and went on to suggest that
"it is unlikely that there is spare money around for this luxury, unless *we are
all* [my emphasis] willing to pay higher taxes". Similar financial concerns
were expressed in a letter by Barbara Stuart. (*Toronto Star,* May): "Surely,
from a financial standpoint, there is a matter of priorities here. If so much as
a single dollar extra can be found in any budget for the implementation of the
Third Language Report, should that dollar not be spent on the more urgent
of our problems?" Another correspondent (Steve Gurian, *Toronto Star,*
May) asked "How are these ethnic children ever going to integrate and
assimilate into the Canadian culture stream if they do not possess English?"

It is clear that this most recent Toronto debate escalated far beyond the
specific proposals contained in the Work Group report. The concerns of
opponents were not diminished by the presence of almost 30 000 students in
integrated heritage language classes in the Metropolitan Separate School
Board at no extra cost to taxpayers, with no hint of ghettoization nor
academic difficulties as a result of the programme.

VII Conclusion

The issues in the heritage languages debate go to the core of Canadian
identity and illustrate why the "persistent ambiguities" in the federal
multiculturalism policy remain unresolved. The demographic strength and
increased economic security of the ethnic minority population in Metropolitan Toronto appear to have allowed them to reject the two options proffer-
red by the dominant societal group, namely, to give up their languages and
cultures and become invisible and inaudible through assimilation or, alternatively, to maintain their languages and cultures but to do it "quietly", at their
own expense, without in any way affecting the linguistic and cultural status
quo. Instead, the ethnic communities have articulated *their* priorities as
Canadian taxpayers and have shown themselves willing to fight for these
priorities in the political arena. What is being challenged, both visibly and
audibly, is the core value of Anglo-conformity which persists underneath the
veneer of "multiculturalism" among a significant proportion of the Canadian
public. The outcome of this continuing debate will very likely help define
what "multiculturalism" really means in the Canadian context.

Notes

1. A French immersion programme involves teaching anglophone students through
   the medium of French for a considerable part of the school day with the aim of

developing fluent skills in French at no cost to acquisition of English or other academic skills. These programmes have been highly successful and have spread rapidly across Canada. Currently about 80 000 students are enrolled in some form of French immersion programme.

2. According to Lind (1974) "when Grande first made his proposal in April, the New Canadian Committee went apoplectic" (pp. 48–49).

References

Abella, I. and Troper, H. (1982). *None is Too Many*. Lester and Orpen Dennys, Toronto.

Anderson, J. T. M. (1918). *The Education of the New Canadian*. Dent, Toronto.

Berry, J. W. (1981). Multicultural attitudes and education. Paper presented at symposium, "Perspectives on Multiculturalism in Education", Queen's University.

Berry, J. W. and Kalin, R. R. (1979). Reciprocity of inter-ethnic attitudes in a multicultural society. *International Journal of Intercultural Relations* **3**, 99–112.

Berry, J. W., Kalin, R. and Taylor, D. M. (1977). *Multiculturalism and Ethnic Attitudes in Canada*. Supply and Services, Ottawa.

Bhatnagar, J. (1981). Multiculturalism and the education of immigrants in Canada. In *Educating Immigrants* (Ed. J. Bhatnagar). Croom Helm, London.

Black, N. F. (1913). *English for the Non-English*. Regina Book Shop Limited, Regina.

Burke, M. E. (1982). The heritage languages program. Paper presented to the Association of Women of Indian Origin, Toronto.

Chapman, E. (1981). *An Evaluation of the First Two Years of the English-Ukrainian Bilingual Program: Summary Report*. Manitoba Department of Education, Winnipeg.

Cummins, J. (1979). Bilingualism and educational development in anglophone and minority francophone groups in Canada. *Interchange* **9**, 40–51.

Cummins, J. (Ed.). (1982). *Heritage Language Education: Issues and Directions*. Minister of State for Multiculturalism, Ottawa.

Cummins, J. and Mulcahy, R. (1978). Orientation to language in Ukrainian–English bilingual children. *Child Development* **49**, 1239–1242.

Cziko, G. (1975). The effects of different French immersion programmes on the language and academic skills of children from various socioeconomic backgrounds. M.A. Thesis, Department of Psychology, McGill University.

Deosaran, R. and Gershman, J. S. (1976). An evaluation of the 1975–76 Chinese–Canadian bi-cultural program. Research report #137, Toronto Board of Education.

Deosaran, R., Wright, E. N. and Kane, T. (1976). Students' background and its relationship to student placement. Research Report, Toronto Board of Education.

Edmonton Public Schools. (1979). *Evaluation of the Bilingual (English–Ukrainian) Program*. Edmonton Public Schools, Edmonton.

Edmonton Public Schools. (1980). *Summary of the Evaluations of the Bilingual English–Ukrainian and the Bilingual English–French Programs.* Edmonton Public School Board, Edmonton.

Edwards, H. C. and Casserly, M. C. (1976). *Research and Evaluation of Second Language (French) Programs.* Ontario Ministry of Education, Toronto.

Egyed, C. (1973). The attainment of English language skills as a function of instruction in the mother tongue of Italian Kindergarten children. Paper presented at Canadian Psychological Association Conference, Victoria, B.C.

Ewanyshyn, E. (1979). *Evaluation of a Ukrainian–English Bilingual Program, 1977–78.* Edmonton Catholic Schools, Edmonton.

Ewanyshyn, E. (1980). *Evaluation of a Ukrainian–English Bilingual Program, 1978–79.* Edmonton Catholic Schools, Edmonton.

Feuerverger, G. (1982). Effects of the heritage language program on the ethnolinguistic vitality of Italo-Canadian students. Unpublished Master's Thesis, Ontario Institute for Studies in Education.

Fishman, J. (1976). Bilingual education: What and why. In *English as a Second Language in Bilingual Education* (Eds J. E. Alatis and K. Twaddell). TESOL, Washington, D.C.

Genesee, F. and Lambert, W. E. (1980). Trilingual education for the majority group child. Unpublished research report, November.

Genesee, F., Tucker, G. R. and Lambert, W. E. (1978a). An experiment in trilingual education: Report 3. *Canadian Modern Language Review* **34**, 621–643.

Genesee, F., Tucker, G. R. and Lambert, W. E. (1978b). An experiment in trilingual education: Report 4. *Language Learning* **28**, 343–365.

Grande, A. (1975). A transition program for young Italian children. In *Education of Immigrant Students* (Ed. A. Wolfgang). Ontario Institute for Studies in Education, Toronto.

Gregg, A. (1980). *A Study of Ethnicity and Attitudes Toward Multiculturalism in Canada.* Decima Research Limited, Toronto.

Harney, R. and Troper, H. (1975). *Immigrants: A Portrait of Urban Experience 1890–1930.* Van Nostrand Reinhold, Toronto.

Hébert, R. *et al.* (1976). *Rendement Academique et Langue d'Enseignement Chez les Élèves Franco-Manitobains.* Centre de Recherches du Collège Universitaire de Saint-Boniface, Saint-Boniface, Manitoba.

Henderson, K. (1977). A report on bilingual transition programs for Italian and Portuguese immigrant students. Unpublished research report, Ontario Institute for Studies in Education.

Henderson, K., Silverman, H., Toscano, S. and Giallonardo, F. (1973). *A First Language Reception Program for Immigrant Students.* Ontario Institute for Studies in Education, Toronto. Final Report (0N0030).

Kamin, L. F. (1974). *The Science and Politics of I.Q.* Erlbaum, New York.

Keyser, R. and Brown, J. (1981). Heritage language survey results. Research Department, Metropolitan Separate School Board.

Lambert, R. and Curtis, J. (1980). The French and English–Canadian language communities and multicultural attitudes. Unpublished Research Report.

Lenskyj, H. (1981). Historical attitudes towards the education of new Canadian students. Unpublished paper, Ontario Institute for Studies in Education.

Lind, L. J. (1974). *The Learning Machine: A Hard Look at Toronto Schools*. Anansi, Toronto.

Lupul, M. (1976). Bilingual education and the Ukrainians in Western Canada: Possibilities and problems. In *Bilingualism in Canadian Education: Issues and Research* (Ed. M. Swain). Canadian Society for the Study of Education, Edmonton.

Lupul, M. (1981). The political implementation of multiculturalism. Paper presented to the Ninth Biennial Conference of the Canadian Ethnic Studies Association.

Masemann, V. L. (1978–79). Multicultural programs in Toronto schools. *Interchange* 9, 29–44.

O'Bryan, K. G., Reitz, J. G. and Kuplowska, O. (1976). *Non-Official Languages: A Study in Canadian Multiculturalism*. Minister Responsible for Multiculturalism, Ottawa.

Rocher, G. (1973). *Le Québec en Mutation*. Hurtubise, Montreal.

Royal Commission on Bilingualism and Biculturalism (1970). *Book IV. The Cultural Contribution of the Other Ethnic Groups*. Ottawa, Canada.

Shapson, S. and Purbhoo, M. (1977). A transition program for Italian children. *Canadian Modern Language Review* 33, 486–496.

Sissons, C. B. (1917). *Bi-lingual Schools in Canada*. Dent, London.

Toronto Board of Education (1975). Draft report of the work group on multicultural programs.

Toronto Board of Education (1976). Final report of the work group on multicultural programs.

Toronto Board of Education (1982). *Towards a Comprehensive Language Policy* (Final report of the Work Group on Third Language Instruction).

Yeung, E. (1982). The linguistic pendulum swings in Vancouver schools. *Language and Society* 8, 16–18.

4
Ethnolinguistic minorities and multicultural policy in Australia

Brian M. Bullivant

The emergence of multiculturalism as the dominant ideology of pluralism guiding official policy towards ethnic and linguistic minorities in Australia is a very recent trend in the history of its attitudes towards those from non-Anglo-Celtic backgrounds. In this respect Australia is no different from many other pluralist societies around the world where multiculturalism has become the dominant ideology (see Bhatnagar, 1981; Bullivant, 1981a). However, Australia's remoteness from centres of Western "civilization", its unique demographic, ethno-cultural and educational make-up, and the circumstances surrounding the adoption of the multicultural ideology, coupled with the vacillations and ambiguities which have followed, give a typically antipodean flavour to the way multicultural policy is now being applied.

Such a state of affairs is quite usual in Australia. For decades the education system has gladly seized on successive educational philosophies and ideologies from overseas systems—usually those of the United States or Britain—but some years after they were current in those countries. When they failed to solve Australia's particular educational problems—something that might have been anticipated but rarely was—the philosophies were speedily jettisoned in favour of their successors. Such has been the strength of educational faddism. Multiculturalism may well follow a similar fate.

LINGUISTIC MINORITIES
ISBN 0-12-232760-8

I Demographic and ethnocultural composition

A The general pattern of ethnic groups

Thanks to successive waves of immigration, particularly in the post-World War II period, plus the presence of a well-established majority of settlers built up since colonial times, together with a much smaller number of Aboriginal inhabitants, the composition of the Australian population shows considerable variety. The majority group of *Staatsvolk* (Connor, 1973) is generally of Anglo-Celtic origin, speaking English, and sharing broadly similar Judaeo-Christian values, but, because of the influence of television, with a strong and growing admixture of American "chromium plated culture". Although this group is part of the supposed multicultural society that official policies are attempting to foster, it is not of major concern here.

There are also several long-settled ethnic groups such as Jews and Chinese. They have similar colonial origins and, while not constituting distinct groups, have maintained their *ethnic* boundaries more or less intact through emphasizing markers like language, religion, historical loyalties, kinship and intermarriage ties, even though they also speak English and share other aspects of the majority culture. To some extent these groups are more affected by current multicultural policies where these have been utilized to consciously foster ethnic group revitalization or to gain financial benefit from government funding.

Of most relevance for this discussion are two groups which, to some extent, are both culturally and linguistically different from the longer-established settlers. The first comprises Australian Aborigines and Torres Strait Islanders, who are also racially different. The second comprises those recent, post-World War II immigrants from non-English-speaking countries. They may habitually speak a language other than English, may foster their own cultural traits, and "conceive themselves as being alike, by virtue of their common ancestry, real or fictitious, and who are so regarded by others"—these being the distinguishing characteristics of an ethnic group according to Shibutani and Kwan (1965, p. 47). It is to the second of these two ethno-linguistic groups that most official multicultural policies are directed.

Given the delays that can be expected in obtaining even incomplete data from the 1981 Census (if the experience of its 1976 counterpart is any guide), the numbers of persons in the various ethno-linguistic categories and groups are difficult to establish precisely. At the Census of 30 June, 1976, the total population of Australia was 13 548 448. Subsequent Bureau of Statistics (1981) figures put the total on 30 June, 1981, at 14 856 100 and the population passed 15 million later that year.

TABLE 1
Composition of Australian population according to birthplace on 30 June, 1976

Birthplace	Number	Percentage
Australia	10 829 616	79·93
Europe (including UK and Eire)	2 210 817	16·30
(excluding UK and Eire)	1 093 218	8·07
UK and Eire	1 117 599	8·25
Asia	240 622	1·78
America	80 732	0·60
Africa	70 510	0·52
Oceania	115 829	0·85
Other—at sea	322	0·02
Total born overseas	2 718 832	20·07
Total population	13 548 448	100·00

Source: Australian Bureau of Statistics, 1976 Census: Population and Dwellings: Summary Tables, p. 2, Table 8.

The composition of the 1976 total can be divided according to birthplace (Table 1). On this basis 79.93% of the population were born in Australia, and the remaining 20.07% were born in a great variety of English- and non-English-speaking countries. In the official literature supporting multiculturalism, and in mass media pronouncements generally, it is commonly claimed that at least a quarter to a third of the population comes from non-English-speaking backgrounds. However, the figures suggest otherwise. If the numbers of those from the United Kingdom, Eire, Canada, New Zealand, and South Africa are taken into account, the figure of a third or a quarter cannot be supported empirically.

Included in the Australian-born population is a small number of Aborigines and Torres Strait Islanders. These were asked to identify themselves by race in the 1976 Census, and totalled 160 912 persons or 1·19% of the population. Due to difficulties in collecting data on this group it cannot be claimed that this figure is fully accurate.

Lack of more up-to-date figures and the broad divisions in Table 1 conceal the changing composition of the population, due particularly to the considerable influx of refugees and settlers from Indo-China (all commonly but erroneously termed the "Vietnamese"), Malaysia and Singapore that has occurred since the 1976 Census. The greater detail of Table 2 indicates the dramatic decrease in the percentage of settlers from European countries and a corresponding increase in settlers from Asia, especially South East Asia;

TABLE 2
Settlers arriving in Australia by country of last residence

Country	1970 %	1979 %
South Africa	0·9	4·0
Other Africa	2·1	1·5
Total Africa	3·0	5·5
Canada	1·1	1·3
USA	2·7	2·0
Other America	2·3	2·9
Total America	6·1	6·2
Bangladesh, India, Pakistan, Sri Lanka	2·2	1·3
Lebanon	2·1	1·4
Malaysia, Singapore	0·8	13·9
Turkey	2·4	1·0
Other Asia	2·2	16·6
Total Asia	9·7	34·2
UK and Ireland	41·8	17·0
Austria	6·9	1·0
Germany	2·8	1·5
Greece	5·4	1·2
Italy	4·8	3·3
Yugoslavia	8·5	1·6
Other Europe	7·6	4·9
Total Europe	77·8	30·6
New Zealand	3·0	21·4
Other Oceania	0·4	2·0
Total Oceania	3·4	23·4

Source: Australian Bureau of Statistics, *Overseas Arrivals and Departures Australia,* 1979.

prior to 1970 the proportion of settlers from Europe made up more than three quarters of the settler intake. Another figure of interest is the substantial increase of settlers from New Zealand.

More recent figures for the year ended December 1980 show that numbers of settlers from South Africa, Malaysia and Singapore are continuing to increase compared with the corresponding period in 1979. However, settlers from the UK and Ireland also show a marked increase, while those from New Zealand, again emphasizing the shift away from European source countries, show a slight decrease (Bureau of Statistics, 1981). Despite these short-term fluctuations from year to year the general trend of increasing settlement from Asian countries and decreasing settlement from the more traditional European source countries seems set to continue. It has obvious implications for any multicultural policy as it injects into the Australian society a "racial" component that had largely been absent or at least minimal up to the official demise of the so-called "White Australia" policy in 1975. As United States and British experience suggests, racial dynamics in society may have no cultural origins but can be generated by differences of "colour" and other purely phenotypical features—aspects that a *multicultural* model of society can gloss over.

B Linguistic groupings

The 1976 Census asked for details regarding the regular use of community languages other than English (CLOTEs) by all persons aged five years or more. Those using English only totalled 83·25%, 4·4% did not state their language, 12·35% reported using one or more CLOTEs. This includes 4·2% who are Australian-born and 1·42% who stated they used no English at all.

A wide variety of foreign languages was reported, bearing out the large number of CLOTEs found among primary and secondary students in Australian schools (Committee on the Teaching of Migrant Languages in Schools, 1976). In the 1976 Census the CLOTEs with over 25 000 persons, in decreasing order, were Italian, Greek, German, Slovene, French, Dutch, Polish, Spanish, Maltese, Chinese, Aboriginal and Serbo-Croat. However, this order and selection may not represent the current (1982) pattern as they are based on figures which are now too old to be reliable. In particular, "there have been significant recent arrivals of Chinese, Vietnamese, and Russian speakers" (Clyne, 1981, p. 18). For example, settler arrivals from Vietnam for the years ended December 31, 1979 and 1980 were 2 796 and 12 460 persons respectively (Bureau of Statistics, 1981).

Two features of community language use that have a bearing on policy making are the differences between the sexes and the uneven distribution of CLOTEs throughout Australia. As Clyne (1981, p. 15) notes from census data, "the percentage of women not using English regularly is higher than that of men, and this must be taken into account in the development of multilingual social welfare facilities". The distribution of CLOTEs through-out the States has similar implications. Not only do some languages predomi-nate in a particular State (e.g. Dutch has overproportionate numbers in Tasmania and Western Australia), but there are differences between State capitals. For instance, more people use the largest community languages in Melbourne than in Sydney. Of the smaller languages, however, three times as many Arabic speakers, $2\frac{1}{2}$ times as many Spanish, and twice as many Chinese speakers are found in Sydney compared with Melbourne (Clyne, 1981). Forming policies on the assumption that CLOTEs are uniformly distributed throughout Australia would be an obvious oversimplification.

A similar mistake might well occur if the Census language classification

Aboriginal is taken at face value and assumed to be one CLOTE. In contemporary Australia there are numerous languages and dialects.

"Aboriginality" means one thing to a tradition-oriented Aborigine and quite another to "the urban Aboriginal man who pursues a way of life indistinguishable in many ways from that of his white neighbours but who, at the same time, is different from them because of certain identifications he makes and certain values he holds" (Watts, 1981, p. 79).

This heterogeneity also has important implications for policy making especially in a multicultural society with its implied corollary of a variety of sub-cultures, which the education system and curriculum need to cater for (see discussion in Bullivant, 1977, 1979, 1981b). As Watts suggests (1981, p. 79):

> As educationalists, it seems appropriate to recognize the common cultural membership of all Aborigines, accepting however that being Aboriginal has different meanings for different Aboriginal people and accepting, also, that wide diversity of life styles and particular aspirations that have a marked significance for education.

II The historical context of current policies

In November 1978 the Report of the Review of Post-Arrival Programs and Services for Migrants (The Galbally Report) was formally accepted by the Federal Government. It marked a milestone in the evolution of official thinking about migrants, and has been the basis of subsequent government funding and expenditure in this field. So influential was the Galbally Report that it serves as the dividing point between two eras: the pre-Galbally era of vacillations and general neglect of migrants' needs, and the post-Galbally era that, if official claims are to be believed, will lead to the multicultural millennium in which all will be sweetness and light in relations between the dominant Anglo-Celtic *Staatsvolk* and the ethno-linguistic minorities. Those more conversant with, and inured to, the pragmatism, expediency and political opportunism that historically have characterized the government's policies towards such groups may see the Galbally Report and multicultural ideology as the latest in a long line of palliatives and window-dressings.

A The Pre-Galbally era

Immigration has been a feature of Australian history since first settlement, and until World War II successive waves of mainly British immigrants came into Australia. Many of them were assisted by the British government, and the waves continued through the 1920s under the Empire Settlement Act of 1922. They were halted both by the failure of land settlement schemes—

British being more suited to urban settlement—and by the 1930s Depression. Many British returned home, where at least the dole was available. However, the waves of British migrants did superimpose strongly pro-British sentiments on the existing Australian nationalism which had become apparent since the 1890s, and resulted in establishing the basis of the official pre-and immediate post-World War II policies towards immigration (Jupp, 1966). They conceived of the Australian population as being predominantly of British origin, and expected both British and European immigrants to fit into the social and economic structure as quickly as possible. To this end, in the immediate post-war period, non-British migrants were selected not only for their potential as factory workers, but also because they matched Australian physical characteristics as far as possible. As Calwell, the chief architect of this policy, has commented (1972, p. 103):

> Many [Balts and other Nordic types] were red-headed and blue-eyed. There was also a number of natural platinum blondes of both sexes. The men were handsome and the women beautiful. It was not hard to sell immigration to the Australian people once the press published photographs of that group.

Desirable immigrants fitting this image came from Scandinavian and northern European countries adjacent to Britain. Only when these sources dried up were southern European countries such as Greece, Italy and Yugoslavia tapped.

The official policy towards all immigrants was thus strongly Anglo-conformist and assimilationist in the 1950s and 1960s. An emphasis was also placed on migrants becoming naturalized as soon as possible, thus confirming the act of assimilation. Diversity of any kind was officially discouraged and the need to have a monoculture emphasized (Snedden, in Cigler, 1975).

Despite this, official policy did soften in the late 1960s and early 1970s, bowing to the fact, which was becoming all too clear, that migrants were not assimilating. The successor to this policy was that of integration. This too was given a public justification by the then Minister for Immigration, Phillip Lynch. The rhetoric is easy to detect in the Minister's claim: "The earlier desire to make stereotype Australians of the newcomers has been cast aside. The use of the word 'integration' instead of 'assimilation' is not mere semantics—it is the outward sign of a fundamental change in attitude of the Australian government and people" (Lynch, 1972, p. 10).

These were fine words indeed, but they may not have struck a responsive chord in those many migrants suffering from the effects of the chauvinism, xenophobia and prejudice that research by Beswick and Hills (1969) has shown to be characteristic of Anglo-Celtic Australians. Even less would they have been appreciated by those "Asians" excluded since the mid-1800s from Australia under what was unofficially termed the "White Australia" policy.

Their reaction might have been understandably cynical, despite the progressively more liberal laws introduced in 1966 to allow more non-Europeans into Australia. Laws were further liberalized in 1971 by the same Minister for Immigration, Phillip Lynch, but the emphasis was still placed on maintaining a cohesive Australian community by "avoiding substantial 'undigested minorities . . . very different from the host community' . . . In short, the ultimate goal was presented as something very close to assimilation, though that word was carefully avoided by Mr Lynch". (Mackie, 1977, p. 11.) The Racial Discrimination Act passed by the Australian Parliament in 1975 marked the official demise of the "White Australia" policy, but the accompanying debate generated comments from some parliamentarians which indicated the deep-seated nature of their ethnocentric and, at times, racist attitudes (Kalin, 1978).

In the early 1970s the policy of integration came under attack from a number of academics who considered it to be a form of disguised assimilation, and the term *multicultural* began to appear in their writings as an alternative model of Australian society (e.g. Bullivant, 1972, 1973a, 1973b; Martin, 1972; Smolicz, 1971, 1972). The same period saw a change of Federal government with the election of the Labor Party in 1972 and the appointment of A. J. Grassby as Minister for Immigration. He adopted multiculturalism as the official ideology of pluralism with the publication of *A Multicultural Society for the Future* (Grassby, 1973). It was taken up enthusiastically by teachers and educationists. In subsequent conferences, however, it became all too clear that they were baffled by such concepts as "pluralism" and "multiculturalism", and were in any case not helped by the dogmatic assertions from others that teaching English as a second language would solve all problems in migrant education. This has remained a continuing theme in the debate about multicultural education.

The Labor Government lost office in 1975, but Grassby has continued his advocacy of multiculturalism as Commissioner for Community Relations, heading the office set up under the 1975 Racial Discrimination Act. However, the claims contained in multiculturalism began to be criticized by some academics even in the mid-1970s (e.g. Martin, 1974, 1976; Wiseman, 1974; Bullivant, 1975, 1976, 1977) and alternative models proposed.

At the political level, partly due to ethnic group pressures, the Australian Ethnic Affairs Council (AEAC) was established in January 1977 to advise the Minister for Immigration and Ethnic Affairs on problems related to the migrants in Australia. One of its three constituent committees is concerned with Multicultural Education. In August 1977 the Council published a submission to the Australian Population and Immigration Council on its Green Paper, *Immigration Policies and Australia's Population*. The submission's title, *Australia as a Multicultural Society* (AEAC, 1977), clearly indicates commitment to a multicultural ideology. The same year saw the commissioning of the Committee to Review Post-Arrival Programs and Services for Migrants (The Galbally Committee) on 1 September, 1977. Its brief was to "examine and report on the effectiveness of the Commonwealth's program and services for those who have migrated to Australia, including programs and services provided by non-government organizations which receive Commonwealth assistance, and shall identify any areas of need or duplication of programs or services" (Galbally, 1978, p. 1).

B The Galbally Report and policies for ethnolinguistic minorities

The Galbally Committee submitted its Report to the Government in May 1978, and it was formally presented to the the Australian Parliament by the Prime Minister, Malcolm Fraser, on 22 November 1978 (Fraser, 1978). He stated that the government agreed with the general findings of the Report, and saw the need "to change the direction of its services to migrants and that further steps to encourage multiculturalism are needed" (1978; p. 3). He also endorsed the multicultural model of society originally proposed in the Australian Ethnic Affairs Council's (1977) submission, and adopted by the Galbally Committee, by agreeing that "Australia is at a critical stage in developing a cohesive, united, multicultural nation" (1978, p. 3).

Recommendations in the Galbally Report are far-reaching and cover virtually every aspect of governmental and non-governmental provisions for migrants. Although "multicultural" is used from the outset and freely cited throughout, possibly, one suspects, as a token description, it is not until Chapter 9 that multiculturalism is explicitly considered and then only in relation to education. This is surprising if it is supposed to be the ideological foundation for the whole Report. Instead of an early consideration of what it might entail, a series of general guidelines is provided which could apply to any society concerned about the welfare of its immigrant population, and the question-begging assumption made that multiculturalism is what is required (Galbally, 1978, p. 3):

1.5 That Australia is at a critical stage in relation to migrant services and the need to encourage multiculturalism was brought home to us also in the many submissions we have received and the many discussions we have been privileged to have during the past eight months. We believe that the commissioning of this Review was timely.

1.6 We have concluded that it is now necessary for the Commonwealth Government to change the direction of its involvement in the provision of programs and services for migrants and to take further steps to encourage multiculturalism. In taking these new directions, we stress at the outset that the closer involvement of ethnic communities themselves, and of other levels of government, is essential.

Guiding principles

1.7 In developing our recommendations, we have adopted the following guiding principles:

(a) all members of our society must have equal opportunity to realise their full potential and must have equal access to programs and services;

(b) every person should be able to maintain his or her culture without prejudice or disadvantage and should be encouraged to understand and embrace other cultures;

(c) needs of migrants should, in general, be met by programs and services available to the whole community but special services and programs are necessary at present to ensure equality of access and provision;

(d) services and programs should be designed and operated in full consultation with clients, and self-help should be encouraged as much as possible with a view to helping migrants to become self-reliant quickly.

Many of the recommendations that follow are enlightened and praiseworthy, but they do not need the support of multiculturalism or the reiterated catchphrase "multicultural society". When it is finally discovered late in the Report how the Committee views the multicultural ideology, one must have serious reservations about the likelihood of it ever achieving for migrants the "equal opportunity to realise their full potential . . . [and to] have equal access to programs and services" that forms one of the guiding principles. This issue is the crux of the post-Galbally debate, considered in more detail later in this chapter.

The debate hinges on the attributes delineated by the term "multicultural", and at this point it is helpful to know the Committee's views (Galbally, 1978, p. 104):

9.1 We recognise the extensive cultural and racial diversity existing in Australia and we are conscious of the problems and the advantages to the nation such diversity presents.

9.2 Our ethnic groups are distinguishable by various factors. For our purposes we need only identify the two major relevant varying attributes of ethnicity as culture and race.

9.3 It is desirable to define our concept of culture. We believe it is a way of life, that "complex whole which includes knowledge, belief, art, morals, law, customs, and any other capabilities and habits acquired by man as a member of Society".[1] The concept of race is clear.

9.4 It is obvious that a society which has multilingual, multireligious and multicultural groups will encounter problems in solving the inevitable friction and tension and perhaps divisiveness between groups. We are firmly of the opinion that these problems can be overcome . . .

In passing, it should be noted that these comments were formulated under severe time constraints by a small committee, none of whose members is an anthropologist or specialist in ethnicity. Surely such background is necessary for making official pronouncements on technical and contentious concepts like culture and race, especially if what flows from them will influence the direction of Australian education and social welfare institutions for years to come. One must immediately suspect the level of expertise available when confronted by the mind-boggling claim that the "concept of race is clear", especially when one recalls the years of debate and polemic it generated in the United Nations. Similarly, the adoption of Tylor's outmoded definition of culture may be the result of ignorance of more up-to-date definitions, or, equally likely, may reflect well the Committee's naive preconceptions of what multiculturalism is all about. It is also significant, in view of what follows in the section on education, that multiracial groups do not rate a mention with the "multilingual, multireligious and multicultural groups" that are considered to suffer problems. The whole Report in fact virtually ignores Australian Aborigines in its pre-occupation with migrants. The Committee's view of the composition of "multicultural Australia" is correspondingly limited, and it is left to other bodies to devise policies for Aborigines.

It is unlikely that the Chairman, Frank Galbally himself, has the degree of expertise necessary to have directed his Committee to more productive avenues of research into race and culture. He is a well-known Melbourne criminal defence lawyer, with something of a Perry Mason's charisma. Apparently a former Labor Party supporter, he was offered the opportunity of chairing the Committee of Review by the Liberal Party leader and Prime Minister, Malcolm Fraser. The ideological foundations of the Report are thus not an irrelevant issue. As Stockley has commented (1978, p. 23): "Galbally is a clever lawyer and he has produced an astute Report tailored to what the Fraser Government wanted."

From the outset it is apparent that one major concern of the Review Committee involves the English language deficiencies of newly arrived immigrants, as lack of English is considered to be a major cause of disadvantage in many areas (Galbally, 1978, pp. 5–6):

1.16 . . . For example, the main areas of need (such as for fluency in English and for better communication and information) are common to virtually all areas of program and service delivery, such as health, welfare, education, employment and law. Accordingly the majority of the initiatives proposed are directed at these general areas of need rather than at specific services or programs. Moreover, a balance must also be struck between those services and programs directed at the newly arrived (which can be costly at the time but can save significantly in the longer term because they reduce the need for later special programs) and those directed at the established community of migrants where there is a backlog of needs.

1.17 Accordingly we have developed what we believe is an appropriately integrated package of measures for introduction over a period of three years.

English language training is heavily emphasized in what follows. A comprehensive initial settlement programme is proposed, (in section 1.21 of the Report), to include classes in English and formal advice and assistance in housing, education, employment and other areas of need. The classes are made available through new community centres or existing residential migrant hostels, with a living allowance paid during a specified initial settlement period. Teaching of English to migrant adults and children is increased through extra funding for the existing Child Migrant Education and Adult Migrant Education Programs.

The communication problems of both recently arrived and long-established migrants are acknowledged and recommendations are made to ease the difficulties. They take the form of financial incentives for bilingual staff in official positions, whose duties involve substantial contact with migrants, to up-grade their qualifications. Intensive English courses are also recommended so that migrants with overseas professional and sub-professional qualifications can have them recognized in Australia.

The Review Committee also acknowledged that it is not possible to solve every communication problem by using bilingual staff. Accordingly, it recommends that the Commonwealth government translating and interpreting services should be extended and brought together. The wider problem of lack of information concerning migrants' rights, entitlements and obligations *vis-à-vis* the legal and political systems is also catered for by a proposal to strengthen the Information Branch of the Department of Immigration and Ethnic Affairs. The provision of better information about industrial safety for migrant workers in the workplace is also recommended.

A number of measures are proposed that directly involve the ethnic communities themselves. Multicultural resource centres are to replace existing government agencies and the Good Neighbour Councils, and should be supplemented by increasing the numbers of ethnic welfare workers through an extension of existing grant-in-aid schemes. Special provisions are also recommended for workers to be employed by ethnic communities "to work in child-care centres and pre-schools to foster a multicultural approach and to help bridge the gap between school and home" (Galbally, 1978, p. 11).

Two institutions in particular—school and the ethnic media—are seen as having particular responsibility for "encouraging a multicultural attitude in Australian society by fostering the retention of the culture heritage of different groups and promoting intercultural understanding . . . and fostering multiculturalism" (1978, pp. 11–12). Schools in particular are seen as "the key element in achieving such a goal", and it is proposed to allocate $5m over the three years following the Report to develop "multicultural education programs".

Given the Committee's views on the concept of multiculturalism outlined above, its prescriptions for these programmes are predictable. Firstly, they hinge on the importance the Committee places on the maintenance of ethnic and other forms of identity (1978, p. 104ff):

> We are convinced that migrants have the right to maintain their cultural and racial identity and that it is clearly in the best interests of our nation that they should be encouraged and assisted to do so if they wish. Provided that ethnic identity is not stressed at the expense of society at large, but is interwoven into the fabric of our nationhood by the process of multicultural interaction, then the community as a whole will benefit substantially and its democratic nature will be reinforced.

Secondly, importance is placed on avoiding the "cultural gap" and alienation between migrant parents and their children which cause them to "lose their native languages and much of their culture in this process" (1978, p. 105). Without bringing evidence to support the assertion, the Committee claims that the "cultural gap has other effects. It is damaging psychologically and is an impediment to education thus preventing individuals from achieving their full potential."

The general education aims that schools and school systems should be encouraged to develop are (Galbally, 1978, p. 106):

> . . . initiatives aimed at improving the understanding of the different histories, cultures, languages and attitudes of those who make up our society. This greater understanding can be achieved in a range of ways—for example through greater allocation of resources to the teaching of histories, cultures and languages (both English and other languages), through development of bilingual teaching, through better teacher education in these fields . . . through development of curriculums and essential materials and through greater involvement of parents and the community.

It is recommended that a large part of the $5m funds advocated for multicultural education in the first three years following the Report should be applied to the kinds of initiatives in schools that would encourage the teaching of community languages and cultures and bilingual education. This emphasis is essentially similar to earlier recommendations of the Australian Ethnic Affairs Council (AEAC, 1977), which also considered that an emphasis on community languages and cultural heritage in multicultural education would enhance the self-esteem and ethnic identity of students of ethnic origin.

Fostering ethnic cultures would not only be the task of schools, however, as local ethnic communities are encouraged to help maintain their cultural heritage. They would be assisted by municipal libraries, which could provide facilities such as collections of books, slides and tapes about aspects of various migrant cultures, particularly those most prevalent in the local area. The Australia Council is encouraged to develop closer links with ethnic communities and to increase the financial support for ethnic festivals, singing and drama groups that already exists in its community art programme.

C The structural–organizational features of multiculturalism and multicultural education

An important aspect of the Galbally Report, and of others that followed, is the structures and organizations which were given the task of implementing the recommendations. Some were already available; others had to be established. The history of how the final arrangements were achieved would make a chapter in itself—a story of opportunism, inter-organization rivalries, and sheer expediency—but only a brief outline can be given here (see also Bullivant, 1981a).

1 New organizations

Three new organizations were proposed by the Galbally Committee to facilitate the implementation of its programmes. The first (Galbally, 1978, p. 108) was a "small committee of educators experienced in areas of cultural and racial differences . . . to consult with State, Commonwealth and non-government authorities and to draw up within three months proposals as to how the recommended $5m for multicultural education can be used most effectively in the three years ahead". In most uncharacteristic haste, the Commonwealth Minister for Education accepted the Schools Commission's nominations and appointed a small Committee on Multicultural Education on 30 June 1978, just one month after the Report itself was tabled in Parliament. Its brief was to advise the Schools Commission for the allocation of $·05m which had been provided under the Multicultural Education Program for 1979. The haste was to enable the Schools Commission to include the recommendations in its Report of 31 July 1978 to the Government (Schools Commission, 1978).

The Committee's Final Report (1979) was presented to the Schools Commission by 5 January 1979. For its definition of culture it adopted without apparent reservation the "most common, popular usage in education which equates culture with a social group's heritage, i.e. traditions, history, language, arts and other aesthetic achievements, religion, customs and values" (1979, p. 68). Popular usages are scarcely the basis for formulating technical policies on multicultural education, but a committee lacking expertise in cultural anthropology could hardly have been expected to know the respected theorist Bidney's (1967, p. 27) opinion that to equate culture with a group's heritage is "a serious error". The Committee was also unduly influenced by Government policy in making its recommendations on community languages, but took care to point this out in its Report (1979, pp. 3–4):

> The fact that the Government had decided that the funds to be made available in the first year of the three year program were to be used for the fostering of the teaching of community languages had a considerable influence on the work of the Committee and on the recommendations made in relation to 1980 and 1981.

The Australian education system is renowned for working in most mysterious ways. But this example of how to make far-reaching policy decisions that might determine the direction education takes for years ahead is exceptional even by Australian standards, and all, it should be remembered, initiated by the Galbally Committee—also with limited expertise in relevant sociological, anthropological and educational areas.

That the Galbally Committee rushed into such fields is not really surprising as it was under the impression that "there is very little information available on multicultural developments in Australia and overseas" (Galbally, 1978, p. 108). Had the Committee taken the trouble to do even a limited ERIC or library search it might not have made such a remarkable statement. However, maintaining the fiction that little information exists provided a ready if spurious reason for recommending the establishment of the second new organization, the Australian Institute of Multicultural Affairs, which was speedily set up at the end of 1979. Its Council is chaired by Mr Frank Galbally himself, and its director is a former member of the Prime Minister's press corps. Both appointments were criticized by members of ethnic groups at the time, for the apparent patronage they displayed, and because neither of the incumbents is an expert on migrant issues. Mr Galbally has continued his acquisition of such prestigious positions, having been appointed chairman of the Ethnic Television Review Panel and, following that, chairman of the Special Broadcasting Services Board of Directors (discussed below). Both are considered to be government appointments.

The functions of the Australian Institute for Multicultural Affairs are (Galbally, 1978, p. 109):

(a) the commissioning of research into multiculturalism and related issues;
(b) the dissemination of information to Commonwealth, State and local governments, to non-government organisations, and to the community as a whole, on all aspects of multiculturalism and related issues;
(c) the preparation of material on cultural and racial backgrounds, and other factors affecting migrant settlement, for use in training courses for professional people, schools, tertiary institutions etc.;
(d) the provision of advice on multicultural and migrant issues to government

departments and other bodies to assist them in developing programs and
policies appropriate to a multicultural society;

(e) the education of the community in all aspects of multiculturalism through
such methods as seminars, lectures, conferences etc.

The Institute was also empowered by the Galbally Committee (1978,
p. 109) to appoint "a small but highly skilled research and administrative
staff" which would supplement the work undertaken by outside academics
through some commissioned research projects. This seemed unobjectiona-
ble at the time of the euphoria that greeted the Galbally Report. However,
when positions ranging from professorial to lecturer rank for the research
group were advertised in the national press in October 1980, a number of
reservations were expressed by established researchers in migrant and
ethnic matters about the degree of government control that could be
exercised over the work of the research group.

They have grounds for concern. Although in the Galbally Report (a freely
available document) it is recommended that the Institute provide "high level
technical advice to government" (1978, p. 109) on a variety of issues, the
degree of government control is nowhere apparent. When one reads the
enabling Act of Parliament (1979, No. 54; a much less available document)
setting up the Institute, however, it is clear that the Minister for Immigration
and Ethnic Affairs is empowered to determine the policy issues the Institute
can investigate, and can circumscribe its autonomy to conduct or commission
independent research that might challenge the official ideology of multiculturalism. The first major publication issued by the Institute, its (1980)
Review of Multicultural Education, was not only based on an unrepresenta-
tive sample of tertiary institutes, but was a hastily prepared and ill-informed
document in the opinion of academics and members of ethnic groups. They
also criticized the rush to produce the Report in time for the Prime Minister's
election speech during the Liberal Party's 1980 election campaign.

There could thus well be grounds for interpreting the Institute as an arm
of the Australian Government's "ideological state apparatus", to use
Althusser's (1971) terms. It could have been hoped that its more extreme
activities would be curbed by its Council, which partly consists of a number
of prominent academics and public figures, invited to become members.
However, even their power seems to be severely circumscribed. At the
inaugural meeting of the Council in 1981, the Chairman of the Institute
apparently made it quite clear that the Council was there to do what it is told
to do, rather than play an independent role in determining or guiding
activities[2].

The third organization supported by the Galbally Committee is the ethnic
radio and television system (see also Bullivant, 1981c). According to the
Committee (1978, p. 12) the system is justified because:

The ethnic media play an important part in fostering multiculturalism and we support the Government's decision to extend ethnic radio through the Special Broadcasting Service to all States . . . For ethnic television we recommend the establishment of a pilot station drawing on existing technical resources which would assist in the assessment of public reaction and in working out the details of programming and administration of the permanent service which we consider should be developed over the next three years.

Developments since these recommendations were made have been slow, and ethnic television is still in its infancy. After protracted experimental trial programmes in 1979–80, multicultural—multilingual television began on Channel 0 and Channel 28 UHF from Melbourne and Sydney partly as a symbolic gesture on United Nations Day, 24 October 1980. It provides a wide variety of programmes: news and current affairs segments in English; a small number of English language lessons; fictional films, documentaries, variety shows and cartoons in a number of ethnic languages. Many of the films are historical, one recent (1982) example in Spanish being on the life and times of Miguel Cervantes. If it is intended that ethnic television will assist everybody in Australia to understand the *present* cultures of its constituent ethnocultural groups, emphasis on the past is likely to be counterproductive. Nevertheless ethnic television is probably the most successful of the organizations supported by the Galbally Committee. It is free from commercial advertising, and its world-wide news coverage is even more comprehensive than that of the Australian Broadcasting Commission's service.

However, these are early days, and the structure of the Special Broadcasting Service also contains within it the potential for government interference, as media commentator Myles Wright has warned (1980, p. 7):

In all, the SBS is entirely a political creature: no other branch of the broadcasting services in Australia is so totally able to be dominated by the government of the day. The members of the service are, of course, appointed by the government in the usual way, and predictably the members change with the government. However, the members do not have the right to appoint their executive director. He is a government appointee.

Following the introduction of the Broadcasting and Television Amendment Bill of 1980, in which some of Wright's criticisms are met, the situation has not changed substantially. "The government has given some lip service to the ideal of independence, but examination shows this to be an illusion." (Wright, 1980, p. 9).

2 Existing organizations
The fate of several existing government agencies approved by the Galbally Committee is evidence enough that Myles Wright's warning may not be

merely a flight of fancy. The Committee laid considerable emphasis c
education as the main way of building multiculturalism and noted wit
approval "the priority given to multicultural education in the forwar
research program of the Education Research and Development Committe
and within the Schools Commission and the Curriculum Developmer
Centre" (Galbally, 1978, p. 107). Of these only the Schools Commissic
survives, and even its work has been curtailed by government fundir
arrangements.

Like the Schools Commission itself, the Curriculum Development Con
mittee (CDC) was established in 1973 during the heady days of the Labc
Government's socialist-oriented, egalitarian, reformist zeal. Initially CD
was enthusiastic about the Galbally Committee's recommendations, as
was already conducting a major multicultural education project backed t
substantial funding from the government, and this was given a boost in 197'
It administered a scheme disbursing small grants to schools or communi'
groups "aimed at building up expertise in the area of education for
multicultural society, e.g. programmes in bilingual education, communi'
languages, Teaching English as a Second Language, ethnic studies" (Adam
1978, p. 2). It also ran a Curriculum Information Service which dre
material from some of the projects completed with grant aid, and made
more widely available to other schools and communities across the countr
Such a scheme was very similar to, and overlapped with, the Schoo
Commission's innovations programme and may have been a reason for tr
decision to close CDC. This effectively occurred at the end of 1981 aft
months of fruitless negotiations with the States to obtain funding to replac
that cut off by the Federal government, ostensibly as part of its econon
drive (the so-called "Razor Gang" cuts) in April 1981. A small, token un
dealing with curriculum development has been incorporated into tl
Department of Education in Canberra.

The Education Research and Development Committee's (ERDC) fa
was less protracted and it closed in mid-1981, apparently as part of the san
economy drive. It had also been involved in multicultural education to
significant degree through the work of its Priority Area Advisory Grou
(PAAG) on this aspect of Australian education. This was one of fot
PAAGs given the task of mapping out their respective areas in educatio
commissioning and funding research, and through their findings keeping tr
government informed of developments in several fields of education. Pr
jects that involved materials or curriculum development were referred 1
CDC, and established a closer link between that body and ERDC than wit
the Schools Commission. This may help to explain why both bodies wer
axed together.

D Policies towards Aborigines

1 Evolution of advisory bodies

A major omission, already noted, in the Galbally Report is a total absence of policies and provisions for Aborigines. As this group provides useful comparisons with American and Canadian Indians and, in any case, forms an important part of the Australian scene, a brief consideration of the present situation regarding Aborigines seems justified.

Like the situation for migrants, it has evolved historically through a number of stages. Prior to the late 1930s, the educational provisions for Aborigines had been generally inadequate, and were coupled with government policies of segregation and separation from the white education system (McConnochie, 1981). However, the late 1930s and 1940s saw a change of government policy to paternalistic assimilation, which had a corresponding effect on educational provisions. These were comparable to those which dominated thinking about migrants until the 1960s—Aborigines had to fit into Australian society. As Rowley (1970, pp. 4–5) explains:

> Since Australian governments adopted the "assimilation" policy emphasis has remained on promoting changes among the Aborigines. Though increasingly aware that colour prejudice against the Aborigines is basic to this syndrome, governments still devote administrative efforts to making Aborigines "acceptable", to achieve which, paternal control is still widely used.

Consequently, educational policies were geared to "civilizing and Christianizing" Aborigines through the school and educational systems, which were actually quite unsuited to this task. Nevertheless, despite considerable administrative delay and opposition from local white communities in country areas, by the mid-1960s the assimilationist policy had been largely achieved. Almost all Aboriginal pupils were in state schools, even though this did not lead to commensurate academic successes.

A far-reaching development occurred in 1967 when a national referendum on Aboriginal rights gave the Commonwealth Government powers to legislate in respect of Aborigines concurrently with the State Governments. A three-man Council for Aboriginal Affairs, assisted by a small office within the Prime Minister's Department, was set up to advise the Government on policies, and in 1972 this was expanded to become a Ministerial Department of Aboriginal Affairs. In the years immediately following, agreements were made with all states (excepting Queensland) "whereby, subject to specific provisions with each state, the federal government assumed responsibility for the administration of Aboriginal Affairs within the state" (Watts, 1981, p. 25).

As with changes in policies towards migrants, the Labor Government elected in 1972 produced another radical change in policies towards Aborigines, when "self-determination" signalled the demise of the assimilation ideology (McConnochie, 1981, p. 17):

> Accompanying the self-determination policy were clear statements supporting local autonomy and decision making, substantial increases in access by local communities to federal funding, an improved Aboriginal participation in advisory and decision-making structures, and greater awareness within the wider community of the presence, problems and demands of Aboriginal people.

Paradoxically, these new ideas emerged in a period which also saw the rapid urbanization of Aborigines. "From 1971 to 1976 the percentages of the Aboriginal population living in urban areas rose from 43·5% to 59·6%" (Schools Commission, 1981, p. 133). Despite this trend, the numbers of Aborigines living in rural settlements—reservations, out-stations[3], missions, pastoral homesteads, etc.—remain considerable. Their need to be heard and have a say in their own destiny was becoming all too apparent.

To provide such a "national aboriginal voice" (Watts, 1981, p. 58) and to encourage self-determination, a National Aboriginal Consultative Committee (NACC) was inaugurated in November 1973 and, following general elections among Aborigines, held its first meeting in December of that year. It consisted of 80 members elected for a two-year term. During the next three years it held a number of national meetings at which motions were passed embracing "advice to the government on policies and programs in Aboriginal affairs, advice to the government on other matters and matters affecting the role and function of the NACC" (Watts, 1981, pp. 59–60).

However, it became clear that the NACC had only an advisory role and was largely ineffective in bringing about major policy changes, particularly when faced with obvious Federal Government intransigence. Accordingly, in 1974 the NACC endorsed a constitution for a new body, the National Aboriginal Congress, and devoted a great deal of its energies to getting this accepted by the Government. After several years of often acrimonious exchanges with successive Ministers for Aboriginal Affairs, and protracted procedural discussions (see Watts, 1981), elections were held throughout Australia on 12 November 1977 (19 November in Queensland).

The new body comprises some 35 elected members who meet annually at the national level. Its role is (Watts, 1981, p. 63):

> . . . to provide a forum in which Aboriginal views may be expressed at State and National level and, in particular, to express Aboriginal views on the long term goals and objectives which the Government should pursue and the programs it should adopt in Aboriginal affairs, and on the need for new

programs in Aboriginal affairs. The NAC will also participate, through its entitlement to choose 5 of the 19 members, in the work of a new body the Council for Aboriginal Development.

The Council for Aboriginal Development was duly set up in 1980 under the name Aboriginal Development Commission. Its 10 members are all Aborigines, 5 chosen by the NAC and 5 by the Minister of Aboriginal Affairs, thus symbolizing yet another change in Government policy—from self-determination to self-management, which had begun to crystallize in the late 1970s. It is this policy that, in theory at least, governs the operation of, and Government involvement in, the organizations concerned with educational programmes for Aborigines.

2 Organizations concerned with Aboriginal education
The need for coordination of efforts to improve Aboriginal education at the federal and state levels had been recognized by the Schools Commission from its inception in 1973. In 1974 it appointed an Aboriginal Consultative Group to help it obtain representative views from Aboriginal communities and groups, as it was concerned that these were not being sufficiently recognized at the federal and state policy-making levels. The Group presented its Report, *Education for Aborigines,* in June 1975, and it has since been a major influence on the formation of policies that will implement its broad philosophy of Aboriginal education (Watts, 1981, p. 65):

> We see education as the most important strategy for achieving realistic self-determination for the Aboriginal people of Australia. We do not see education as a method of producing an anglicised Aborigine, but rather as an instrument for creating an informed community, with intellectual and technological skills, in harmony with our own cultural values and identity. We wish to be Aboriginal citizens in a changing Australia.

Two specific matters were of particular concern to the Group: technical education for Aborigines and the need to set up a national-level funding body. The Group undertook its own investigation into the former, and its 1976 *Preliminary Report on the Investigation of Aboriginal Use of Technical and Further Education Resources* has helped shape developing initiatives at the Technical and Further Education (TAFE) level for Aborigines (Watts, 1981). In its 1975 Report the Group recommended the setting up of a separate, statutory funding body to be called the National Aboriginal Education Commission. Discussions between the Group, Department of Aboriginal Affairs, the Australian Department of Education and the Schools Commission, during 1975 and 1976, led to the establishment of the National Aboriginal Education Committee (NAEC) in March 1977. Its full-time chairman and 18 part-time members were and still are all Aborigines.

When the Minister for Education, Senator Carrick, announced the establishment of the Committee he outlined its responsibilities (Watts, 1981, p. 67):

> . . . providing him and his department with informed Aboriginal views on the educational needs of Aboriginal people and appropriate methods of meeting these needs; its advice would also be available to the Department of Aboriginal Affairs and other authorities concerned with the education of Aboriginal people . . . assist the Department of Education and other agencies in monitoring existing programs and in developing programs and policies, and . . . undertake and promote investigations, studies and projects on which to base its advice.

In a very active pursuit of these responsibilities since 1977 the Committee has worked closely with the two Departments specifically referred to, and established a "consultancy framework" with the Education Committee of the Australian Institute of Aboriginal Studies, the Curriculum Development Centre, the Education Research and Development Committee. Since the closure of CDC and ERDC, the major emphasis in Aboriginal education is directed through the Schools Commission with which the NAEC maintains close liaison. The Schools Commission has also encouraged the formation of State Aboriginal Education Consultative Groups through its Special Projects Program and through these the NAEC has "developed rapport" with education authorities at state level (Watts, 1981). It has also produced its *Rationale, Aims and Objectives in Aboriginal Education* (NAEC, 1980). This "recognizes the need for Aborigines to achieve academic or technological skills, and the desire of parents of Aboriginal children to be able to function effectively in the wider Australian community. Equally they stress the need to enhance Aborigines' knowledge of and pride in their cultural heritage" (Schools Commission, 1981, p. 135).

For its part, the current Liberal Federal Government's policy objectives and their implications for funding Aboriginal education are published in detail each year in a Ministerial Directive from the Minister for Aboriginal Affairs. Its central theme is that "Aboriginal communities have the central place in all aid programs" (Watts, 1981, p. 35). The Directive also sets out a number of criteria used for considering projects to be funded. They include explicit recognition of "self-management", "self-sufficiency" and of "Aboriginality". Detailed functional guidelines and objectives are provided for thirteen "functional areas": housing; health; prevention of alcohol abuse and rehabilitation; education; training; employment; welfare; community development employment projects; town management and public utilities; outstations; enterprises; culture, recreation and sporting activities; legal aid.

The objectives for education illustrate how far Government policies have changed since the 1960s assimilationist period. In the Ministerial Directive for 1979–80 cited by Watts (1981, p. 38) four objectives are listed:

1) To ensure that educational opportunities at all levels, from pre-school to technical, further and tertiary education are available to Aboriginals and are in no way inferior to those available to the general community.

2) To enable Aboriginals to overcome educational disadvantages they may suffer, including those created where existing educational services are inappropriate or inaccessible to them for economic, social and cultural reasons, by the provision of special education facilities.

3) To ensure that Aboriginals receive an education which is in harmony with their cultural values and chosen lifestyle in order to restore in them a pride in their identity and enable them to acquire the skills they desire.

4) To promote education within the whole Australian community in the culture and lifestyle of the Aboriginal people.

It is interesting that nowhere in the statement of Objectives and Guidelines does the concept occur of multicultural Australia and Aboriginal relationships within such a society. The Schools Commission, on the other hand, fully appreciates this issue and maintains that the principles it now follows in respect of multiculturalism apply equally to education responses to meet the needs of Aborigines. However, it is also aware that Aboriginal education poses "special and significant challenges which are not yet being adequately met" (Schools Commission, 1981, p. 134). Such arrangements as the Aboriginal Secondary Grants Scheme designed to encourage Aboriginal and Torres Strait Islander students to stay on at secondary school, Aboriginal Studies programmes and kits, bilingual education, parent-aid programmes, out-station education and black community schools, together with pre-service and in-service teacher training courses for Aborigines, are some of the practical ways adopted by federal and state governments to cope with the challenges.

III New directions in the post-Galbally period

In the four years since the Galbally Report was published, some progress has been made in improving provisions for both immigrant and Aboriginal groups but, as is often the case in Australia, much more could have been achieved had relationships between state and federal levels been less complex and administratively cumbersome than they are. What has been achieved owes much to the work of the Schools Commission, which has emerged not only as an accomplished "survivor" in a period notable for the number of axed or, more appropriately, "razored" educational organizations, but also as the major source of advice on Federal Government funding for the education of ethno-linguistic minorities. In its rationale for this function, the Schools Commission has significantly modified the multicultural ideology to some extent, but in a way that adds fuel to what might be termed the post-Galbally "pluralist debate" (Bullivant, 1982b). Both issues are discussed in the remainder of this chapter.

A The role of the Schools Commission

Australia's education system is the context in which the Commission functions. Unfortunately the federal composition of the Australian political system makes for considerable complexity and diversity in many institutions; education is one of them. States' rights are jealously guarded and every attempt to set up centrally controlled enterprises (e.g. in curriculum development, which might exercise *direct* control over syllabuses and teaching in each state's schools) is vigorously, even bitterly, opposed.

The Australian Commonwealth Government is directly responsible for education in the Australian Capital Territory; otherwise, the six State Governments are responsible for their own education systems, and education in the Northern Territory is now the responsibility of its own government. Education at all government-controlled primary and secondary schools in Australia is free, with each state providing the major portion of funds for its own school system from general revenue sources. The other source of funds is the Commonwealth Government. Payments for the education of ethnolinguistic minorities are made directly by the Department of Education, indirectly through appropriations by the Departments of Immigration and Ethnic Affairs, and by the Department of Aboriginal Affairs. The Schools Commission also administers a variety of grants, some of which are for migrant education. Finally, each state also contains a number of non-government schools which are funded privately and also receive both state and federal assistance. It is current policy of the present Liberal Government to assist such private schools more generously than in the past, a policy which also applies to the funding of the growing number of ethnic schools.

Ethno-linguistic minorities (Aborigines and migrants) are catered for in a number of ways through these education systems. Special Commonwealth Government funding is available to assist Aborigines from pre-school level upwards, throughout Australia, by means of study grants, secondary grants, grants to private non-profit organizations, grants to states and other means. Responsibility for administering the grants is shared between Ministers of State, acting on the advice of the NAEC and Schools Commission. The Department of Aboriginal Affairs also disburses appropriations from Commonwealth revenue for such educational activities as bilingual schooling, Aboriginal teacher education, Aboriginal teacher aide training, apprenticeship technical education, Aboriginal language and culture, pre-schooling, community development and the like.

The State Governments provide resources for migrant education, especially at the school level. The Commonwealth Government has responsibility for two kinds of migrant education programmes. The Child Migrant

Education Program is designed to provide English-as-a-second-language teaching for migrant children, mainly through "withdrawal" classes, although a number of other methods are now being adopted. These include bilingual programmes and language assistance programmes within the general classroom. There is a slowly growing recognition that English language teaching should be supplemented by multicultural education which acknowledges migrant identity and self-esteem within the overall framework of Australian society. Child Migrant Education at the primary and secondary levels is funded through the Schools Commission which also provides supplementary assistance to schools with high-density migrant populations. The Commission also administers funds for the in-service training of teachers of migrant education. In all cases payments are not made directly to schools, but to government and non-government education authorities in each state. These have the responsibility of determining priorities and allocating the funds.

In contrast, the Adult Migrant Education Program is nationally funded and coordinated by the Commonwealth Department of Immigration and Ethnic Affairs, through its local office and Adult Migrant Education Branch in each state. This programme aims to help adult migrants and refugees from non-English-speaking backgrounds to learn English and obtain essential information about Australia. The programme comprises a variety of full and part-time courses and classes. Special arrangements are made, such as English classes in the work-place, the Home Tutor Scheme and some English education through television and radio. For instance, the Commonwealth-funded Special Broadcasting Service television channel runs regular English lessons during the week.

The Schools Commission, a Federal body, occupies a key advisory and administrative role in this kind of state/federal system, although this has not prevented concern being expressed recently that it would suffer the fate of other Labour Government innovations and be axed, partly for economic and partly for ideological reasons. Secure for the present, it continues to carry out four major groups of activities: collection and dissemination of information on needs; developmental programmes, in particular the Special Projects Program; studies and publications on education; administration of grants. One of its important functions is to prepare and publish triennial reports which put before the public and governments the Commission's "assessment of the needs of schools and the way in which these needs might best be met, after taking into account the prevailing economic and social conditions which influence the level of resources the community may be prepared to provide for schools" (Schools Commission, 1981, pp. 1–2).

The Schools Commission is also something of an ideological pacemaker in educational policy advocacy. Reports "are written within a conceptual framework setting out educational matters which the Commission considers to be of current importance. For this reason, the triennial report is necessarily as much an educational ideas document as a statement about physical resources" (1981, p. 2.) As such ideas are often taken up as the basis for policy, it is from the current *Report for the Triennium 1982–84,* that one can obtain a view of the possible direction of future policies towards ethno-linguistic minorities and multiculturalism.

1 Aboriginal education

The Schools Commission played a major part in the development of the National Aboriginal Education Committee and the State Aboriginal Consultative Groups, which are both intended "to help Aborigines to take more responsibility for their own advancement" (Schools Commission, 1981, p. 138). However, it sees a weakness in the present state and federal structural/organizational arrangements whereby funds are allocated and distributed to Aboriginal education. The NAEC has little direct involvement in this task, and the Commission suggests that the time is now opportune for giving responsibility for disbursing commonwealth funds wholly to the Minister for Education, rather than persist in the present arrangement of shared responsibility with Minister of State. However, this proposal does not entirely remove the possibility of inter-Departmental collaboration, for "there would, of course, be due consultation with the Minister for Aboriginal Affairs" (1981, p. 139).

Greater involvement of Aborigines in the actual allocation of funds disbursed by the Department of Aboriginal Affairs is advocated, and the Schools Commission recommends that the NAEC should be more directly involved in this responsibility. In the area of determining policy, ways should be found to increase the involvement of the Aboriginal Consultative Group in each state and the NAEC and its State Branches (1981, p. 142):

> There now exists, in the Commission's judgment, a basic set of structures to provide for Aboriginal viewpoints to be heard in the framing of educational policy at the State and Commonwealth levels. The next phase should be one in which the National Aboriginal Education Committee and the consultative groups consolidate and enlarge on these structures and become involved in developing practical strategies for the development of education which are consistent with the aims set out in *Rationale, Aims and Objectives of Aboriginal Education.*

The Commission also suggests that inservice education activities be increased to encourage and improve the teaching of Aboriginal students, and, in line with its multicultural ideology, learning about Aboriginal society and the place of Aborigines in Australia by all students. The Commission's recommendation (1975), in its previous *Report for the Triennium 1976–78,* to set up the NAEC may have played some part in this organization's ultimate establishment. It remains to be seen how the Commonwealth Government will respond to the Commission's latest suggestions to increase Aborigines' control over matters that affect their own life chances.

2 Migrant education and multiculturalism

The Commission's recommendations for migrant education and multiculturalism are set out as part of one of the main themes in its *Report for the Triennium 1982–84* (1981, p. 10): "(a) the fostering of policies which promote equal opportunities, encourage structural and curricula reform in schools, foster pluralism and respond to the changing world". One of the educational challenges of the 1980s is considered to be the "greater demands from ethnic groups for recognition of the value of their culture [which] render even more urgent current efforts to foster and support viable forms of cultural pluralism" (1981, p. 12). However, accomplishing these efforts poses a greater "essential challenge [which] is to promote diversity and choice while maintaining social cohesion" (1981, p. 15)—in effect, the pluralist dilemma in a nutshell (see Bullivant, 1981a). The challenge is scarcely new, however, as it was posed by the Australian Ethnic Affairs Council (1977) and, after it, by the Galbally Committee.

In pursuit of the complementary values of equality and diversity, the Commission suggests (1981, p. 64) that, given acceptance of its interpretation of a viable multicultural policy, "individuals ought to be exposed to the teachings of community languages and cultures not only in regular schools but, where appropriate, in ethnic schools or in other types of learning situations". Reference to support for ethnic schools is an endorsement of a policy which was first proposed in detail by the Australian Institute of Multicultural Affairs (1980) rather than by the Galbally Committee. Since then the numbers of ethnic schools have expanded, even though they have numerous weaknesses (see Bullivant, 1982a). In part this is due to the policy of the Commonwealth Government to assist all non-state, independent schools. Ethnic schools attract a subsidy of A$30 per pupil provided they are open to students from any ethnic background, and operate on a non-profit basis. This policy is to continue.

The Commission's support for community languages stems from its conviction (1981, p. 117) that "it is an important affirmation of the rights of individuals from a cultural background which is not Anglo-Celtic to be able to find expression of that culture in their schools, especially in the form of language maintenance. The Commission believes that educational policy should state this unequivocally as a right". However, this statement implies a consensus about the value of community language maintenance which the Commission acknowledges is not shared by many, whether Anglo-Celtic or migrant, in the wider community. It thus suggests that the Commonwealth Government launch a general national inquiry into present and desirable language teaching policy in Australia.

This appears to have been taken up by the Government. In a speech on 1 May 1982, the Minister for Immigration and Ethnic Affairs foreshadowed a National Language Policy "which will enable future Australians to acquire a fluency in languages other than our national language . . ." (Ward, 1982, p. 5). Pressure to adopt such a policy at federal and state levels is a far cry from the assimilationist and integrationist ideas that dominated thinking as few as ten years ago. The pressure also acknowledges the proliferation of community languages but with no matching provisions for language teaching in schools and tertiary institutions. A related policy supported by the Schools Commission is to provide schooling in a bilingual setting if parents desire it. A few bilingual schools have been established in various states, but it is unlikely that their number will increase as "there is no widespread desire in the community for all students to have a second language: for this to occur a major shift in attitudes would be necessary" (Schools Commission, 1981, p. 118). There are obvious social engineering overtones in the Commission's comment that it "sees this as a possible later stage in the realisation of a multicultural policy" (1981, p. 118).

Given the Commission's eclectic and somewhat confused view of multiculturalism, one may wonder just what multicultural policy is being envisaged. It is certainly much broader than the naïve "cultural heritage" view proposed by the Galbally Committee, as it is not confined to immigrants but also includes other ethnic groups, especially Aborigines, their languages and cultures. "Indeed, the need is to define a policy in such a way that it relates to the whole population of Australia and responds to the pluralist needs within the population". (1981, p. 111).

What these needs are likely to be is not entirely clear from the Commission's views on pluralism and the kind of educational provisions needed to encourage it. "The plurality of Australian society is demonstrated by the variety of values, life styles, political viewpoints, beliefs, and roles which operate. This holds true too in a racial and ethnic sense . . ." (1981, p. 14). Eclecticism begins to get out of hand when the Commission recommends (1981, p. 16): "The intellectual content of all schooling should reflect plurality—for class, race, ethnicity, gender and community are ever-present realities".

One searches in vain for clarification of these views in the Commission's formulation of multiculturalism. After the trivializing treatment in the Galbally Report, it is refreshing to see it officially recognized (1981, p. 16) that consideration of ethnic foods, dance, festive clothing and national days "are relatively superficial aspects of cultural difference and may moreover reinforce the notion that multiculturalism is merely acceptance of some exotic strangeness". But understanding what multiculturalism really should entail is scarcely advanced by the Commission's view (1981, p. 112):

> Broadly, the term merely connotes differences of ethnic origin, race, religion and socio-economic class among the people of Australia. Narrowly used, it often refers to the presence of ethnic communities within the population. The specifics of what is needed to achieve equal opportunity for all of those people have yet to be worked out, but most groups realise that this will not be achieved without political action and struggle.

A number of aspects are puzzling in this formulation. Bracketing socio-economic class with other causes of pluralism is theoretically and empirically difficult to sustain despite conventional sociological wisdom that class "cultures" can be identified. One suspects that their inclusion is an attempt to meet one frequent objection to the multicultural model (e.g. Birrell, 1978; Bullivant, 1980, 1981a), namely, that it cannot take class differences into account. Including differences of ethnic origin under multiculturalism begs the question that ethnicity is solely determined on cultural grounds, while the inclusion of racial differences implies that the Commission has made the common error of equating race—strictly a genetic concept—with culture. For a supposedly technical treatment this is indefensible and, like the comments levelled at the Galbally Committee, does not suggest that a great deal of expertise in anthropology and ethnicity theory was available on which to base the Schools Commission's Report. The final caution about ethnic communities not achieving equal opportunity for all without political action and struggle does not sit easily with the frequently parrotted slogan of achieving "social cohesion".

B The pluralist debate

It has been reservations like those above that have led some theorists to challenge the claims made about multiculturalism and multicultural education in the official literature and in the writings of those academics who support the ideology. The result has been a pluralist debate (see Bullivant, 1982b) which is not yet exhausted. One side of the debate, as exemplified by Smolicz (1980, 1981), advocates multiculturalism and multicultural education as vehicles for preserving ethnic groups' cultural core values and community literary languages, and thus, it is claimed, for enriching and contributing to the diversity of Australian culture.

The other side (e.g. Bullivant, 1980, 1981a, 1981d, 1982b) agrees that these are intrinsically worthwhile aims but strongly challenges official claims that multicultural education programmes will produce equality of educational opportunity and ultimately more equitable access to social rewards and economic resources. Multiculturalism and multicultural education may even be unwittingly or deliberately obscuring the fact that socio-economic disadvantage for ethno-cultural groups in pluralist societies is due to structural and institutional causes that do not relate to cultural or ethnic differences. This view, the "politics of multiculturalism", follows modern social and cultural reproduction theory, and adds an ethnic dimension to show how ethnic hegemony can be maintained by the *Staatsvolk* through the education system.

Other critics of multiculturalism hold comparable views. Atchison (1981, p. 13) suggests that multiculturalism, in particular, has been so abused as a term by incompatibly diverse groups as to become meaningless. It has been increasingly replaced by the cumbersome term "social cohesion with cultural diversity". This needs careful definition. On one interpretation, it could be virtually synonymous with assimilation. Martin (1978, p. 216) has pointed out that "the proposition that we are, or are in process of becoming, a culturally pluralist society has a specifically ideological aspect . . . [having] been created by established institutions looking for a way to accommodate ethnically diverse populations with the minimum of change on their part". Martin also adds a warning containing clear implications that either the present policy of multiculturalism (cultural pluralism) will collapse or generate inter-ethnic structural tensions and conflict over access to social rewards and economic resources (Martin, 1978, p. 216):

> . . . the thesis of cultural pluralism rests on the unspoken assumptions that ethnic culture can be sustained without ethnic communities and that a culturally diverse society is something different from a structurally pluralist one, assumptions that defy the weight of historical experience.

I have attempted (1981a, 1982b) to resolve the pluralist dilemma and incorporate the cultural and structural dimensions into a model of pluralism called *integrated polyethnicity*. For this I draw on Enloe's (1981) distinction between the *vertical* structure of public authority that comprises the state and the *horizontal* network of trust and identity in the nation, together with Higham's (1975) concept of "pluralistic integration". The integrated polyethnic model suggests that, at the horizontal level of trust and identity, multicultural and polyethnic diversity are compatible with the idea of nationhood. However, they are essentially private-domain lifestyle concerns that do not necessarily involve challenges to the power of the state. In this vertical dimension a plurality of competing ethnic structures and institutions is clearly incompatible with the state's control over power; thus in the public domain integration should be the goal to maximize the survival capacity of the state.

Inevitably this also enhances the power and control of the *Staatsvolk* and the essential problem for education is one of maintaining cultural diversity in the private domain, while preparing all children to compete for rewards and a share of power in the public domain. The strategy of a "polyethnic survival curriculum" is advanced as a possible solution (Bullivant, 1977, 1981b). Such a curriculum would contain five core elements to provide all children with a common body of "survival" knowledge and skills. These elements are: communicative competence, political and economic competence, numeracy (including the social consequences of such developments as micro-processors and computers), moral and social education and environmental awareness. In addition to the compulsory core elements, academic electives and enrichment electives should be provided. The former comprise those academic subjects taught in senior years which would equip students who wish to go on to tertiary studies with the necessary entry qualifications. The latter comprise a wide variety of activities providing students with opportunities to develop personal interests and skills. They would also include such activities as learning ethnic languages and cultures, so that children from such backgrounds can learn something of their heritages if they wish.

Whether any of these and other challenges to the official ideology of multiculturalism will influence future policy making remains to be seen. The Australian education system is not noted for being kind to homegrown "tall poppies" of whatever variety, being more inclined to lop them down to size—the great egalitarian myth—and import foreign ones. At the moment multiculturalism, largely copied from Canada and the United States, flowers in a fertile ideological soil. Whether it will continue to do so or will generate social fragmentation and structural conflict in the kind of "ghetto and the ethnic cauldron" feared by Knopfelmacher (Warnecke, 1981) lies ahead in Australia's uncertain economic, ethnocultural, and political future.

Notes

1. Source cited by Galbally is "Taylor (*sic*), *Primitive Culture*, London 1891 (*sic*)". See reference section for proper citation (Tylor, 1871).
2. Personal communication from one of the Council Members present at the inaugural meeting.
3. Out-stations are self-governing Aboriginal communities, which Aborigines have established usually some miles distant from the reservations and missions where they formerly lived. The trend to this new pattern is generally known as the "out-station movement".

References

Adams, I. J. W. (1978). *Small Grants for Projects in Multicultural Education* (Ethnic Education Centre Circular).

Althusser, L. (1971). Ideology and ideological state apparatuses. In *Lenin and Philosophy and Other Essays*. New Left Books, London.

Atchison, J. F. (1981). The immigration policy background to multicultural education. *Journal of Intercultural Studies* **2**, 5–16.

Australian Ethnic Affairs Council (1977). *Australia as a Multicultural Society*. Australian Government Publishing Service, Canberra.

Australian Institute of Multicultural Affairs (1980). *Review of Multicultural and Migrant Education*. A.I.M.A., Melbourne.

Beswick, D. G. and Hills, M. D. (1969). An Australian ethnocentrism scale. *Australian Journal of Psychology* **21**, 211–223.

Bhatnagar, J. (Ed.) (1981). *Educating Immigrants*. Croom Helm, London.

Bidney, D. (1967). *Theoretical Anthropology*, 2nd edition. Schocken Press, New York.

Birrell, T. (1978). Migration and the dilemmas of multiculturalism. In *The Immigration Issue in Australia* (Eds R. Birrell and C. Hay). La Trobe University, Department of Sociology, Melbourne.

Bullivant, B. M. (1972). The cultural reality of curriculum development. *Education News* **13**, 14–16.

Bullivant, B. M. (1973a). Is there a hidden curriculum in curriculum development? *Twentieth Century* **27**, 239–253.

Bullivant, B. M. (Ed.) (1973b). *Educating the Immigrant Child: Concepts and Cases*. Angus and Robertson, Sydney.

Bullivant, B. M. (1975). Implications of the Australian Schools Commission for the education of immigrants. In *Australian Schools: The Impact of the Australian Schools Commission* (Ed. L. M. Allwood). Australia International Press, Melbourne.

Bullivant, B. M. (1976). Social control and migrant education. *Australian and New Zealand Journal of Sociology* **14**, 174–183.

Bullivant, B. M. (1977). Education for the poly-ethnic society. *Forum of Education* **36**, 27–31.

Bullivant, B. M. (1979). Curriculum problematics in a poly-ethnic context. In *Mosaic or Melting Pot: Cultural Evolution in Australia* (Eds P. R. de Lacey and M. E. Poole). Harcourt Brace Jovanovich, Sydney.

Bullivant, B. M. (1980). Multiculturalism—No. *Education News* **17**, 17–20.

Bullivant, B. M. (1981a). *The Pluralist Dilemma in Education: Six Case Studies*. George Allen & Unwin, Sydney.

Bullivant, B. M. (1981b). *Race, Ethnicity and Curriculum*. Macmillan, Melbourne.

Bullivant, B. M. (1981c). Multiculturalism and media in Australia. *Multiculturalism* **5**, 13–17.

Bullivant, B. M. (1981d). Multiculturalism—pluralist orthodoxy or ethnic hegemony? *Canadian Ethnic Studies* **13**, 1–22.

Bullivant, B. M. (1982a). Are ethnic schools the answer to ethnic children's accommodation in Australian society? *Journal of Intercultural Studies* **3** (forth-coming).

Bullivant, B. M. (1982b). Pluralist debate and educational policy—Australian style. *Journal of Multilingual and Multicultural Development* **3**, 129–147.

Bureau of Statistics, Australian (1981). *Australian Demographic Statistics Quarterly, June*. Australian Bureau of Statistics, Canberra.

Calwell, A. A. (1972). *Be Just and Fear Not*. Lloyd O'Neil, Melbourne.

Cigler, M. (1975). History and multicultural education. *Australian History Association Bulletin* **4**, 23–29.

Clyne, M. (1981). Community languages and language policy: A demographic perspective. In *Community Languages—Their Role in Education* (Ed. M. Garner). River Seine Publications, Melbourne.

Committee on the Teaching of Migrant Languages in Schools (1976). *Report*. Australian Government Publishing Service, Canberra.

Committee on Multicultural Education (1979). *Education for a Multicultural Society*. Schools Commission, Canberra.

Connor, W. (1973). The politics of ethnonationalism. *Journal of International Relations* **27**, 1–21.

Enloe, C. H. (1981). The growth of the state and ethnic mobilization: The American experience. *Ethnic and Racial Studies* **4**, 123–136.

Fraser, M. (1978). *Migrant Services and Programs, Statement* (Commonwealth of Australia Mimeo).

Galbally, F. (1978). *Migrant Services and Programs*, Vols 1 and 2. Australian Government Publishing Service, Canberra.

Grassby, A. J. (1973). *A Multi-cultural Society for the Future*. Australian Government Publishing Service, Canberra.

Higham, J. (1975). *Send These to Me: Jews and Other Immigrants in Urban America*. Atheneum, New York.

Jupp, J. (1966). *Arrivals and Departures*. Cheshire-Lansdowne, Melbourne.

Kalin, K. (1978). Where do we stop this discrimination business? *Ethnic Studies* **2**, 32–41.

Lynch, P. (1972). Australia's immigration policy. In *Australia's Immigration Policy* (Ed. H. Roberts). University of Western Australia Press, Perth.

Mackie, J. A. C. (1977). Asian migration and Australian racial attitudes. *Ethnic Studies* **1**, 1–13.

Martin, J. I. (1972). *Migrants: Equality and Ideology* (Meredith Memorial Lectures). La Trobe University, Bundoora.

Martin, J. I. (1974). The changing nature of Australian society: Pluralism today. In *The Multicultural Society* (Proceedings of the National Seminar for Teacher Educators, Macquarie University). Australian Department of Education, Canberra.

Martin, J. I. (1976). The education of migrant children in Australia. In *Australian Immigration: A Bibliography and Digest* (Eds C. A. Price and J. I. Martin). The Australian National University, Department of Demography, Institute of Advanced Studies, Canberra.

Martin, J. I. (1978). *The Migrant Presence*. George Allen & Unwin, Sydney.

McConnochie, K. R. (1981). Background notes on Aboriginal education. Paper given to the NZARE-AARE Seminar, Massey University.

National Aboriginal Education Committee (1980). *Rationale, Aims and Objectives in Aboriginal Education*. National Aboriginal Education Committee.

Rowley, C. D. (1970). *The Destruction of Aboriginal Society*. ANU Press, Canberra.

Schools Commission, Australian (1975). *Report for the Triennium 1976–78*. Australian Government Publishing Service, Canberra.

Schools Commission, Australian (1978). *Report for the Triennium 1979–81*. Australian Government Publishing Service, Canberra.

Schools Commission, Australian (1981). *Report for the Triennium 1982–1984*. Australian Government Publishing Service, Canberra.

Shibutani, T. and Kwan, K. M. (1965). *Ethnic Stratification: A Comparative Approach*. Macmillan, London.

Smolicz, J. J. (1971). Is the Australian school an assimilationist agency? *Education News* **13**, 4–8.

Smolicz, J. J. (1972). Integration, assimilation and the education of immigrant children. In *Australia's Immigration Policy* (Ed. H. Roberts). University of Western Australia Press, Perth.

Smolicz, J. J. (1980). Multiculturalism—Yes. *Education News* **17**, 12–16.

Smolicz, J. J. (1981). Cultural pluralism and educational policy: In search of stable multiculturalism. *Australian Journal of Education* **25**, 121–145.

Stockley, D. (1978). The Fraser government, migrants and education. Paper given to the Australasian Political Studies Association Annual Conference, Adelaide.

Tylor, E. B. (1871). *Primitive Culture*. John Murray, London.

Ward, P. (1982). The vanishing language resource. *The Weekend Australian Magazine* May 8–9, 5.

Warnecke, R. (1981). Do we really want a multi-culture? *The Age* October 2, 13.

Watts, B. H. (1981). *Aboriginal Futures: Review of Research and Developments and Related Policies in the Education of Aborigines*. Schonell Education Research Centre, Brisbane.

Wiseman, R. (1974). Some issues involved in ethnic pluralism and education in Australia. *Forum of Education* **33**, 146–163.

Wright, M. (1980). Alternative institutional frameworks for ethnic broadcasting. In *Television in a Multicultural Society* (Eds M. Liffman and J. MacKay). (Multicultural Australia Papers, No. 9). Clearing House on Migration Issues, Melbourne.

5
Problems of language planning in the United States

Glendon F. Drake

Language planning in the United States is overwhelmingly focussed on what is termed "bilingual education", and I have come to be known as a critic of this (Edwards, 1980a, 1980b). In my opinion, I am actually an advocate of something that can be called bilingual education, but I understand why the label has stuck. My relationship with other advocates of bilingual education reminds me of the story of the customer—and let that customer represent bilingual education—who went into a store to buy a suit. After buying and being fitted for the suit, the customer left the store and on his way out noticed that the right sleeve was a bit long. He complained to the salesman who told him that if he would just draw up his arm a bit the sleeve would fit just fine. The customer left again, only to notice that the left pant leg was a little bit long. Again he returned and was told by the very persuasive salesman that everything would be all right if he would just draw up his leg a bit when he walked. The customer left for the third time, limping noticeably. He looked at his reflection in the store window and noticed that the jacket was just a bit short. He returned once again. He was told that he simply had to slouch slightly and the coat would reach down to the right length. Many more times the customer noticed little imperfections in the fit, returned and was told by the intrepid salesman how to make the necessary adjustment. Finally, the customer made all the necessary adjustments and walked down the street in

LINGUISTIC MINORITIES
ISBN 0-12-232760-8

a painfully cramped, lurching motion. I then approach him, along with another advocate of bilingual education. I say, "Look at that poor, pathetic creature and how painfully he's walking. How disabled and handicapped the poor man is". To which my companion, the bilingual education advocate, replies, "Yes, but notice how nicely his suit fits".

In my view, the problems that beset bilingual education and cause it to lurch along in the United States are: definitional confusion, ideological conflict, technical difficulties, failure to inform public opinion, and an ahistorical stance.

The term "bilingual education" in the United States has no clear reference. Its meaning is in the eye—or rather the ideology—of the beholder. To advocates of cultural pluralism, bilingual education may mean maintenance and promotion of a mother tongue. To assimilationists, bilingual education may mean transitional programmes which aim for the acquisition of English without regard to the maintenance of the mother tongue. To many Americans, bilingual education refers to a compensatory education programme for underclassed ethnics, part of the general run of "poverty programs" from the 1960s.

One of the problems has been that professional educators and sociolinguists who may have a clear reference, an operational definition, for bilingual education have fallen victim to "Mannheim's Paradox". This paradox arises from the inevitable social element in the pursuit and perception of truth and knowledge. Mannheim (1954, p. 3) pointed out that sociopolitical thought "is always bound up with the existing life situation of the thinker". Thus, a scientific observer observes from his location in history and social structure. Sociolinguists are more prone to confront the paradox than other linguists because we generally seek application of knowledge in areas of great ideological loading and motivation: ethnic inclusion or exclusion, minority/majority rights, class differences, economic and educational opportunities, social mobility, etc. All of these elements are related to bilingual education programmes. Because we attempt to apply our knowledge, we tend to become participants as well as observers. Consequently, we often find ourselves on the "side" of an issue. Usually our knowledge is for use in some presumed social good such as, in the area under discussion here, the educational success, economic opportunity and human rights of a minority group. As citizens with well-developed moral sentiment, we can hardly remain aloof from the humanitarian dimensions of the causes our discipline exposes us to. However, as social scientists we need to detach ourselves from the ideological themes and discern the "facts" and "truths", and here we find ourselves frustrated by the paradox.

To suppose that we can be objective observers and pay no heed to our own ideological involvement in the data with which we work is simply to reject the substance of the sociology of knowledge. Yet, some investigators appear to virtually celebrate Mannheim's Paradox. Here, for example, is a sociolinguist writing: "Never before in this country has the linguist had a greater opportunity to do social engineering. . . . Many of us who are involved with the linguistics of bilingualism have been, and will continue to be, called upon to represent the linguistically and socially repressed minorities. . . ." (Keller, 1976, p. 17). At first glance, this statement seems straightforward. To represent a repressed minority is, indeed, a high calling and to perform social engineering a suitable and rewarding activity for the knowledgeable social scientist and concerned citizen. At the same time, Keller is a person whose role it is to critically examine evidence about bilingualism gained from careful objective observation, to sceptically test his hypotheses and to draw valid inferences based upon the evidence—all of this within the stated content of his ideological advocacy. This is a difficult dilemma indeed. Sociolinguists and other linguists involved in the bilingual education movement are interested in language diversity, tolerant of it to the point of celebrating it, and convinced of the general benefit and social good to be derived from bilingual behaviour. These elements began as scientific inferences, evolved into values and beliefs, and ended as an ideological system. In such a subtle and generally nonconscious process, it becomes increasingly difficult for the scientific side to account for evidence that does not accord with ideology. Objectivity declines in the heat of social passion, except in those sociolinguists who have cultivated the ability to be at once critical and apologetic towards the same situation.

Social passion is an important characteristic of language planning in the United States, as well as elsewhere. This may be an appropriate place to state that ideology may serve a useful function, especially in areas in which we are likely to seek application of our sociolinguistic skills, such as bilingual education. It is the fashion in recent years to attach a pejorative meaning to ideology, but there is no reason that this should necessarily be so. Ideologists may distort the nature of things, but they also call attention to problems and mobilize groups to action, which, of course, is one of the themes in the story of bilingual education in the United States. It has been the political mobilization of such groups as Chicanos in the United States that has brought attention to the linguistic problems of minorities. Linguists have only followed in the wake of these movements, which have facilitated a climate of opinion which allows for the application of linguistic knowledge. Science tends to be a handmaiden to ideology. That is the opportunity, the problem, and the paradox.

Moreover, there exists the distinct possibility that to be a participant as well as an observer leads to greater knowledge. Hymes (1974, p. 209) on this point quotes Mao Tse-Tung's remark that: "If you want to know a certain thing or certain class of things directly, you must personally participate in the practical struggle to change reality, to change that thing or class of things, for only through personal participation can you uncover the essence of that thing or class of things and comprehend them". Since linguists, especially those involved with bilingualism and bilingual education, are apt to be vexed and confounded by ideology, it is surprising we have not been more active in admitting the study of the operation of cultural symbols to our analysis of the things we are studying. For example, I find it curious that the general approach to ethnicity in the United States by most, but not all, scholars and educators concerned with bilingual education is out of touch with the reality of the history, nature, and symbolism of the ethnic groups with which they deal. I have in mind concerns for such matters as the effect of bilingual education on power and status, knowledge of the long history in the United States of the fundamental tension between assimilation and pluralism, the belief that somehow this tension was a new phenomenon emerging in the 1960s, the history and nature of linguistic maintenance and shift in the United States, the tension between the leaders of minority groups and the attitudes of those minority groups being led and the alternation of ethnic mobilization and assimilation (Drake, 1979).

Perhaps those involved professionally in bilingual education in the United States, like all applied linguists, should realize that they are in a relationship that is analogous to that of a psychiatrist with his patient. In this relationship, the psychiatrist plays a dual role of participant and observer. As "participant/ observer" (see Percy, 1961, pp. 39–40), a psychiatrist must note not only the patient's behaviour but his own behaviour as well. For the psychiatrist will crucially affect the situation by eliciting responses from the patient and by motivating the patient's further behaviour. As applied linguists we are necessarily in "participant/observer" relationships with out "clients". As linguists we are good at understanding and conceptualizing our observer role; but as applied linguists, I submit, many of us on the same level do not understand our participant role. I believe the problems of bilingual education in the United States would somewhat diminish if we could bring our special relationship into some conceptual order.

Let me provide an illustration. It is common to read in the sociolinguistic literature that we must choose either the assimilationist's or the pluralist's side as a policy base for bilingual education (Kjolseth, 1973; Rubin, 1977). The problem is that neither position in its pure form is acceptable or has been found to be acceptable historically. The assimilationist in seeking the elimination of ethnic boundaries—and language is seen as a boundary maintenance device—teaches rejection and contempt for things that resist rejection and deserve respect. The assimilationist trades affection and loyalty for autonomy and mastery, achieves the pursuit of individual success at the cost of identity, and assumes that an individual needs only the opportunity to prove his worth. This leads to alienation and self-hatred on the part of those who fail to prove their worth in the assimilationist's terms (Abrahams, 1972; Higham, 1975).

Pluralism, on the other hand, insists on a rigidity of boundaries and a commitment to group that American society simply will not permit. Pluralism limits the autonomous, the adventurous, and the ambitious. It breeds suspicion, narrow-mindedness, and prejudice against the outside world—a deadly environment in which to educate. An individual is at the mercy of the group. Thus, in our zeal for spreading the benefits of linguistic diversity, many of us have defined the conflict and picked a side that assures that we will lose even if we win.

It may be worth examining the proposition that ethnicity *per se* and language *per se* are much too general explanations for most of the phenomena dealt with in connection with bilingual education. Differences in the location and age of ethnic group members are not controversial or ideologically loaded but may explain more in terms of income, education, or occupation than mere ethnic membership or language usage (Sowell, 1978). The same may be said of religious and political factors. Indeed, the evidence regarding educational success can be read in such a way that social class has much more explanatory power than ethnicity (see Epstein, 1977; Paulston, 1974). Linguists consistently lament the fact that most bilingual programmes in the United States are assimilationist (Kjolseth, 1973; Rubin, 1977); however, the fact that they are assimilationist accords with the dominant value structure of American society and with its singular history of linguistic shift. Linguists also lament the fact that public opinion feeds the fear that the country may lose its national unity in the face of widespread bilingualism. While linguists and intellectuals find this view simplistic at best and wrong at worst, it is clearly the public opinion. Moreover, many intellectuals and political elites share the view. Indeed, American historians, as a rule, think that the United States has been extremely fortunate in not having to deal with the intractable problems of some genuinely bilingual societies. While linguists may view bilingualism as liberating, many policy makers view language as one of the most crucial means of maintaining ethnic boundaries—as a means of keeping people in. The prevailing ideology of Americans is not to keep people in. For any bilingual education policy based upon a pluralistic model to be expected to work, public opinion would have to be informed of the benefits of bilingualism, societal and psychological, in order to provide the basis for such a policy. Language planners have failed to inform public opinion. Characteristically, they have even dismissed public opinion as ill-informed and unimportant. Ill-informed or not, public opinion is a potent force in the success or failure of bilingual education programmes.

By and large, public opinion has not been favourable to anything but transitional programmes, and it has been suspicious of these, especially when supported by public funds.

The historical context of bilingual education in the United States has had two aspects. First of all, bilingual education advocates have tended to see the tension between assimilation and pluralism as a new phenomenon emerging in the 1960s. In point of fact, the problem of the one and the many had become important before the ethnic issue added the dimension of reconciling ethnic diversity with national unity. The present argument about bilingual education represents a continuity with the dilemma with which Americans, old and new, have struggled since the Puritans founded a city on the hill in the seventeenth century. A knowledge of this history would have prevented many of the blind alleys that bilingual education programmes have turned down. For example, a general twentieth-century experience shows us that, in Higham's words: ". . . cultural pluralism would appeal to people who are already strongly enough positioned to imagine that permanent minority status might be advantageous. It was congenial to minority spokesmen often enough to visualize themselves at the center rather than at the periphery of American experience. Accordingly, cultural pluralism proved most attractive to people who were already largely assimilated. It was itself one of the products of the American 'melting pot'." (Higham, 1975, p. 211.) It is a genuine irony of bilingual education policy in the United States that, as Edwards (1981) has pointed out, the desire for cultural pluralism is in many cases an ideal of the élite, and not in accord with the desires and ideology of the masses of "ethnics", who have demonstrated over our history a desire for mobility and integration.

A second aspect of the context of bilingual education programmes is that the history of linguistic maintenance and shift has been ignored. The best predictor of future social behaviour is past social behaviour, all other things being equal. Clearly, in the United States, the pattern of linguistic shift of ethnic groups is clear. With few exceptions, this shift has occurred completely by the third generation and has been in progress during the second generation, with the greatest degree of bilingualism during the childhood of the second generation. In general, the reliance of many bilingual education programmes upon ethnic solidarity, commitments and boundaries does not have much, if any, historical relevance in the United States. If there is a reason to assume there are new factors at work in our society which would alter this historical continuity, it is hard to think of what they might be. Most likely, the argument from this position would be that a new social situation has asserted itself in the last two decades. Indeed, there has been a widely acclaimed shift in the values and ideology of the American system, but I would submit that this shift is more proclaimed than established; I do not believe that this alleged shift in ideology toward pluralism is rooted in social reality. I have written elsewhere (Drake, 1979) that there is widespread evidence that American values have changed since the 1960s to reject restrictions based on race, religion, or nationality (see also Sowell, 1978). These changes are signalled by social behaviour, survey responses, and voting data. In general, there has been a breakdown of employment, educational and intermarriage barriers. Values have shifted towards tolerance of "ethnics", but not necessarily in favour of pluralism. Attitudes favouring ethnic inclusion do not necessarily promote the maintenance or even the acknowledgement of ethnic difference. There is a growing impatience with programmes providing benefits based upon ethnic categories. Impatience with quotas and goals in affirmative action has been widely manifested in the last few years. I do not want to be judgemental about these matters but I *do* wish to indicate that they belie the assumption of a tilt in the social landscape, or a break in the continuity of linguistic shift in the United States (Drake, 1979).

The technical success or failure of bilingual education programmes is not the subject of this chapter. However, one point I would make is that from a pragmatic point of view the widespread failure of minority children to respond successfully to bilingual education does, to some degree, signal technical failure as well as ideological confusion and the complication of sociocultural factors. Therefore, while I have not discussed these technical linguistic matters here, I want to point out that, in my opinion, we in the United States are getting better at the linguistic and pedagogical technology for creating bilingualism and that there is an accumulation of evidence that successful bilingualism can be created in bilingual programmes. Cummins (1979, 1981) has recently summarized much of this evidence. Some of the successful programmes include the Rockpoint Navaho project, the Nester School Bilingual Program, the Manitoba Francophone study, and the Saint Lambert experiment (Lambert and Tucker, 1972). This is just a partial list. There are some common threads running through many recent success stories in bilingual education that seem to give some hope for the future. For one thing, many programmes show success with thorough training initially in the mother tongue; second, there is increasing evidence of easy transfer of skills from one language to another; and there is also evidence, at a certain level of proficiency, of cognitive, intellectual and attitudinal benefits that bilinguals have over monolinguals. If such evidence continues to accumulate and become significant, it would seem to be possible that a bilingual programme that accords with dominant ideology and public opinion could evolve. If bilingual education could come to be seen as an enrichment process rather than a social engineering scheme for minority ethnic children, as a benefit to the entire community and an asset to all individuals, and if it should become clear that bilingualism could offer the intellectual and cognitive advantages that middle-class Americans seek for their children in schooling, advantages which make for mobility and autonomy, and if attitudinal advantages of bilingualism can be shown to serve to blunt ethnic conflict and promote openness in society, then bilingual education may evolve and find success. Above all, it may be bilingualism itself which is the best means of addressing the ethnic dilemma in America which forces many to choose between the emotional health and security of pluralism and the autonomy and adventure of assimilation. If bilingualism can serve as a bridge which connects a person with his group and at the same time allows him to achieve the more cosmopolitan outlook and behaviour of the larger society, then I suppose that a stronger policy could evolve.

One of the most fundamental debates about the American character is whether the American is an idealist or a pragmatist. The American philosopher, George Santana, in responding to this, said that "an American is an idealist working on matter". I think that my view of the problems of language planning in the United States is very neatly covered by this insight. It is our idealism, in my view, that has thwarted our efforts to create a viable, bilingual programme in the United States; and, in my view, it is our working on matter (i.e. our pragmatic drive to find out what works) that may make a viable language-planning policy. The reason for this is that it would appear that the programmes that are working may prove to be those which both accord with our ideology in allowing for change and mobility and openness and, at the same time, address the needs of the ethnic individual to maintain ties with his ethnic identity.

References

Abrahams, R. D. (1972). Stereotyping and beyond. In *Language and Cultural Diversity in American Education* (Eds R. Abrahams and R. Troike). Prentice-Hall, Englewood Cliffs, New Jersey.

Cummins, J. (1979). Linguistic interdependence and the educational development of bilingual children. *Review of Educational Research* **49**, 222–251.

Cummins, J. (1981). The role of primary language development in promoting educational success for language minority students. Unpublished manuscript.

Drake, G. F. (1979). Ethnicity, values and language policy in the United States. In *Language and Ethnic Relations* (Eds H. Giles and B. Saint-Jacques). Pergamon Press, Oxford.

Edwards, J. R. (1980a). Bilingual education: Facts and values. *Canadian Modern Language Review* **37**(1), 123–127.

Edwards, J. R. (1980b). Critics and criticisms of bilingual education. *Modern Language Journal* **64**, 409–415.

Edwards, J. R. (1981). The context of bilingual education. *Journal of Multilingual and Multicultural Development* **2**, 25–44.

Epstein, N. (1977). *Language, Ethnicity and the Schools.* Institute for Educational Leadership, Washington, D.C.

Higham, J. (1975). *Send These to Me.* Atheneum, New York.

Hymes, D. (1974). *Foundations in Sociolinguistics.* University of Pennsylvania Press, Philadelphia, Pennsylvania.

Keller, G. D. (1976). Constructing valid goals for bilingual education: The role of the applied linguist and the bilingual educator. In *Bilingualism in the Bicentennial and Beyond* (Eds G. Keller, R. Teschner and S. Viera). Bilingual Press, New York.

Kjolseth, R. (1973). Assimilation or pluralism. In *Bilingualism in the Southwest* (Ed. P. R. Turner). University of Arizona Press, Tucson.

Lambert, W. E. and Tucker, G. R. (1972). *Bilingual Education of Children: The St. Lambert Experiment.* Newbury House, Rowley, Massachusetts.

Mannheim, K. (1954). *Ideology and Utopia.* Harcourt Brace Jovanovich, New York.

Paulston, C. B. (1974). *Implication of Language Learning Theory for Language Planning: Concerns in Bilingual Education.* Center for Applied Linguistics, Arlington, Virginia.

Percy, W. (1961). The symbolic structure of interpersonal process. *Psychiatry* **24**(1), 39–52.

Rubin, J. (1977). Bilingual education and language planning. In *Frontiers of Bilingual Education* (Eds B. Spolsky and R. Cooper). Newbury House, Rowley, Massachusetts.

Sowell, T. (1978). Ethnicity in a changing America. *Daedalus* **107**, 213–337.

6
Bilingual education and its social implications

William F. Mackey

The locus of bilingual schooling is the community. Bilingual education may be a matter of policy, a matter of need or a matter of desire. Policy depends on principles like language parity, territoriality, freedom of choice and the like. The need for bilingual schooling may be simply the consequence of differences in language status and language standardization. A desire for bilingual schooling may be the result of a belief that one's children may have certain economic or social advantages if they become fluent in a certain language.

The relation between school and community is not the same for language as it is for other subjects. In any community, the school is the place where one goes to acquire knowledge about history, geography, arithmetic, social studies, and the like. Although one may have to go to school to become literate in one's home language, the school has no monopoly on language learning. It may indeed be the repository of knowledge; it is not the repository of language. And yet many bilingual education programmes seem to be based on such an assumption. Parents whose children have been schooled in such programmes are surprised that the impressive bilingual balance achieved since kindergarten as the result of the cumulative effects of bilingual schooling often disappears in early adolescence, as the young person becomes integrated into the wide uni-ethnic universe of an adult world. Society and its set of community forces have begun to exert more pressure than the school and the family could maintain.

LINGUISTIC MINORITIES
ISBN 0-12-232760-8

Since the implementation of the Bilingual Education Act by the United States Congress in 1968, and the propagation of a bilingual education policy in Canada in the sixties and seventies, there has been a phenomenal increase in the number of writings devoted to bilingual education, as a comparison of the listings under that heading in the index of the 1972 edition of the International Bibliography on Bilingualism with the corresponding terms in the index of the 1982 edition will demonstrate (Mackey, 1982b).

Much of the literature, however, is discipline oriented, in that it mostly comprises studies by psychologists, linguists, educators and other specialists reporting that their observations of uses of bilingual schooling seemed to mean that it has such and such an effect on the personality, or on performance, or on the linguistic or educational achievement of individuals. The effects observed depend on the issue which the writer or investigator wishes to study within the context of a particular discipline. Some of these studies have led to findings and generalizations about bilingual education which, in reality, are applicable only to the cases studied. Much of the experimental work on bilingual education has been based on situations common to the most typical urban North American Anglophone environment, where the only home language or the dominant one is English, and the only contact or the main one is with another standard language as taught in school. Since such situations affect so few countries and fewer of the world's many languages, generalizations based on them, if at all valid, must have limited value.

There is a difference, however, between the invalid generalization based on these regional studies and the study of common problems faced by most bilingual communities (Mackey, 1981b). In some countries of the world, where the speech of the home is not the language of schooling, any estimate of the social implications of a particular type and degree of bilingual schooling on a given community rests on an understanding of the variables involved. To begin with, one must identify the type of speech community one is observing—from the point of view of language use and language dominance. Since a language is not necessarily dominant in both speech and writing, a first distinction is necessary, between bilingualism and biliteracy; any community may follow one of several patterns of inter-ethnic distribution of speech and literacy.

The type and extent of interpersonal and intergroup contact between two ethnic communities are factors in determining what sort of bilingual education is possible. The fact that two ethnic groups live in the same city does not mean that they are socially any nearer than if they lived in separate towns. In the towns and cities of Quebec, for example—especially in the smaller ones—contact between English and French in the past had been either professional or perfunctory. Even in the sociable atmosphere of sports, the different attitudes toward games had discouraged contact; the English seemed to take them seriously, the French regarded them as mere amusements or pastimes—with the possible exception of organized and professional spectator sport, which from time to time would act as an inflated symbol of civic solidarity.

This segregation of the English and French communities did not, however, prevent a certain number of intermarriages taking place. The mobile Anglo-Canadian and American bachelor discovered that he could improve his economic standing by accepting a transfer to Quebec towns and cities. Since the sons of the town's French-speaking élite were away for professional training, the stay-at-home daughters found fewer marriageable men who were equally educated and French-speaking. A number of resulting French–English marriages supplied the schools with bilingual children whose language dominance, it was seen, depended on the socio-economic level of their parents. It was likely to be French if the income was lower and English if the income was high since children in the latter group, having fathers of the mobile managerial class, were committed to English.

One cannot assume that the closeness of two ethnic groups leads to interaction between them, for population mobility and segregation attenuate the effects of nearness. In Montreal the mobile English had been segregated from the more élite French majority—educationally, socially, professionally, economically and even geographically. In fact, the bilingual schools that did exist had an entirely English-speaking school population, the only French-speaking person in the class being perhaps the teacher. This resulted in the type of school dubbed "immersion" in Montreal, one which had been the norm in most colonies of Asia and Africa. It was a monoethnic type of bilingual school in which one language was used as a medium of instruction and a different language as the home language of the pupils. Studies purporting to discover social advantages or disadvantages of this or any other type of bilingual schooling sometimes simply took for granted that each language must have a fixed norm. This is not generally true, however, either for a language or for the group who speak it.

Not all language communities are norm-conscious. Some languages show a higher degree of tolerance of mixture than do others. In some communities, like the new republic of Belize, the acceptable mixture of creolized forms may vary from one day to the next in the speech of different social groups—without loss of communication (Le Page, 1968). At the other end of the scale we have languages like French whose long tradition of standardization has created an attitude of intolerance for anything which does not conform to the accepted norm (Mackey, 1982a).

On the basis of experiments where such normalized languages are involved one can hardly generalize results as being applicable to all language communities. Nor can one attribute the language norms for age-groups established in one community to those language norms of other communities. In bilingual societies, the normal distribution of bilingual competence may vary from a certain degree of dominance in one language to levels of balance in both languages; and, the distribution may be different for the written language.

When one has identified the linguistic pattern and the language distribution of a community one can consider the social implications of a national language policy, its language objectives, its type of control, its implementation at the level of the community and its effects on the local social environment.

I Language education in national policy

Since human environments differ so much, it is not surprising that language education policies should also differ. The language education problems of Europe are not those of Africa, and those of Asia are not those of America. There are a number of reasons why this is so. Areas of the globe differ in the number of languages they harbour, the number of speakers (and what they do, who they are, and where they live), the status and standardization of their languages and the degrees of resemblance among neighbouring languages. Superimposed upon a distribution of some three thousand languages are the national boundaries of some two hundred countries fashioned by the desire of man to expand or consolidate the communities in which he lives.[1] Within these few hundred boundaries are housed all the languages of the world. In most instances, however, only one language is considered to be the language of the country—the number of officially multilingual nations being very few indeed (and even these do not recognize *all* the native languages of all of their citizens). It is inevitable that most countries should be faced with problems of language education. But these problems and their solutions will differ from country to country since, in addition to the number, similarity, status and standardization of the languages concerned, they are determined by the nature of the population speaking them, the degree of literacy, educational facilities, and by the national priorities of the country as a whole.

A The number of languages

Some countries are blessed (or cursed) with more languages than others. In planning for the progress of a country as a whole—in power, prestige or prosperity—the pressure of different groups clinging to their own language may become an embarrassment.

Some national leaders have asked whether linguistic heterogeneity is necessary, or whether it is a luxury they can ill afford. Many of the new nations have even found it expedient to adopt the language of their former colonial overlords as their national tongue, and a few have even adopted two such languages. The only official languages in Cameroon, for example, are English and French, although neither is among the hundred or so native languages spoken in the country. Yet all public schooling is done in one or both of these two foreign tongues, as it was in the past when one of the colonial languages was German.

It is not so much the number of languages in a country, however, which causes the problems, as their demographic and geographic distribution. We could argue that more languages are spoken in the United States than in most countries. In addition to English, there are at least a hundred languages spoken within the frontiers of the country by populations ranging from one thousand to more than three million, if we count all the immigrant and native Amerindian languages. But not one of these languages is the mother tongue of more than 3% of the population (Kloss and McConnell, 1978a). The overwhelming numerical majority of English speakers has made it possible to impose English, until recent years, as the sole language of education in the United States. If, however, the number of English speakers had been comparable to that of the other languages, the history of bilingual education in the United States would undoubtedly have been quite different.

As a case in point, take the Soviet Union whose population is comparable to that of the United States, but whose language demography has a different distribution pattern. Here, despite state control and the predominance of Russian, more than seventy other languages have had to be recognized as media of education in the schools. The Soviet Union is a large and populous country and some of the language minorities represent large populations. In smaller and less populous areas, language diversity can create problems of a different order. Take, for example, the Netherlands West Indies. In the Netherlands Antilles (Curaçao Group), more than 75% of the population speak Papiamentu, less than 25% speak Dutch or English and less than 10% speak Spanish. In other parts of the Netherlands Antilles (the Leeward Islands), Papiamentu is used by less than 25% of the population, as is Dutch, whereas English accounts for more than 75%. In Surinam, however, some 18 different languages are used, 12 of them by less than 5% of the population, two by about 5%, two by about 10%, one (Hindustani) by about 25% and only one (Taki-Taki) by more than 50% of the population (Kloss and McConnell, 1978b). It was obviously necessary for the Dutch government in The Hague to take these language facts into consideration in the planning of its educational policy for this area, where Dutch is not understood by more than a quarter of the population. As a matter of fact, the

Netherlands government in the 1960s had an executive director in The Hague responsible for education in Papiamentu.

Numerical distribution, however, is not all; there are also the differences in geographic repartition. If nearly all the speakers of a language live in one part of the country, it is easier for the State to recognize a local language as a medium of instruction. This is a factor which distinguishes the colonial from the immigrant languages. For example, although the number of native speakers of Spanish, German, and Italian in the United States is comparable—between three and four million each—Spanish, the first colonial language, is historically associated with a certain American region, unlike German and Italian, the main immigrant languages (Fishman, 1966). In some countries, like Belgium, Canada, Switzerland and Yugoslavia, the geographical repartition of languages has been so marked as to permit the division of the country into linguistically autonomous regions each with its own language of schooling. Language division along geographic lines is not always territorial in the sense that part of the country is inhabited by people speaking another tongue. It may also be a division between town and country, producing comparable effects. When Malaysia achieved its independence in 1957, some 80% of the population were almost equally divided between Chinese speakers (39%) and Malay (41%), but the Chinese speakers were concentrated in the cities, with their progressive Chinese schools and colleges (besides a large Indian minority), whereas the Malay speakers chose to remain on their lush and fertile land.

B Similarity of languages

In some countries, however, adjacent languages are so similar as to be mutually comprehensible. In such cases, the more useful one may have been selected as a language of education, with the assurance that all the pupils will be able to understand it. This is the case in areas where dialects are spoken at home and corresponding standardized languages used in the school. It is also the case for certain closely related languages, like Galician and Portuguese or Frisian and Dutch. Since there is no structural line of demarcation between different languages and different dialects, interlingual distance is a matter of degree, and this is measurable; some languages being closer than others, they may be more or less interintelligible (Mackey, 1979b). There are different types of interlingual distance, however, and different types of interintelligibility (Mackey, 1971, 1976). This is reflected in the observation that attitudes towards intelligibility are not always reciprocal. For example, although 87% of Swedes think they are understood by Danes, only 40% of the latter agree that they in fact understand Swedish; 76% of the Danes said they were understood by Norwegians, while only 50% of these admitted understanding Danish (Haugen, 1966). English-speaking tourists have often acted as if everyone could understand them even though they could understand no other language.

Interethnic attitudes, however, may inhibit interintelligibility of similar languages. In highly bilingualized areas, speakers will admit to understanding the language of highest status and not to understanding an inferior although closely related dialect of their mother tongue. Few Angas speakers admit to understanding the highly similar and nearby Sura language, but will claim to understand Hausa, the lingua franca of a great area in the Northern region of Nigeria (Wolff, 1959). These attitudes, however, may be conditioned by the relative status of the languages in contact.

C Language status

The fact that a language is easy to understand as a medium of instruction or that it is spoken by a good proportion of the population does not mean that it will be accepted by all. People are also interested in the value of the language as expressed in its status; they do not want to invest part of their lives learning what they might consider as unimportant languages. It makes a difference whether the language of instruction—especially if it is not the language of the home—happens to have international status, whether it is an official or national language, or whether it is only a language of an ethnic minority.

A language of high international status, even though it is that of a minority, may be preferred as a medium of instruction—especially at the secondary level—over a national majority language. In the past, the French population of Belgium has been averse to having its children do their schooling in Flemish. Language status is a reflection of economic and cultural power. A powerful language may be preferred by the educated élite of a nation because it has so much to offer (Mackey, 1973). If an ex-colonial language is chosen as an official language in a country where only a small fraction of the population has completed secondary school, only the élite is then able to enjoy the fruits of independence. The élite maintains control at the national level by perpetuating its class through schooling, while some of the born leaders remain at the local level using only local languages. Some of the first fruits of independence, however, may include mass communication and the consequent acculturation of the country through its bilingual élite. For only they may be able to afford such media as television—although all the television these people can afford may be in the form of canned programmes. Since it may cost thousands of dollars a minute to make an original commercial videotape or television film, but only a fraction of this to broadcast it, it is often more economical for the country to buy the package, than to produce its own. In this way rich countries propagate their culture, their cultural values, and their information through local élites who understand their language. Yet many of these same languages may still happen to be good instructional media, not only because they have so much available, but also because they are so standardized.

D Language standardization

Language skills are a fundamental prerequisite of education at any level. The teaching of reading and writing in school supposes not only the alphabetization but also a certain degree of standardization of the language to be read and written; it also supposes the existence of things in print. The extent of standardization and publication necessary to operate a worthwhile education programme in a given language is not known; facts of standardization for the languages of the world started to become available only in the 1970s (Kloss and McConnell, 1978b). Some useful typologies, however, have been developed. In a bilingual community, the use of the languages in school may depend on whether one or both of the languages are standard, classical, vernacular, dialectical, creole, pidgin—in a descending order based on presence or absence of four characteristics: standardization, autonomy (e.g. dialect acting as a language), historicity (e.g. association with a national tradition) and vitality (e.g. use as the mother tongue of an isolated community) (Unesco, 1973). A highly standardized language like Spanish, English, or Dutch may be more attractive to parents and local educators than a semi-creole like Papiamentu, even though the latter might be the home language of the majority. For a standardized language, with its written code of correct usage enshrined in its grammars, dictionaries, pronunciation and style manuals, can be handled in the sort of curriculum planning which public education requires in a more orderly and less ambiguous fashion than can a language where the difference between what is correct and what is unacceptable has not been established. It may also make literacy worthwhile.

E Literacy of the population

The choice, proportion and use of two or more languages in an educational system may depend on the type and amount of literacy of the population. If the educated have been traditionally literate in a classical or regional language, this literacy may have to be continued, along with a reading programme, to make a more useful international language available to the population. This may be more difficult in some areas than it is in others. In countries with ancient civilizations embodying traditional scripts, as exist for example in Asia, a primary school pupil may have to master three entirely different scripts, one of which may not even be alphabetic.

Differences in script make different languages seem more distant in their written forms and make biliteracy for the masses difficult to achieve. Because of this, some nations have done away with the traditional script, adapting a Roman alphabet to the national tongue. The phenomenal creation of modern Turkey is associated with such a move. Here, in the space of a few years in the mid-twenties, Mustafa Kemal Attaturk succeeded in transforming written Turkish from an Arabic to a Roman alphabet and in giving it permanence through a mass literacy campaign. This was accompanied by the elimination from the language of Arabic and Persian forms so prevalent in Ottoman Turkish. As a result, for most Turks reading their language in the 1980s, everything printed before 1928 has become unintelligible. And even when transliterated into modern Turkish, much of it is still unintelligible in content—replete as it is with Ottoman idioms, ideas and values. The maintenance of an old literary tradition can thus become a new educational burden. In balance, however, this may have seemed a small price to pay for a modernization designed to meet the needs of the population for new social structures.

F Social structure of the population

The type and formula of a multilingual educational system may depend on the social structure of the population, as control passes from the hands of an educated élite to those of the people and their elected representatives; and the educational system may be forced to change as well, especially if the élite has been educated extensively through a foreign language. That is, the educational systems, operated exclusively in the colonial language, were designed to produce a small number of well-educated persons capable of specialization in the home country. These comprised not only administrators but professionals as well, including some highly trained teachers. Their number, however, was insufficient to meet the popular demand for schools which followed independence. The unilingual curricula of such schools were suited to an élite, not to the needs of the masses for universal and fundamental education. To adapt the schools to these needs of a multilingual population, without sacrificing the continued and growing needs of the nation for well-educated professional people, presented schooling problems which were vaster, more complex and more urgent than those of most other countries in Europe and America.

The problems were made even more complex by the presence in multilingual societies of co-occurring characteristics such as race, religion and occupation. In Malaysia, for example, language had been associated with both race and occupation, reinforcing the group loyalty and linguistic nucleation of the urban Chinese on the one hand and the rural Malay on the other. In Quebec education, language has traditionally been associated with religion—so much so that the entire educational system was designed for a population made up exclusively of English Protestants and French Catholics; so that, except in private schools or big cities, some French-speaking Protestants and some English-speaking Catholics had to choose between their language and their religion. Many of the other ethnic groups, Italian in particular, wishing to educate their children in the language of their choice might have had to give up both, that is, as far as public education was concerned. With the rise of ecumenism among Christian religions, however, and the great decline in the influence of the Church in the secular life of contemporary Quebec, divisions along language lines began to overshadow those of religion (Mackay *et al.*, 1961). Failure to accommodate others, excepting the language communities of English-speaking Catholics, was often attributed to lack of facilities.

G Educational facilities

For the viability of a bilingual policy, what may be most crucial is the presence or absence of educational facilities—schools, books and teachers. If they are not available in one language, the system may have to function in another tongue. Since raising the standard of living may depend on a more educated work force, which in turn depends on schooling and eventually on a sufficient number of teachers trained in a world language, some young countries may have to put teacher-training on the top of their list of national priorities.

H National priorities

In the multilingual societies, national priorities are often language-related. A need for technicians may be more urgent than is secondary education in the vernacular. Or, a lingua franca may be widespread enough to risk its implementation as a national tongue, being given the highest priority. In Tanzania, for example, Swahili has been chosen as a national tongue, and a new culture is being developed around it. In other countries, the highest priority may be that of national unity. In India, in the quarter century following independence, concession after concession had to be made to regional languages in order to prevent secession. In other areas, education of a whole generation may have to be sacrificed. Planning for future generations at the expense of the present one has been a common trait of reformers, and this tendency must be taken into account in the evaluation of national linguistic objectives.

II National language objectives

It is in relation to these national priorities and the limitations imposed by available educational facilities, the social structure and literacy of the population, the status, standardization, similarity, number and distribution of the languages within its territory that a society must determine the language objectives attainable through its educational and political institutions. These may include such aims as the political, economic or cultural autonomy of the country, national unity, interethnic harmony, or the control of interethnic tensions, the influx of technical knowledge from the outside, and integration into a supranational organization. The objectives may be determined by certain national principles—assumed or overt. Since it is a tendency of all establishments to maintain the *status quo,* and that of minorities to lend themselves to emotional exploitation of their national sentiments, it has been the practice in the older bilingual societies to base national language policies on certain overtly stated principles. The two main ones are the principle of territoriality and the principle of personality. According to the principle of territoriality the individual accommodates to the language of the state; according to the principle of personality, the state accommodates to the language of the individual.

In practice, these principles generate contradictions. A state cannot give all individuals an open choice of language for education, the courts, and government administration, whereas the application of the territorial principle may infringe on basic rights. Both principles may have to be applied with certain restrictions. The choice of objectives may also be dominated by the political structure of the country. In loosely centralized national states the preservation of ethnic languages and cultures may be the aim, so that in regions where ethnic minorities dominate bilingual maintenance will become the educational policy. In Italy, such bilingualism affects only the populations of the areas of Trieste, Bolzano, and Gorizia. In Great Britain, it affects schools in parts of Wales and Scotland. In the Netherlands, it is confined to Friesland, whereas in Norway, regional dialect apart, it is limited to the Finns and the Lapps. A political structure of segmented pluralism as found in certain Central European states will also favour language maintenance through bilingual education—a child of the politics of accommodation.

Contrariwise, in highly centralized nation-states, the objective may be the forging of a strong unified nation with a mobile superstructure of trained cadres. Here the educational policy has been one of transfer from one home language to the national tongue. France has given a remarkable example of an educational policy of language integration, and many of her former African colonies have followed suit without, however, adapting to an indigenous language. For them, bilingual education may be only a concession to their unsurmounted problems, especially in primary education—the desire and ultimate objective being to make French the national vernacular. Some former British colonies have had similar objectives. In Canada and the United States, it has long been the aim to transfer the community language of Amerindian and immigrant populations, through the school, from the home language to English. A transfer policy may start abruptly and fully in the first grade, as it has in France and her colonies, in a subsequent primary grade, or it may extend gradually through primary and secondary school years. As a national policy, it may cover one or more generations. Some countries may have a monolingual nation as a long-term objective, but may be obliged to settle for a bilingual policy for a generation or so. In such countries—Israel, for example—a long-term transfer policy is not to be confused with one of bilingualization.

A policy of bilingualization is characteristic mainly of bilingual or multinational federations. It generally arises out of the two-fold objective of cultural autonomy of federated states on the one hand and sharing of national responsibility on the other (Mackey and Verdoodt, 1975). Such a policy has been applied in Yugoslavia and in the Soviet Union, where Russian has been adopted as the second language of the autonomous Soviet republics and used as the all-union language. With fewer languages in question, Canada and South Africa have tried to apply such a policy at the federal level. In countries where economic development has priority over language maintenance, people will tend to use one language (that of the economically dominant group) at the expense of the other. This may lead, however, to the complete domination of a single language.

In countries where the primary national values are economic, the vast majority of the population in any or all of the language groups may be more interested in economic than in linguistic policies. Imposition of language policies by force, however, may arouse stronger opposition than the implementation of economic ones, especially if the former threaten the employability of a group. In implementing language policy objectives, four different types of bilingualism have been considered: traditional bilingualism (teaching the national language just long enough to permit its use as a medium of instruction); monoliterate bilingualism (where both languages are used orally but only one in writing); partial bilingualism (literate in both languages, with one language limited to certain subjects); and full bilingualism (with all subjects in both languages) (Fishman and Lovas, 1970).

III National and regional control

Countries with bilingual education policies differ greatly in the degree and amount of control which they exercise, the flexibility allowed at each level and the extent and effects of interaction between various levels of society. The control from the central government may be one of executive edicts or one of advice or persuasion. In some federated states there is little central control of language policy. The over-all principles are simply stated in the federal constitution, as they are in Yugoslavia, and the constituent states are required in their own constitutions to elaborate their application of these principles in their own language and educational policies (Mackey and Verdoodt, 1975). Whether these policies are centrally or regionally controlled, they are at the heart of an interaction network whereby the society through its government and its education agencies may affect and be affected by language policy. But the implementation of curriculum through the teachers and the materials may indirectly reach the individual language learner and user, who comes to school from that same population whose language environment has shaped him and determined what he does and learns (Mackey, 1970). The realities of the environment, however, may modify a policy as it is implemented at the community level and eventually in the school.

Since language distribution throughout any country or area is rarely homogeneous, the success or failure of a bilingual education policy depends largely on its implementation at the community level. The type of adaptation necessary and the ability to implement the policy depend on the social structure of the community, its language distribution pattern, the political and educational criteria of the administrators, the attitude of the population and the motivation of the parents. In much of what follows, I shall draw upon the useful example of Montreal.

A Social structure of the community

The type and number of possible bilingual schools in a community will depend on whether the language groups are segregated or unsegregated and to what extent. In Montreal the degree of segregation of the population has been reflected in two systems of unilingual schools. When language segmentation is congruent with segmentation upon religious and socio-economic lines it encourages the creation of a system of segregated schools as, for example, existed in Montreal, where there was one segregated public city school system for English-speaking Protestants and another for French-speaking Catholics. This latter school system maintained English-speaking Catholic schools, in which were found the bulk of European immigrant children, all supported by public funds. Another segregation factor is one of status—most of the managerial posts in business, industry and finance had been held by English-speaking Protestants and by some bilinguals. The English-speaking commercial elite of Montreal did business with half a continent; its members regarded North America, not Quebec or Canada, as their domain; they came from and move to a variety of Canadian and American cities and, being connected with large firms and corporations, they found it easier to move than did their French professional counterparts. One could estimate that their replacement rate was as high as a fifth of their number every year, if based on the over-all average Canadian telephone disconnect rate of 25%, which is almost identical to the American one (Packard, 1972). In this context it is not surprising that these people, Montreal Anglophones, have insisted on a North American education for their children and not a bilingual one, where much of the time would be devoted to instruction in a language they might never use.

Closer to the base of the socio-economic pyramid are other groups equally averse to bilingual education, and for similar reasons. These are the immigrants who had regarded Montreal as a North American city and had not wanted to be hindered from moving to other Canadian cities for better jobs. As with their cousins in Toronto, they found it only natural to send their children to English-speaking schools, thereby integrating them into Montreal's Anglo community and eventually sharing its privileges and prestige. In this way they achieved both vertical and horizontal mobility.

For the French-speaking élite, especially in the less anonymous small cities of Quebec, these two highly mobile sociolinguistic classes represented a threat both to the stability of the community and to the survival of its language. For the French-speaking élite of professional and local entrepreneurs had been more stable, not only because of the restricted area covered by its language but also because of the nature of its professions, the success of which depended on personal relationship with local clients and regional clientele. Contrariwise, their mobile English-speaking social counterparts were of a different kind. The typical one was a hired manager, dependent on others and, if a newcomer, of uncertain social background. In a community where independence of income and family tradition were held in very high esteem such persons could not aspire to the highest status. In fact the English-speaking managerial class in Quebec did not enter the social circles of the French-Canadian traditional élite. And the Quebec professional élite had little in common with the English-speaking managerial class; they rarely sent their children to English schools. Yet most members of this élite were usually quite at ease in English, for second-language ability in Montreal had long been directly proportional to the number of years of schooling for Francophones, while for the English-speaking population it was inversely proportional. The lower the education level of the families, the less the mobility and the longer the contact with French-speaking workers, giving a type of French which was not the same as that taught in the English high-schools.

B Types of language and dialect

Willingness of one language group in a community to have its children adopt the language of the other group will depend on its estimate, not only of the national or international status of their language, but also of how close the local dialect comes to the parents' idea of the standard. If the local variety of a language—even one of great international prestige—is considered to be dialectal or impure, it may be rejected as a medium of instruction. Many English-speaking communities in Canada rejected the teaching of Canadian French because of a belief that it was dialectal. Since they had been acquainted with only a single language, Canadian English—one of unusual regional and social uniformity—they failed to realize that French, like most of the world's standard languages, was an abstract of regional and social dialects, and that Canadian French contained ranges from the professional accents of radio announcers to the dynamic *joual* of unskilled workers. It is not the linguistic facts, but rather the language attitudes of the parents which comprise the critical criteria. These attitudes may be affected by the availability in bilingual communities of radio and television channels using different languages.

C Attitudes of the population

In implementing a bilingual education policy, local school administrators may not use the same criteria as did the policy makers. The latter may have acted on a criterion of national survival of the language or some other nationwide objective. The administrators, however, being more interested in the fate of the child than in the future of the language, might have limited themselves to the use of educational criteria. This has led to conflict between the government and the educators.

In such cases, the issue may well split the population. Although a majority of people may favour the retention of a national language, they may oppose it being forced upon their children as a medium of instruction; the appearance of the Language Freedom Movement demonstrated this in Ireland, where many parents insisted on the right of the individual to choose between Gaelic and English as the language of instruction. On the other hand, the population may strongly oppose the granting of such freedom. Witness, for example, the demonstration in 1968 of the *Mouvement pour l'intégration scolaire* in Montreal and the vigorous opposition of the French-speaking population of Quebec to a bill (Bill 63) granting parents the freedom to choose the language in which their children should be instructed (Egretaud, 1970). Thus there has been, in both cases, the force of attraction of a powerful language (English) which could only be diverted, in Ireland and in Quebec, by government edict.

Even the threat of bilingualism may split an otherwise peaceful and congenial town where ethnic relations may have been ideal. In 1971, the trilingual town of Bonnyville, Alberta (English, French and Ukrainian speakers), split into opposing factions after the ethnic French minority of about 40% discovered that the town might be given official recognition as a federal bilingual district.

The success or failure of a programme of bilingual education depends enormously on public enthusiasm and support. In Texas, for example, the presence of this feature in Laredo and the lack of it in San Antonio may have been the cause of the success of the former and the failure of the latter in launching successful bilingual education programmes (Andersson, 1972).

In estimating the effects of public attitudes on the creation of bilingual schools, one must know whether the event is likely to split or unite the community along lines of ethnic versus national, or to divide one generation against the other; whether the support is total or partial or conditional, being the result of general consensus or ethnic concession; whether the local dialect has a high and desirable status or a low and tolerated one; and what the motivation of local authorities really is.

D Motives of the parents

In the last analysis, it will be the motives of parents who send their children to the bilingual school that may be decisive. The motives may be economic, in the sense that a better language means better education means better jobs. In North America, this had long meant English—even in French Canada. But after the Quiet Revolution in Quebec, French became more attractive to English-speaking parents. In the past, the law may have forced parents who wanted to be religiously right in their choice of schools to be at the same time ethnically wrong, or vice versa. As a result of the Quiet Revolution, Quebec began to make the English minority feel like one. There was then pressure from the parents for bilingual education for their children. How they succeeded in the context of modern Montreal would make an excellent case study (Mallea, 1977).

It is true a small minority of English-speaking Catholics in small Quebec towns had sent their children to French (Catholic) rather than English (Protestant) schools; but that was only for a few years, that is "long enough to learn some French". As religious importance decreased ethnic identity dominated; and at a time when government began exercising more and more control over society, and the social environment of each community.

IV Environmental determinants: a case study

The community being the real locus for the application of a bilingual education policy, it constitutes the environment with and within which most interaction takes place. This environment changes—sometimes slowly, sometimes quickly. To understand these changes as they affect the planning of bilingual education, it is useful to construct drift models of language communities. The direction of the drift may be towards a greater and greater use of one of the languages—from incipient to progressive bilingualism; or to a decline in the use of the home language—from regressive to residual bilingualism. There is nothing deterministic, however, about such drift. A strong language policy or a change in the demographic structure of an adjacent community may modify a situation of *laissez-faire* language transfer to one of controlled language maintenance.

By way of example, consider again the evolution of the linguistic situation in the Montreal Urban Community in the half-century preceding the year 1975 and the relationship among the three main ethnic groups, French, English and immigrant. The movement of population into the urban community of Montreal built up the sort of interethnic tensions that lead to open conflict. Montreal is a good example of how interlingual tensions can build up over the years. A city of two and a half million, about 70% French-speaking, it already had by mid-century one of the largest segregated school systems in North America. To illustrate the social implication of bilingual education, let us examine the linguistic evolution of this city and the fate of attempts to solve through education its main language problems.

The sociolinguistic patterns of this urban community were the results of changes that had built up over more than half a century, from a time when the linguistic distribution had been that of a predominantly rural French-speaking majority, as against a large urban English-speaking population. At the turn of the century, the French-speaking population of Quebec was twice as rural as it was urban, whereas English speakers were more urban than rural by a ratio of three to two—and Montreal was their citadel. The two populations coexisted fairly peacefully in two worlds well separated by language, culture, religion and area.

The bulk of the French-speaking population lived in small towns, villages or on farms clustered around a parish church. The parish was not only a place but an institution and its head, the curé, had close ties with each member, especially through the head of the family who was generally a farmer, artisan or professional man—all self-employed and of modest but independent income. Each was responsible for both the welfare and the historic continuity of his family and hoped to hand over his farm, trade, or clientele to one of his sons—most often to only one son, especially if it were a landed family, since the type of farm constituted a single, largely self-sufficient, and indivisible economic unit. All the other children—and there were many—had to find careers elsewhere. If the family could afford to educate them, some of these children might end up as professionals, priests, nuns or trades people.

The family head paid for the education of his children himself and it was the family who would have the honour of producing a professional man. There was no question of a boy working his way through college as was common in North America. If he could afford it, the head of the family sent the girls to be educated in a convent—not in a public high-school. In fact, the rural French-speaking family head was distrustful of all public expenditures—even for education. He preferred to be frugal and independent, and to pay for things himself.

His English-speaking counterpart was quite different, preferring business to farming and starting modern business enterprises in the towns, forming companies and corporations to promote industrial expansion, in sum, doing what all other English-speaking North Americans were doing at the time and sharing their culture, their attitudes and beliefs. In addition to this, the English-speaking Quebecer was generally Protestant, believed in change, and had fewer children. He more often than not lived in a town, and dominated its economy—and that included the city of Montreal where he occupied all levels from that of the factory worker to that of the executive.

The city, however, began absorbing more and more French speakers, as the many farmless children of the rural areas drifted into the towns, and from there to the rapidly industrializing metropolis. The trend was accelerated by the continent-wide phenomenon of urbanization whereby the farming population was greatly reduced, as it was elsewhere, in favour of urban living. By mid-century, with only 10% of the population still living on the farms, the population drift had created in Montreal a mass French-speaking population of unskilled workers having entered the city at the base of the socio-economic pyramid, thus permitting the more experienced English-speaking industrial workers to become specialized; by this time, three quarters of the entire English-speaking population was living in Montreal and English-speaking business people already occupied the upper half of the economic pyramid. They had become the metropolitan element of Canada's metropolis from which they operated vast economic enterprises extending beyond the borders of Canada. This population dominated in all areas where capital counted; it controlled merchandizing, the wholesale trade, big business, and the executive suite. On the other hand, the French-speaking population constituted the city's majority in the professions, small business and the labour force.

Although a numerical minority, the English-speaking population controlled almost 90% of the city's wealth, including all the large corporations—some three hundred in number. This, of course, did not exclude their presence in all sectors of society. As a professional man, however, the English-speaking Montrealer was more likely to be a specialist. As a group, English-speaking Montrealers were business-oriented. They rarely spoke in public on local political issues, leaving politics to the French. Indeed, while Quebec business belonged to the English, Quebec politics belonged to the French.

The French-speaking population of Montreal gave more prestige to intellectual and artistic accomplishments than did their English counterparts. They developed a greater urbanity in Montreal, which quickly developed into the secular centre of French Canada, with a highly sophisticated French-speaking élite. This included intellectuals, professional men, lawyers, writers and artists.

Although they constituted a numerical majority, with a cultural élite, the French-speaking population of Montreal had really minority status, in the sense that they did not control the forces which decided their fate. For it is the fate of minorities to have changes foisted upon them by aliens; so Montreal became the staging area for the acculturation of French Canada. It was from there that French-Canadian entrepreneurs and promoters carried such dubious blessings as bingo, the beauty contest, and the junior chamber of commerce—to name only these—to the towns and villages of Quebec.

But what was more profoundly disturbing to the traditional French culture of Quebec was the introduction by the English of new forms of enterprise and the extremest stage of industrialism which threatened the traditional way of life and invalidated the aims and content of French-Canadian education. By 1960, these evolving forces had developed all the internal conflicts of a major revolution. Surprisingly, it was a fairly quiet one, and its basic elements were succinctly stated as follows:

> Revolutions thrive on contradictions and the Quiet Revolution is filled with contradictions. The French are a majority in Quebec and a minority in North America; the English are a minority in Quebec and a majority outside. The French have political power in the Province; the English have economic power. Cultural and explicit ties are strengthened with France; economic and implicit ties bind Quebec more closely with Ottawa and New York. A language and culture must be preserved; the birth rate is declining, urbanization increasing, social and geographic mobility becoming typical, and immigrants to Quebec are being assimilated into the English culture. An organic culture and value structure are being replaced by a machine model of North American economic and social development; elsewhere this model is being challenged by the effects of new media, by countercultures, and by new forms of consciousness.

> Henchey, 1972, p. 96

In the sixties there came a sudden realization among the French of Montreal that they had been swept into the very life against which their leaders had always preached and that they themselves had been condemning the modern economic world while working hard to advance in it. The resolution of these conflicts came about in a fundamental shift in the goals, conduct and style of Quebec society which became known as the Quiet Revolution. By 1970 there was hardly an institution left in Quebec which had not undergone a fundamental change—politics, government, education, and the Church. In the process, the French-speaking majority had learned how through political power it could control its own fate. It accepted and often insisted on government intervention, even in the control of language usage, pointing out that whereas only 6% of English speakers found difficulty in working only in English, 46% of the French speakers found it difficult to work in French in their own city.

As the French population assumed the posture of a majority, the formerly dominant English-speaking population took on the protective behaviour of a minority, defending rights which had never before been questioned. They also saw the need to adapt to the new distribution of language power, as French-dominated political forces of society took precedence over the English-dominated economic forces.

This adaptation was reflected in the desire of parents to provide for their children an assurance that they would be able to work in French. As a result, from the mid-sixties, pressures were put by parents organizations on their almost autonomous English-speaking school council in an effort to create schools in which teaching would be done exclusively in French.

Meanwhile, half a continent away, similar French-medium schools were also being organized—but for a different clientele and for a different reason. Here the French-speaking urban minority of the Winnipeg area was attempting to promote the survival of their language through the schools in an area dominated by English, and one in which French speakers constituted only 6% of the over-all population. But the degree to which the French-speaking parents, when put to the choice, were willing to commit their children to a French education in an English-speaking area varied so much that four types of schools had to be recognized to permit a range from almost unilingual irredentism to unilingual assimilation (Mackey, 1981a). The change which made possible the creation of such schools was the creation by the federal government of official minorities, English and French, on a national basis, and the recognition by the Manitoba government, after a century of struggle by their French-speaking minority for language rights in matters of education. Not all members of the French-speaking minority, however, reacted in the same way to these changes in the political environment. Although many were willing to adopt an educational formula that would give the optimal guarantees for the survival of the language, some were unwilling to compromise the future of their children in an English-speaking world, and still others were willing to split the risks. In this context, an official policy was forged (Mackey, 1979a).

Changes in the political climate of Montreal were of a different nature and affected not a numerically small minority but one twenty times the size of Winnipeg's French minority population. Moreover, the Montreal minority was not French but English and it had long enjoyed majority status in a metropolis whose great industrial and financial institutions it controlled. This status began to diminish, however, as Quebec's Quiet Revolution placed the innovation initiative in the hands of a new and secular class of French-speaking progressives. As the men, and especially the women, of English-speaking Montreal found themselves surrounded by social and cultural changes instituted with the support of a French-speaking political majority over which they had no control, they began to realize the implications of living in a new sociolinguistic environment in which the initiative for change and innovation had passed into the hands of a new French-speaking urban élite. In this new climate, the more settled English-speaking population of this cosmopolitan city, feeling that it was now a minority in function as well as in number, realized that a continuation of the linguistic isolation of the past would only reinforce its minority status and work to its own disadvantage and especially to that of its children. Prevented from sending these children to French schools, which were entirely Catholic, it was led to organizing bilingual education in its own schools and with its own resources. The pressure for the creation of bilingual schools came directly from the parents, who, after several years of planning, succeeded in convincing a reluctant administration to start experimental classes in which all instruction was given, not in English, the language of the home, but in French, the language of the majority. The first experimental classes—called "immersion" classes—were started in kindergarten and continued with the first class as it progressed through the primary school years. The innovation was handled as a fully fledged psycholinguistic experiment, with testing and evaluation by an outside body (Lambert and Tucker, 1972).

As evidence mounted that education through the French language of children from English-speaking homes was neither mentally retarding nor academically harmful, more and more parents began to organize similar immersion classes. Those with children who had already completed a number of years of schooling, however, did not want their sons and daughters to be entirely deprived of the reported advantages of bilingual education, and they conceived the idea that a complete home-school language switch could be attempted in any grade; on this notion programmes called "Grade-Four immersion" and "Grade-Seven immersion" were instituted. These were later used as what became known as a "booster year", the function of which was to permit pupils to join a continuing immersion programme the following year. By secondary school, the proportion of instruction in French was reduced by less than half and the programme became known as "post-immersion" or "secondary immersion".

In the space of a few years, these various types of monoethnic bilingual schools—all voluntary and locally initiated—had proliferated to such an extent that by 1973, they comprised 10% of the school population under the jurisdiction of Montreal's English Protestant School Board (Mackey, 1978). It was indicative of the two solitudes, however, that not one of these schools was designed to include Quebec-French speakers, although a few of them did include pupils from French-speaking Protestant, Muslim, and Jewish families. The schools remained essentially segregated English-Protestant organizations: the difference was that some of them were operating entirely in French. Being voluntary, however, not all parents in any given school wished their children to be instructed in a language other than that of the home, so that the recruits for immersion classes had often to shift schools as well as language. This posed administrative problems the solution of which resulted in a system of "feeder schools" for the immersion classes.

As the English-speaking minority was initiating bilingual schooling through voluntary participation, the French-speaking majority proceeded to impose it through government edict. In 1968, the Ministry of Education published a regulation (Regulation 6) whereby English-speaking schools would henceforth be required to do part of their teaching in the French language (Article 4) (Ministère de l'Education, 1971). The effect was to accelerate the proliferation of various types of immersion programmes to such an extent as to give pauses to the authorities. It was therefore decided that any proposed programme be approved and tested before being authorized, thus slowing down the application of the new regulation.

After experimenting with different dosages of the language at different years, two formulas became more or less standard. One of them, called "primary immersion", started at kindergarten entirely in French, gradually introducing a little more English year after year until the proportion became stabilized in mid-primary school at 60% English and 40% French. The other basic formula, called "secondary immersion", or "Grade-Seven immersion" or both, started with a booster year, most often the first year of secondary school, in which almost 100% of the teaching would be done in French, to be followed, the next year, by the same proportion of French (40%) as that included in the continuing programme of primary immersion. This part of the programme which covered the remaining years of secondary school became known as "post-immersion". In addition, the regular programme, from Grade One up, had long included at least 20% of French in each year.

These patterns, it should be noted, like the ones which evolved in Winnipeg, were the results of the adaptation of a language community to changes in its environment. Just as organisms tend to select from their environment the most favourable circumstances for the survival of their species, human adults tend to seek for their young the training best suited to cope with their surroundings (Wilson, 1975). In a multilingual environment, this means the acquisition of the languages which provide the child with the best chances of success in later life. As the environment changes, the relative importance of the languages may also change. Yet since the educational system does not change or adapt at the same rate, some parents in an attempt to do what is best for their children will try to outwit the system as they long have in bilingually regulated cities like Brussels (Swing, 1980). They may, for example, take their children out of one school and put them in another, send them to another part of the country or move themselves to another part of town.

These moves are reflected in the school statistics, which are often interpreted in the abstract, and without taking into account this natural tendency of parents to seek the best training for their children. In Quebec, as we have seen, while the influence of the French-speaking majority increased through government control, some parents in the English-speaking minority group adapted to the change by attempting to have their children educated in French in special kindergarten and primary immersion classes. Knowing that their own inadequate high-school French had not enabled them to function in a French-speaking community and that they could not rely on the effectiveness of the second-language teaching programmes of their schools to give their children the bilingualism they needed to get ahead in Montreal, they decided on hiring French teachers to immerse their children in the second language from the very beginning. Yet they were not prepared to do so at the expense of the children's education in English, the dominant and most useful language in North America and still an important one in Montreal.

Like any group moving into a new area, they proceeded with caution, as a few innovators boldy sounded new ground—more and more of them making the move as word came back that it was a safe one. Educational innovation seems to follow this pattern of hesitant development in other bilingual societies (Mackay and Beebe, 1977). Some parents, however, with their future less committed to life in a French-speaking city, were unwilling to go all the way, so they transferred their children to regular English-language schools after a few years of this intense, early exposure to the French language. Since the number of such cases sometimes totalled a quarter of the enrolment in kindergarten and first-year immersion, the false impression was created that the system was unsuccessful and that parents were not satisfied, whereas studies of the achievement and attitudes of pupils and parents indicated the contrary. The English-speaking parents were simply trying to do what they thought best for their children in a changing sociolinguistic environment, as they have done elsewhere (Mackey and Ornstein, 1979). So were the French-speaking parents.

Intent on preserving French as the language of the home, that of the schools, and if possible the language of their work, many French-speaking parents nevertheless believed that in certain fields like business and industry a knowledge of English could be a great help. Equally unsatisfied with the achievement of the schools in second-language teaching as were their English-speaking opposite numbers, these parents planned and executed their own immersion programme for their children, by trying to transfer them to all-English schools for one or two years of intense exposure to the language at some point during their school career. For many of them, this seemed most easily achieved at the end of secondary school, and in fact many French-speaking families in Montreal used this juncture to send their children to an English business school. The switch, however, appeared in the school statistics as an increase in the transfer of French-speaking children from French to English-medium schools—and as a consequent threat to the linguistic integrity of the Francophone population—when in fact it was not a question of language disloyalty, but one of the concern and response of parents to the economic and sociolinguistic environment in which their children might have to work.

To the third group of Montrealers, who spoke neither French nor English at home—and there were many—both English and French appeared as necessary for a successful career. Many also insisted on maintaining the home language. In other words, their children would have to become trilingual. To achieve this threefold objective under the best possible environmental conditions a different language was used in the home, in the community and in the school. But which language would be the school language and which the neighbourhood language? Since their children would want to profit from job and educational opportunities in other parts of North America, the vast majority of speakers of other languages in Montreal sent their children to English-medium schools. But these families did not for that reason necessarily live in an English-speaking part of the city. On the contrary, almost a quarter of a million people living in the inner city of Montreal proper have neither English nor French as their mother tongue, and according to the 1971 census form almost 18% of its population, as against 15% English and 67% French. There are also third-language concentrations in Montreal North and St-Léonard, where they make up almost 32% of the population, outnumbering the English 5 to 1 but being themselves outnumbered 2 to 1 by the French. They tended therefore to inhabit French-speaking areas and often to become part of the French-speaking community, where their children learned a spoken French which blended well with that of their environment. In the school statistics, however, this third-language population appeared as English-speaking, creating the impression that few of the third-language group took the pains to learn French. As a matter of fact, the sociolinguistic behaviour of third-language groups varied somewhat according to ethnic origin. Most Italians lived close to French-speaking neighbourhoods, where they learned French; but they sent their children to the Catholic English-medium schools where their number in 1973 accounted for more than 18 000 (about 50%) of the entire English-Catholic enrolment, as against 2000 (about 1%) of the French-Catholic school population. This did not mean, however, that the population of most English-Catholic schools in Montreal was half Italian. Not at all. In fact the Italian population tended to congregate in a few schools some of which had an Italian home-language population of almost 100%, thus reinforcing the maintenance of the home language while undergoing formal school instruction in English. Such schools were too preoccupied with English as a second language to attempt experiments in French immersion. This explains why nearly all bilingual schools in Montreal were English and Protestant.

We have seen how three ethnic groups have adapted to sociolinguistic changes in their environment by creating new patterns of language distribution in the education of their children. This adaptation expressed itself in the school—indeed at the classroom level—where the feasibility of such new patterns generally meets its test.

V Concluding remarks

The adaptation of ethnic groups within a community to various types and degrees of language contact is difficult to predict. So many critical but unstable factors can combine to modify the sociolinguistic environment that it would be hazardous to make generalizations on what will determine what. That is why descriptive, quantitative and ecologically oriented case studies like that, briefly sketched here by way of example, for the Montreal community seem to give a better understanding of the complexity of the real-life contexts of bilingual education.

Such real-life case studies often reveal how the delicate balance within a community among ethnic attitudes, administrative requirements, general educational practice and the concern of parents for the future of their children may lead to compromises resulting in some type of bilingual schooling. Which school language is used for what subjects may depend on the relation between the social structure of the community and the distribution of its dialects. The options of a community for bilingual compromises may in turn depend on the extent to which control of education programmes is distributed between regional and national authorities. The implementation of the policy, however, no matter what the national priorities may be, can be hampered by economic and social forces within the country, the lack of educational facilities, the degree of literacy and, above all, by the languages themselves, their number, status, similarity and standardization. All this would seem to indicate that the social implications of bilingual education may severely limit the options of curriculum developers bent on applying isolated linguistic or psychological criteria to some abstract formula of bilingual schooling.

Note

1. Since linguists have no objective method of distinguishing between a dialect and a language, estimates of the number of languages in the world have varied widely—ranging from under 3000 to over 9000, depending in large part on how the dialects are classified. In 1929, the French Academy identified 2796 different languages; in 1931 Kieckers (*Die Sprachstämme der Erde*) counted more than 3000. Since then, the tendency has been to recognize more and more distinct languages. In the recent classification of the Voegelins there are some 9000.

References

Andersson, T. (1972). Bilingual education: The American experience. In *Bilingual Education: Some Experiences in Canada and the United States* (Ed M. Swain). Ontario Institute for Studies in Education, Toronto.

Egretaud, H. (1970). *L'Affaire Sainte-Léonard*. Société Education du Québec, Montréal.

Fishman, J. A. (1966). *Language Loyalty in the United States*. Mouton, The Hague.

Fishman, J. A. and Lovas, J. (1970). Bilingual education in sociolinguistic perspective. *TESOL Quarterly* 4, 215–222.

Haugen, E. (1966). Semicommunication: The language gap in Scandinavia. *Sociological Inquiry* 36, 280–297.

Henchey, N. (1972). Quebec education: The unfinished revolution. *McGill Journal of Education* 7, 95–118.

Kloss, H. and McConnell, G. (1978a). *Linguistic Composition of the Nations of the World* (Vol. 2, North America; Vol. 3, Central and South America). Presses de l'Université Laval, Québec.

Kloss, H. and McConnell, G. (1978b). *The World's Written Languages: A Survey and Analysis of their Degree and Modes of Use: Vol. 1, The Americas*. Presses de l'Université Laval, Québec.

Lambert, W. E. and Tucker, G. R. (1972). *Bilingual Education of Children: The St. Lambert Experiment*. Newbury House, Rowley, Massachusetts.

Le Page, R. B. (1968). Problems of description in multilingual communities. *Transactions of the Philological Society of Great Britain* 189–212.

Mackey, W. F. (1970). An interaction model of language learning, language teaching and language policy. In *Foreign Language Teaching* (Ed. L. A. Jakobovits). Newbury House, Rowley, Massachusetts.

Mackey, W. F. (1971). *La Distance Interlinguistique*. Centre International de Recherche sur le Bilinguisme, Laval University, Québec.

Mackey, W. F. (1973). *Three Concepts for Geolinguistics.* Centre International de Recherche sur le Bilinguisme, Laval University, Québec.

Mackey, W. F. (1976). *Bilinguisme et Contact des Langues.* Klincksieck, Paris.

Mackey, W. F. (1978). *Le Bilinguisme Canadien: Bibliographie Analytique et Guide du Chercheur.* Centre International de Recherche sur le Bilinguisme, Laval University, Québec.

Mackey, W. F. (1979a). Prolegomena to language policy analysis. *Word* **30**, 5–14.

Mackey, W. F. (1979b). Distance interlinguistique et interintelligibilité des langues. *Innsbrucker Beitrage Zur Sprachwissenschaft* 691–695.

Mackey, W. F. (1981a). Safeguarding language in school: The effects of mixed French/English schools—assimilation or bilingualism? *Language and Society* **4**, 10–14.

Mackey, W. F. (1981b). Urban language contact: Common issues in Brussels and abroad. *Taal en Sociale Integratie* **3**, 19–37.

Mackey, W. F. (1982a). Intégration, interférence et interlangue: Rapports entre bilinguisme et didactique des langues. *Langues et Linguistique* **8**, 45–64.

Mackey, W. F. (1982b). *International Bibliography on Bilingualism: With an Analytic Index to 19,030 Titles.* Presses de l'Université Laval, Québec.

Mackey, W. F. and Beebe, V. N. (1977). *Bilingual Education in Binational School: Miami's Adaptation to the Cuban Refugees.* Newbury House, Rowley, Massachusetts.

Mackey, W. F. and Ornstein, J. (Eds) (1979). *Sociolinguistic Studies in Language Contact: Methods and Cases.* Mouton, The Hague.

Mackey, W. F. and Verdoodt, A. (Eds) (1975). *The Multinational Society.* Newbury House, Rowley, Massachusetts.

MacKay, J. *et al.* (1961). *L'Ecole Laïque.* Editions du Jour, Montréal.

Mallea, J. (1977). *Quebec's Language Policy: Background and Response.* Presses de l'Université Laval, Québec.

Ministere de L'Education (1971). *Le Règlement Numéro 6.* Bulletin du Ministère de L'Éducation du Québec, 1/3.

Packard, V. (1972). *A Nation of Strangers.* McKay, New York.

Swing, E. S. (1980). *Bilingualism and Language Segregation in the Schools of Brussels.* Centre International de Recherche sur le Bilinguisme, Laval University, Québec.

Unesco (1973). *Linguistic and Cultural Diversity.* Canadian National Commission for Unesco, Ottawa.

Wilson, E. O. (1975). *Sociobiology: The New Synthesis.* Harvard University Press, Cambridge, Massachusetts.

Wolff, H. (1959). Intelligibility and interethnic attitudes. *Anthropological Linguistics* **1**(3), 34–41.

7

More than tongue can tell: linguistic factors in ethnic separatism[1]

Colin H. Williams

Introduction

One of the main difficulties in accounting for the linguistic component of many ethnic separatist movements is the very wide variation in the character and scope of such movements. Even by limiting our analysis to separatism within the advanced industrial state we are still faced with the dual problem that the forces which promote separatism affect states in very different international positions, and that the domestic strength of such states can alter, sometimes quite rapidly, making prediction in this field a dubious and humbling task. It is nevertheless true that the most virulent manifestation of the contemporary ethnic revival is the widespread demand for autonomy, such that virtually all the constituent states of Western Europe are troubled in some degree or other by autonomist nationalism. My intent, in this chapter, is to examine the manner in which questions related to linguistic grievances are woven into the fabric of separatist rhetoric and action.

In many ways, separatist movements provide the classical paradigm of nationalism, for they desire the *de jure* independence and sovereignty of the unit on whose behalf they operate. For my argument it will be assumed that nationalism, both in general and in particular cases, is something contingent and historically recent and not, as nationalists themselves have argued, an expression of primordial identity. Local and regional loyalties are indeed historically common, but the belief that political boundaries should coincide

LINGUISTIC MINORITIES
ISBN 0-12-232760-8

with such identities, and that they divide up the world in a mutually exclusive and exhaustive fashion is recent, and very far from the realities of many parts of the world. The national construction of social identity is a complex phenomenon, and we should be wary, right from the outset of our discussion, of collapsing such intricacies into standard questions relating to the operation of broad categories, transcendental structures, modes of production and cultural reproduction, social formations and the like. Too often we reify the very substance which makes ethnic separatism such an enigmatic subject.

Theorizing about separatism might proceed in several ways. One is to ask what factors precondition the general emergence of secessionist movements in such diverse contexts as Corsica, Euskadi (Basque region), Québec and Wales. A second is to ask what motivates some members of certain territorially discrete ethnic groups to attempt to leave the states of which they are a part, whereas other members and groups, also regionally concentrated, make no such attempt. Horowitz (1981) has cautioned that as the former question calls for a general explanation of aggregate trends, it aims to compare the present with some period in the past. The second question, by contrast, calls for an explanation that can discriminate among individuals and classes of cases, and thus it entails comparison not across time but across space.

As a general guide to the analysis of linguistic factors relating to separatism, I propose the following agenda. The theory we seek must account for:

1. the preconditions of separatism, namely the factors which are necessary (but not necessarily sufficient) for the beginnings of separatist alienation;
2. the bases of separateness, namely the materials of distinctiveness and uniqueness;
3. the rise of separatist movements and the effectiveness of their attempts to achieve the goal of sovereign independence;
4. the response of central governments and the effectiveness of their attempts to prevent secession and maintain the integrity of their states;
5. the direct precipitants of separatism, in the form of confrontational developments and conflict issues;
6. the likelihood of success, with reference to both domestic and international factors affecting outcomes.

(Orridge and Williams, 1982; Wood, 1981).

Preliminary distinctions

For heuristic purposes nationalism may be divided into three broad categories. *State Nationalism* is manifested by groups close to the centre of well-established states. Culture and state will have developed hand in hand over many centuries and be mutually reinforcing. The population of smaller old-established states may be almost entirely composed of groups whose national identity is of this sort, such as the Netherlands, Denmark and Sweden, but in larger states these groups will be preponderant rather than all-encompassing, as with the English in the United Kingdom, or the French in France. *Unification Nationalism* and *Irredentism* may be defined as attempts to unite culturally similar groups and territories into a larger and more powerful state. In the case of irredentism a fragment is not politically independent and must be detached from an already existing and culturally alien state. Common culture precedes political structure in these sorts of nationalisms and their political embodiments are typically a mixture of parties or movements and the state of one of the more important and politically dynamic fragments, such as Prussia or Piedmont. *Autonomist Nationalism* or *Separatism* is my primary concern. It has certain similarities with irredentism, for in this type also a part of a larger state rejects the state and claims to belong to a separate national group, but in this case it claims to be the core of a nationality, not a detached fragment. I shall treat the difference between autonomist nationalism and separatism as a matter of degree for movements can move rapidly from one to the other.

Despite the apparent ease with which we have identified clear differences in types of nationalism, we should be wary, for many citizens of advanced industrial states express a dual nationality. That is, they often possess two types of loyalty which the literature often fails to distinguish. The historical circumstances surrounding usage are critical here. As we shall see below, before the rise of the bureaucratic state in Europe, nation and nationalism were not widely used terms (Smith, 1981). They are now legitimized in terms of loyalty to the state. Given successful political socialization, threats to the integrity of the state become threats to the nation. In these circumstances nationalism is in effect statism, as in the contemporary USA. Separatism and sectionalism are internal threats to the state and its integrity (Williams, 1982c). They may be anarchic or disintegrative rather than statist in character, but they are, in common terminology, regional scale rather than state scale in focus, and hence threaten the state and its nationalism. In essence the tendency in the sociolinguistic literature to switch from discussions of French or British nationalism to Corsican or Scottish nationalism involves a terminological confusion that betrays a lack of interest in differentiating meaning and causes of nationalism at different scales and at different epochs (Orridge and Williams, 1982). Typically such instances of dual nationality (e.g. Welsh and British) are treated as conflicting rather than as harmonious identities. In terms of the dominant functionalist approach to nationalism the persistence of minority identities in multinational societies represents a barrier to social progress and economic development. During the period of state-building the position of the political majority and its satellite minorities becomes articulated most often within a dependency relationship. In common with other social cleavages, that between majority and minority is conceptualized as a "strain" within the social and political system. Hence the emergence of minority nationalist movements within an established state speaks of wider social tensions within the existing order. Social friction is reproduced at the level of the individual citizen as psychological strain, produced by the inability of the personality system to cope with the demands of both the established state value system and the dissenting challenges which issue from the mobilized nationalist intelligentsia.

In such a context, nationalist resurgence, like any other manifestation of social protest against the state, is treated as a form of cultural disorder. It is seen to represent a patterned response to social strain, economic decline, instability, and emotional uncertainty. What is absent in such an approach to the analysis of political change is the explanation of the link between stimulus and response, between structural change and cultural effect. Strain theory provides a promise of precision in the identification of the structural origins of the social grievances which fuel nationalist discontent. But it is far less effective in explaining the meaning of such grievances for those who express social concern, and for accounting for the consequences of discontent.

The key problem with the epistemological framework we have inherited from earlier theory, especially modernization theory, is its deterministic assumptions underlying the diffusion of nationalism. We are beginning to realize that nationalism does not develop automatically, nor does it develop in isolation. It develops and is *created* in response to certain social and economic structures, but even within the confines of these structures, nationalism is not the sole nor often the most attractive response. As Rawkins (1979) cautioned, there is no inevitability that a given set of cultural factors, psychological dispositions or economic inequities will produce a politics of group conflict, based on ethnic differences, and legitimized by nationalist ideology.

With these caveats in mind let us now examine the manner in which the states of Western Europe have attempted to make the state and nation co-extensive territorial and psychological entities and thereby identify those areas most prone to separatist incursions.

The state development process

Political development when considered coincident with state-building, often involves the institutionalized denial of minority group rights in such spheres as language maintenance, education, religious liberty, the franchise, and employment opportunities. In the past the internal conception of separateness which many ethnic groups professed was often crystallized by their external stigmatization at the hands of state agencies and powerful private institutions such as the Church or Universities. Discrimination within the private sector was often imitated in the public sector. This trend accelerated in post-Enlightenment Europe when state-building came to be associated with modernization, progress and civilization. For a variety of reasons, some strategic, others related to conceptions of morality or the common good, state-building involved the subordination of "primordial" ties of language, religion and land to the allegedly more rational, and therefore more acceptable, class-based relationships which characterize modern polities. In such a perspective, shaped by the implicit Marxism of so many Western intellectuals, such differences (of language, ethnie etc.) were either irrational and not to be taken seriously, or a disguised attempt by the oppressor class to justify continuing oppression by deflecting conflict away from the "true" bases of social organization (viz. the ownership of the means of production, land, resources and capital) to a spurious and mystifying "cultural" conflict. A society, it was reasoned, divided along class lines and along lines of essentially economic political issues was an acceptable society, but there was to be no room for divisions on issues that were ethnic, particularistic and personal. Consequently the chief goal of state-building was to produce a united citizenry out of a disparate multinational populace. In essence this process could be summarized as the successive resolution of a series of crises through time (Binder, 1971; Young, 1976; Williams, 1980):

1. *Identity:* the extension of an active sense of membership in the national state community to the entire populace; in essence this is the issue of making state and nation coterminous.
2. *Legitimacy:* securing a generalized acceptance of the rightness of the exercise and structure of authority by the state so that its routine regulations and acts obtain compliance.
3. *Participation:* the enlargement of the numbers of persons actively involved in the political arena, through such devices as voting for parties and extending involvement ideally to the entire polity.
4. *Distribution:* ensuring that the valued resources in society such as material well-being and status are available on equal terms to all persons regardless of creed, colour or language and that the redistributive policies inhibit the heavy concentration of wealth in a few hands or in a specific region.
5. *Penetration:* extending the effective operation of the state to the farthest periphery of the system.

In combination, this development syndrome is a far-reaching normative statement of the role of the nation-state which has obvious implications for those minorities who perceive the existing state system as a threat to their group distinctiveness and solidarity. In multi-ethnic polities ethnic separatism often takes the form of a reactive response to the erosion of a minority's identity, a claim that ethnic discrimination can only be halted through the separation of the minority territory to form a sovereign state co-equal with other nation-states.

Preconditions of separatism

Under what circumstances can élites cause part of a population of a state to believe that it is a potential independent nation? First, there must be some *core territory* in which the group is concentrated and is sufficiently high a proportion of the total population for the region to be seen as a national homeland. The élites of a potential autonomist nationalism argue that the group occupies the core of a possible national state and this argument will carry little weight if most of the inhabitants will clearly never express attachment to the putative nation.

Secondly there must be one or more characteristics that provide the basis for separateness and community in the potential nationality. I shall call these *bases of community* for they provide that cultural infrastructure which is a distinctive feature of ethnic separatism. Language, clearly the most frequent basis of community in Europe, and religion, important in certain cases, are perhaps the most appropriate. Economic divisions, on the other hand, often fail to meet both criteria, that of regional concentration and of cultural infrastructure, whether they be class divisions or differences between regional economies. In general, economic divisions act as reinforcements for characteristics such as language and religion in defining nationalities, not as substitutes for them. In part this may be because linguistically or religiously defined communities share certain features of a pre-existent status group in Weber's sense (Weber, 1968). Unlike class-defined groups they necessarily carry some awareness of their common existence because they are elements of a life style. This is not to deny that nationalist élites often have to devote much effort to convert regional dialects into a national language, and transform parochial loyalties into a wider sense of identity. It need hardly be stressed that these bases of community are not "givens" which of themselves create a widespread sense of common identity.

A third structural precondition is to some extent a deduction from the first two. If there are sizeable groups in the territory which are closely associated with the dominant power, they should either be concentrated at the top of the social hierarchy, especially in political administration or land ownership, or, if they spread further down the social structure than this, they should themselves be regionally concentrated (e.g. the Protestants in Ulster or the Germans in the Sudetenland of Bohemia). In the first case, they can then seem dispensable; in the second case, despite their numbers, they still leave a substantial territory in which the autonomist nationality can feel itself to be overwhelmingly in the majority.

These structural preconditions, a core territory, bases of community and opposition groups, locate those areas vulnerable to autonomist nationalism, the places where it is a possibility (not the actual cases). But they say nothing about the circumstances or the period in which they may be converted into autonomist nationalism. These matters will be explored below. Let us now turn to the bases of separateness, those features which evoke an awareness of a common identity amongst a people.

Bases of separatism

Ethnic separatism rests its case on the cultural distinctiveness of the community pressing for independence. Frequently, but not necessarily, there are "renewal movements" seeking to recover the cultural identity of a formally independent unit. For nationalist leaders imbued with the uniqueness of their destiny, the incorporation of their group into a multinational state is inherently contrary to nature and a severe impediment to the full realization of that group's developmental potential. As Smith (1979, p. 22) has demonstrated:

> . . . the watchwords of ethnic separatism are identity, authenticity and diversity . . . it seeks through separation the restoration of a degraded community to its rightful status and dignity, yet it also sees in the status of a separate political existence the goal of that restoration and the social embodiment of that dignity.

It follows that for independence to be achieved the primary requirement is to translate the goal of separate ethnic identity into a political ideology which will animate a movement for national freedom. The remarkable feature of many contemporary separatist movements is their ability to combine ethnic and territorial-based grievances so that the movement itself appeals to a wider target group than would one based upon language preservation or religious freedom alone. For example, many of the current European movements are active in the ecology/anti-nuclear campaigns, and see themselves as the heralds of a new world. They identify themselves as the Fourth World, those subject peoples who have long been forgotten or dubbed regressive by the media of the modern state. Their appeal to community politics incorporates love for the land/environment of that community and they demand to garner their *own* produce from their *own* soil.

Ethnicity and territory are the key materials of separateness. Ethnic separatism is a powerful if somewhat vague sentiment. It incorporates descent as a basis of group and of individual status, and of spiritual confirmation. We need to know to whom else we belong, and ethnic separatism can thus provide a *myth of origin*. It can also provide an historic explanation for the tragic events of past conquest and subordination, and a rationale for group superiority achieved through the pain of suffering—a *myth of development*. Underlying all this are issues of isolation, self-sufficiency and the relative infrequency of sustained intercultural contact—a *myth of uniqueness*.

Cultural separateness reinforces the sense of unique descent and provides a "mission/destiny" view of historical development. It is reflected through three salient markers, the meanings of which can vary in different social settings. The first is group customs and institutions which serve as group boundaries, as modes of exclusion and as sustainers of special routines and distinctive procedures. A second is language, for not only is it a functional means of communication, but also an instrument for cultural division. Often, as we shall see, it provides the most tangible barrier to assimilation. The third is religion, a phenomenon which, like language, is capable both of uniting and dividing populations. A sense of separateness itself is insufficient, however, to generate the dynamism involved in nationalist struggles. The movement from communal consciousness to political action requires two further preconditions: (1) a perception of inequality in the distribution of, and competition for, resources and rewards, and (2) a political organization to articulate group demands along explicitly national lines.

Not all symbols of group identity are of equal value as mobilizing agents in separatism. Often, nationalists tend to emphasize one symbol above all others and strive to bring other symbols into congruence with it (Brass, 1974). I shall be arguing that in the cases covered here, language has been accorded primary group-defining significance. Why should this be so? The orthodox explanation is that, as language is a natural barrier separating cultural groups, language conflict is both inevitable and peculiarly unamenable to compromise. In multilingual societies differentiation as regards to language is unavoidable. In addition, the competing interest groups in language conflict are also communication groups. Since coalitions rarely form across communication barriers, this pattern reinforces the language divide, predisposing both parties to conflict rather than cooperation.

From separateness to separatism: the ethnic revival

The explanation above fails to take account of the larger structural changes which have affected European society and political organization. It is simply not good enough to impute to language a naturally divisive role. This model of language as a barrier to cross-cultural political cooperation between core and periphery might be feasible in some multilingual polities which are comprised of a number of *discrete unilingual regions*. It is less applicable to those cases where the ethnic élite, and a good proportion of the populace in minority areas, are functionally bilingual, and to those in which ethnic status does not necessarily act as a barrier to full participation in the political system of the state. In such circumstances it is more profitable to treat language as a political resource which can be used as a grievance factor to mobilize mass support for the separatist cause.

In order to provide a satisfactory account of language as a political resource we must look at its role within the wider social processes underpinning ethnic revival in advanced industrial states. From the Reformation to the Industrial Revolution, Europe underwent a number of transformations which, in combination, served to undermine the traditional socio-political structure of a universal Christian order. The most profound transformations were modernization, secularization and centralization (Gerhard, 1981; Wallerstein, 1974, 1979, 1980). Together these structural changes in the European economy and society challenged the previously dominant universal axioms derived from the Judaeo-Christian basis for law and behaviour. One alternative interpretation of the relationship between an individual and political authority was the particularistic conception of a nation, rooted in time and space, a link in the chain of human evolution. Burke provided a classical definition of a nation when he wrote, ". . . a nation is not an idea of local extent and individual momentary aggregation but it is an idea of continuity in time as well as in numbers and space . . . it is a constitution . . . made by the pecular circumstances, occasions, tempers, dispositions and moral, civil and social habitudes of the people which disclose themselves only in a long space of time." (Burke, 1782, quoted in Berry, 1981, p. 83.) Thus the identity of a nation is bound up with the individual and collective memory. For Burke, and others influenced by English common law, historical continuity was expressed primarily through legal and political institutions and this is clearly an important source of national identification for historically autonomous states such as Scotland, France and Sweden.

But for non-state peoples such as the Germans, Welsh, Slavs, Basques and other nationalities, this attempt to make nation and state coterminous is not possible. Accordingly they had to exploit another resource. The grounding of temporal value in political continuity being barred to them, they sought this ground and legitimacy in cultural continuity and collective memory (Berry, 1981). A prime element in this form of identity appeal is language. Fichte expressed the classic form of linguistic self-determination when he claimed, " . . . it is true beyond doubt that wherever a separate language is found there a separate nation exists which has the right to take independent charge of its affairs and to govern itself." (Fichte, 1968, p. 190.) He and Herder, in particular, link language to the wider cultural complex, the whole fabric of social existence. Two implications derive from this switch from universalism to specificity and temporality (Berry, 1981). The first is that this location of a nation's identity in temporally acquired customary behaviour gives to it an inclusivity; it is constitutive of co-nationals as members and welds together the principles of fraternity, equality and liberty under the banner of democracy. To use language and customs is precisely to render conceptually unacceptable an internal us/them division and to render alien and improper governors not possessing the same marks of culture or nationality as the governed. The second implication involves the rejection of the previously dominant modes of thought, individualism, rationalism and mechanism (Berry, 1981). To allot to custom and language a decisive role is to see this mechanical mode of thinking inappropriate. Language is not invented, nor is it a matter of choice. It is a gradual constitutive legacy, or in Herder's words, language and the nation are "natural organisms": ". . . a nation is as natural a plant as a family only with more branches. Nothing is more manifestly contrary to the purposes of political government than the unnatural enlargement of states, the wild mixing of various races and nationalities under one sceptre . . . such states are but patched up contraptions (*Zusammengeleimt*), fragile machines for they are wholly devoid of inner life." (Herder, in Barnard, 1969, p. 324.) The great transition in state-formation and nationality-formation which the age of nationalism ushered in is of tremendous import as a precedent for the use of language as the prime cultural marker in the definition of political territories. Though obviously not a complete process this attempt to co-relate nationality and statehood in the nineteenth century has provided the framework within which our more current concern with ethnic separatism may be set.

Emergent issues in ethnic separatism

The contemporary significance of language politicization may be summarized under six major topics—equality of status, state education, access to public services, public employment, territorial unilingualism and ethnic self-determination. Despite a now voluminous literature related to language and ethnic politicization there are no obvious solutions to these ethnic problems, thus proving the essential truth of Maine's dictum that "democracies are quite paralysed by the plea of nationality. There is no more effective way of attacking them than by admitting the right of the majority to govern, but denying that the majority so entitled is the particular majority which claims the right." (Maine, cited in Bogadnor, 1982, p. 291.)

A major thrust of language activists in the territories we shall be discussing has been the search for collective equality. For centuries, as a result of their political incorporation into dominant European states, national minorities in such places as Wales, Euskadi, Flanders, Brittany and elsewhere were legally barred from using their mother tongue in matters of state and public life. The last century has witnessed a sometimes tragic, sometimes heroic, struggle by linguistic minorities to achieve parity of status in a variety of socio-cultural and political domains. In the case studies which follow I want to examine the manner in which language-related grievances have been politicized in three quite different contexts: Wales, Euskadi and Québec.[2] It should be clear that although separatism has been central to the demands of certain interest groups in each of these countries there is no reason to assume: (a) the majority of the inhabitants of each territory desire political independence; (b) the majority of language activists necessarily endorse a separatist programme; (c) that separatism is the only avenue by which minorities may effect change in their political and economic situation. The truth of the matter is, as always, somewhat more complex than the convenient linking of linguistic grievances and ethnic separatism would imply. Nevertheless, there can be no doubt that without the central threat of political separation which nationalist parties in these countries pose, many of the linguistic and socio-political reforms of the past thirty years would not have been instituted. Let us turn then to an examination of the different styles of social change afforded by each of these case studies.

Wales

The fundamental principle of government in Wales has been its treatment as an incorporated territory of England. The basic demand of separatists has been a formal recognition of the separate nationhood of Wales. This is not a new source of tension but one of the most enduring conflicts in European history. The fact that it has not dominated English–Welsh relations over the centuries may be attributable to the incorporation of Welsh territory, customs and loyalties in the emerging English state in the sixteenth century. Conquered in the thirteenth century, Wales was not formally annexed by England until after the victory of the Tudor Prince Henry, at Bosworth Field. The basis of legal provision in Wales is the Tudor system of English

Minority areas
1 Scots
2 Welsh
3 Scotch–Irish(Protestant); Northern–Irish(Catholic)
4 Flemings
5 Walloons
6 Bretons
7 Alsatians
8 Corsicans
9 Basques
10 Catalans
11 Galicians
12 Jura Swiss
13 South Tyroleans
14 Sardinians
15 Sicilians

Selected ethnic minority areas is Europe.

law and administration consolidated in the reign of Henry VIII. The Act of Union in 1536 imposed English law upon Wales and the statute of 1542 applied the English county system of local administration to the Principality. The Act of Union, while acknowledging that "the people of (Wales) have and do daily use a speech nothing like nor consonant to the natural mother tongue used within this realm (of England)", went on to provide that the language of the courts should be English, and that "from henceforth no person or persons that use Welsh speech or language shall have or enjoy any manner office or fees within the realm of England, Wales or other of the King's dominions . . . unless he or they use English".

Although barred from ceremonial and formal life, Welsh continued to be used after 1536 in local legal and administrative matters, since the vast majority of the population were monoglot Welsh speakers. Its role was compartmentalized in the everyday functions of home, work, prayer and entertainment, a dominance which was greatly aided by the translation of the Bible in 1588 and the diffusion of a standard Welsh form thereby. There was little sustained criticism of this policy by the landed gentry since as a class they were effectively anglicized and institutionalized by the Tudor ascendancy—so much so, in fact, that the general view of the Act of Union and its subsequent legal pronouncements was one of a liberating, enfranchizing programme to bring to the élite of Wales all the benefits, both fiscal and political, of the developing English aristocracy.

In the past century, however, attempts have been made to disentangle Wales from English/British administration and allow various measures of separate but equal treatment, especially in cultural and educational matters.

This drive towards linguistic and cultural equality is often associated with the development of the Welsh Nationalist Party (Plaid Cymru). However, attempts to establish separate Welsh national institutions, and even Home Rule, pre-date the formation of Plaid Cymru by at least 50 years. It was the radical Liberal ascendancy of the 1880s which promoted the ideal of Welsh nationhood. Welsh departments were created in a number of UK ministries (e.g. Board of Education), a federal University of Wales was chartered in 1896 and in 1905 the Unionist government under Balfour sanctioned a National Library of Wales, to be established at Aberystwyth. The cultural awakening of the first decade of this century brought an immense surge of self-confidence, in spiritual as in political realms. The native language, which in the later years was to become a symbol of oppression and survival, seemed in 1910 more vigorous that ever before. The fact, as Morgan (1982) observes, that a smaller proportion of the people spoke Welsh did not arouse much concern at this time (49·9% in 1901; 43·5% (of whom 35% were bilingual) in 1911; Williams, 1980). The linguistic and literary dimensions had never been stronger. Further, the numbers of those who spoke their

TABLE 1
Welsh speakers by geographic county

| | Thousands / Census figures | | | | | | | | | | | | | | Percentages 1901–1971 Summation of inter-censal percentage changes |
| | 1901 | | 1911 | | 1921 | | 1931 | | 1951 | | 1961 | | 1971 | | |
	Welsh only (1)	Total (2)	Welsh only	Total	Welsh only	Total	Welsh only	Total	Welsh only	Total	Welsh only	Total	Welsh only	Total	
Anglesey	22·8	43·6	17·4	42·7	15·1	41·5	11·2	41·0	4·6	38·4	2·8	37·1	2·6	37·1	15·1
Breconshire	4·7	23·1	3·0	22·9	2·6	21·4	1·1	20·5	0·3	16·3	0·3	14·9	0·6	11·7	62·2
Caernarvonshire	56·0	105·3	42·1	101·2	32·7	93·7	24·9	91·9	10·6	85·1	5·8	79·9	5·1	73·1	35·2
Cardiganshire	29·1	53·6	19·5	51·1	15·2	47·6	10·6	46·3	3·8	40·6	2·4	38·5	2·0	35·8	31·8
Carmarthenshire	44·9	113·9	30·7	127·2	27·1	135·5	15·7	141·1	7·3	127·3	4·0	120·9	4·5	103·8	6·6
Denbighshire	22·4	75·6	13·6	76·9	12·4	70·6	8·1	73·1	3·7	62·5	2·2	57·9	3·2	49·6	39·2
Flintshire	5·7	37·3	2·9	36·5	2·3	32·8	1·0	34·1	0·4	29·1	0·4	27·2	1·4	24·4	39·7
Glamorgan	52·5	344·9	31·7	393·7	25·5	368·9	9·1	355·4	3·5	231·7	4·1	201·1	8·7	141·0	73·4
Merioneth	23·1	42·8	15·9	39·0	12·7	35·2	9·1	35·5	3·7	30·0	2·0	27·8	2·6	24·9	50·9
Monmouthshire	2·0	35·1	1·5	35·2	1·0	26·9	0·5	25·0	0·6	14·1	0·9	14·4	0·6	9·3	108·5
Montgomeryshire	8·0	24·3	5·4	22·4	4·3	20·4	3·2	18·8	1·4	15·3	0·6	13·6	0·5	11·6	69·3
Pembrokeshire	9·8	28·3	6·5	27·4	5·0	26·2	3·3	25·5	1·4	23·2	0·8	21·8	1·0	19·5	36·0
Radnorshire	0·1	1·4	0·0	1·1	0·1	1·4	0·0	1·0	0·0	0·9	0·6	0·8	0·0	0·7	61·2
Wales	280·9	929·8	190·3	977·4	156·0	922·1	97·9	909·3	41·2	714·7	26·2	656·0	32·7	542·4	48·7

(1) Persons aged 3 and over speaking Welsh only.
(2) All persons aged 3 and over speaking Welsh.
Primary source: Office of Population Census and Surveys.

native language were steadily increasing (Table 1). In 1911, the total reached 977 366; if Welsh emigrés to England were added, then the total of Welsh speakers would be over a million.

At the end of the First World War, with the decline of the Liberal strength nationwide and the rise of the Labour Party, socialism brought different types of Welsh actors to the forefront of the British political stage. No longer were the nation's heroes promoting disestablishment, Home Rule all round and the independent farmer, but rather they denounced international capitalism and emerged as the voice of protest and radical change in opposition to the Coalition government after the armistice, and the Conservative government that followed it. Profound economic and social change transformed industrial Wales, producing a Labour ascendancy which is with us yet. The details of this transformation are well known (see Morgan, 1982; Foot, 1962, 1973). Its implication for our study is that the Liberal decline left a partial vacuum which was filled by a Nationalist Party dedicated to the conservative task of defending both Welsh culture and Christian morality in a country undergoing depression and industrial conflict (Williams, 1982c). One of the prime considerations of Plaid Cymru, established in 1925, was the incorporation of Welsh into the machinery of local government as a mandatory language for bureaucracy, by making the Welsh language the only official language of Wales, and thus a language required for local authority transactions and mandatory of every official and servant of every local authority in Wales. Increased political and cultural pressure from a wide range of political movements within Wales after the Second World War brought the language issue into the mainstream of political debate, but it was still largely related to the problems of a rural, nonconformist hinterland. That is, until the development of a small but articulate body of language activists who sought the twin reforms of Welsh medium education and equal status for Welsh and English forced the attention of local government politicians. By and large, this concern was confined to the anglicized areas of the industrial south-east and north-east, and channelled through the Labour Party councillors who were sympathetic to the cause.

As a result of pressure from within the established political parties, and reaction to popular protest largely inspired by Plaid Cymru, the Conservative Government in 1963 established a Committee on the Legal Status of the Welsh Language chaired by Sir David Hughes Parry. The committee reported in 1965 and two years later the Welsh Language Act was passed.[3] Although the Act (with subsequent local interpretation) has assisted in the introduction of Welsh into hitherto unilingual domains (e.g. the supply of statutory forms and the judicial proceedings of Welsh courts), it has not kept pace with the growth of administrative law and the vast field of subordinate legislation (Williams, 1982a). Nevertheless the past two decades have seen the establishment of the principle of "equal validity" of Welsh and English in public life. More importantly this principle has become routine practice within the public administration. Welsh has moved from the realm of conflict politics to the compromise politics of administrative execution, with varying degrees of success. The net result of this campaign for equal validity, waged in a non-violent manner by a largely middle-class intelligentsia, is that Welsh administrative life is now more distinct from its English counterpart than at almost any other period in modern history.

Yet, the language census figures for each decennial count continued to show a decline (Table 1). Language activists declared that Welsh was facing a crisis and mobilized support in defence of it. Defence turned to attack, with the now familiar tactics of peaceful resistance, non-violent protest and more militant demonstrations in government and private offices throughout Wales and beyond. The tactics of the Welsh Language Society may be debatable, but its effect in mobilizing large segments of Welsh-speaking youth is not in doubt (Williams, 1977). By the mid-sixties "Welsh youth was now caught up emotionally in the heady rebellion of student youth all over Europe and North America. With the riotous students of Berkeley and Columbia, the Sorbonne and Nanterre, with the terrors of the mass bombings on North Vietnam and the heady days of freedom in Czechoslovakia, there was no shortage of idealistic causes to fire the imagination of students and school children in Wales. In truth, the Welsh language movement had virtually nothing in common with any of these overseas movements; but in so far as it inspired the young and seemed to appeal to a traditional folk culture in contrast to the shoddiness and false glamour of commercialized capitalism, it helped speed on militancy." (Morgan, 1982, p. 384.) Exposure to the outside world had strengthened rather than weakened the language cause and had shown that the Welsh problem was neither unique nor irrelevant; for the quest for peace, identity and community was the universal hallmark of the culture of protest in the advanced industrial state and only the details varied from place to place.

Education

The most tangible manifestation of the language revival has been the development of a Welsh-medium educational sector (Welsh Office, 1978). This is the one area where both élite and mass pressure have combined in an effective manner. Local authorities have responded to such pressure in the anglicized areas by establishing Welsh-medium junior and high schools (Table 2). Today there are thirteen formally designated Welsh-medium high schools, supported by a network of scores of primary schools and, most encouraging of all, close to four hundred nursery schools. In addition

TABLE 2
Designated bilingual secondary schools

Authority	School	Year of establishment and number of pupils		Pupils September 1978
Clwyd	Glan Clwyd	1956	94	1212
	Maes Garmon	1962	221	882
	Morgan Llwyd	1962	38	370
Dyfed	Bro Myrddin	1978	213	213
	Penweddig	1973	144	548
	Y Strade	1963	392	426
Gwent	——	——	——	——
Gwynned	Tryfan	1978	386	386
	Llandudno/ Colwyn Bay[a]	1981		
Mid Glamorgan	Cwm Rhymni[a]	1981		
	Llanhari	1974	146	1010
	Rhydfelen	1962	80	1107
Powys	——	——	——	——
South Glamorgan	Glantaf	1978	98	98
West Glamorgan	Ystalyfera	1969	323	1243
Wales	Thirteen schools	1956–1981	94	7495

[a]Both schools opened in September 1981.

students may take University and college-level subjects through the medium of Welsh at a number of national institutions. The education question, though not of course a direct product of separatist agitation, does nevertheless raise new sources of conflict in relation to Wales's two cultures. Opponents argued that separate Welsh-medium education was divisive, retrograde and irrelevant to a modern society. Proponents, who were often identified as ardent nationalists by their critics, countered such claims with the advantages of bilingualism and the very high academic attainment records of the initial bilingual students as proof of the scholastic merit of such education. Indeed, so successful were Welsh-medium schools in establishing both an academic and a community reputation in anglicized areas that they are now a conventional feature of state education. It is only within the primarily Welsh-speaking districts of the north and west that unilingual English opposition is still a real threat to the expansion of Welsh-medium education (Fig. 1). Thus although the initial struggle for legitimacy has finally been won by Welsh language supporters there are nevertheless other conflict issues which have arisen.

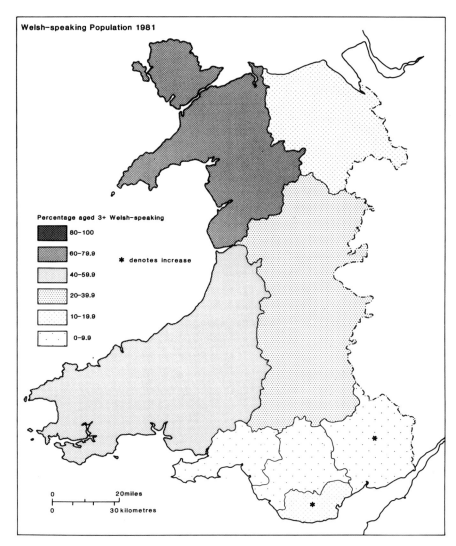

Fig. 1. Welsh-speaking population, 1981.

The widespread support for Welsh-medium education has now been tempered by a realization that, although the language of instruction is Welsh, the messages now conveyed in some schools tend to be middle-class and statist. Such schools are becoming more "normal" in a British context. This may be a disappointment for the earlier generation of language activists, but sociolinguists have long identified education as a crucial determinant of state socialization. Central to this process is the struggle for control over the agencies of cultural reproduction, since it is culture which serves as the medium for the institutionalization of power and inequality in language contact. Rather than being the basis for liberation and mobility, Glyn Williams (1980) reminds us that education can be seen as the basis for social control through its legitimizing ideological function. At a more general level, the development of Welsh-medium schools does lead to a value conflict over the role Welsh should play, between areas where Welsh is a "natural" language (and, paradoxically, where Welsh-medium education was resisted) and those areas where it is largely intrusive, and dependent on educational institutions.

The discussion so far has reflected the main source of conflict, namely the legitimacy of language promotion in Wales (Williams, 1982b). Educational reforms and the attendant institutionalization of para-public concerns (e.g. broadcasting, the legal system and public administration) all increase the effectiveness of Welsh as a functional language in new domains. However, while such developments are a major breakthrough they also bring their own related tensions which are often ignored by virtually all involved with Welsh language promotion. In previous generations, minority language communities strove for freedom *from* interference by state agencies. Today the institutionalization of Welsh is a reflection of current demands for freedom *to* govern, and be served, through Welsh wherever possible. This accession to language demands places a new obligation on the state and increases the minority's dependence upon government agencies for legitimization and financial support. Hence, an entirely new relationship between the state and the minority language community is being fashioned. Were Wales unilingually Welsh, or even predominantly Welsh-speaking, this trend would be welcomed, for sheer demographic and socio-economic power would guarantee the functional utility of Welsh as a medium of governance. However, Wales is overwhelmingly English in speech, and its bilingual population is too small and ineffective to insist on that full realization of language rights envisaged by the initial nationalist leaders (Williams, 1982a).

In essence I am arguing that the widespread attempt to legitimize the separateness of Welsh culture may have come a generation too late. For the traditional socio-economic character of a Welsh-speaking environment is being eroded as the formal incorporation of Welsh into the para-public sector is being realized.[4] This disjunction of habitual language context and formalized language role is likely to polarize tension between a declining core and a not-yet-established counter-node based on Cardiff, and also between a proletariat dependent on a diminishing primary and secondary economic base and an emerging middle class dependent on the very institutions the language revival has created. Our common linguistic heritage may yet divide us more than at any other period in modern history. In times of economic decline, when other types of minority (defined by need, inequality and deprivation) may well compete for the scarce resources now invested in language promotion, our very dependence upon a Westminster-controlled state machinery may prove something of a Trojan horse. *Laissez-faire* economic and state interventionist policy has already combined to transform the socio-economic structure of the core which threatens language survival there (Rees and Rees, 1980). In the future the language may become so marginalized that its role and function in real terms will be severely restricted. If that does happen then social conflict and even violence are to be expected if other European cases of language contact and conflict are allowed as precedents.

Brittany

A parallel, if arrested, sequence characterizes the Breton struggle for equality of status. Estimates by French and Welsh scholars suggest that in 1928 there were some 1·4 million Breton speakers and that, despite population increase in Brittany, this number had declined to about a million in the sixties. The limited incorporation of the Breton language into the functions of the French state has resulted in a number of political movements being formed to redress language and economic grievances. Thus, as early as 1911, a Breton nationalist party had been formed, and more recently several nationalist and educational organizations have emerged. In an attempt to weld these disparate groups into a common focus the "Charte Minimale Bretonne" was drawn up in 1967; it demanded that Brittany be recognized as a nation within France, that the Breton language be taught at all levels, that a Regional Assembly be organized out of the five existing departments and that a regional economic and social council with a Breton executive be formed (Anderson, 1980). Some attempts have been made of late by the central government to decentralize its functions to various regions within the system, but they mostly relate to functional, not formal, regionalism and typically include the encouragement of private investment and state projects within the marginal, peripheral areas (Kofman, 1982). It is likely that the short term will see a greater recognition on behalf of the central government of the needs of its constituent national minorities but, compared with the Welsh case, the Breton situation is in a very early stage of development. It is doubtful whether the Breton language and culture will flourish without a greater degree of local autonomy and a firmer economic base to support the development of bilingual public services and to stem the population outflow to the more prosperous regions of France and Europe.

Euskadi

After generations of discrimination Spain's linguistic minorities are also seeking collective recognition for their rights. The Basque country (Euskadi) provides perhaps the best example in Europe of the interweaving of language and separatism. The status of Euskera (the Basque language) is the product of a complex interaction of political oppression, social stigmatization, economic development and civil war. The early history of Basque–Spanish relations was based upon suspicion, exploitation and oppression (Medhurst, 1982). Intransigent attitudes were commonplace on both sides of the ethnic divide but rarely have such attitudes been so transformed into group violence as they have in the Basque provinces during this century. "These abominable separatists do not deserve to have a homeland", raved the Spanish military governor of Alava, General Gil Yuste, during the Civil War. "Basque nationalism must be ruined, trampled underfoot, ripped out by its roots." (Clark, 1979, p. 80.) Under Franco's regime the language issue was to become a symbol of Basque oppression and opposition to the centralist, neo-fascist policies of Madrid.[5] Clark (1979) shows that from 1937 to the middle 1950s the Spanish policy was one of total suppression of the Basque language. After the fall of Bilbao, the Basque university created a year earlier by the Statute of Autonomy of 1936 was closed. Libraries and documents held by social and cultural organizations were seized by troops and there was a mass burning of books in Euskera. The teaching of the language was prohibited in all schools, in all public places (even the most casual conversations in the street), and in the media. This attempt at linguistic genocide was especially crucial in rural school districts, since the children there did not speak or understand Spanish. Euskera was prohibited in all religious publications and was banned from Church ceremonies. A decree was issued that required the translation into Spanish of all Basque names in civil registries and other official documents. Basque names could not be used in baptism, and all inscriptions in Euskera were ordered removed from tombstones, funeral markings and public buildings.

The revival of Basque nationalism

Concern with the reclamation of Basque autonomy and the maintenance of a distinct Basque identity were the twin mobilizing forces in the development of both the Basque Nationalist Party—El Partido Nacionalista Vasco (PNV)—in 1894 and the more recent ETA movement, established in 1959. Under the early years of the Franco regime the systematic attempt to eradicate local political dissent and to destroy Basque cultural identity provoked only limited opposition, led from outside Spain by members of the exiled regional government. The PNV contributed to Pyrenean-based guerilla operations but their activities were little more than irritants, especially after the Second World War when Basque hopes for Allied military intervention to topple Franco were dashed.

After the war the PNV's difficulties pointed to their inability to adjust to changing political realities. It had developed as a Christian Democratic Party without the organization or experience needed to prosper in an underground situation. Its exiled leaders increasingly tended to lose contacts and adherents in Euskadi, where local opposition was now being organized by Communist or Socialist factions. Disillusioned by the lack of political penetration a splinter group of younger PNV activists broke away in 1952 and by 1959 had eventually re-grouped with other dissident sections of the Basque intelligentsia and working class as *Euzkadi'ta Askatasuna* (ETA: Basque Homeland and Liberty).

This development reinvigorated Basque nationalism. A series of spectacular urban guerilla operations in the early 1960s produced government repression of immediate post-Civil War proportions. This repression came to affect large sections of Basque society and helped to precipitate major political crises throughout Spain (Medhurst, 1982). The pattern of escalating violence and increased retaliation by central government was largely in conformity with the political strategy of ETA's leadership. It was the classic tactic of using government repression as a means of alienating Basque opinion and so attracting sympathy for the ideals, if not necessarily the methods, of ETA. The extension of repression beyond the region's major urban centres and into the semi-rural hinterland served to broaden the social base of opposition so as to include larger sections of the area's middle and lower classes.

Two often conflicting aims animated the movement. One was the long cherished separatist aim of Basque independence, to guarantee cultural survival and promote regional economic development. Some in the movement, however, saw the independence issue within the context of a wider struggle conducted ultimately in the interests of the entire Spanish working class. Basque independence was seen as a necessary stage in the creation of a Spanish socialist state. The former aim tended to emphasize the ethnic dimension, separating Basques from Spaniards, while the latter saw social class as the "true" political cleavage. Both Medhurst and Clark provide detailed evidence of this tension, which may be identified in a number of ethnic autonomous movements; quite often ethnicity is counterposed against class as the legitimate political axiom. Clearly there is a need to discuss *both* ethnicity and class even if, as Glyn Williams (1980) posits, this is only to root the problem in social rather than cultural terms.

This need becomes critical when we come to an analysis of why social movements engage in political and violent activity in the name of a linguistic minority. It is too facile to assume that it is the language *per se* which is the generator of such passion and drive. Rather it would seem more realistic to view language as a group marker, one which is intimately related to the total determination of a group's position within a state. This certainly seems to be the basis upon which Spanish repression was predicated. Destroying the language was an instrument by which political superiority and control could be demonstrated. Conversely, promoting the language and other ethnic markers was a means of resisting such power, and separatism became the logical alternative to submission.

In classic social theory the fundamental basis of social class involves the relationship of social groups to economic resources. It is customary to establish the existence of such groups by considering the relationship of actors to economic resources, regarding the resultant social formations as somehow "natural". Any other characteristics are subsumed under the economic order. In contrast, ethnic groups are established by a consideration of their unique (usually cultural) attributes and the groups are then located in the economic order (Willams, G., 1980). Either the ethnic group is treated as socially homogeneous, or the problem of ethnicity is reduced to a problem of class. This has been the conventional manner of treating the differences within the Basque nationalist movement. A more realistic approach has been developed by Glynn Williams (1980) who argues that if we accept that groups exist because of an institutionalized discrimination which is manifested in terms of access to economic resources and with the markers of ethnicity being the basis for the legitimization of that discrimination, then ethnic stratification becomes a "natural" order in the same sense as social class. The ethnic group thus is seen as a social rather than a cultural one.

When viewed from this perspective, the bases for political mobilization in Euskadi are the markers of ethnicity and the institutions which serve as the basis for minority cultural reproduction (i.e. the Catholic Church and the *ikastolas* system of illegal primary education). Such institutions are sustained and vitalized by their function as welfare agencies for an oppressed minority which is only weakly connected to the State. There ensues a struggle between the State and the community which is the essential *raison d'être* of ethnic politics. Central to this struggle is the control over the agencies of cultural reproduction, since it is culture which serves as the medium for the legitimization and institutionalization of power and inequality. For Basque

TABLE 3
Evolution of Basque-speaking population, 1860–1970 (in thousands)

Year	Population of Basque provinces	Estimated Basque-speaking population	Percentage
1860	750	400	53·3
1930	1200	500	41·7
1970	2300	455	19·8

Sources:
1. Beltza (1976). *El Nacionalismo Vasco, 1876–1936*, pp. 10, 217–223. Editorial Txertoa, San Sebastián.
2. Pedro de Yrizar (1973). Los dialectos y variedades de la Lengua Vasca: Estudio Linguístico-Demográfico. *Separata del Boletín de la Real Sociedad Vascongada de los Amigos del Pais,* **29** (1/2/3).

nationalists state education is seen as the basis for social control through its legitimizing ideological function. Thus the struggle over Euskera education involves, in part, a struggle over ideological control at the heart of which lies the revolutionary potential of a minority language which can be employed to transmit a radical ideological position. This is surely the meaning behind Sartre's now famous phrase, after the Burgos trial, that to speak Euskera is a revolutionary act.

The control of the State over education constitutes an attempt to control this potential and to expropriate the cultural role. Such expropriation limits the ability of the minority to reproduce its culture except within the context of the dominant ideology. The effects of such expropriation and outright repression are evident in Table 3 which highlights three base points for the period 1860–1970 and suggests an overall decline of some 45 000 speakers, a decline largely related to the passing away of an older age cohort and the refusal or inability of younger elements to learn the language. This linguistic decline is accelerated by the continued high immigration into the region of unilingual Spaniards. This trend had a twofold effect. First, it diluted the specific Basque social communication networks which once dominated the older industrial heartland towns, and led to an erosion of traditional Basque homogeneity. In the provinces of Alava, Guipuzcoa and Vizcaya about 38% of the residents are not indigenous Basques (see Table 4). In the 1975 del Campo survey, 20% of the residents of these provinces claimed to feel no sense of identification with their region (Table 5). One of the primary reasons for the low absorption rate of Spaniards into Basque culture is their inability or refusal to learn Euskera; typically, only some 2–4% of non-Basque immigrant communities can converse effectively in Euskera. This leads to heightened language tension at the workplace and in social situations and fuels the linguistic animosity of Basque "cultural nationalists".

TABLE 4

Percentages of Basque-speaking persons in total population of four Basque provinces
(Based on work of Pedro de Yrizar, c. 1970)

Province	1970 population (in thousands)	Estimated numbers of Basque speakers	%
Alava	204	1 863	0·91
Guipúzcoa	631	276 843	43·87
Navarra	465	36 143	7·77
Vizcaya	1 043	140 229	13·44
Total	2 343	455 078	19·42

Sources:
1. Population: Amando de Miguel (1974). *Manual de Estructura Social de Espana*, Table 3, pp. 64–65, Editorial Tecnos, Madrid.
2. Basque-speaking population: Pedro de Yrizar (1973). Los dialectos y variedades de la Lengua Vasca: Estudio Lingüístico-Demográfico. *Separata del Boletin de la Real Sociedad Vascongada de los Amigos del Paris* 29 (1/2/3), 74–76.

TABLE 5

Percentage of use of Basque language among native-born Basques and among
general population of three Basque provinces, 1975 (*N* = 350)

Response	Understand		Speak		Write	
	Native-born	General population	Native-born	General population	Native-born	General population
Yes	39·3	26·2	30·4	19·1	8·9	5·8
Yes, with difficulty	12·4	12·2	13·3	*	12·9	7·9
A few things	—	*	—	*	6·6	*
Nothing	45·6	54·3	53·7	61·3	62·4	*
No answer	2·7	*	2·7	*	9·3	*

Notes: *Indicates data not reported in source.
  Survey deals only with Alava, Guipúzcoa and Vizcaya provinces. Native-born Basques are those respondents who reported their province of birth as one of three surveyed provinces, regardless of province of then-current residence.
Source: Salustiano del Campo, Manuel Navarro and Felix Tezanos (1977). *La cuestión regional espanola*, p. 212. EDICUSA, Madrid.

The second effect of large-scale immigration was to strengthen the position of Socialist and Communist factions at the expense of the Nationalists. During the 1950s and 1960s, as working-class dissent renewed throughout Spain, workers from the Basque region were in the vanguard of illegal strike movements. ETA was particularly disturbed by this trend, for sections of its élite were Marxist, and their attempt to combine class and ethnic appeals confused the largely immigrant populations of industrial areas in the cities, and annoyed ardent Basque "cultural nationalists" who claimed, incorrectly, that the essence of the nationalist struggle was linguistic, cultural and religious. By failing to recognize the interrelationships among politics, economics and culture the PNV old guard lost the opportunity to radicalize a new generation of Basque youth on their terms and through their organization.

Language reforms 1960–82

By the early 1960s the Spanish government had realized the inadvisability of trying to eliminate the language, and instead concentrated on regulating its use. Sermons were now preached in Euskera and, after Vatican II permitted the use of vernacular languages in the celebration of the Mass, it was used for this ceremony as well. Indeed the Church has played a significant role in the revival of Basque culture especially since the radicalization process after Vatican II which was to affect the entire Spanish Church. Part of this process was due to domestic Catholic politics, but part was also due to the more specifically Spanish experience of disruptive economic change within the context of an authoritarian political system—an experience that had especially dramatic consequences for the Basque region. In Spain at large, the result was a questioning of established economic inequalities and of traditional political alliances. In the particular circumstances of Euskadi, the result was a reassertion and, for some, a reinterpretation of traditional links between Catholicism and Nationalism (Medhurst, 1982).

In practical terms the language could be used on certain radio stations that were owned or used by the Church for religious broadcasts. More importantly the local clergy expanded the operation of the first Basque schools, the *ikastolas* (which had been teaching clandestinely, as they were still prohibited by law) up until the most important reform of this period, the 1968 Law of General Education which authorized (but did not encourage in any way) the teaching of regional languages at the primary level, thus legalizing the *ikastolas* (Clark, 1981).

A third phase of Spanish policy towards Euskera dates from May 1975 when the government issued a decree allowing the teaching of Euskera on an optional basis, after school hours, and at the full discretion of the school principal. In October of the same year a second decree provided for the protection of the regional languages, although it was made clear that Spanish would continue to be the only official language permitted in government offices, courts and legislative assemblies. Nevertheless, the two decrees do represent a relaxation of the stranglehold Madrid exercised over the language practices of the Basques. This trend continued through the decade, reaching its peak in 1979 when two significant events heralded a marked change in the political support for the language. In May, the Spanish government issued its long-awaited decree on bilingualism in which the Ministry of Education accepted responsibility for programmes of instruction in Euskera at all levels of education in the Basque region.[6] The decree also confirmed the Spanish government's responsibility to provide financial assistance to the private *ikastolas,* where all instruction is conducted in Euskera.[7]

The second major event was the approval of the new Basque Autonomy Statute, wherein the Basque provinces (except Navarra) were granted considerable autonomy.[8] The first Basque Parliament was elected in March 1980. Article 6 of the Statute established Euskera as a co-official language with Spanish in the Basque provinces, and gave to the regional government the authority to regulate its use and make provisions to strengthen the language. Clark suggests that since this latter provision is regarded as giving the new Basque government authority over the mass media as well as the schools, it seems likely that the Basque language will enjoy a much improved political and social future. Of this there can be little doubt. What is in doubt is the ability of the Nationalist parties to translate their success in cultural fields to economic control or, at least, direction of the Basque region. It is evident from recent election results that the PNV continues to draw a considerable proportion of its votes from the small towns of Vizcaya and Guipuzcoa and from the predominantly Euskera-speaking districts, although its recent improved form in the provincial capitals of Bilbao, Vitoria and San Sebastian may herald a new electoral pattern in industrial/ urban areas. As Clark (1981) cautions, these elections do not constitute a trend, but they may reveal a shift in the orientation of the Basque nationalist movement away from the language issue as the central cultural symbol of political oppression, towards more general socio-economic issues. Evidence for this shift is the rise of the *abertzale* left wing faction of the movement, with its attempt to appeal to the electorate on primarily economic or class-based issues set within the context of a colonized culture and a beleaguered minority territory. And this may very well be the most promising direction for change in Euskadi, for, after all, its position within the Spanish economy has suffered acute structural strain of late.[9]

The Basque case demonstrates *par excellence* that nationalist revival within the ethnic periphery is not necessarily related to economic underdevelopment, for Euskadi has long been one of Spain's leading industrial regions, and the scene of much immigration as Spaniards display increased occupational mobility. Arguing that nationalism is not the direct response to "underdevelopment" does not mean that uneven economic development is negligible—quite the reverse. For, with the extension of state intervention in regional planning and the development of monopoly capitalism in the periphery, we see the marginalization of the existing capitalism in the periphery. This marginalization produces a class fragmentation which derives from the contrast between the enclave and marginalized sectors and, together with distinctive social mobility patterns and relations of production, militates against the emergence of a uniform proletarian consciousness (Williams, G., 1980). This in turn facilitates the mobilization of political alignments which cross-cut class affiliation. The very bases of such mobilization are the markers of ethnicity, including a shared historical memory of past and present oppression, such that the State and its agencies become an anathema to the Basque population.

However, the future may encourage a diminution of cross-cutting affiliations, as Euskadi's economic position worsens, and as the grievances of the working classes are directed at the Regional Assembly rather than Madrid. Increased autonomy in other cases has produced two quite distinct trends— the acceleration of demands for complete independence, or the reintegration of the periphery into the state structure on more sophisticated neo-colonial terms. This latter would constitute a more "perfect" imperialism—at least in theory—since anti-internal colonial feeling would be deflected onto a comprador, bourgeois–nationalist class with all the formal trappings of autonomy, but no real economic muscle to affect changes in the regional economy and in collective development. In either case the struggle for the Basque language will remain central as its economic and political role becomes increasingly instituted in the affairs of the region. Tension will continue between Euskadi and the state, and between Basque speakers and non-Basque immigrants in Euskadi.

Québec

From Confederation to the present the pattern of ethnic accommodation between French and English in Québec has developed within the context of rapid industrialization. Historically, ethnic accommodation had been based on Québec's segmented character, with separate ethnic schools, religious organizations, trade unions, social communication networks and residential differentiation.

This perpetuated institutional separation serving both linguistic communities. What disturbed this arrangement and fuelled the separatist case was provincial modernization and the new "scientific bureaucrats". In the immediate post-war period, the growing discontent with the character and policies of the Duplessis regime (as evidenced by the asbestos workers strike of 1949) hardened the split between the secularizing intelligentsia and the defensive clerico-nationalist ideology which had underpinned relations between Church and State. The attack on church-dominated education, health, and welfare services which the Quiet Revolution heralded was spearheaded by the expanding provincial bureaucracy created by Premier Paul Sauvé. In Québec, unlike Wales and Euskadi, it was an arm of government which was to be used as the reforming instrument allowing the province to "catch up" with neighbouring Ontario and providing employment, status and a future political role for the ambitious ethnic bureaucrats. "The aspirations of the new middle class and the growth and development of the institutions they staffed were to become the political priorities of the provincial state." (Guindon, 1978, p. 214.)

Having replaced the Church as the main source of authority, the new élite now successfully challenged the leadership of the traditional, conservative Francophone hierarchy by restricting the management prerogatives of the authorities of such institutions as local school boards and hospital administrations. They espoused a politically centralized bureaucratic model which, apart from curtailing the authority of French institutional managers, transformed the Anglophone institutional managerial élite into a minority dependent upon the state. Modernization pointed to the pivotal role of the state as the focus of reform, initiative and enterprise. State financed ventures such as Hydro Québec, the Sidbec Steel complex and the pension and investment fund represented instruments for extending Québécois control over economic development. But, increasingly the leaders of the Lesage and successive governments recognized that Québec's drive towards autonomy would clash with federal priorities, especially as the federal government was playing a more aggressive role in regional development and cultural affairs— a role which did not always accord with Québec's interests.

Social mobilization and state modernization created a brand of nationalism quite distinct from previous Québécois self-assertion. The new nationalism embraced the logic of social and economic modernization as the key to a dynamic and prosperous future. While traditional nationalism had been conservative and engaged in the politics of cultural defence, the new nationalism was activist and interventionist and engaged in the politics of cultural promotion. Where the old nationalism was content to maintain ethnic institutional separation, even if this meant that Anglophones had the upper hand in certain sectors, the new nationalism now sought to penetrate all sectors. Where the old nationalism had challenged the legitimacy of federal jurisdiction only when it infringed upon Québec's legal rights, the new nationalism called into question the very basis of Confederation, challenging Ottawa's right to determine revenue levels and resource allocations. Finally, the traditional nationalism's suspicion of the state as an instrument of reform was displaced by an ideological commitment to state intervention and planning, such that it became the key sector in the struggle for ethnic survival and the springboard for group development (Williams, 1981).

Inherent in this cultural process has been the attempt to use language as an index of group power and autonomy. Many observers who claimed that language and cultural questions were receiving a disproportionate share of government attention in the late 1960s and early 1970s failed to appreciate the pervasive role which language plays in almost all aspects of public life (most notably in education, the work-place and government).

Given the pre-eminent concern to preserve the "French fact in North America" (2·5% of the total population), it is not surprising that language, the essence of French Canadian identity, should be the prime political concern of the new nationalists. The concern with *survivance* is related to the fact that in time the language of the business élite will come to dominate the language of the passive majority, if the state does not intervene. The differences between the élite and the masses could be managed so long as Québec's birth rate remained high. The "revenge of the cradle" would undo the Conquest. However, the province's birth rate has changed from one of the world's highest to one of the world's lowest, lower than all other Canadian provinces. The post-war trend of immigrants assimilating into the Anglophone community has led to emotional charges that, without restrictive language policies, only a tiny proportion of immigrants and their children would opt for French immersion classes offered by education boards. Demographic forecasts predict that the French proportion would fall from 79·0% to 70.5% of the provincial population, if such trends continue within the 1980s. There is one qualification which makes all the difference. The non-French population are disproportionately concentrated in the Montreal metropolitan area (Hamilton and Pinard, 1982). Within this area (containing 45·5% of Québec's population) the French versus Others proportion is 5:3. Demographers argue that if the current trends continue unabated the metropolis will lose its French majority within two decades, the heart of the nation would be lost, and provincial, rural Québec would provide only a partial defence of Francophone culture in an increasingly urban age. The solution, according to the leaders of the Quiet Revolution, was to compel immigrants in Québec to acculturate to the French language and to educate their children in French medium schools. Parental freedom of choice about the medium of education, a longstanding practice in Québec that the Bilingual and Bicultural Commission endorsed, would have to be eliminated. In this way the risks of eventual minorization would be reduced (Esman, 1982; Williams, 1981).

One explanation for the centrality of language policies in the 1970s relates to the growth of the public sector in Québec. The new middle class is overwhelmingly concentrated in the public sector as a consequence of the expansion of French-medium municipal and provincial civil service departments which recruited Francophone social science, engineering and business graduates. Unlike the private sector, the public sector did not insist on bilingualism as a criterion for employment. However, once the state sector began to be adequately manned in the mid- to late 1960s, language became a prime political issue. The aspiring middle classes, blocked in their attempts to swell the state bureaucracy, looked to the Anglophone-dominated private sector for employment. Disadvantaged linguistically, and experiencing blocked mobility in both sectors, the thwarted intelligentsia reinforced its determination to seek in separatism a collective, and then political, solution to its problem. Only in a separate, independent nation-state could the full aspirations of the Francophone be realized. "Maître chez nous" was to become a reality, le Parti Québécois its champion.

The Parti Québécois in power

In November 1976 the Parti Québécois won the provincial election and formed the government in Québec. It was a party dedicated to separatism, to the creation of a new state in North America where French culture would be secure and where socialist principles could be enacted to achieve a more equitable distribution of resources. One of the earliest policy commitments was to a unilingual regime in the province. One of the earliest laws enacted by the National Assembly, now dominated by the Parti Québécois, was a new Official Language Charter (1977) which superseded former language legislation. Many federalists in Ottawa and elsewhere, who had dedicated their efforts to the policy of two official languages for Canada, felt betrayed by a move toward one official language in Québec (Cartwright and Williams, 1982). Five months after the election, the Minister of State for Cultural Affairs, Camille Laurin, provided his government's analysis of the language situation (1977). The efforts of the federal government to promote bilingualism were dismissed. Although the federal policy was based upon institutional bilingualism rather than personal bilingualism, to the government of Québec this did not accord with the fact that Canada was truly an English-speaking state. Institutions and the entire social fabric of Québec were recognized as essential to the extension of the use of French. The new provincial programme was designed to give these elements a thoroughly French character:

> The Québec we wish to build will be essentially French. The fact that the majority of its population is French will be clearly visible—at work, in communications and in the countryside. It will also be a country in which the traditional balance of power will be altered, especially in regard to the economy; the use of French will not merely be universalized to hide the predominance of foreign powers from the French-speaking population; this will accompany, symbolize and support a reconquest by the French-speaking majority in Québec of that control over the economy which it ought to have. To sum up, the Québec whose features are sketched in the Charter (of the French language) is a French-language society.
>
> Laurin, 1977

The separatist case is based upon the premise that ethnic majorities within a multi-ethnic polity have the right to constitute national governments in their own sovereign states. This is of course the right of national self-determination. Initially such claims appear to be framed in majoritarian terms, and hence inherently democratic. Closer examination suggests much ambiguity in the justification of majoritarian independence, and this is one of the prime pitfalls in using language as the cultural marker for separatist mobilization (Williams, 1982c). Despite a clear victory in the 1976 election, the PQ opted for a referendum to endorse their mandate for Sovereignty–Association. Opponents of separatism argued that, given the importance of the issue to Québec and to Canada, a 50–55% vote to separate was an inadequate endorsement. From the PQ perspective a 55% positive vote would suggest acceptance of the principle by a "huge majority" of Francophones, somewhere around 65% of the French-speaking citizenry. The implication is that a genuine victory of the majority of Francophones is assured. Note that the interpretation defines the majority not in terms of a collection of individuals, but by cultural groupings. What this suggests is that it is not the majority which ought to rule but the majority of the dominant culture. This represents a claim to rule on behalf of a certain group within society, not simply by virtue of its being a majority, but by virtue of its cultural characteristics, chiefly language. The result of the referendum was clear-cut and decisive—59·5% no and 40·5% yes; 80% of Québec's 4·4 million voters cast their ballots.

Historically, it has always been argued that it is the special responsibility of Québec to represent the interests not simply of individuals *per se*, but of French culture; the corollary of this is that it is the Francophone nation which has the right to separate if it so chooses. Now, this is a right which is claimed irrespective of majoritarian status for if we change the spatial context and consider Canada rather than Québec, the culture which is said to have this right is clearly a minority one. Majority–minority rights are determined by the political context as we have already seen in this chapter. Analytically they are quite distinct from the collective claims to independence as a right *per se*. This emphasis on the appropriate political context provides further illustration of the tensions inherent in the separatist ideal. In the past the PQ leadership, and Camille Laurin in particular, have pressed the claim of the Francophone nation to independence because it is the *only* nation in Québec (implying that only territorially defined majorities have rights to constitute nations); other ethnic groups have a responsibility to participate and to cooperate to develop the national culture of Québec (Knopf, 1980). However, Laurin also uses the term nation in a way which is synonymous with the state, and not the ethnie. Separatist rhetoric refers to Québec as a nation struggling for independence. In order to do so this argument must maintain that the Québec state represents not only the embodiment of the French nation in North America (as used to be argued) but of all the people within it. The "national culture" of Québec, though decidedly French, is the common inheritance of all its citizens.

The extension of the doctrine is that the state, which is primarily responsible for the promotion of national culture, has the responsibility to ensure that every citizen learns the single official language. Thus the preamble to the original version of the Language Charter declared that "the French language has always been the language of the Québec people, that it is, indeed, the very instrument by which they have articulated their identity". To maintain this identity through the province the language was to be used as the instrument of French cultural promotion. Québec's non-Francophone population saw in this formulation the establishment of an official state culture, with the implication that they would become disadvantaged citizens within their own province. Recognizing this fear, the preamble to the new bill (Bill 101) was modified, referring to French as "the distinctive language of a people that is in the majority French-speaking . . . the instrument by which that people has articulated its identity". This awkward reformulation does not remove the inherent ambiguity which gave rise to the legal enforcement of French culture in Québec, and forces the nationalist to embrace a majoritarianism which negates a fundamental premise of nationalism, namely that nations and states should be coextensive (Knopf, 1980).[10]

The difficulty facing the Québécois government was that their rise to power had been based upon appeals to ethnic nationalism. But rather than redefine Québec's boundaries so that they now coincided with the Francophone nation, thus making state and nation co-extensive, they referred to the Québécois nation's right to self-determination, thereby converting an ethnic nationalism into a territorial nationalism. The party hopes to persuade non-Francophones that its conception of nationalism is territorial and state-based, one in which they may partake if they will choose to exercise their newly-acquired right to assimilate into the "national culture" and become Québécois citizens rather than hyphenated ethnic Canadians (e.g. Italian-Canadians).

I have refrained from providing a detailed summary of language-related legislation and its impact on the Québec electorate since 1976 (See Esman, 1982; Cartwright and Williams, 1982; Clift, 1982; McRoberts and Posgate, 1980, for details). What is evident is that Bill 22 (1974) and Bill 101 (1977), although sponsored by different parties have *together* enabled a social and economic reform to be effected within Québec in the guise of linguistic reform.[11] As McWhiney observes (1982), the French-as-language-of-work stipulations have been rather more important in their impact than the French-as-official-language sections. They opened the way to access, and on some equitable basis, by the French-Candian majority in Québec to economic decision-making in the province. It seems that executive prag- matism has won the day in the field of language policy, for there was a time when Canada was mounting two radically different and mutually irreconcil- able language policies—federal official bilingualism policies, expressed in the Official Languages Act of 1969 and resting on the personality principle, and Québec government policies which effectively "territorialized" the French factor within the province of Québec (McWhiney, 1982). Federal self-restraint in not sabotaging Québec's language policy by court appeals and litigation was balanced increasingly by flexibility and humanity in Québec's own application of its language-of-work stipulations. Pragmatic adjustments and mutual accord have produced a system of federal and provincial language policies with distinct and separate, but not conflicting, zones of application for each. In time, an optimist could argue, the two language policies may conceivably emerge as complementary and mutually supportive. McWhiney, for example, suggests that the Québécois voters have already appraised the situation as one of mutual accommodation and voted accordingly in the Sovereignty–Association referendum. Knowing that many of their grievances were already being allayed by a powerful and reforming provincial government, why should they risk the possible collapse of this arrangement in an as yet untried and unmapped independence? Further evidence for the sophistication of the electorate's assessment may be found in the next provincial election of 15 April 1981. After defeating the specifics of the referendum of 20 May 1980, the electorate endorsed the general trend of the Parti Québécois policies and returned them to office for another term. Confident that Premier Lévesque would not hold another referendum during any new term, the electorate did what they nearly always have done in the Canadian federal system; they tempered their strong support for Trudeau's Liberal Party in the federal elections of February 1980 with an equally vociferous mandate to the rival party at the provincial level, thereby maintaining the operation of the checks and balance form of Federal–Provincial democracy.

Territorial language planning

Recognizing the need to implement its policy of bilingualism and biculturalism as a counter to the growing discontent within Québec since the early 1960s, the federal government attempted to design a federal-provincial framework which would allow for the full implementation of language rights. After a century of independence, the federal government promulgated the Official Languages Act in 1969, in which English and French were accorded equal status as official languages of the Parliament and Government of Canada. The national significance of this statute, in the view of the government, was expressed by the federal Minister for Secretary of State when it was before the House of Commons. "The measure is extremely important . . . because it touches the very foundation of Canadian unity . . . this bill is a gesture of faith in the future of Canada". To effect the spirit of this legislation the government adopted the concept of bilingual districts, territorial units in which people would be entitled to obtain full services from federal government agencies in French and English (Cartwright and Williams, 1982).

After more than a decade of research, legislation and discussion, the federal government has been unable to implement its state-wide policy of bilingual districts. This is largely due to Québec's intransigence, but also to opposition from western Canadian interest groups. Its significance is that it was the primary instrument for demonstrating to French speakers that the federal government was committed to the protection and promotion of their language rights, thus serving to reduce the appeal of the separatist case, at least in relation to linguistic matters.

The original concept of bilingual districts was developed to solve a practical problem, viz. at what threshold of concentration should an official language minority receive federal services in its own language? In the event, it came to be interpreted as a primary instrument for achieving parity between both official languages. This was a major error, for critics had questioned whether the socio-political imbalance between French and English could be reduced by the establishment of bilingual districts, especially when different solutions for the francophone and anglophone minorities were proposed (Cartwright and Williams, 1982). The fundamental issue, of course, is that the very conception of Canadian society has changed markedly since the early 1960s when the bilingual and bicultural programme started. The federal government's explicit recognition of the francophone community's rights and the determination of its status relative to the anglophone raised the basic question of how it was to be defined and served. What were to be its boundaries?

The answer depended upon the resolution of a prior question. Was Canada one nation or two? Historically, two conceptions of the linguistic communities have been confronting each other, and the official language districts have failed to satisfy either conception. On the one hand, there is a Pan-Canadian view that identifies the francophone community as consisting of francophones in all parts of Canada (and similarly the anglophone community). This view, dominant until recently, underpins the initial conception of bilingual districts as an instrument for guaranteeing francophone rights throughout Canada. On the other hand, the segmentalist view identifies Québec as the francophone heartland and the rest of Canada as the anglophone domain. This view underpins the separatist movement's programme of sociolinguistic reform in Québec since 1976. Despite causing difficulties for francophones outside Québec and problems for anglophones within, this view does at least focus on the central political question of whether Canada is comprised of two coequal nations. The Parti Québécois' judgement is that the Canadian confederation is a partnership which has failed. Thus, in most respects the bicultural and segmentalist concepts are apparently irreconcilable within a federal framework. This is especially damaging because each conception is articulated in defence of a particular distribution of opportunities and power.

Must we therefore conclude that federal and provincial language policies are doomed and that the "dialogue of the deaf" will continue to characterize French–English relations? I think not. We have already seen that the Québécois government, having established the structure of a quasi-autonomous state, is not foolhardy enough to push its language regime to unpalatable ends. Mediation is in progress on many of the language rights of the non-francophone, non-anglophone ethnic minorities. Similarly, at the federal level, despite the rebuff to the bilingual districts policy, there is a recognition that rather than attempt a state-wide programme of sociolinguistic reform, a more sensitive and localized policy might prove feasible. It is within local communities that a pattern of language use can be identified, urban and rural alignments established and, in consequence, the most appropriate type of bilingual service enacted. The cooperation of the local population is more likely to be forthcoming if there is an awareness of the perceived need of the minority and the precise patterns of cultural erosion that occur within the community. This assessment may be considered applicable to the bilingual zone of Canada as well. Although identified as the zone of transition between the French and the English unilingual zones, analysis indicates that the zone consists of a number of "islands" that are in geographical proximity. The extension of services should have spatial as well as temporal components that will minimize conflict and maximize ethnic contact and cooperation. Through flexible and imaginative implementation of the Official Languages Act or the new Canadian Constitution, "two solitudes" need not be a lasting epitaph for Canada (Cartwright and Williams, 1982).

Conclusion

This chapter has demonstrated that linguistic concerns are often central to ethnic political activity, especially separatism. Language is a means of mediating between the past and the present; it is the repository of a group's collective identity, rooted in a national territory. Attempts to challenge this arrangement through state and private incursions often lead to reactive ethnic assertion. I have also shown that the nature of ethnic assertion varies over time and space. In the three detailed case studies it was evident that language promotion was not mere cultural attachment, but often a rational and instrumental attempt to reduce socio-economic inequality, to wrest more power from the state and opposition groups, and to determine an increasing amount of the ethnic group's role in the wider political structure. Strategies adopted by the various political movements relate to the strength of their parties, the nature of their political incorporation into the state system and their economic resource base. Clearly, Wales presents a remarkable example of how a small, highly articulate interest group can promote its language such that it becomes incorporated into the machinery of government. However, it is very doubtful that independence will ensue from the nationalist struggle, partly because of the small target group that can be mobilized on the basis of the language and related issues and partly because of the sophistication of Welsh voters—they recognize that in order to bring about fundamental economic changes a wider political base needs to be established which cross-cuts the ethnic segmentalist basis of purely Welsh parties. The promotion of the Basque language is of a different order of magnitude, for incorporated within the language struggle is a power struggle between Euskadi and Madrid. Unlike Wales, where members of the periphery have aspired to key political and economic positions within the British state, Basque aspirations have never been channelled through state-wide parties. Regional autonomy seems likely to encourage the wider adoption of Euskera and also refocus class tensions, as socialist elements within the region attempt to reintegrate Euskadi with other Spanish regions and nationalist leaders resist such integrative moves.

Of the three studies it is Québec which has come closest to realizing its separatist ideal. Having established a Francophone dominance within the state public sector and penetrated far into the private sector, economic issues are likely to outweigh linguistic considerations in the future as successive Québécois governments grapple with the problems of resource development, industrial regeneration and social welfare priorities. As the realities of the decline of the Ontario–Québec economic axis take their course, the Québécois leadership will recognize that the common market which underpinned the Sovereignty–Association programme is no longer feasible. Commentators within Québec already point to the decline in the salience of the language issue as Québec moves towards a new equilibrium in her relationship with neighbours within Canada and across the border. Though nationalism remains the dominant ideology, counter manifestations are evident, viz. the rise of individualism and the desire for personal achievement, a greater interest in economic management, and a temporary rejection of the historical collectivism that has animated the drive for survival over the centuries. The experience of governing has blunted the pristine quality of separatist rhetoric and logic. For the short term at least, it is likely that consolidation of the language gains will dominate domestic language planning. Once that is achieved, and once economic management is placed on a sound socialist footing, Québec may well return to the old cause of championing the rights of French speakers, wherever they live in North America.

Notes

1. I am grateful to North Staffordshire Polytechnic for granting me a sabbatical leave, and to the Pennsylvania State University for hosting me, during 1982–83 when this chapter was written. I acknowledge the encouragement of A. D. Smith and Don Cartwright, and the cartographic support of Mrs Jane Perks. Part of the discussion of the Quebec case here is a reworking of material in my "Identity through autonomy", in *Political Studies from Spatial Perspectives* (Eds A. D. Burnett and P. J. Taylor), Wiley, London, 1981, and is used with the publisher's permission.

2. It is not my intention to provide a complete chronological account of the rise of separatism in each of these cases (see Clark, 1979; McRoberts and Posgate, 1980; Williams, 1982c).

3. The Report contained 31 recommendations, but the policy of both Report and Act may be said to make statutory "the Principle of Equal Validity" whereby Welsh may be used by any person in any court proceeding in Wales and Monmouthshire (see Williams, 1982c).

4. I do not imply that all Welsh-medium governmental agencies are necessarily enthusiastic in their embrace of the language as a medium of government. As this is still quite a novel feature there exists in many interactions a deep-seated

linguistic/psychological aversion to the discussion of bureaucratic matters through Welsh.

5. At the turn of the century Euskera underwent a minor cultural revival (see Clark, 1979). By 1931 there were an estimated 400 000 Basque speakers in the seven provinces (570 000 in 1934). By the outbreak of civil war, then, about half the population of the Basque provinces spoke, understood, or regularly used Euskera. The Autonomy Statute of 1936 gave to the Basque provincial assemblies the authority to promote Euskera as a co-official language. Thus, had the civil war and Franco not intervened, it seems that Euskera would have continued to adapt and grow.

6. According to the decree these programmes of instruction would be obligatory in regions where Euskera was still a functioning language. In other areas (like Navarra and Alava), where Euskera is dying, programmes would be initiated on a gradual and voluntary basis.

7. Another crucial post-Franco development has been the cultural revival. About 200 books are published annually by ten firms, and there are six daily newspapers (and others periodically). The greatest difficulty is lack of access to the mass media; television in Euskera is minimal and lacks continuity and appeal. This seems likely to become one of the major conflict issues (as in Wales) over the short term.

8. Medhurst (1982) offers little hope for outright independence. France is likely to cooperate with Spain to resist this; the possibility of independence could precipitate conflict between indigenous Basques and immigrants; the possibility of secession would likely provoke military intervention.

9. I have deliberately avoided analysing the influence of violence on Basque mobilization, but it should not be underestimated.

10. See also my "Identity through autonomy" (note 1).

11. It is interesting to note that, in a recent development (September 1982), the Quebec Superior Court—having reference to Canada's new Charter of Rights—ruled as unconstitutional certain provisions of Bill 101 that require French-medium education for anglophone children. The case, launched by two Montreal school boards and some parents, upheld the priority of tne new Charter's Section 23 which acts as a guarantee for minority-language education throughout Canada.

References

Anderson, A. B. (1980). The problem of minority languages: Canadian and European contrasts. Paper presented to the First International Conference on Minority Languages, Glasgow University.

Barnard, F. (1969). *Herder on Social and Political Culture.* Cambridge University Press, Cambridge.

Berry, C. J. (1981). Nations and norms. *The Review of Politics* **10**, 75–87.

Binder, L. (1971). *Crises and Sequences in Political Development.* Princeton University Press, Princeton.

Bogadnor, V. (1982). Ethnic nationalism in Western Europe. *Political Studies* **30**, 284–291.

Brass, P. R. (1974). *Language, Religion and Politics in North India*. Cambridge University Press, Cambridge.

Cartwright, D. G. and Williams, C. H. (1982). Bilingual districts as an instrument in Canadian language policy. *Transactions of the Institute of British Geographers* **7**, 474–494.

Clark, R. P. (1979). *The Basques: The Franco Years and Beyond*. University of Nevada Press, Reno.

Clark, R. P. (1981). Language and politics in Spain's Basque provinces. *West European Politics* **4**(1), 85–103.

Clift, D. (1982). *Quebec Nationalism in Crisis*. McGill-Queens University Press, Montreal.

Esman, M. J. (1982). The politics of official bilingualism in Canada. *Political Science Quarterly* **97**, 233–253.

Fichte, J. (1968). Addresses to the German nation. In *Addresses to the German Nation* (Ed. G. Kelly). New York.

Foot, M. (1962 and 1973). *Aneurin Bevan* (Volume 1, 1962). MacGibbon and Kee, St. Alban's, (Volume 2, 1973). Davis-Poynter, London.

Gerhard, D. (1981). *Old Europe: A Study of Continuity, 1000–1800*. Academic Press, New York.

Guindon, H. (1978). The modernization of Quebec and the legitimacy of the Canadian state. In *Modernization and the Canadian State* (Eds D. Glenday, A. Turowetz and H. Guindon). Macmillan, Toronto.

Hamilton, R. and Pinard, M. (1982). The Quebec independence movement. In *National Separatism* (Ed. C. H. Williams). University of Wales Press, Cardiff.

Horowitz, D. L. (1981). Patterns of ethnic separatism. *Comparative Studies in Society and History* **23**, 165–195.

Knopf, R. (1980). Democracy versus liberal democracy: The nationalist conundrum. *The Dalhousie Review* **58**, 638–646.

Kofman, E. (1982). Differential modernisation, social conflicts and ethno-regionalism in Corsica. *Ethnic and Racial Studies* **5**, 300–312.

Laurin, C. (1977). *Quebec's Policy on the French Language*. Ministry of State, Québec.

Maine, H. (1897). *Popular Government*. John Murray, London.

McRoberts, K. and Posgate, D. (1980). *Québec: Social Change and Political Crisis*. McClelland and Stewart, Toronto.

McWhiney, E. (1982). *Canada and the Constitution 1979–1982*. University of Toronto Press, Toronto.

Medhurst, K. (1982). Basques and Basque nationalism. In *National Separatism* (Ed. C. H. Williams). University of Wales Press, Cardiff.

Morgan, K. O. (1982). *Rebirth of a Nation: Wales, 1880–1980*. University of Wales Press, Cardiff.

Orridge, A. W. and Williams, C. H. (1982). Autonomist nationalism: A theoretical framework for spatial variations in its genesis and development. *Political Geography Quarterly* **1**(1), 18–39.

Rawkins, P. (1979). The gobal corporation, ethno-nationalism and the changing face of the West European state. In *Ethno-Nationalism, Multi-National Corporations and the Modern State* (Eds R. M. Grant, E. Spencer and J. Wellhofer). University of Denver Press, Denver.

Rees, G. and Rees, T. L. (Eds) (1980). *Poverty and Social Inequality in Wales.* Croom Helm, London.

Smith, A. D. (1979). Toward a theory of ethnic separatism. *Ethnic and Racial Studies* **2**, 21–37.

Smith, A. D. (1981). *The Ethnic Revival.* Cambridge University Press, Cambridge.

Wallerstein, I. (1974). *The Modern World System: Capitalist Agriculture and the Origins of the European World Economy in the Sixteenth Century.* Academic Press, New York.

Wallerstein, I. (1979). *The Capitalist World Economy.* Cambridge University Press, Cambridge.

Wallerstein, I. (1980). *The Modern World System,* Vol. 2. Academic Press, New York.

Weber, M. (1968). From Max Weber: Essays in Sociology. In *From Max Weber* (Eds H. H. Gerth and C. Wright Mills). Routledge and Kegan Paul, London.

Welsh Office (1978). *Primary Education in Rural Wales.* The Welsh Office, Cardiff.

Williams, C. H. (1977). Non-violence and the development of the Welsh Language Society. *Welsh History Review* **8**, 426–455.

Williams, C. H. (1980). Ethnic separatism in Western Europe. *Tijdschrift voor Economische en Sociale Geografie* **71**(3), 142–158.

Williams, C. H. (1981). Official language districts. *Ethnic and Racial Studies* **4**, 334–347.

Williams, C. H. (1982a). Language planning and minority group rights. *Cambria* **9**(1).

Williams, C. H. (1982b). Social mobilization and nationalism in multicultural societies. *Ethnic and Racial Studies* **5**, 349–365.

Williams, C. H. (Ed.) (1982c). *National Separatism.* University of Wales Press, Cardiff.

Williams, G. (1980). Review of E. Allardt's *Implications of the Ethnic Revival in Modern Industrial Society. Journal of Multilingual and Multicultural Development* **1**, 363–370.

Wood, J. R. (1981). Secession. *Canadian Journal of Political Science* **14**, 107–134.

Young, C. (1976). *The Politics of Cultural Pluralism.* University of Wisconsin Press, Madison.

8
Pluralism and assimilation: a conceptual history

Philip Gleason

Students of ethnicity in the United States are agreed that the terms *pluralism* and *assimilation* designate two quite different concepts. Pluralism, generally speaking, affirms the existence and persistence of diversity, and prescribes its preservation. Assimilation is associated with unity; it concerns itself with and generally approves of the processes by which various elements have been blended into the overall national culture.

I would not deny the broad differences between pluralism and assimilation, but I believe they have been greatly exaggerated and handled much too rigidly. The tendency to dichotomize the two viewpoints includes the moral aspect as well as the theoretical; in many discussions of the so-called new ethnicity they were treated as mutually exclusive categories, and pluralism was associated with everything good in social policy and assimilation with everything bad. This is unfortunate from the viewpoint of theoretical understanding because the two concepts, as they have been used historically, overlap and relate to each other in a dialectical manner. The failure to appreciate this fact confuses matters grievously, especially in respect to policy debate, because it beclouds the issues and prevents people from recognizing what their agreements and disagreements actually are.

In the pages that follow I will sketch the way these two concepts have been used in 20th-century discussions of American ethnic affairs. This review will show that at the very beginning of its theoretical career, and in the last few

LINGUISTIC MINORITIES
ISBN 0-12-232760-8

years, pluralism was strongly anti-assimilationist; from the late 1930s through the 1960s, however, pluralism resembled assimilation much more closely.

Assimilation was the first of the two terms to come into general use. It emerged around 1900 in the context of concern over the nation's capacity to absorb the millions of immigrants who were pouring into the country, and referred in the broadest sense to the blending of different elements into one people. *Assimilation* was used interchangeably with *Americanization*, and the production in 1908 of Israel Zangwill's drama, *The Melting Pot,* introduced a vivid image which gained immediate and widespread popularity as a symbol for the process of assimilation. Intermarriage was often linked with assimilation, but it was usually distinguished from *amalgamation*, or biological mixing. As one writer put it, the end product of assimilation was nationality, and that implied not "unity of blood," but "unity of institutions and social habits" (Mayo-Smith, 1894, p. 670; see also Commons, 1920; Gleason, 1964a; Simons, 1900–01).

But while assimilation was an elastic term that could accommodate a wide variation of interpretations, it became more closely identified with a narrow nativistic insistence that immigrants had to conform closely to the prevailing American norms before they could be considered satisfactorily assimilated. This development is reflected in Fairchild's *Immigration* (1913), a work by a leading sociologist of old American stock who accepted the prevailing scientific racialism of the day and was deeply troubled about the implications of immigration for the national culture. Basing his discussion on the "physiological analogy" of the digestion of food by the body, which he believed underlay the concept of assimilation as a social process, Fairchild (1913, p. 398) said that "true and complete assimilation of the foreign elements in the United States involves such a complete transformation and unification of the new constituents that all sense of difference between the new and the old completely disappears". Fairchild added that assimilation presupposed the existence of a national type which the immigrant was to conform to, and the "native American" was that national type.

This version of assimilation was not only offensively ethnocentric, it also proposed a standard impossible to meet in practice. First generation immigrants simply could not make themselves over so completely, even if they had been willing to do so (which most of them were not), and even if the receiving society had been willing to regard them as unqualified Americans after they had done so (which it was not). It was therefore natural that spokesmen for immigrant groups would reject assimilation altogether if this was what it meant. The work that prompted their boldest champion to step forth was not Fairchild's book, but Ross's *The Old World in the New* (1914), a veritable diatribe against the new immigrants. Ross, a progressive sociologist at the University of Wisconsin, did not discuss assimilation systematically, but his disbelief that immigrants could come up to American standards was patent throughout, and in the chapter entitled "American Blood and Immigrant Blood" he really let himself go. Even the physical appearance of the newer immigrants betrayed them as a "sub-common" people of obviously low mentality who really belonged in animal skins, beside wattled huts, at the end of the great ice age. Ross was appalled by their "sugar-loaf heads, moon-faces, slit mouths, lantern jaws, and goose-bill noses". Jews he singled out as puny and sissified, the saddest possible contrast to the type of the American pioneer.

This was too much for Horace M. Kallen, a German-born Jew, a Zionist, a Harvard PhD, and a colleague of Ross's at the University of Wisconsin. The appearance of *The Old World in the New* prompted him to set forth a radically anti-assimilationist interpretation of American nationality in an article entitled, "Democracy *versus* the Melting Pot". Originally published in *The Nation* in February 1915, this essay was reprinted with very minor changes in 1924, at which time Kallen gave the name "cultural pluralism" to his position. Since he was reacting to extreme "100-percent Americanism", it is perhaps understandable that Kallen went to the opposite extreme in his formulation of cultural pluralism. His statement was long and diffuse, downright obscure in places, but the overall argument may be summarized as follows.

First, Kallen denied that there was an American nationality as such, a generic national identity defining the whole people considered as a collectivity, to which the immigrants could be assimilated. Such a generic national culture had at one time existed, he stated, but it had been dissipated by the great waves of immigration. As a result, the United States in the 20th century was not really a nation, but a political state within the borders of which there dwelt a number of distinct nationalities.

Secondly, Kallen assumed that these distinct nationalities would perpetuate themselves indefinitely. Although the language here was vague, his thinking was clearly rooted in a romantic kind of racialism. "Like-mindedness" was the key to nationality, and it was "inward, corporate and inevitable" because it sprang from "a homogeneity of heritage, mentality and interest". Members of an ethnic group shared a "prevailing intrinsic similarity" that Kallen seemed to regard as forever fixed. "What is inalienable in the life of mankind", he declared, "is its intrinsic positive quality—its psycho-physical inheritance". Because a person "cannot change his grandfather", ethnic nationalities were destined to perdure indefinitely through a kind of biological determinism.

The third feature of Kallen's thinking brings us to the policy question.

Given the existence of many nationalities in the same country, and the prospect of their remaining permanently distinctive, what should be done? Kallen saw two alternatives, which he designated the options of "unison" or "harmony". By unison he meant the effort to make everyone conform to a common pattern—essentially the 100-percent Americanization policy. By harmony he meant the glad embrace of the existing multiplicity. Kallen opted decisively for harmony; indeed, he affirmed that it was the truly American and democratic policy, whereas the effort to enforce conformity to a common pattern actually violated democratic ideals and the spirit of American institutions.

Kallen had turned the tables on the Americanizers very neatly, but as a policy presciption his cultural pluralism amounted to little more than a lyrical vision. The following rhapsodic passage is the closest he ever came to describing how cultural pluralism would be operationalized, how his "great and truly democratic commonwealth" would function in practice (1924, p. 124):

> Its form would be that of the federal republic; its substance a democracy of nationalities, cooperating voluntarily and autonomously through common institutions in the enterprise of self-realization through the perfection of men according to their kind. The common language of the common-wealth . . . would be English, but each nationality would have for its emotional and involuntary life its own peculiar dialect or speech, its own individual and inevitable esthetic and intellectual forms. The political and economic life of the commonwealth is a single unit and serves as the foundation and background for the realization of the distinctive individuality of each *natio* that composes it and of the pooling of these in a harmony above them all. Thus "American civilization" may come to mean the perfection of the cooperative harmonies of "European civilization"—the waste, the squalor and the distress of Europe being eliminated—a multiplicity in a unity, an orchestration of mankind.

As this passage reveals, the assumption of automatic harmony among a multiplicity of permanently distinct ethnic nationalities should be added as the fourth feature of Kallen's original formulation of cultural pluralism. It was, in fact, precisely this assumption that permitted Kallen to disregard entirely the need for assimilation to American ways that other commentators stressed so heavily. For although he denied the existence of American nationality as such, and repudiated the Americanization programmes of the day, Kallen silently included assimilation in his theory by postulating a degree of consensus adequate to assure cooperation and harmony among all elements in his contemplated federation of nationalities. Kallen thus made tacit provision for the *Unum* of the national motto, although his rhetorical stress was altogether on *Pluribus* and his theoretical assumptions seemed to rule out any kind of fundamental merging-into-one of the many immigrant nationalities that made up the American people.

The publication of Kallen's article in 1915 attracted the attention of a few intellectuals, but its republication and the introduction of the term *cultural pluralism* in 1924 passed almost completely without notice (Powell, 1971; Higham, 1975). No doubt the principal reason for this neglect was that the passage in 1924 of a stringent immigration restriction law removed ethnic concerns from the forefront of public discussion. More than a decade passed before the expression *cultural pluralism* entered into circulation, even in the limited universe of scholarly observers of intergroup relations.

Before examining the way cultural pluralism was understood in the late thirties, however, we must pause to catch up on what was happening to the concept of assimilation. As the examples of Fairchild and Ross attest, cultural anxieties on the part of old-line Americans caused them to formulate the concept in a narrow and nativistic way even before the outbreak of World War I intensified the atmosphere of social and cultural crisis. The outburst of ethnic nationalism and the manifestations of immigrant loyalty to old-world homelands that marked the neutrality years (1914–1917), convinced many more Americans that "hyphenation" was a danger and lent greater urgency to programmes of Americanization. But as these efforts at forced assimilation took on a chauvinistic character that bordered on the hysterical, a reaction against them set in. Not only were liberal intellectuals put off by their hypernationalism; thoughtful observers also recognized that they were counter-productive—rather than facilitating the integration of immigrants into American life, forced Americanization programmes left them more alienated than ever. In these circumstances, a more liberal version of Americanization was set forth.

Its most impressive embodiment was the series of "Americanization Studies" sponsored by the Carnegie Corporation and published by Harper Brothers in the immediate postwar years (Bernard, 1971). According to this interpretation, Americanization did not mean forcing immigrants into a predetermined "old American" mould. Rather they were to be assisted towards full partnership in the national life by means of "a mutual giving and taking of contributions from both newer and older Americans in the interest of the common weal". Far from demanding the suppression of immigrant languages and societies, the liberal Americanizers looked upon these elements of the immigrant's heritage as the vehicles that made it possible for him to play a role in society. Though outwardly "foreign", ethnic newspapers and organizations brought the individual into contact with his new homeland in countless ways and thus acted as agencies of Americanization in spite of themselves. In time, the immigrant (or his children) would be fully incorporated into the national life, which was, by definition, assimilation. The process was "as inevitable as it is desirable"—inevitable because it was the natural outcome of on-going social interaction; desirable because by its workings immigrants eventually became full participants in a democratic social order (Park and Burgess, 1969; Thomas *et al.*, 1971).

This understanding of assimilation was quite in line with the most authoritative sociological thinking of the day. The congruence was natural since Park of the University of Chicago was a major participant in the Americanization Studies project *and* the principal author of the standard treatise on sociology in the period between the two world wars. This was the famous *Introduction to the Science of Sociology* (original, 1921) by Park and E. W. Burgess, which served as "the green bible" for generations of graduate students as sociology came of age in the American university.

Assimilation figured here as the culminating phase of "the four great types of [social] interaction", which were competition, conflict, accommodation, and assimilation. This sequence in slightly modified form was soon christened "the race-relations cycle", and took on special importance for students of intergroup relations in the United States. Park did not restrict his focus to this country, however; rather he regarded assimilation as "central in the historical and cultural process" on the broadest scale. But while he and Burgess gave great prominence to assimilation, their discussion left certain ambiguities as to the meaning of the concept (Park and Burgess, 1969, pp. 506, 735–736).

They defined assimilation as "a process of interpenetration and fusion in which persons and groups acquire the memories, sentiments, and attitudes of other persons and groups, and, by sharing their experience and history, are incorporated with them in a common cultural life". This definition, and the preponderence of the discussion in the 1921 volume, seemed to make assimilation primarily a psychological and cultural process, a matter of the subjective consciousness of people who come to think of themselves differently from the way they had before the process began. Yet the authors played down the degree to which "like-mindedness" was required for assimilation, indicated that it might leave fundamental cultural patterns or racial characteristics unchanged, and talked in one place as though assimilation was more a matter of interdependence in social relationships than of subjective disposition or cultural orientation. This left the degree of cultural cohesion required for assimilation quite indeterminate; yet being "incorporated in a common cultural life" was central to the definition.

Park continued to grapple with the problem, and by the time he wrote the entry on "Assimilation, Social" for the *Encyclopedia of the Social Sciences* (1930) he had grown definitely sceptical about cultural cohesion as a defining feature of assimilation. In fact he began his "most concentrated theoretical discussion of assimilation" by saying that it was more a political than a cultural concept. It was simply the name of the process by which people of diverse backgrounds who occupied a common territory "achieve[d] a cultural solidarity sufficient at least to sustain a national existence". Culturally speaking, the process was to be understood in minimalist terms. "The common sense view of the matter", Park reported approvingly, "is that an immigrant is assimilated as soon as he has shown that he can 'get on in the country'." Indeed, he added, it was questionable whether culture as anthropologists conceived it could be said to exist at all in a complex modern society with its highly refined division of labour, specialization of roles, and so on. In these circumstances, assimilation did not mean close conformity to a definite cultural pattern, but merely the acceptance of "those ideas, practices and aspirations which are national . . . the generally accepted social customs and political ideas and loyalties of a community or country. . . . " (Park, 1930, pp. 281–283; see also Matthews, 1977).

This loose and largely political interpretation of assimilation left much room for diversity among the subgroups of a population, all of whose constituent elements accepted a minimum of general norms that enabled them to get along together, to undertake essential collective tasks, and to discuss their differences in a free and open manner. Indeed, this was a version of assimilation that could be understood "pluralistically"!

More detailed research would be required to establish in detail just how the concept of assimilation was used by social scientists and commentators on intergroup relations in the 1930s, but it is safe to say that it had become somewhat problematic (Gleason, 1981). On the one hand, assimilation was regarded in the abstract as a very significant process; it was also believed to be proceeding inevitably in American society, and with generally beneficent results since it operated to reduce the likelihood of intergroup conflicts and to facilitate the participation of minorities in American society. At the same time, however, assimilation still carried nativist overtones as a result of its association with chauvinistic "100-percent Americanism" and the racial xenophobia of the early 1920s. Virtually all informed commentators in the 1930s deprecated efforts at forced Americanization, and increasing attention was being paid to the costs of assimilation considered as a natural social process. The "marginal" situation of the second generation, for example, was thought to exact a heavy psychological toll, and there were also more generalized murmurs of regret at the decline of diversity in American culture.

Complicating the picture further was the enhanced cognitive authority of the anthropological concept of culture, which was rapidly coming to be regarded as "the foundation stone of the social sciences" (Chase, 1948, p. 59). One result of this development was that the term "acculturation" was often used more or less interchangeably with assimilation; but it was not clear whether the two terms meant precisely the same thing or, if not, wherein they differed. Park, as we have seen, was moving towards a differentiation of assimilation from cultural incorporation, but the preponderance of usage was in the other direction, and two of Park's students later remarked that "assimilation" and "acculturation" illustrated the way in which the terminologies of sociology and anthropology "half-blended in a grand confusion" (Hughes and Hughes, 1952, pp. 30–31).

The growing prestige of the anthropological concept of culture had two other notable effects: it discredited the idea that differences in group ways of life were explainable in racial terms; and it inculcated the ethical imperative of tolerance for diversity, which was assumed to follow as a corollary from the empirical finding that cultural values and norms differed from group to group. The latter point was often spoken of as "cultural relativism", and it had a good deal more in common with cultural pluralism than mere verbal similarity. But both developments, along with the general influence of the anthropological outlook, were important background factors in the reintroduction of the expression *cultural pluralism* in the late 1930s and its popularization in the next decade. And if acculturation stood in a somewhat ambiguous relation to assimilation, the status of cultural pluralism was considerably more paradoxical, for it was no longer posited as an alternative to assimilation; rather it was usually presented as an enlightened and liberal means of achieving the goal of assimilation, a harmoniously united society.

The 1937 volume, *Our Racial and National Minorities,* edited by Brown and Roucek, was the earliest major landmark in the reintroduction of the term. The evidence it provides indicates clearly that Kallen was not the source from which the new version of cultural pluralism stemmed, although he was the one who put the expression into circulation in the first place. Part IV of this compendium of specialized studies by different authors was headed "The Trend Toward Cultural Pluralism", but not one of the contributors to this section referred to Kallen and his name was missing from the 66-page bibliography of the book. The chapters included in this section emphasized the positive contributions to American life made by Indians, Negroes, and immigrants, and urged preservation of "the best that each group has brought". But while it was portrayed as desirable to preserve "the fundamentals of [group] heritages . . . for generations" (Brown and Roucek, 1937, p. 762), the writer who discussed these matters most explicitly denied flatly that cultural pluralism meant "the ultimate preservation of different cultural streams in our civilization". Payne, a prominent educational theorist at New York University, did not regard such an eventuality as harmful; it was simply that inevitable acculturation ruled it out and pointed toward the emergence of "a new and superior culture". Cultural pluralism, Payne explained, "does not imply that the special cultures will continue unchanged for all time. The theory involves essentially a technique of social adjustment which will make possible the preservation of the best of all cultures . . ." (Brown and Roucek, 1937, p. 763).

This version of cultural pluralism differed sharply from Kallen's original formulation since he did assume that distinct ethnic cultures would perdure indefinitely, not as contributors to a common American culture, but as equal participants in a federation of nationalities. Despite the fact that he was using the same term, Payne's cultural pluralism was actually a liberal variation of assimilation theory much like that of the post-World War I "Americanization Studies". As such it strongly resembled the approach that many earlier commentators had associated with the melting pot, although Kallen wrote his piece as a corrective to melting-pot thinking.

Brown and Roucek's volume (of which two later editions were published) opened the era in which *cultural pluralism* entered into general usage and eventually became a conventional touchstone of liberal enlightenment among commentators on American society. The most thorough investigation of the subject, done by Powell (1971), identifies some sixty-four persons who wrote about cultural pluralism between 1940 and 1955. Powell distinguishes three versions of cultural pluralism in that era: Kallen's original federation-of-nationalities type; the liberal Americanization version; and a third variety that combined elements of the other two in seeing the retention of ethnic cultures as supplements to, rather than as substitutes for, an overall American culture. The third type, which was sometimes called *cultural democracy*, differed from the second only hazily in stressing diversity-within-unity as a permanent, rather than a temporary, condition. Both of these versions made explicit provision for assimilation while simultaneously calling for toleration of diversity; the federation-of-nationalities type, however, was strongly anti-assimilationist. But according to Powell, no one who interpreted cultural pluralism in the federation-of-nationalities sense applied the concept to American society; rather it was used exclusively in reference to the "minorities problem" of Eastern Europe. This is a most important finding because it means that when cultural pluralism attained popularity in commentary on the American scene, it designated a variety (or two varieties) of assimilationist theory rather than constituting a significant alternative to assimilationism.

Even more striking is the fact that by midcentury Horace Kallen himself had abandoned the federation-of-nationalities version of cultural pluralism. Although he touched on related matters in the forties, Kallen's first major statement on the subject in three decades was *Cultural Pluralism and the American Idea* (1956), a volume consisting of three essays by Kallen and responses to his ideas (overwhelmingly favourable) by nine other scholars.

He was still glowingly committed to cultural pluralism, but it was a very different thing from what he had outlined in 1915 and 1924. All hint of racialism was, of course, gone; and there was no suggestion that immigrant nationalities would perpetuate themselves indefinitely. Indeed, pluralism was no longer specifically related to ethnicity at all. It embraced the "diverse utterance of diversities—regional, local, religious, ethnic, esthetic, industrial, sporting, and political . . ." (Kallen, 1956, p. 98).

Kallen had also enlarged his terminology: besides cultural pluralism he spoke now of "the philosophy of Cultural Pluralism", and of philosophical pluralism more generally; of spontaneous pluralism, of fluid, relational pluralism, of the actual pluralism of experience; and, with very negative overtones, of absolutist pluralism and isolationist pluralism. The relationship between pluralism and Americanization had also changed. In the twenties, Kallen attacked Americanization vehemently; but now he spoke approvingly of an "Americanization, supporting, cultivating a cultural pluralism, grounded on and consummated in the American Idea" (Kallen, 1956, p. 97). "American Idea" was appropriately capitalized, since Kallen regarded it with religious awe and declared (pp. 204–205) that it represented "that apprehension of human nature and human relations" to which all must be converted if they were to live together peaceably. But despite erecting Americanism into a civil religion, Kallen still thought he was opposed to assimilation! When an admiring commentator hailed him for discerning "that our country is a true melting-pot", he indignantly disavowed all sympathy for the melting pot.

As Kallen's performance suggests, the concept of cultural pluralism had by the mid-fifties become highly elusive and contradictory, not to say hopelessly muddled. The most important factors in bringing this situation about were the great revival of the democratic ideology in World War II, the postwar critique of conformity, and the popularization of pluralism as an interpretation of American politics.

The war of course created an urgent need for national unity (see Higham, 1975; Gleason, 1980, 1981). Since assimilation is associated with unity, while pluralism implies differentiation, one would naturally expect the war to generate a strong push for assimilation. That did happen, although it seemed that just the opposite development was going on. What obscured matters was the fact that the demand for unity was usually couched in the language of pluralism and diversity, instead of being talked about in terms of assimilation or Americanization. The explanation for this seemingly paradoxical state of affairs was that unity was sought on the common ground of ideological consensus, and the principle of tolerance for diversity was heavily stressed as a key element in the democratic ideology behind which all were supposed to rally in the wartime crisis.

Unity was sought on the basis of ideological consensus because, as Gunnar Myrdal (1962, p. 1004) insisted at the time, "This War is an ideological war fought in defense of democracy". It pitted the United States against totalitarian regimes that denied the premise of human equality and perverted the ideals of freedom and self-determination beyond recognition. Confronted by the monstrous contrast of Nazism, it was quite understandable that Americans were galvanized to a deeper appreciation of democracy, and that their leaders should reaffirm the nation's collective commitment to freedom, equality, and respect for human dignity. To be an American was to identify oneself with these values. Race, religion, or ethnic background were secondary issues; true Americanism was defined by ideological commitment.

But if ideological consensus was to serve as an effective basis for national unity, Americans would have to do more than profess democratic principles—they would have to live up to them, which was something they were notoriously *not* doing in the area of race relations. This was the reason that tolerance for diversity came to be regarded as so vital an element of the democratic creed. It was bad enough that racial prejudice and discrimination were embarrassing inconsistencies that invited exploitation by enemy propagandists; even more distressing was the fact that intergroup hostilities weakened national unity and thus hampered the war effort. The need for mutual tolerance and good will among all segments of the population was recognized even before the United States became involved in the fighting. But the outburst in 1943 of race riots in Detroit and mob violence against Mexican-Americans in Los Angeles lent much greater urgency to the task of reducing intergroup tensions. According to one count (Williams, 1947), there were no fewer than 123 national organizations working for better intergroup relations by the end of the war. This sort of "action for unity", as one study called it, carried over into the postwar era. At the same time, programmes of "intercultural education" were widely adopted in the schools, and the study of race and minority problems became major specialties among social scientists (Vickery and Cole, 1943; Watson, 1947; Rose, 1968; Montalto, 1978).

Cultural pluralism and *cultural democracy* became part of the standard terminology of this broad movement to improve intergroup relations, but its goals were social harmony and national unity, not heightened consciousness of the differences between peoples. On the contrary, differences among population groups were precisely the problem, and the real message of many of the preachments about diversity was that fundamentally people were more alike than different, and that the failure to be guided by recognition of that fact was what constituted prejudice. Thus in 1944 almost four thousand American psychologists subscribed to a "Psychologists' Manifesto" which stated, among other things, that prejudices could be reduced by teaching people "that members of one racial, national, or cultural group are basically similar to those of other groups, and have similar problems, hopes, aspirations, and needs" (Murphy, 1945, pp. 455–456).

The world *assimilation* was not generally used in discussions of race relations—no doubt because it was too closely associated with the sensitive issue of intermarriage—but the goals of the struggle for civil rights and integration were, as Killian (1981, p. 43) puts it, "fundamentally and unrelentingly assimilationist". In these circumstances, the original anti-assimilationist version of cultural pluralism, vaguely racial in its assumptions and open to a segregationist interpretation, simply could not be admitted (Rose and Rose, 1953). But as it gained currency in the loose tolerance-for-diversity sense, the concept of cultural pluralism became quite blurry and moved in the direction of self-contradiction. Verbally it seemed to celebrate differences between groups; actually it rested on the assumptions that basic consensus made Americans one people in essentials, that the differences between groups were relatively superficial, and that toleration of those differences was required by the value system on which consensus was grounded.

But while assimilationist assumptions and goals were thus fundamental to the campaign for better intergroup relations, those who were committed to the good cause did not think of themselves as assimilationists. On the contrary, the word *assimilation* had a disreputable air about it. Those concerned with the most serious problem, race relations, had good reason to avoid using the term. In the area where it had been traditionally used—discussions of immigrant adjustment—the conventional wisdom of the day held that assimilation had done its work, and perhaps overdone it. Immigration had been virtually cut off for a generation, and it was widely held that the children and grandchildren of the earlier immigrants were becoming completely Americanized (Smith, 1939). Hence assimilation was no longer a problem: Americans could relax on that score. And being able to relax, a good many felt embarrassed about the extremes to which assimilationist efforts had sometimes been carried. Awakening to the realization that our minorities were vanishing, social commentators in the postwar years were clearly uncomfortable with the concept of assimilation (Borrie, 1959). Cultural pluralism was much more attractive. It took unity for granted—and why not, if assimilation was an accomplished fact?—and combined with it an appealing invocation of diversity.

Rising postwar concern over the evils of "mass society" highlighted certain negative consequences of assimilation and, by doing so, reinforced the appeal of cultural pluralism (Bell, 1963). The critics of mass society were, after all, champions of diversity; they bemoaned its decline and the concomitant homogenizing of society into a bland, standardized sameness. Assimilation was clearly one of the main culprits here; it was hardly more than another name for homogenization.

Even more troubling, however, was the linkage between immigrant assimilation and a constellation of socio-psychological morbidities that the critics discerned in mass society—alienation, anxiety, anomie, over-conformity, ethnocentrism and, most ominously, authoritarianism. It was a commonplace in those days that immigrants and their children were to some extent "marginalized" by the process of assimilation, and plunged as a result into a kind of "psychological civil war" (Gleason, 1981). The bearing of this phenomenon on the symptomology of mass society was not developed in a systematic way, but there is evidence that it was perceived by observers at midcentury. Erik H. Erikson, for example, mentioned immigration in connection with identity problems, and other influential writers portrayed immigrants as archetypically American in their being uprooted and cut off from the past (Erikson, 1950). Being rootless, ethnic Americans were vulnerable to status-anxieties; they might easily become ethnocentric, and they were almost bound to be conformists. In short, they were prime candidates for recruitment into irrational, authoritarian social movements, and their support for McCarthyism was interpreted by several commentators along the lines suggested by this sort of mass-society analysis (Shils, 1956; Bell, 1964).

No one argued that immigrant assimilation was primarily responsible for the evils of mass society. But given the linkages just outlined, it was obviously part of the problem rather than being a solution to it. The antidote for tendencies towards massification was diversity; hence pluralism was bound to be stressed. And that is what happened: a group of political analysts emerged in the 1950s who offered *pluralism* as an interpretation of the American system and as a preventative for the dangers of extremism inherent in the politics of a mass society (Nicholls, 1974). These writers drew on an intellectual tradition different from that of students of intergroup relations; they seldom, if ever, referred to cultural pluralism as such, and the focus of their interest was different. Yet their approach was compatible with the midcentury versions of cultural pluralism, and since the latter had become extremely vague anyhow, the newer political pluralism merged with existing tradition of usage to make *pluralism* more diffuse and generalized than ever.

Pluralism, in the new sense, designated a theory of interest-group politics. It portrayed the American system as an interplay among different groups— labour unions, business associations, religious bodies, professional societies, and so on—which mobilized their resources to influence political decision-making by means of publicity, lobbying, and other forms of pressure.

Alliances were forged and dissolved according to the changing needs of the groups involved. Political parties functioned as coalitions of interest groups. Since they were naturally desirous of attracting as much support as possible, parties inclined towards comprehensiveness; this made them reluctant to embrace rigid ideological positions or to identify themselves with extremist solutions to problems. The fact that interest groups (sometimes called "veto groups") often nullified each other also worked against domination of the system by extremist elements. Moreover, the individual citizen belonged to a variety of different interest groups, and the "crosscutting pressures" set up by multiple group loyalties likewise militated against all-out commitment to an overriding ideological goal.

According to the pluralists' interpretation, the diffusion of power and influence among a multitude of shifting groups thus forestalled many of the dangers of a mass society in which atomized individuals were apt to be swept up in irrational movements that promised a totally new order. But their theory also excluded totalitarian extremism by definition—that is, they insisted that for pluralism to work, all the groups involved had to exercise moderation, had to abide by the rules of the game. This meant, in general, accepting the constitutional framework, following agreed-upon democratic procedures, and being guided by the conventions of civility and basic decency in the political struggle. Without this kind of democratic consensus, pluralism would not imply an acceptable and indeed healthy "limited warfare", but a brutal contest in which naked force would quickly dominate political life and democratic government would be impossible (Truman, 1951; Shils, 1956; Kornhauser, 1959; Lipset, 1960).

Ethnic groups did not have a distinctive place in this theory, as they had in respect to cultural pluralism. Yet it certainly covered the case of ethnic groups along with all others that opted to participate in the political process. And we have already seen that Horace Kallen had by 1956 vastly extended what he still called cultural pluralism to embrace a whole range of diversities besides those of ethnic origin. These points of contact make it understandable that the two versions of pluralism blended together. Yet there was another similarity between them that is even more significant from our perspective. *Each was predicated on consensus around the American value system, despite the fact that verbally each seemed to place a premium on diversity.*

The consequence of this double dose of pluralism, as we might call it, was that Americans tended to mislead themselves as to how deeply they were committed to diversity. In discussions of the political system and of the key social issue of intergroup relations, pluralism and diversity were endlessly extolled. Indeed, pluralism was made virtually synonymous with the democratic social and political order (Kallen, 1943; Kornhauser, 1959). This inevitably gave rise to confusion as to the relation of cart and horse because it obscured the point that pluralism and toleration for diversity did not *define* democracy, but were *corollaries* that flowed from the prior acceptance of democratic values as the basis of national unity. For, in spite of all the celebration of diversity, it was not pluralism as such that constituted the American identity; rather it was ideological consensus, a common commitment to the ideals of freedom, equality, and democratic self-government.

All of this was clear enough in the realm of ideology as such. It was notorious that "unAmerican" ideas, movements, and organizations were beyond the pale of tolerable diversity. In the era of the Cold War there was no question of applying to Communists the principle of pluralistic acceptance: they were a part of a totalitarian movement that was excluded by virtue of its self-definition and its intrinsic nature. But there was another group, bitterly opposed to Communists but sometimes likened to them anyhow, whose situation was more ambiguous—American Catholics. As a religious minority they presumably belonged in the pluralistic picture. But their Americanism seemed very questionable to some influential observers including, incidentally, Kallen (1951). The controversies that arose between Catholics and elements of the Protestant, Jewish, and liberal communities often featured charges of "divisiveness", and are highly revealing of the complexities of pluralism and assimilation in the 1950s. This whole area takes on added importance in view of the fact that cultural pluralism seemed to be resolving itself into religious pluralism. We must therefore look briefly into the relation of pluralism to American Catholicism, despite the complications it entails.

The case for regarding Catholics as full partners in the pluralistic experiment was strong. They had been in the land since early colonial days; freedom of religion was a basic American postulate; religion itself was a key element in the culture of many ethnic groups; and the American Catholic community was made up of a large number of ethnic subgroups. Besides these important points, Catholics had often been victims of nativist hostility, which gave added force to their claim for tolerance as fully accredited actors on the pluralistic scene.

At the same time, the Americanism of Catholics seemed doubtful to many, just as it had in the past. Uneasiness at midcentury centred primarily upon the Church's internal organization and discipline, which was hierarchical and authoritarian; her teachings on the union of Church and state and various moral issues like divorce and birth control, which were conservative if not reactionary; and her doctrinal dogmatism and generally absolutist intellectual stance. In view of these characteristics, many American liberals (Protestant, Jewish, and secular) found Catholic professions of commitment

to American principles unconvincing. The Catholic Church was too undemocratic to be trusted; according to her severest critics, she was too close to
being totalitarian to merit unqualified admission to the theatre of American
pluralism (Blanshard, 1949, 1951).

These doubts were brought into focus in the late 1940s and early 1950s as
sharp religious controversy broke out, pitting Catholics against libertarians
(religious and non-religious) with the latter being supported by others who
entertained a more generalized religious suspicion of Catholics (Kane,
1955). A number of factors were involved, but the most important and
enduring source of friction centred upon the question of public support for
religious education and particularly the use of public funds for Catholic
parochial schools. It was in this context that the issue of divisiveness was
raised.

The term had been used earlier, but it was given special prominence when
Conant, the president of Harvard University, warned against the dangers to
a democratic unity posed by a "dual system" of public *and* private schools.
Affirming his commitment to the "fundamental belief in tolerance for
diversity so basic to our society", and denying that he advocated suppressing
private schools, Conant nevertheless contended that the public schools
should serve "all creeds and economic groups within a given geographic
area", and he pointed out that many foreign observers had commented on
the function of public schools in "assimilat[ing] so rapidly the different
cultures which came to North America in the nineteenth century". Then
Conant added two sentences that attracted wide attention: "The greater the
proportion of our youth who fail to attend our public schools and who
receive their education elsewhere, the greater the threat to our democratic
unity. To use taxpayers' money to assist private schools is to suggest that
American society use its own hands to destroy itself". (Conant, 1953,
pp. 80–81; see also Conant, 1970).

Catholics naturally resented the implication of divisiveness; and they
made the point that it was the very existence of Catholic schools, not just
public support for them, that Conant (1953) branded as a threat to democratic unity. From their viewpoint, the maintenance of a separate school system
reflecting their distinctive religious and moral values was a legitimate
expression of pluralism, thoroughly in line with American principles, and in
no way a threat to democratic unity. On the contrary, they interpreted the
exclusive equation of democratic education with the public schools as
evidence of a "statist" or even totalitarian tendency in American life. As one
of the most respected Catholic spokesmen put it, "the notion of 'public
education' as meaning a unitary and monolithic school system which singly
and alone is entitled to public support has rightly been called . . . 'an
aberration in the general picture of our society, which is pluralistic'."
(Murray, 1960, p. 147).

Now the pertinent question for us is not whose interpretation here was correct; the question, rather, is: What distinguishes the "divisive" from the "pluralistic"? The two terms are practically interchangeable in denotation, for that which is divided has thereby been made plural, and if something is pluralized it must necessarily have been somehow divided.

Perhaps there were attempts to draw analytical distinctions; if so, they did not attract widespread notice, to say nothing of gaining general acceptance. The real difference between divisiveness and pluralism as it comes through in the literature is strictly connotative, rather than denotative; that is, divisiveness was an invidious term for forms of social differentiation one disapproved of, while pluralism was a positive label for differences one found acceptable or good. The tacit criterion for distinguishing good from bad forms of social differentiation was presumably the democratic ideology or, more precisely, whether the difference in question was or was not compatible with the democratic value system. Catholics and their antagonists differed on this basic question and that was why institutions that were "pluralistic" to the former were "divisive" to the latter. But the terminology in which the controversy was carried on tended to conceal, rather than clarify, what was really at issue, namely, differing interpretations of democracy and what it permitted, or required, in the sphere of education. Discussions carried on in this fashion, as Murray (1960) once observed, seldom reached the arduously attained level of clearcut disagreement. Instead they floundered in confusion.

On rare occasions pluralism as such was evaluated negatively in connection with the Catholic threat. On 13 June 1951, the *Christian Century* ran a lengthy report on what was perceived as an effort to mobilize Catholics in Buffalo into religiously segregated associations with the goal in mind of "mak[ing] this a Roman Catholic city". Accompanying this alarmist account was an editorial headed "Pluralism—National Menace", which began by warning that Buffalo was not the only city "facing the threat of a plural society based on religious differences". "The idea of a plural society", the editors continued, "is so new to Americans that many will not even understand the term". They might have added that those familiar with current thinking on cultural pluralism would have been the most shocked of all, for what the *Christian Century* was talking about differed radically from the benign versions of pluralism to be found in the American literature. This species was described in unrelievedly negative terms. It applied to a situation in which different elements existed side-by-side in the same polity without mingling, each pursuing its own group interests as far as it could. A pluralistic society of this sort had no national will; anarchy, instability, or the domination of one element by another was to be expected; and materialistic economic considerations were exalted above all else because nothing of a more elevated nature united the various groups of the society.

This version of pluralism derived from the writings of Furnivall, the earliest of the "plural society" theorists, a group whose work did not become generally known, even to American social scientists, until the 1960s (Powell, 1971; Van den Berghe, 1973). The work of these scholars dealt with colonial and newly post-colonial lands, and was quite negative in assessing the social costs of internal cleavages deriving from differences in race, language, religion, and so on. It was a kind of nightmare vision of Kallen's original federation-of-nationalities pluralism gone sour, and its application to the American scene was anomalous in the extreme. What the episode indicates is the degree to which growing Catholic strength and assertiveness disturbed spokesmen for Protestantism. Confronting this kind of pluralism, the editors of *Christian Century* (1951, p. 703) felt no embarrassment in calling universal public education "the *sine qua non* of a homogeneous society", and in urging "straightforward, uncompromising resistance to any efforts by any group to subvert the traditional American way of life".

Although the *Christian Century*'s editorial attracted much attention among observers of the religious scene, interreligious feeling mellowed in the mid-fifties and the fearsome variety of pluralism it presented left no trace on subsequent usage. In January 1958, *School and Society* even ran an article entitled "Subsidized Pluralism", which argued that the time had come to provide public funding for private schools which were set up to meet special group needs not adequately provided for by the public schools. The author, Robert F. Creegan, was affiliated with a state teachers' college in New York; he regarded pluralism as "a philosophy of freedom" that merited public support, and he felt that a way could be found to provide it without contravening constitutional prohibitions in respect to Church/State and desegregation (see also Creegan, 1959).

This proposal caught the attention of Joshua A. Fishman, then at the University of Pennsylvania, who arranged a symposium on the topic at the 1958 meeting of the American Psychological Association. Most of the participants (whose papers were published in the 23 May 1959 issue of *School and Society*) were unsympathetic to the idea of subsidized pluralism. Marshall Sklare (1959) of the American Jewish Committee seemed bemused by the fact that the topic was being discussed at all, and he suggested that it might be more timely to think about moderating pluralism rather than strengthening it. Subsidized pluralism would deepen "divisiveness", and cause concern among Jews because "greater support for parochialism" might increase the dangers of authoritarianism and anti-Semitism. Other black and Jewish participants were firmly opposed to the idea, alluding to the evils of segregation, *apartheid,* and "cultural *parallelism*" (sic). It was even suggested that by expanding the welfare state, Creegan's proposal would reinforce tendencies toward totalitarianism, and thus imperil genuine diversity and freedom (Chworowsky, 1959; Plaut, 1959). Only Creegan himself and Charles Donahue, a Catholic professor from Fordham University, argued that the proposal was justifiable in terms of the nation's tradition of religious pluralism (Creegan, 1959; Donahue, 1959).

In reviewing the discussion, Fishman (1959) brought out several points highly relevant to the relation of pluralism and assimilation. Despite verbal adherence to cultural pluralism, he observed, Americans were not really in agreement about what groupings in society were viable candidates for permanent survival and merited public support along the lines visualized by Creegan's proposal. Racial and religious groupings seemed permanent, but were ineligible for public support on account of constitutional prohibitions; immigrant ethnic groups were eligible, in Fishman's view, but assimilation worked against the likelihood of their survival, and they were "not popularly defined (or even self-defined) as meriting permanent existence in American society". The latter groups were thus too far gone along the road to assimilation to make group maintenance feasible; and, leaving the constitutional issue aside, Americans did not want to encourage religious diversity because it might cut too deeply, upsetting the existing *modus vivendi*. For although they had learned to live with diversity, Americans were not really committed to promoting it. "The kind of diversity we have come to respect", Fishman wrote, " . . . [and] to proclaim via brotherhood weeks, interrelations committees, assembly programs for school children, and hollywoodized fiction is a respectable, westernized, protestantized diversity—a diversity of agreeable sorts and proportions. Above all, it is a participationist diversity and not a separatist diversity" (1959, p. 267).

The tone of Fishman's analysis left some doubt as to whether he approved or disapproved the national taste in diversity, but he had put his finger on the underlying paradox of pluralist thinking in the 1950s, viz. its assimilationist substructure. Almost equally striking is the aptness of the labels "participationist" and "separatist" for designating the divergence that developed among American Catholics themselves in reference to pluralism.

Catholics were virtually at one in regarding religious differences as the key differentiating elements in a pluralistic society. By religious differences they understood "divergent and incompatible views" with respect to basic questions like the existence and nature of God, the ontological order of reality, the nature and destiny of man, and the sources of moral obligation. Because it involved differences so fundamental, pluralism necessarily implied "disagreement and dissension within the community"; but it also implied "a community within which there must be agreement and consensus". This, as Murray (1960) observed laconically, constituted "no small political problem", for some way had to be found whereby all religious groups could participate in the oneness of the community, despite their dissensions; yet the common principles of participation could not be such as to interfere with the maintenance by each group of its distinctive religious identity.

With this formulation of the pluralistic problem nearly all Catholics would have agreed. Where they differed among themselves was in their assessment of the relative importance of these dialectical contraries, and in the inferences they drew as to policies to be followed in the practical order. The traditional and still predominant approach in the 1950s can be called "separatist" in that it gave priority to preserving the religious identity of Catholics by means of Catholic schools and other religiously based associations that performed a boundary-maintaining function. Such an approach was, in the minds of its supporters, required by the facts of the pluralistic situation and justified by American pluralistic principles.

The contrasting "participationist" interpretation of pluralism rose to prominence in the 1950s when it won the support of the liberal Catholic intelligentsia, whose principal organ was the weekly journal, *Commonweal.* The great concern of these *Commonweal* Catholics, as they were sometimes called, was to bring the Church out of its "Catholic ghetto" and into "the mainstream" of American life. From their standpoint, separatism was precisely what was wrong with American Catholicism; they were therefore highly critical of "ghetto organizations" that sealed Catholics off from interaction with their fellow citizens of other (or no) religious background. According to their understanding, American society was pluralistic because it consisted of persons and groups of diverse origin and character, all of whom worked together in the common enterprise of national life. The appropriate response to this situation was for Catholics, *as individuals,* to involve themselves in "pluralistic" activities (i.e. organizations, causes, and movements in which Catholics took their places alongside Protestants, Jews, and secular liberals in working for goals that would advance the common good of society).

The assimilationist tendency of this approach is obvious. It was further reflected in the sympathetic interest shown by Catholic liberals of the fifties in the historical tradition of ecclesiastical "Americanism", which was recovered by a great outpouring of scholarship in the postwar era. But the term *assimilation* was never used in reference to the participationist strategy—at least not with positive connotations. Rather it was simply called *pluralism.*

American Catholics thus collectively espoused two sharply contrasting versions of pluralism—one that justified the self-segregation of Catholics in denominationally based social and cultural associations, and another that justified the mixing together of Catholics and non-Catholics in every sort of social context except those relating directly to worship. This naturally gave rise to confusion. And as pluralism came to be closely identified with democracy in general American usage, Catholic confusion took on a more impassioned polemical quality because spokesmen for both versions inter-preted pluralism as a *normative* concept, one that should guide behaviour. In other words, the separatist and the participationist version—each simply described as "pluralistic"—was offered as *the* democractic prescription for how Catholics should respond to the conditions of American life. It was difficult at best for Catholics to decide how they should respond to American life; by using the same equivocal term to designate opposite strategies, they made it an almost insoluble problem (Gleason, 1964b; Callahan, 1963; Canavan, 1963).

As Catholics thrashed about in this semantic muddle, their situation *vis-à-vis* pluralism was becoming a matter of more general theoretical interest. Herberg's *Protestant-Catholic-Jew* (1955) was the first major land-mark in this development. Glazer and Moynihan's *Beyond the Melting Pot* (1963) and Gordon's *Assimilation in American Life* (1964) continued to emphasize the importance of religion as a key element in pluralism, but the appearance of these books presaged an era in which race and ethnicity came to dominate the consciousness of those who talked and wrote about pluralism.

Herberg's brilliantly provocative analysis of the postwar "revival of religion" gave the factor of religion unprecedented salience as the key element in American cultural diversity. Yet if Herberg articulated a new form of pluralism, as Powell (1971) maintains, he did so largely in the process of tracing the workings of assimilation, and the moral he drew from his investigation was that religion itself was in danger of being assimilated to the American Way of Life. He was a determined religious pluralist in resisting such an eventuality, but he clearly regarded assimilationist forces as much stronger in American society than those tending to preserve cultural or religious diversity.

Assimilation figured in Herberg's argument in at least three ways, which are distinguishable but closely related. The problem he set out to explain was how it could be that American society was experiencing a great revival of religion, while in every other respect it seemed to be growing more sec-ularized than ever. To solve this paradox he turned to the social psychology of an immigrant-derived people. The religious revival, he suggested, was their response to the psychic malaise induced by contemporary mass society. People felt rootless and alone in mass society; religion gave them a sense of where they belonged by providing a link of continuity with the past and a meaningful location in the world of the present. Religion was the only viable linkage with the past because assimilation had eroded all the other elements of immigrant culture. In identifying themselves with organized Protestan-tism, Catholicism, and Judaism, persons of immigrant background were therefore giving expression to their residual loyalties and at the same time protecting themselves from anomie, alienation, and the other ills of mass society (Herberg, 1955).

Its role in leaching away the non-religious elements of immigrant heritages (language, societies, etc.) is the first way in which assimilation figures in Herberg's analysis. The second relates to the Americanization of immigrant religious heritages, for, while they survived, they did not survive unchanged by assimilation. Herberg devotes separate chapters to the history of Protestantism, Catholicism, and Judaism showing how each tradition was modified in interaction with New World circumstances, with the last two being most clearly Americanized as they all moved towards equal standing as "the three great faiths of democracy".

The mention of democracy brings us to the third dimension of assimilation in Herberg's interpretation, and the only one towards which he adopted a definitely critical stance. The democratic ideology, or what he called the American Way of Life, was, in Herberg's judgement, the *real* religion of Americans; he thought they prized traditional organized religion because it was functionally useful in buttressing the national ideology. Protestantism, Catholicism, and Judaism, in other words, enjoyed public approbation because they provided three equally acceptable ways for the individual to manifest his or her commitment to the "spiritual values" underlying the American Way of Life, not because they were looked upon as embodiments of autonomous religious truth. Herberg had great admiration for democracy as a socio-political ideology, but he resolutely opposed the tendency to erect it into a civil religion. His conviction that such a tendency existed, and that it threatened to denature the true religious quality of the "three great faiths of democracy", is a measure of the degree to which he believed assimilation was carrying everything before it.

Herberg's analysis of religious pluralism thus testified to the pervasive influence of assimilation. In the racial sphere, the assimilationist-oriented drive for integration and civil rights assumed new importance after the mid-fifties and soon demanded equal time with religion from those who discussed the sources of diversity in American life. In 1963 Glazer and Moynihan's *Beyond the Melting Pot* brought the convergence of these elements into full articulation by proposing that religion and race were the two most important organizing principles in American society. In the nation's great cities, they said, "four major groups emerge: Catholics, Jews, white Protestants, and Negroes, each making up the city in different proportions". Looking into the future they ventured the prediction that religion and race would "define the next stage in the evolution of the American peoples" (pp. 314–315).

This forecast was based on a study of New York City which had shown that group identity among Negroes, Puerto Ricans, Jews, Italians, and Irish was a powerful force in shaping the social and political life of the metropolis. Only the racial half of the prediction was borne out by events, but the book has been so closely linked to the great upsurge of racial and ethnic consciousness that followed its publication that the reader today is startled by the importance attached by the authors to religion. The same linkage with the new ethnicity has probably misled those only casually acquainted with the book into thinking that it provides an unqualified confirmation of the cultural pluralist interpretation of American society. The position taken by the authors is considerably more complex, although it is pluralist in a general sense.

Glazer and Moynihan (1963, p. 290) invited an oversimplified reading by the title they chose and by the statement, repeated twice, that "the point about the melting pot is that it did not happen". For, despite this seemingly categorical assertion, they did not deny the reality of assimilation. On the contrary, they regarded assimilation as a powerful solvent that washed out immigrant languages, customs, and "the specifically *national* aspect" of ethnic cultures in two or three generations. For that reason they looked upon "the dream of 'cultural pluralism'" as no more realistic than "the hope of a melting pot'" (pp. 12–14). Glazer and Moynihan might therefore have said with equal justice that cultural pluralism "did not happen" either; what their analysis actually suggested was that the processes designated by both terms had really taken place, although neither had worked out as people seemed to expect. The melting pot did change immigrants and their descendants quite profoundly; yet ethnicity persisted in American society despite the transformation wrought by assimilation. Pluralism did exist and was based on ethnicity; but ethnicity itself had been reshaped by the assimilative forces of American society and no longer constituted itself clearly around identifiable cultural traits or foreign nationality. Thus the ethnic group was "not a survival from the age of mass immigration but a new social form" produced by the interaction of group heritage and American conditions (pp. 16–17).

This subtle analysis underscored the dialectical relationship of assimilation and pluralism, but it was usually portrayed by later spokesmen for the new ethnicity as having completely discredited the "fearful and contemptuous" theory of melting-pot assimilation (Paulding, 1963). Something of the same sort happened to Gordon's *Assimilation in American Life*, which appeared the year after Glazer and Moynihan's book and which presented an interpretation congruent with theirs in certain respects.

Gordon's work was the most ambitious theoretical study till then undertaken of the role played in American society by ethnicity, assimilation, and pluralism, and any attempt to capture its main points in a few words runs the risk of distortion. Nevertheless, we must confine ourselves to three aspects of the book: the salience it accords to race and religion; the treatment of assimilation and pluralism as such; and the nature of its contribution to later thinking about these matters. The first point will not detain us long, but it is important to note that, like Glazer and Moynihan, Gordon treated religion and race as the main sources of diversity in American life. He also referred to *Protestant-Catholic-Jew*, and in one place made use of Herberg's image of multiple melting pots, the most important of which had religious or racial labels. And a long chapter entitled "The Subsociety and the Subculture in America" is divided into subsections devoted to Negroes, Jews, Catholics, white Protestants, and intellectuals (whom Gordon considered a kind of incipient ethnic group).

Gordon began his treatment of assimilation proper with an informative review of the way social scientists had defined it and related concepts like acculturation and amalgamation. On the basis of this review and his earlier discussion of social structure and culture, he then elaborated a seven-stage model of the assimilation process. The crucial distinction was between the first stage, "cultural or behavioral assimilation", and the second, "structural assimilation". The former, which Gordon equated with acculturation, referred to the adoption by those undergoing assimilation of the cultural patterns of the host society. He left the meaning of "cultural patterns" vague, but in general cultural assimilation meant adopting the English language and conforming to other visible, external features of American culture. Structural assimilation, on the other hand, meant large-scale entry into the "cliques, clubs, and institutions of [the] host society" on the level of primary-group relationships. In other words, structural assimilation was not a matter of how one acted, but of who one interacted with.

The remaining stages involved in the process Gordon listed as follows: *marital* assimilation, marked by large-scale intermarriage; *identificational* assimilation, marked by the development of a sense of peoplehood based exclusively on the host society; *attitude receptional* assimilation, which referred to the absence of prejudice against the group being assimilated; *behaviour receptional* assimilation, referring to the absence of discrimination against those assimilating; and *civic* assimilation, meaning that there were no political differences concerning issues of power and values between the assimilating group and the host society.

Gordon referred variously to this scheme as an ideal type, an analytical model, and an array of assimilation variables, but the reader could hardly be blamed for assuming that it was being presented as a description of social reality. For, by applying the model to American society, Gordon was able to elicit facts that led him to conclude that cultural assimilation was the first to take place, but its taking place did not necessarily mean that structural assimilation would follow. These conclusions were said to be borne out by the history of immigration, from which one would infer that social reality did conform to the model. Moreover, the variables were interrelated causally from structural assimilation on down. For although cultural assimilation did not necessarily bring structural assimilation in its wake (and had not done so historically, according to Gordon), structural assimilation *was* indissolubly linked to marital assimilation, which led in turn to identificational assimilation, and so on down the line, "like a row of tenpins bowled over in rapid succession by a well placed strike". This insight led to a formulation that sounded as much like a fact of nature as an analytical relationship: "Structural assimilation, then, rather than acculturation, is seen to be the keystone of the arch of assimilation" (Gordon, 1964, pp. 80–81).

By analogy with the distinction between cultural and structural assimilation, Gordon also distinguished between cultural and structural pluralism. The concept of *cultural pluralism* was appropriate before cultural assimilation took place, when the intergroup situation was characterized by diversity of languages, customs, and other visible manifestations of cultural differences. *Structural pluralism,* however, was the proper designation after the various groups involved had undergone acculturation but were not yet structurally assimilated. The reader who followed all this could hardly have been surprised by Gordon's assertion that structural pluralism was "the major key to the understanding of the ethnic makeup of American society". And he certainly would have been justified in assuming Gordon (1964, pp. 157–159) was making a statement about social reality when he said that structural pluralism was "a more accurate term for the American situation . . . than cultural pluralism, although some of the latter also remains".

Now whatever he may have intended, and despite language suggesting here and there that his conceptual scheme was a purely theoretical construct not meant to be taken as a description of social reality, Gordon's analysis implied that such assimilation as had actually taken place was shallow and superficial—being largely confined to the first of seven possible stages—and that pluralism was a much deeper and more meaningful reality in American society than assimilation. This brings us to the influence the book had on subsequent thinking about pluralism and ethnicity. I have not systematically surveyed the literature with that question in mind, but, as one professionally interested in ethnicity during the entire period since the book was published, my impression is that Gordon's work was, like Glazer and Moynihan's, generally regarded as having discredited the "assimilationist myth". His distinction between cultural and structural pluralism, although noted by serious students of ethnicity, had no impact on popular usage, an area where the ethnic revival was soon to make *cultural pluralism* more of a shibboleth than ever. By offering scholarly confirmation of the persistence of some sort of pluralism based on ethnicity, Gordon's work doubtless reinforced this outcome, despite the fact that it argued that cultural pluralism was passing from the scene as a result of cultural assimilation.

Passi (1971) touched on this matter in professing puzzlement at what he deemed Gordon's inconsistency. He could not understand how Gordon could perceive the reality of pluralism as fully as he did and still maintain that cultural assimilation had actually taken place on a large scale. In Passi's view, cultural pluralism was as much a continuing fact as structural pluralism, and he interpreted Gordon's obtuseness on this point as evidence of the "transitional nature" of his book. Passi wrote as an advocate of the new ethnicity, and he was certainly correct that thinking on pluralism and assimilation had changed dramatically in the years since Gordon's book had appeared.

The transition towards which *Beyond the Melting Pot* and *Assimilation in American Life* pointed was the great upsurge of ethnic feeling that arose as an aspect of the radical social and cultural changes of the late 1960s. These developments are too complex to enter into; and what was variously called the ethnic revival, the new ethnicity, or the new pluralism produced a literature too extensive to review (Weed, 1973; Colburn and Pozzetta, 1979; Mann, 1979). All we can do here is highlight a few of the issues most directly related to assimilation–pluralism polarity.

The assertion of ethnic claims in many parts of the world suggests the inadequacy of a strictly national explanation, but in this country the most important single factor in the ethnic revival was the new spirit of group-centred militance shown by American blacks. The mid-sixties shift from the assimilationist-oriented drive for integration and civil rights to a more aggressively particularistic emphasis on black power, black pride, and black culture legitimatized "ethnicity"—a word that only came into widespread use in the late 1960s as the designation for the kind of "we-group" feeling that would have been branded in the 1940s or 1950s as "ethnocentrism". After it was legitimatized by blacks, ethnicity was quickly taken up by other groups in American society.

The rapid emergence of red power, brown power, and white ethnic movements underscores another important point about the assertion of ethnicity, namely that it served group interests. Ethnicity became a means for mobilizing group energies to enforce group demands, and it was generally associated with a claim on public authorities for the redress of wrongs or some other kind of action designed to benefit the group in question. Glazer and Moynihan pointed out in 1963 that ethnic groups were also interest groups, and as national policy moved towards affirmative action, the significance of the group-interest dimension of ethnicity stood forth more clearly than ever. Students of the "plural society" type of pluralism, whose work was becoming more widely known in the 1970s, also stressed the group-interest angle, some even portraying it as the basic element in the whole phenomenon of ethnicity and pluralism (Despres, 1975; Glazer, 1975; Glazer and Moynihan, 1963).

The persistence of ethnicity (as qualified by Glazer and Moynihan and Gordon), the influence of the black example, and the group-interest angle all figure as positive factors in the enhanced salience of pluralism that marked the revival of ethnicity. But there was an equally important negative factor: the discrediting of assimilation that was an inevitable by-product of the revulsion from traditional Americanism brought on by the racial upheaval and the Vietnam War. The crisis engendered by these and related developments (e.g. urban riots and campus disruptions) severely shook the confidence of Americans in their national values and institutions. Few, it is true, accepted the extreme view that "AmeriKKKa" was fundamentally vicious and oppressive, but the damage to collective self-esteem was sufficient to discredit assimilation because assimilation means identification with national values, ideals, and institutions. In the distemper of the sixties, "Americanization" became a term of abuse, and the melting pot was held up to scorn as a hateful symbol for a contemptible goal which had, however, not been realized because of the enduring ethnicity of our pluralistic population.

The new ethnicity thus accentuated the ostensible contrast between pluralism and assimilation; and by associating the former with admirable social goals and the latter with disreputable goals it made the terminology more value-laden and rigidly judgemental. This aggravated the semantic obscurities of the past and generated some new ones as pluralism was ritualistically invoked in support of the most diverse positions. Critics of the new ethnicity soon appeared, and the picture grew more complicated in the mid-1970s (Patterson, 1977; Stein and Hill, 1977). From the vantage point of the present (1982), the most significant development seems to have been the emergence of a radically "separatist" interpretation of pluralism, which is associated with a revival of racialist thinking, and which is likely to arouse a reaffirmation of assimilation as a respectable social policy.

In the early stages of the ethnic revival, most people seemed to have a "participationist" version of pluralism in mind when they used the term. Participationist here means the kind of pluralism that embodies a healthy chunk of assimilation without labelling it as such. It envisages loosely defined groups interacting on a basis of consensus about basic social values, showing mutual respect and tolerance, each conceding the right of others to be different, but none in fact differing significantly enough to constitute a "divisive" element in the overall harmony of society. This was the kind of pluralism promoted by the American Jewish Committee, the most influential single force in the white ethnic movement. Its National Project on Ethnic

America was intended to ease the confrontation between blacks and working-class whites and thereby to "help polarization dissolve into pluralism" (Friedman, 1971; Mann, 1979). The leaders of this "depolarization project" were alert to the dangers of ethnocentrism and destructive separatism, and sensitive to the "difficulty of going beyond fragmentation toward a genuine pluralism". The same notes are sounded repeatedly in the hearings on a 1970 bill to establish "ethnic heritage studies centers". The sponsor, Congressman Pucinski of Illinois, disavowed any intention of promoting separatist ethnic consciousness. "The main thrust of this legislation", he declared, "is to try to eliminate the differences [between people] by letting people know about each other and recognizing their differences" (Ethnic Heritage, 1970). A Sunday-supplement book review suggests the bland and innocuous manner in which this participationist version of pluralism came across to the general reading public: "Cultural pluralism means that each culture within a country will have its respected place, and every individual will be free to choose the elements he may find attractive in another life style." (Stanton, 1975.)

Pluralism meant more than that to many spokesmen for ethnic groups, and the rise of black nationalism in the late sixties legitimatized demands for *militant pluralism* all along the line. This term was used by Hare (1969), the embattled organizer of a Black Studies programme at San Francisco State University, who defined it as "the right [of a group] to exist as an equal, akin to parity, as a distinct category". Paralleling the rhetoric of black separatism, if not directly inspired by it, was the call for "community control" of institutions like schools that served a black clientele (Fein, 1970). Chicano separatists envisaged a "Plan of Aztlan" whereby all the territories ceded by Mexico to the United States in 1848 would be restored to Chicano control (Scott, 1972). Separatism and tribal autonomy had always figured prominently in the relationship of American Indians to the national society, and as the new ethnicity gathered momentum Vine Deloria proposed that tribalism be applied across the board to guarantee "the basic sovereignty of the minority group", strengthen its bargaining position, and guard against the dangers of "co-optation". The contrast between this approach and the participationist vision of individuals freely choosing elements of other life-styles was brought out starkly in Deloria's comment that, in the arrangement he urged, everyone would have his or her special enclave, and "alienation would be confined to those times that people stray from their own neighbourhood into the world of other peoples" (Friedman, 1971).

Ethnic activists pioneered in separatist pluralism, but it eventually affected academic studies too. Among scholars, the tendency towards a more militant pluralism first took the form of increasingly strident rejection of "assimilationist values, with their connotations of elitism and a monocultural society", and an insistence on the perduring quality of ethnicity

(Metzger, 1970–71; Novak, 1972). These were the main themes of Passi's historical critique of academic studies of ethnicity, and the cultural pluralists were his heroes. However, Powell's dissertation, done in the same year (1971), showed that most advocates of cultural pluralism had really been liberal assimilationists or, at best, advocates of unity-*cum*-diversity. Powell reported this finding with detachment; by the late 1970s others were reacting more indignantly. Nicholas Montalto (1978, 1982), for example, branded the cultural pluralism of many involved in the intercultural education movement of the 1940s as "almost hypocritical"; theirs was "a pluralism of deception". Another historian charged that those seeking reform in Indian educational policy in the 1930s were not real cultural pluralists because they did not believe "in the indefinite preservation of cultural qualities requiring political self-determination or permanent self-separation". Their thinking was "flawed or insidious", and the cultural democracy they offered was merely a "softer version" of "crass assimilationism" (Goodenow, 1980).

Writers of this persuasion tend to be highly critical of the liberal democratic assumptions of the earlier cultural pluralists. In this respect their outlook reflects the alienation from national values and institutions that pervaded social commentary in the late sixties and early seventies. Montalto brings out the connection in a frank avowal of the "biases which may have shaped his perceptions" of the issues involved in intercultural education and pluralism. "I believe that the disorders of our society, the spiritual unrest, the materialism that provides the only confirmation of self-worth, the loss of creativity and freedom, are consequences of an outmoded social system, which attempted to suppress those centers of valuation and opinion in conflict with the 'core culture'. In its uncorrupted form", he continues (without elaborating on corrupted forms), "the revival of ethnic consciousness is but one aspect of a larger movement for social change, a movement to protect the environment, to adapt technology to human needs, to find satisfaction in work, to regain power over our lives, to eliminate racism, and to reorder relations among the nations." (Montalto, 1978, p. xi.)

Montalto included the elimination of racism among the goals associated with the ethnic revival, but the new pluralism has in fact been accompanied by a strong resurgence of racial thinking. "Racial thinking" as used here does not mean holding that one race is inherently superior or inferior to another. It refers rather to the outlook that regards race as a valid social category, that accepts the classification of individuals into racial categories on the basis of ancestry or the "rule of descent", and that justifies differential treatment of individuals according to their racial classifications. The development of this sort of racialism has been closely linked to affirmative action and other forms of "benign quotas" that are predicated on the assumptions spelled out above (Glazer, 1975; Van den Berghe, 1971, 1978; Killian, 1981). It is thus to be understood primarily as the unanticipated by-product of policies intended to overcome the effects of America's historic racism. But there were also more positive factors in the development of racial thinking. One was the heavy emphasis by black nationalists and their counterparts in other groups on the distinctive racial qualities, "soul", or consciousness of *la raza,* that marks the group in question. Another was the insistence of the new pluralists that ethnicity is a "primordial" quality that deserves more adequate recognition in the institutional arrangements of society (Eisinger, 1978; Van den Berghe, 1981). In this harking back to something like Kallen's original federation-of-nationalities pluralism, the new pluralists found themselves being led almost irresistibly to the vaguely racialist interpretation of ethnicity that Kallen himself entertained in the early years of this century.

   In view of the extent to which racialist assumptions have been accepted *de facto,* it is not surprising that one can now discern the beginnings of a new theoretical interest in the subject which treats seriously the possibility that genetically determined factors in social life are real and demand scientific attention. Van den Berghe's *The Ethnic Phenomenon* (1981) is the most explicit manifestation of this tendency and the most fully elaborated. Van den Berghe grounds his interpretation in sociobiological theory, arguing that "ethnic and racial sentiments are [an] extension of kinship sentiments. Ethnocentrism and racism are thus extended forms of nepotism—the [genetically-based] propensity to favor kin over nonkin". From this it follows that "ethnocentrism and racism, too, are deeply rooted in our biology and can be expected to persist even in industrial societies, whether capitalist or socialist" (pp. xi and 18). Van den Berghe is well aware that this view is flagrantly at odds with both liberal and radical ideologies, as well as with the scholarly consensus on race that has prevailed for half a century, and he is at pains to make clear that he does not *approve* of ethnocentrism and racism. His position, rather, is that to be able to deal with these unattractive aspects of our nature, we must understand how deeply they are embedded in our evolutionary history.

   Van den Berghe (1978) is "adamantly universalist" in ideological orientation and has written critically of the American revival of ethnicity, but another writer sympathetic to the new ethnicity hints at a somewhat similar biologically linked racialism. This is Fred Wacker, who seems to regard the abandonment of Lamarckian racialism, not as a clear scientific advance, but as a problem requiring explanation. He interprets the shift away from Lamarckianism (by which is meant the belief that the cultural traits of a people are transmitted by hereditary mechanisms) as resulting from two kinds of factors: ideological considerations, such as a commitment to democratic reform and the elimination of prejudice; and changes in scientific assumptions, specifically "a movement toward a stronger and more dogmatic environmentalism". Wacker takes explicit note of Kallen's racialism, but does not treat it as a scientific error or a faulty basis on which to erect a theory of cultural pluralism. He is, however, sufficiently embarrassed by Kallen's sharing the same assumptions as the nativist racists of the day to add: "One can argue . . . that it makes an important and even vital difference whether a person looks at racial or group stereotypes as positive heritages or marks of backwardness". Obviously "one can argue" this way, but only by reducing the scientific question to the level of ideological preference; for what the argument implies is that racialism is scientifically unacceptable only if the wrong social inferences are drawn from it (Wacker, 1979, 1981).

Wacker's writings illustrate how the logic of the new ethnicity leads its proponents towards a scientific rehabilitation of racialism. But they are not the only ones tending that way. Certain critics of "the myth of ethnicity" start from the other side of the street, so to speak, but they contribute to the same result by drawing so sharp a distinction between race and other heritage-related social groupings as to make the conclusion inevitable that only race is real and deserving of recognition. They sometimes, but not invariably, add the allegation that the revival of ethnicity is merely a cover for white racist backlash against affirmative action (Van den Berghe, 1981; Takaki, 1982).

A recent and authoritative example of this general line of interpretation is provided by Smith, a West Indian scholar prominent in the study of plural societies. Although he does not accuse the editors of the *Harvard Encyclopedia of American Ethnic Groups* of being motivated by backlash, he regards their having subsumed race under the more general heading of ethnicity as a "monumental confusion" that vitiates the conceptual foundation of their whole undertaking. According to Smith, race is a reality in nature; it has social consequences; and to disregard these facts, no matter how high-minded the reasons, makes it impossible to understand "those fundamental differences within America between its major racial stocks on the one hand and the multitude of ethnic groups on the other which have exercised and continue to exercise such profound influences on the development and structure of the society from its earliest beginnings" (1982, p. 10).

As a result of the practical and theoretical revival of racialism—in addition to the affirmation of "unmeltable" ethnicity and the discrediting of traditional Americanism—a drastically "separatist" variety of pluralism has developed in the past ten years or so. It resembles Kallen's 1915 version of cultural pluralism, but differs fundamentally from the cultural pluralism that has predominated since the late 1930s and that Kallen himself championed in the 1950s. Not everyone who speaks of pluralism today has this militantly separatist variety in mind, for the term is still used in a participationist sense and invoked to celebrate the blandest sort of diversity. This circumstance, coupled with the vagueness that has always surrounded the expression and the fact that it was used for so long without acknowledgement of the assimilationist substructure it tacitly embodied, tended to mask what was happening for some time. But the recognition that something significant was afoot has gradually dawned, and in 1981 Gordon illuminated the topic brilliantly in an important article entitled, "Models of Pluralism: The New American Dilemma".

As the subtitle indicates, Gordon believes the nation now confronts a situation comparable in importance to that addressed in Myrdal's classic work, *An American Dilemma* (1944). For Myrdal, the dilemma had to do with the unwillingness of Americans to live up to the requirements of the democratic ideology in their actual treatment of blacks. He did not regard the ideology itself as problematic; nor did he find it difficult to specify what "the American Creed", as he called it, actually required in the way of equal treatment of blacks. Today, however, it is precisely these matters that have become problematic: the liberal democratic consensus has been challenged, and Americans disagree among themselves about what would constitute equal treatment and how it should be realized.

The traditional position Gordon designates *liberal pluralism*. This corresponds to the participationist pluralism that flourished in the forties and fifties. Premised on democratic individualism, it envisages ethnic and racial relations as falling outside the scope of legal coercion or direct governmental control, except that the state is supposed to prevent discrimination. Racial and ethnic groups have no standing in the polity and no legal rights as entities in themselves; individuals are free to associate themselves with such groups as they see fit, but their doing so, or not doing so, has no bearing on their status in law or their entitlement to the benefits of citizenship. Equality is understood in terms of equal opportunity for individuals, regardless of racial or ethnic background, not in terms of equality of outcomes for groups considered collectively. Officially, liberal pluralism prescribes tolerance and a *laissez-faire* policy with respect to the perpetuation of structural differentiation and cultural distinctiveness among the groups composing the population. In fact, however, its universalistic premises run contrary to the logic of particularistic distinctiveness, and liberal pluralism deprecates differentiation that tends to become "divisive".

Against the traditional position, Gordon contrasts the newer *corporate pluralism*. This approach corresponds to what I have called the militantly separatist version, but Gordon develops its implications more systematically. It envisages formal standing before the law for ethnic and racial groups; recognizes group rights in the political and economic spheres; and makes the enjoyment of rights by individuals conditional, to some extent, on whether they belong to specified groups. In respect to equality, corporate pluralism would require proportionally equal outcomes for groups rather than equality of opportunity for individuals. And without explicitly rejecting the need for national unity, it would officially foster structural separatism and cultural and linguistic differentiation among the constituent groups in society. Corporate pluralism would not require what Gordon calls "area exclusivism", or the establishing of territorial enclaves, but it would find such a development acceptable, even though it might result in limitations on the rights of outsiders to travel through, or reside in, the areas in question.

Although he lays out the two positions in an abstract, "ideal typical" manner, Gordon is convinced that they correspond to real differences in outlook and policy that now confront the American people and demand a choice. Moreover, he insists that the choice is not between unrelated alternatives in discrete areas of concern; rather "there is an inherent logic in the relationship of the various positions on these public issues which makes the choice one between two patterns—two overall types of racial and ethnic pluralism each with distinctly different implications for the American way of life" (1981, p. 187).

Gordon is correct on these points, in my opinion; and I would add that his spelling out so clearly the contrasting meanings of "pluralism" is a major contribution towards raising the discussion from the morass of semantic confusion to the hard-won level where clearcut disagreement becomes possible. My own belief is that as more people come to realize what the corporate version of pluralism actually implies, there will be a strong reaffirmation of the traditional values of democratic universalism and a frank espousal of assimilation understood as a social policy promoting identification with those democratic values by all Americans, regardless of ethnic or racial background. The beginnings of such a reaffirmation are already discernible (Morgan, 1981; Glazer, 1982; Hollinger, 1982; Thernstrom, 1982); as the illiberal—indeed, anti-liberal—implications of corporate pluralism come to be appreciated for what they are, the reaffirmation will gain in strength.

Until Gordon's analysis appeared, proponents of corporate pluralism could draw on the moral capital accumulated by a whole generation's uncritical celebration of liberal pluralism, despite the fact that it (corporate pluralism) rested on diametrically opposed theoretical foundations and prescribed quite different social policies. Now it should be clear to those committed to the traditional values of liberal democracy that they can no longer endorse any and every call for "cultural pluralism". In the past, the great majority of those who championed cultural pluralism were far more deeply committed to assimilation, understood as ideological consensus on democratic values, than they seemed to realize. Now it is the democratic consensus itself that is at issue—what it consists in and what it implies for government action in the area of racial and ethnic relations. Pluralists may have thought they could take all that for granted, but they cannot. They cannot even begin to discuss these fundamental questions constructively until the terminology of pluralism is demystified, and people realize that it usually confuses rather than clarifies what is really at issue.

References

Bell, D. (1963). Modernity and mass society: On the varieties of cultural and cultural experience. In *Paths of American Thought* (Eds A. M. Schlesinger, Jr., and M. White). Houghton Mifflin, Boston.

Bell, D. (Ed.) (1964). *The Radical Right*. Anchor, Garden City, New York.

Bernard, W. S. (1971). General introduction to the republished series. In *Schooling of the Immigrant* (Ed. F. V. Thompson). Patterson Smith, Montclair, New Jersey.

Blanshard, P. (1949). *American Freedom and Catholic Power*. Beacon, Boston.

Blanshard, P. (1951). *Communism, Democracy and Catholic Power*. Beacon, Boston.

Borrie, W. D. (Ed.) (1959). *The Cultural Integration of Immigrants*. Unesco, Paris.

Brown, F. J. and Roucek, J. S. (eds) (1937). *Our Racial and Cultural Minorities*. Prentice-Hall, New York.

Callahan, D. (1963). The new pluralism: From nostalgia to reality. *Commonweal* 78, 527–531.

Canavan, F. (1963). New pluralism or old monism. *America* 109, 556–560.

Chase, S. (1948). *The Proper Study of Mankind*. Harper, New York.

Christian Century (1951). Pluralism—national menace. *Christian Century* 68, 701–711.

Chworowsky, M. P. (1959). Subsidized pluralism: Its implications for intergroup relations. *School and Society* 87, 257–260.

Colburn, D. R. and Pozzetta, G. E. (Eds) (1979). *America and the New Ethnicity*. Kennikat, Port Washington, New York.

Commons, J. R. (1920). *Races and Immigrants in America*. Macmillan, New York.

Conant, J. B. (1953). *Education and Liberty*. Harvard University Press, Cambridge, Massachusetts.

Conant, J. B. (1970). *My Several Lives*. Harper, New York.

Creegan, R. F. (1958). Subsidized pluralism. *School and Society* 86, 32–34.

Creegan, R. F. (1959). Quality and freedom through pluralism. *School and Society* 87, 248–251.

Despres, L. A. (Ed.) (1975). *Ethnicity and Resource Competition in Plural Societies*. Mouton, The Hague.

Donahue, C. (1959). Religon and state power: The American pattern. *School and Society* 87, 253–256.

Eisinger, P. K. (1978). Ethnicity as a strategic option: An emerging view. *Public Administration Review* 38, 89–93.

Erikson, E. H. (1950). *Childhood and Society*. Norton, New York.

Ethnic Heritage (1970). *Ethnic Heritage Studies Centers*. (Hearings before the general subcommittee on education of the committee on Education and Labor, House of Representatives, 91st Congress, 2nd Session, on H.R. 14910). Government Printing Office, Washington.

Fairchild, H. P. (1913). *Immigration*. Macmillan, New York.

Fein, L. J. (1970). The limits of liberalism. *Saturday Review* **53**, 83–85, 95–96.

Fishman, J. A. (1959). The American dilemmas of publicly subsidized pluralism. *School and Society* **87**, 264–267.

Friedman, M. (Ed.) (1971). *Overcoming Middle Class Rage*. Westminster, Philadelphia.

Glazer, N. (1975). *Affirmative Discrimination*. Basic Books, New York.

Glazer, N. (1982). Politics of a multiethnic society. In *Ethnic Relations in America* (Ed. L. Liebman). Prentice-Hall, Englewood Cliffs, New Jersey.

Glazer, N. and Moynihan, D. P. (1963). *Beyond the Melting Pot*. MIT Press, Cambridge, Massachusetts.

Gleason, P. (1964a). The melting pot: Symbol of fusion or confusion? *American Quarterly* **16**, 20–46.

Gleason, P. (1964b). Pluralism and the new pluralism. *America* **110**, 308–312.

Gleason, P. (1980). American identity and Americanization. In *Harvard Encyclopedia of American Ethnic Groups* (Eds S. Thernstrom, A. Orlov, and O. Handlin). Harvard University Press, Cambridge, Massachusetts.

Gleason, P. (1981). Americans all: World War II and the shaping of American identity. *Review of Politics* **43**, 483–518.

Goodenow, R. K. (1980). The progressive educator and native Americans. *History of Education Quarterly* **20**, 207–216.

Gordon, M. M. (1964). *Assimilation in American Life*. Oxford University Press, New York.

Gordon, M. M. (1981). Models of pluralism: The new American dilemma. *The Annals of the American Academy of Political and Social Science* **454**, 178–188.

Hare, N. (1969). *Chicago Sun-Times*. 25 March.

Herberg, W. (1955). *Protestant-Catholic-Jew*. Doubleday, Garden City, New York.

Higham, J. (1975). *Send These to Me*. Atheneum, New York.

Hollinger, D. A. (1982). Two cheers for the melting pot. *Democracy* **2**, 89–97.

Hughes, E. V. and Hughes, H. M. (1952). *Where Peoples Meet*. Free Press, Glencoe, Illinois.

Kallen, H. M. (1915). Democracy versus the melting pot. *Nation* **100**, 190–194, 217–220.

Kallen, H. M. (1924). *Culture and Democracy in the United States*. Boni and Liveright, New York.

Kallen, H. M. (1943). "E Pluribus Unum" and the cultures of democracy. *Journal of Educational Sociology* **16**, 329–332.

Kallen, H. M. (1951). Democracy's true religion. *Saturday Review of Literature* **34**, 6–7, 29–30.

Kallen, H. M. (1956). *Cultural Pluralism and the American Idea*. University of Pennsylvania Press, Philadelphia.

Kane, J. J. (1955). *Catholic-Protestant Conflicts in America*. Regnery, Chicago.

Killian, L. M. (1981). Black power and white reactions: The revitalization of race-thinking in the United States. *The Annals of the American Academy of Political and Social Science* **454**, 42–54.

Kornhauser, W. (1959). *The Politics of Mass Society*. Free Press, Glencoe, Illinois.

Lipset, S. M. (1960). *Political Man*. Doubleday, Garden City, New York.

Mann, A. (1979). *The One and the Many*. University of Chicago Press, Chicago.

Matthews, F. H. (1977). *Quest for an American Sociology*. McGill-Queens University Press, Montreal.

Mayo-Smith, R. (1894). Assimilation of nationalities in the United States. *Political Science Quarterly* **9**, 426–444, 649–670.

Metzger, L. P. (1970–71). American sociology and black assimilation: Conflicting perspectives. *American Journal of Sociology* **76**, 627–647.

Montalto, N. (1978). The forgotten dream: A history of the intercultural education movement, 1924–1941. Ph.D. Dissertation, University of Minnesota.

Montalto, N. (1982). The intercultural education movement, 1924–1941: The growth of tolerance as a form of intolerance. In *American Education and the European Immigrant: 1840–1940* (Ed. B. J. Weiss). University of Illinois Press, Urbana, Illinois.

Morgan, G. D. (1981). *America Without Ethnicity*. Kennikat, Port Washington, New York.

Murphy, G. (Ed.) (1945). *Human Nature and Enduring Peace. Third Yearbook of the Society for the Psychological Study of Social Issues*. Houghton Mifflin, Boston.

Murray, J. C. (1960). *We Hold These Truths*. Sheed and Ward, New York.

Myrdal, G. (1962). *An American Dilemma*. Harper, New York.

Nicholls, D. (1974). *Three Varieties of Pluralism*. St. Martin, New York.

Novak, M. (1972). *The Rise of the Unmeltable Ethnics*. Macmillan, New York.

Park, R. A. (1930–35). Assimilation, social. In *Encyclopedia of the Social Sciences, Vol. II*. Macmillan, New York.

Park, R. A. and Burgess, E. W. (1969). *Introduction to the Science of Sociology*. University of Chicago Press, Chicago.

Passi, M. M. (1971). Mandarins and immigrants: The irony of ethnic studies in America since Turner. Ph.D. Dissertation, University of Minnesota.

Patterson, O. (1977). *Ethnic Chauvinism*. Stein and Day, New York.

Paulding, G. (1963). Review of N. Glazer and D. P. Moynihan's *Beyond the Melting Pot. The Reporter* **29**, 59.

Plaut, R. L. (1959). The segregational aspects of publicly subsidized pluralism. *School and Society* **87**, 251–253.

Powell, J. H. (1971). The concept of cultural pluralism in American social thought, 1915–1965. Ph.D. Dissertation, University of Notre Dame.

Rose, A. and Rose, C. (1953). *America Divided*. Knopf, New York.

Rose, P. I. (1968). *The Subject is Race*. Oxford University Press, New York.

Ross, E. A. (1914). *The Old World in the New*. Century, New York.

Scott, J. W. (1972). Ethnic nationalism and the cultural dialectics: A key to the future. In *America in Change: Reflections on the 60s and 70s* (Ed. R. W. Weber). University of Notre Dame Press, Notre Dame, Indiana.

Shils, E. A. (1956). *The Torment of Secrecy*. Free Press, Glencoe, Illinois.

Simons, S. E. (1900–01). Social assimilation. *American Journal of Sociology* **6**, 790–822.

Sklare, M. (1959). Ethnic-religious groups and publicly subsidized pluralism. *School and Society* **87**, 260–263.

Smith, M. G. (1982). Ethnicity and ethnic groups in America: The view from Harvard. *Ethnic and Racial Studies* **5**, 1–22.

Smith, W. C. (1939). *Americans in the Making*. Appleton-Century, New York.

Stanton, L. (1975). Review of H. Coy's *Chicago Roots go Deep*. *Michiana Magazine (South Bend Tribune)*, 21 December.

Stein, H. F. and Hill, R. F. (1977). *The Ethnic Imperative*. Pennsylvania State University Press, University Park, Pennsylvania.

Takaki, R. (1982). The myth of ethnicity: Scholarship of the anti-affirmative action backlash. *Journal of Ethnic Studies* **10**, 17–42.

Thernstrom, S. (1982). Ethnic groups in American history. In *Ethnic Relations in America* (Ed. L. Liebman). Prentice-Hall, Englewood Cliffs, New Jersey.

Thomas, W. I., Park, R. A. and Miller, H. A. (1971). *Old World Traits Transplanted*. Patterson Smith, Montclair, New Jersey.

Truman, D. (1951). *The Governmental Process*. Knopf, New York.

Van den Berghe, P. L. (1971). The benign quota: Panacea or Pandora's box. *The American Sociologist* **6**(3), 40–43.

Van den Berghe, P. L. (1973). Pluralism. In *Handbook of Social and Cultural Anthropology* (Ed. J. J. Honigmann). Rand-McNally, Chicago.

Van den Berghe, P. L. (1978). *Race and Racism: A Comparative Perspective*. John Wiley, New York.

Van den Berghe, P. L. (1981). *The Ethnic Phenomenon*. Elsevier, New York.

Vickery, W. E. and Cole, S. G. (1943). *Intercultural Education in American Schools*. Harper, New York.

Wacker, R. F. (1979). Assimilation and cultural pluralism in American social thought. *Phylon* **40**, 325–333.

Wacker, R. F. (1981). The fate of cultural pluralism within American social thought. *Ethnic Groups* **3**, 125–138.

Watson, G. (1947). *Action for Unity*. Harper, New York.

Weed, P. L. (1973). *The White Ethnic Movement and Ethnic Politics*. Praeger, New York.

Williams, R. M. Jr. (1947). *The Reduction of Intergroup Tensions*. Social Science Research Council, New York.

9
Language, ethnic identity and change

Carol M. Eastman

Introduction

Some scholars have suggested that as one acquires a second language and begins to use it one acquires the ethnic identity that goes with the language (Pool, 1979). Reese and I (1981) have suggested that ethnic identity does not always coincide with the language used. We argued that the relationship between a language and an ethnic identity is one of association. A particular "associated language" is a necessary component of ethnic identity but the language we associate ourselves with need not be one we use in our day-to-day lives. It need not even be one we know at all. In the United States Italian-Americans who associate the Italian language with their ethnic identity may know few Italian words. In Alaska, only 36 of 192 native languages associated with ethnic groups are actually used by both adults and children; 47 others are used primarily by adults, while 109 have no child users at all. Still, the Alaskan educational policy of setting up wherever feasible village primary and secondary schools staffed by native teachers trained in Cross-Cultural Education Development (X-CED) programmes is ensuring that ethnic identities are preserved despite such change (Orvik, 1981).

The question we will be dealing with here is whether or not, in the face of language change, language is a proper vehicle for preserving ethnic identities. There are situations in which people associate themselves with many languages and identify themselves as members of a multilingual group. In such situations (often urban) people use their different languages in different

LINGUISTIC MINORITIES
ISBN 0-12-232760-8

circumstances. They do this in common with other members of their group and all feel that they belong, then, to one multilingual group with respect to their urban behaviour—rather than to several unilingual ones. In this sense, for example, people of Nairobi are urban Kenyans rather than European expatriates, Kikuyu or Asian, and have in common the use of English, Swahili and their respective first languages. This does not mean that urban Kenyans (with situational multilingualism) have many ethnic identities. In general, one's ethnic identity remains associated with the language of one's forebears, be they European, Asian or African.

It will be implicit in the argument to be presented here that people who have several languages use them for the same communicative purpose for which one language is used. For example, some complex societies may require one language in the marketplace, another in the schools, and still a third in government; another complex society might require only one language in all domains.

It follows that if second language acquisition and ethnic identity were related in a causal way, *all* governments wishing to foster unity should require that citizens learn and use a national language (and thus become "nationals" in terms of their identity, rather than "ethnics" or "tribals"). In fact throughout the world this is a common type of language policy. But, it appears quite clear that the language and ethnic identity link is more complicated and of a different sort than this policy supposes. Are all school children in the United States "national" Americans because they learn and use English? What about Spanish-as-a-first-language speakers who are taught in Spanish in the United States? Are the schools keeping them from becoming American?

A person may acquire a second language for communicative purposes, whether or not an ethnic identity associated with that language is also acquired. The ethnic identity one associates with a second language is that person's perception of it—seen the way that person has always seen things. When an English speaker learns French, that English speaker's perception of what it is to be French is what the English speaker thinks being French is. When, and if, all Kenyans speak Swahili it will not be the same Swahili spoken by "ethnic" Swahilis (if, indeed, there are such). Opponents to Swahili as a Kenyan national language have objected to the choice of Swahili as a national language because it would *make* people more Swahili or Tanzanian than Kenyan. But, as the implicit Swahili national language policy of Kenya is taking effect we see that what is being acquired and used as Swahili is a peculiarly Kenyan language. This is similar to what happened in the United States where English has evolved into that "bastardized" form, "American". Today defenders of "American" English are beginning to decry a further "bastardization" of their national language because it, too, is changing with society. *Change* happens.

Language planning is impossible if what planners mean by language is a static system of grammar and speech associated with a particular speech community. Edwards (1981, p. 37) made this point when he noted that "supporters of cultural pluralism and language revivalists have often seemed ignorant of this dynamic course of language. That is why language planning has such a queer ring to it". On the other hand, Edwards noted that speakers implicitly understand that language use is changeable and they are the ones who adapt to this. Planners need to realize that what is plannable is not only language in the structuralist sense—i.e. language with a system of grammar, *langue,* exemplified in speech, *parole* (after DeSaussure, 1916)—but also language in its behavioural–cultural usage sense (Eastman, 1979). Thus, if language is to be usefully planned, it must be seen as dynamic. The ramifications of this for the relationship between language and ethnic identity will be explored in the following pages.

In so doing, we will also need to see what is meant by ethnic identity as part of culture in relation to language. The behavioural–cultural usage of language is an aspect of ethnic identity, and ethnic identity is a form of cultural behaviour. The structure of a language and the speech representing it represent the way we make use of our linguistic knowledge. Thus we need to distinguish ethnic identity as a form of cultural behaviour, including the appropriate use of language in association with that identity, from language use as the way we employ linguistic knowledge. Ethnic identity, like language, may be seen to have an underlying system of belief about how to act. Where language has *langue* as an underlying system of rules for grammatical speech, ethnic identity has a primordial belief aspect underlying "correct" ethnic behaviour. The behavioural–cultural usage of language is an aspect of ethnic identity at the surface level, one of the ways we can act "ethnic", but it is certainly not all there is to behaving ethnically—just as using noun classes is not all there is to speaking Swahili. When we stop using the language of our ethnic group, only the language use aspect of our ethnic identity changes; the primordial sense of who we are and what group we think we belong to for the remainder remains intact. For example, if a French person leaves Paris and goes to live in New York, that person may learn to use English and stop using French (and even forget *how* to use it in some situations!). That person remains ethnically French until the unlikely event that *all* factors of that ethnic identity change, including that person's perception of ancestry. When a person says "We've always been . . ." or "Our people come from . . .", what goes in the blanks reflects his or her ethnic identity. So, the person who says "We've always been French" or "Our people come from France" remains ethnically French, no matter what language is now spoken. If the language in which one makes these statements is the language of the group referred to, then it is a factor of that identity. If, on the other hand, one says "We've always been French" in English, then language use is no longer an aspect of one's "French-ness"—instead, other overt behavioural factors, such as morals, values, oral tradition, kinship, religion, dress, or cuisine may mark one as French both to oneself and to others. Here, association with the French language is covert; it relates to ancestry, to legend and history, and in this sense is still possessed, though not as a surface marker of identity.

How language and ethnic identity change

Aronoff (1980), expanding on Clark and Clark (1979), sees linguistic innovation on a continuum from complete to opaque. A complete innovation is familiar and integrated in its context of use while an opaque innovation is perceived as foreign and has not yet been accepted. If no aspect of language use is foreign to members of a speech community, the language *is* its language; everyone uses it and there are no dialects. Here we have a homogeneous speech community. A particular language is perceived as a cultural feature of a particular (ethnic) group. The behavioural–cultural and linguistic use of aspects of language in such a situation coincide. As long as the culture and the language coincide, the speech community and its language attract "no particular notice from anyone" (Labov, 1972, p. 319). As a foreign language begins to be used/acquired within a group that had been hitherto just "aware" of it, it will first affect the social groups closest to the originating group (Labov, 1972). For example, in Kenya, English was perceived as the language of colonial officers (which it was). Eventually the officer's Kenyan deputies, and district and provincial commissioners' staff, began to pick up English terms in the government administration context. Insofar as the language being introduced had prestige, power, and other social values, the persons acquiring it would be encouraged in their efforts to learn it. Where *prestige* was accorded to a "new" language in Kenya, the deputized officials learned to generalize their behavioural–cultural use of the "new" language (English) beyond the administrative domain.

Language contact always assumes culture contact as well, though such contact may be limited (Bynon, 1977). So, in the case of Kenya and English, English could have remained the colonial language of administration had it not become prestigious and been extended to other spheres of Kenyan life. Had African provincial and district commissioners not begun to adhere to English it could not have begun to become a Kenyan language as it is doing today.

As a new language acquires more complexity and scope in its new context of use, people note its incursion. If the new speakers are in the mainstream of society, respected and prominent, then the new language may be incorporated into the speech community at the expense of the older form. However, "if the group is excluded from the mainstream of society, or its prestige declines, the linguistic form or rule [or language] will be stigmatized, corrected, and even extinguished" (Labov, 1972, p. 320). To exemplify this, consider the French language again—this time in Strasbourg after the period of German occupation (Tabouret-Keller, 1968). Prior to occupation, the Germanic dialect known as Alsatian was the first language of the local inhabitants (who thought of themselves ethnically as Alsatians); French was the national language and the language of education, and German was a foreign language attracting "no particular notice from anyone". With occupation, things began to change. Today, Strasbourg is an Alsatian/French bilingual city where German is also used. The socio-economic context of the language change from Alsatian as the major language to French acquisition and German acceptance reflects social and political expedience rather than ethnic change.

Strasbourg is an urban area, and as such is within the network of Paris-originated activity (commerce, education, culture, etc.). Hence, French-as-a-second-language provides access to the very activities perceived as prestigious by urbanized Strasbourg. During the occupation, German, though not imbued with prestige (i.e. linked to valued resources), became "noticed" for pragmatic reasons. Once "noticed" it ceased to be foreign and today is useful to the people of Strasbourg in more favourable contexts such as travel and trade. Outside Strasbourg, in rural areas, Alsatian remained (at least until 1968) the major language although French was desirable for those who had dealings in the urban context. Within Strasbourg the relative use of French and Alsatian differed from neighbourhood to neighbourhood and was associated with age or class. As Tabouret-Keller pointed out, all upper-class people in Strasbourg used a variety of French dialects while members of the lower classes, particularly the very old and the very young, were "dialectal unilinguists" in Alsatian. A native-French-speaking upper-class restaurant proprietor, middle-aged and able to use German with customers, may be as much an Alsatian in terms of ethnic identity (at the primordial level) as is a monolingual elderly Alsatian farmer from outside the city—as long as both share the feeling that (historically) they are descendants of the same group.

Thus, language use (speech behaviour in a cultural context) changes to accommodate communicative needs in mainstream society. Ethnic identity, on the other hand, changes to accommodate individual beliefs about the origin of the group. But, ethnic behaviour, like speech, reflects group needs in mainstream society (rather than group beliefs). If the group can get what it needs to maintain itself using its associated language it will. If it can get what it needs wearing ethnic dress it will. However, necessary changes in dress and language use need not change group identity.

The difference between language change and ethnic change hinges on the notion of *primordiality*. A society characterized by primordial ethnicity is relatively conflict free—and contact free. Its members feel they have a right to exist in society as a group and that feeling goes unchallenged. In such societies "we find a fully integrated set of beliefs, views, and behaviors, a 'way of life' that is 'traditional' in that it invokes timeless custom as the directive guide to all the processes, problems, and perspectives of life" (Fishman, 1972, pp. 179–180).

Once a society is structurally and functionally differentiated, the primordial nature of ethnic identity is transformed—a consciousness of difference arises and people use various cultural attributes (age, social status, occupation, education, religion, and language) to separate themselves, as a group, from others. Associated language (as used in the "homeland") is one of these attributes used to assert primordial ethnicity. Language *use* reflects pragmatic communicative needs, but need not be associated with this ethnicity. When societies become complex, language for the first time becomes "something separately recognized, valued, loved, protected, cultivated and ideologized" (Fishman, 1972, p. 180)—it keeps "us" from "them" whether we use it or not.

However, ethnic identity does not have only a primordial nature, just as language does not have only a systematic grammatical aspect. Ethnic identity has segments or features that are used in society (much as language has both a speech and a systematic grammatical aspect). The surface-use features of primordial ethnicity only show up in a non-homogeneous society affected by sociocultural change. Kikuyu people in Kenya had to "notice" English much as Alsatians had to "notice" German in Strasbourg. Kikuyu people have also had to acquire some form of Swahili to interact in urban Kenya; Alsatians had to acquire some French to get along as French citizens in a modernizing nation. But, the Kikuyu have not had to abandon all of their ethnic attributes to be Kenyan in a vestigial British colony, and Alsatians have not had to give up being Alsatian to be French in a formerly German occupied territory. Both the Kikuyu in urban Kenya and the Alsatians in urban France have transformed or changed certain attributes of their primordial ethnic identity as these are reflected in behaviour—but they have not abandoned them. Kikuyu and Alsatian are still "their" languages but not necessarily the languages they use. Instead they are their associated languages. A transformed language aspect of one's ethnic identity is still an aspect of that identity (and the transformation is from use to association—a change not a substitution) much as are ethnic dress and cuisine, no longer features of daily life but brought out for "special" expressions of group identity. An associated language is one transformed from a language of use by the process of change discussed at the beginning of this section. An associated language in its particular group-reference function may still have remnants in the language used by its adherents. These form a culturally-loaded vocabulary that acts to preserve one's feeling of ethnic identity (Eastman, 1979, 1981a, 1981b). Words and expressions and intonation that go with an ethnic vocabulary are sometimes perceived by others as an ethnic speech style:

> . . . Indeed, Jews the world over speak with a distinctive accent in their host languages, and with words and phrases peculiar to their own culture and experiences. Similarly, the Irish and Scots speak with a very distinctive accent that they would be loathe to relinquish. A distinctive language then need not be a necessary or sufficient symbol of one's ethnicity, but some speech style distinctive to one's group might be.
>
> Giles, Bourhis and Taylor, 1977, p. 327

In contrast, where a group speaks (as well as associates itself with) a particular language, it may be seen as expressing its world view as culturally homogeneous and socio-economically secure. Where a group, instead, retains only a culturally loaded vocabulary or ethnic speech style (or no remnants at all of its associated language) it is generally not at the top of the socio-economic ladder in the complex society in which it is now living (see Eastman, 1982). But, language here primarily functions as an indicator of class and social status—not ethnic identity. The further we are removed from our ethnic origins in our behaviour in a modern urban context, the more "integrated" we are into that society. The "man in the gray flannel suit" who epitomizes urban success provides little clues as to his primordial ethnicity, having abandoned its manifestations in exchange for middle-class status. Yet, people on all "rungs" of the socio-economic ladder may retain their ethnic identity without active (instrumental) use of their language as long as they still have an association (or sentimental attachment) with it. The "man in the gray flannel suit", particularly on holidays, can still go home again.

The process of change of ethnic identity, if it were to be complete, would involve substitition for all the cultural attributes or features of that ethnic identity, both at the level of belief (primordial) and use (behavioural). When this happens ethnic identity becomes national identity or nationality. The "nationals" look to a new common set of "interpretations of experiences and actions of mythical ancestors and/or historical forebears. . . [which] are often presented in the forms of myths or legend in which historical events have been accorded symbolic significance" (Keyes, 1981, p. 8). This process can be seen in the United States where members of various hyphenated American backgrounds are now claiming to have forebears who came over on the Mayflower. The Mayflower charter myth is increasingly depicting the ship (carrying persecuted Puritans fleeing England) as a model of multiethnic transport—the backdrop of American primordiality. Once disembarked from the Mayflower our forebears found that in their new world old patterns of social action no longer worked. Consequently new patterns emerged stimulating "either consciously or unconsciously, a reassessment of the appropriateness of the functions of ethnic group identities upon which these affiliations are predicated. Concomitant with the necessary changes in social patterns, those living in new circumstances may also have to adopt new cultural meanings and practices" (Keyes, 1981, p. 15).

As a relatively complete form of ethnic change, Bentley (1981) documents the case of the Tausug people who migrated to the Sulu Archipelago (Philippines) and are now the dominant ethnic group there. The mythical charter of the three major groups (Tausug, Somal, Bajau) in the region has now been reformulated to accommodate the new order much as we are reformulating the Mayflower myth in America:

> Tausug myths now stress that they are of local origin and link them to Islamic origin themes. Somal, who are probably the aboriginal inhabitants of the region, are characterized in Tausug mythology as poor Muslims who are therefore morally inferior to the Tausug . . . the Bajau are relegated to a pariah pagan status in Tausug mythology. . . .
>
> Keyes, 1981, p. 21

What has occurred to the Somal in Tausug mythology is somewhat akin to the place of the "savage" American Indian in the American myth—the Indian who can hardly claim to have come over with the rest of us, having been here already!

One of the most necessary new practices for the coexistence of groups in contact is communicative speech alteration. In changed circumstances the salience of the cultural basis of the speaking aspect of our group identity is lost and a new interpretation needs to be acquired. An illustration of this may be seen in the differential adaptation of East European Jews to English-speaking communities in the United States and in South Africa. Selipsky (1982) found that where both groups gave up Yiddish and now use English with their ethnic speech style and culture-loaded vocabulary, the custom of *shiva* (visits to the bereaved for a week of mourning following a death and burial) has been reinterpreted differently in the two communities with regard to spoken ritual. Another custom, *schmuisn* (social visits and greetings and talk), in contrast, has been retained intact in both communities. Thus an American Jewish person can schmuisn perfectly well in Johannesburg but will have difficulty in behaving appropriately during a *shiva* visit.

The interrelationship of language and ethnic change

In the previous section we saw that language change and ethnic change are quite different processes. Language is changed for instrumental reasons— we use language to communicate and we communicate to survive. From one perspective we may say that we change the way we use our linguistic knowledge but the mental capacity for language learning underlying our linguistic knowledge remains constant. As humans we are capable of knowing any language. Chomsky (1965) makes a distinction between linguistic *competence* (the speaker-hearer's knowledge of language) and *performance* (the actual use of language in concrete situations). If competence reflects a mental capacity, as Chomsky feels it does, and if different languages are culturally specific manifestations of that knowledge, then to shift language does not entail any corresponding shift in mental capacity but is instead an expedient change.

Our capacity for language is mental; the languages we know and use are applications of our linguistic knowledge in specific cultural contexts.[1]

Ethnic identity, unlike linguistic knowledge, only develops once cultural differentiation takes place. Ethnic identities, then, as are particular languages, are social facts. As Keyes (1981, p. 7) put it, "what constitutes one's ethnic heritage is not determined genetically, it must be learned." Ethnic change to be total, then, would involve a change in root beliefs (Pool, 1979; Eastman, 1981a). To be American we have to have come over on the Mayflower as well as speak English in the society in which we live. In order for us to change our ethnic identity we need to change our beliefs about who we are in society. This total ethnic change is rare in a person's lifetime, and slow to take place for a group. For all practical purposes, then, such primordial ethnicity does not change, though the behaviours associated with it may—given the necessity of functioning in social and cultural reality. Individuals do not give up their "feeling of continuity with the past, a feeling that is maintained as an essential part of one's self-definition . . . intimately related to the individual need for collective continuity . . . a sense of survival" (DeVos, 1975, p. 26). Our primordial, ethnic identity is durable. As with the Tausug example above, it may change but only over a long time. The Tausug are still Tausug but now they have Philippine origin. Irish-Americans are still *Irish*-Americans except that they are beginning to feel they got here on the Mayflower fleeing religious persecution, rather than on an Irish ship fleeing the potato famine. We in the United States are still some time away from removing the hyphen from our multi-ethnicities. Where American Indians are barred from claiming the Mayflower myth, so too, as yet, are Black Americans; but as Afro-Americans, there is still room in the myth for more expansion.

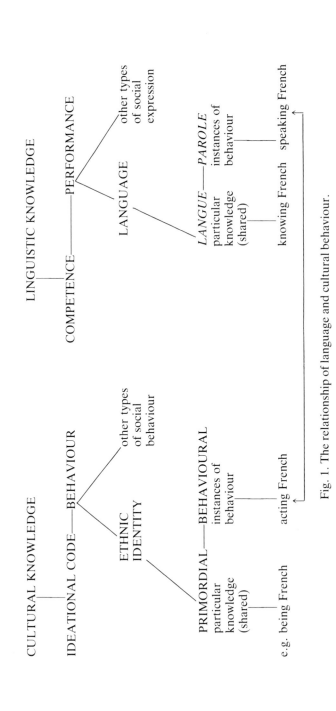

Fig. 1. The relationship of language and cultural behaviour.

Figure 1 shows the relationship of language and cultural behaviour as we have been discussing it. When we compare language and ethnic identity we are comparing different levels of the structure of culture and language respectively—ethnic identity is more a form of social behaviour while language behaviour represents variable use of knowledge. From the figure we can see that the language we acquire has an underlying intrinsic structure derived from our mental capacity (competence) but realized differently in various languages. We use or perform languages in particular speech communities where there exists a shared set of rules for what makes our performance appropriate. We know these rules and when we speak we try to live up to them; if we have them wrong our culture lets us know and we make adjustments. This is the aspect of language that changes under influences from other cultures. When the Germans occupied Alsace, certain aspects of German language use were "noticed" by French and Alsatian speakers. Once these German words or phrases began to enter Alsatian society the behavioural aspect of Alsatian ethnic identity that had to do with language use was somewhat changed. This behavioural–cultural type of language change, as is clear from the diagram, does not affect either the structure of a particular language (i.e. Alsatian is still Alsatian) or what it means to be Alsatian. Thus, what it means to know and be Alsatian remains the same, while speaking and acting Alsatian may be altered. Again, as is clear from the diagram, the part of language that changes in relation to ethnic identity is only its actual use aspect. If a person stops speaking French that person may still act French with regard to food, dress, music and so forth and will still believe that French is the language of his or her group. The person who no longer speaks French may also have retained the higher level performance aspects of it but have lost touch with the shared rules of appropriate use in a French-speaking community. Thus, one may lose one's *langue* by having substituted another form of linguistic knowledge, whereas ethnic identity may not be so transformed. Particular ethnic identity is just one type of cultural behaviour making use of general features of cultural knowledge; linguistic performance is the way we make use of one type of linguistic knowledge (one language). If we lose our ability to behave in a speech community we can still perform linguistically and do. If we lose our ethnic use of language we can still perform ethnically. Thus, from a structural standpoint ethnic identity as a type of cultural behaviour is on the same level as performance (i.e. knowledge and use of a particular language, as a type of linguistic behaviour where other languages represent other instances of linguistic behaviour). From this perspective neither performance nor ethnic identity change. Linguistic performance is a manifestation of linguistic knowledge, while ethnic identity is, in contrast, a manifestation of cultural behaviour. Being primarily cultural or behavioural rather than directly reflecting intuitive knowledge, ethnic identity rests on socio-cultural factors rather than conceptual ones. As such, ethnic identity is comparatively impervious to change in other than its surface behavioural aspects. Hence we don't have to speak French to act French and believe we are French.

Where there is a match between the features of behavioural and primordial ethnicity we have a homogeneous community or a group that is at the top of the socio-economic hierarchy in a community and pays no heed to the other groups around it. Still, not all members of such a group do everything possible to be a member, just as not everyone who is a speaker of a particular language says everything grammatically possible in that language. As language and culture bearers, however, we recognize our own distinct language behaviour and culturally specific behaviour as well as know how to carry it out on our own.

Pluralism and assimilation policies in light of language and ethnic change

If we change the language we know and use without changing our ethnic primordial identity (as I have tried to argue here), what are the consequences of this for people involved in making government language and education policies with regard to linguistic and cultural pluralism and assimilation?

In this section I will argue that pluralism versus assimilation should not be the question. That is, the behaviour or performance aspects of ethnic identity and language are what change in response to contact with other languages and cultures. Such change cannot be legislated. It occurs in response to radical shifts in society. In cases of both contact and radical social change it is the use (behavioural, *parole*) aspect that changes. Language use is more closely related to linguistic knowledge, while ethnic behaviour is tied to cultural belief, socially determined. Language use changes by means of shifts in the linguistic knowledge that reflects our human mental capacity for language. Ethnic change, in contrast, is intransigent due to its closer association with behaviour and cultural beliefs. Our cultural behaviour is not altered if we speak another language; only the language aspect of our ethnic identity changes. It changes from language use to association. The way we use ethnic identity is a reflection of our primordial ethnic identity. The way we use language is a reflection of the system of rules underlying it. While both ethnic and language change have the same cause (contact), the difference in the effect of change lies in the difference in kind of change—i.e. change in the immediate underlying structure of language behaviour (i.e. competence) on the one hand and in ethnic identity (i.e. cultural behaviour) on the other. The primordial aspect of ethnic identity is parallel to *langue*, the systematic underlying aspect of language reflected in speech use. French stays French as a language and as an "ethnic" idea changing only slowly over time. If the prestigious way to act French changes, a change takes place in the primordial belief about what is "good" French behaviour, but the belief in being French remains. Linguistic use of French (performance) is a reflection of one's knowledge of French derived from an innate mental capacity to learn any language; ethnic identity is a particular and learned form of behaviour derived from instances of general cultural behaviour in a specific context. Ethnic identity has a two-part structure: primordial (the belief level) and behavioural (the social level). Actual language use in a cultural context (*parole*) may be one of the aspects of the behavioural level of ethnic identity. It can be a part of what goes into, for example, "acting French". This is what changes when language change takes place. The language we name as an emblem of our ethnic identity when we associate ourselves with a group of people does not change, as long as it remains an aspect of the belief level of our identity.

Banton (1981) defined assimilation as reducing cultural distance between groups in regard to some particular behavioural aspect. Thus, linguistic assimilation need not mean ethnic assimilation; religious assimilation need not mean ethnic assimilation, and so forth. In fact, what is suggested here is that total ethnic assimilation for all practical purposes does not occur. Even with change in the Tausug charter myth, as seen in our earlier example, the people remain ethnically Tausug. They have altered their myth over time— not substituted another for it. Similarly a language's grammatical system (*langue*) will change from one historical period to another by shifting elements within the system, not by substituting one system for another. Even supporters of the idea of ethnic change call the result (i.e. when there is a substituted myth of primordiality) "nationality"—ethnic identity but "bigger", having the same primordial–behavioural structure. That is, the cultural attributes of nationality are the same as the attributes of ethnic identity except that they have coalesced from diversity rather than emerged aboriginally.

The emergence of the idea of a primordial underlying structure to ethnic identity with a surface manifestation is reminiscent of the structuralist view of language in a speech community. For language, the belief system underlying speech behaviour is *langue*—the systematic rules for using language in a community; its behaviour is speech (*parole*). We never say everything our rules account for but we recognize new things others say as obeying them. We never behave as Italians doing all the possible things Italians do, for example, but if we are Italian and think of ourselves as such, we recognize Italian behaviour in others.

In these pages, then, I have been arguing for a particularist behavioural–contextual view of ethnic identity and a generalist view of language. In complex societies it is common for some speakers to have a mixed language (i.e. to use their linguistic knowledge or competence in a way that is not recognized as conforming to any shared set of rules or *langue* associated with a particular speech community—yet) as their main means of pragmatic communication. The ethnic corollary does not occur. Even people of mixed parentage generally adhere to one set of primordial beliefs rather than a composite. A change in primordial beliefs, as in the Tausug case above, can only occur over a long period of time.

Often nationality arises in this way and eventually, where there is also a resulting mixed language, this becomes the national language. This appears to be beginning to happen in urban Kenya today where to be a Kenyan is to subscribe to the idea that all Kenyans were involved together in the struggle for independence. Kenyans are all part of a complex society using a mixture of standard and coastal Swahili with English, pidgin Swahili, and a number of other African and Asian language influences. In contrast, in Tanzania nationality is more closely related to historical Swahili ethnicity and Swahili in a relatively unmixed form can function as the national language.

The idea of primordial and behavioural dimensions of ethnic identity is akin to Mullings' (1978) two dimensions of ethnicity—cognitive and social structural. Mullings asserts that the cognitive (ideological–symbolic; primordial) dimension characterizes all groups but the social structural (behavioural) dimension is different according to discrepancies in the socio-economic position and history of the group in the context in which it exists.

Ethnic problems, Mullings feels, should not be a surprise. "Given the history of unequal constraints, a distinct difference in the contemporary status of the descendants of European immigrants and that of the descendants of captured Africans is to be expected." (1978, p. 15.) Mullings argues that the "characterization of cultural content [of ethnic identity] does not appear to tell us much about how and why people are stratified" and concludes that "the history of US immigration demonstrates that it is not possible to predict which cultural features will become markers for discrimination" (p. 18). He distinguishes "cultural" and "oppressed" minorities; the former maintains only its primordial identity though "it may be mobilized and restructured as an interest group often for political action" (p. 19); Euro-American ethnic groups are of this type. But, "an oppressed minority, on the other hand, is, in general, confined to the lowest levels of the stratification scale with respect to the division of labor and allocation of resources" (p. 19). The differential expression of ethnic identity by cultural and oppressed minorities is due to this division of labour and allocation of resources in the dominant society; groups retaining only the charter myth (altered or not) as an expression of their primordiality are, in Mullings' terms, a cultural minority. Those who continue to express other cultural markers of ethnicity (such as language, dress, costume, etc.) in their behaviour, so as to distinguish themselves from the dominant society, continue to be structurally constrained in the dominant society—in Mullings' terms, oppressed.

From this perspective, language as speech used (as *parole,* often a component of ethnic behaviour) may be seen to be related to ethnic identity insofar as groups without access to the dominant society's form of language for communication purposes are cut off from the upper echelons of the social structure and from access to that society's economic resources. If linguistic competence is the underlying knowledge for a particular language derived from a general human mental capacity for language, and if particular language use can be a factor of oppression, the implication of this for policies of linguistic pluralism is clear. It should not matter what we do with our linguistic competence as long as we are not cut off from access to the resources of our society. Linguistic assimilation, on the other hand, can only take place if it is functionally necessary. Non-oppressing aspects of our linguistic ethnicity (such as our culture-loaded vocabulary, sometimes our ethnic speech style, and always our association of a language with our identity) need never be abandoned in the interest of social mobility. Language behaviour reflects social structural status and changes (or does not change) in response to contact and access to socio-economic resources; but, as knowledge sensitive to a specialized mental capacity, it is constant. Whoever we are and wherever we live we will have language. It is the performance aspect of language that changes, and it changes only in use. At the level of system (*langue*) and belief (primordiality) language and culture change only slowly over time.

As Edwards (1981) observed, in today's world we sometimes find cultural and linguistic pluralism as a desire of socially and structurally assimilated individuals. It is an ". . . ideal of the elite, a top-down phenomenon which affects little the masses of the 'ethnics'" (1981, p. 33). Advocates of pluralism are often those who have lost all of the overt behavioural aspects of ethnic identity and retain only their primordiality. By giving up their cultural "ethnic" (including linguistic) markers these people gained social status, prestige, and access to the dominant economic system and now they want to recover their ethnic identity since they are "safely" in a position to do so. However, those who never lost their behavioural ethnic identity are not advocating pluralism since that is what is keeping them down. They, too, first need to assimilate in order to become a cultural rather than oppressed minority. What is involved in assimilation, however, need not be knowledge (linguistically) nor belief (culturally)—instead assimilation involves change in the way we use our linguistic knowledge (language change) and a substitution of certain forms of ethnic behaviour such as language, dress, and cuisine for others.

Conclusion

In the preceding pages, we have looked at some of the current literature on language and ethnic change in order to see how the change process affects the relationship between language and ethnic identity. To do this it was necessary to define what both language and ethnic identity are in the context of change. Clearly there is no one-to-one correspondence between language and ethnic identity; both are complex structures (see Fig. 1). I have tried to show here that the underlying structure of language and that of ethnic identity are fundamentally different. Language is a context-sensitive system of knowledge manifested differently in particular speech communities as the various languages or language mixtures known and used throughout the world. Ethnic identity is analogous to the behavioural manifestation of a particular language in a particular speech community in terms of what we believe it should be and how it is used. Like particular language, ethnic identity is specific to particular cultures and in each culture it has an underlying system of rules or beliefs (primordiality as analogous to *langue*) and surface behavioural aspects (instances of ethnic behaviour, like *parole* as instances of *langue*). Languages function communicatively in society—the structure of society determines the particular behavioural form of our language in that society. The form our linguistic knowledge takes in a speech community does not change what we believe about "our" people. That is, language knowledge and use do not affect our underlying or primordial ethnic identity. As society changes, language use does as well. As society changes, group belief (primordial ethnicity), like language structure, only does so over long periods of time, although aspects of group cultural behaviour (behavioural ethnicity including language use, dress, food, etc.) may alter greatly. Changing our primordial ethnicity is akin to, for example, changing French grammar. Where we can change our linguistic knowledge (e.g. learn Swahili), we certainly do not change what we believe about our first language in the process.

If we develop a new myth or legend as to the primordiality of our group, and if all the attributes of our "ethnic" behaviour have changed, it is indeed then possible to become a new "ethnic" and belong to a new group—often a nation. But this is as gradual a process, and as arduous, as acquiring the rule or belief that French has no gender and using French that way. Many would say that once this happens the French language is no longer French, just as they would say, analogously, that the "old" ethnic group no longer exists.

If, somehow, a world culture were to emerge with a common charter myth, that "belief" would still be derived from the shared "world" of its people. Who we believe we are and how we act (our ethnic identity and, for example, our language use) are socially determined; what we know (language and culture) is a property of the human mind. What goes into who we are and how we act changes constantly within the different structural frameworks of language and cultural behaviour.

Given the argument here, the question of preserving ethnic identity in the face of language change is moot. Language shift or change can only affect one aspect of our ethnic identity—the language use aspect, which is a very low level manifestation of our cultural belief system. The implication of this analysis of the relationship of language and ethnic identity, and the way change in both occurs, is that there is no need to worry about preserving ethnic identity, so long as the only change being made is in what language we use.

Note

1. According to Chomsky, the *competence–performance* distinction "is related to the *langue–parole* distinction of Saussure; but it is necessary to reject his concept of *langue* as merely a systematic inventory of items and to return rather to the Humboldtian conception of underlying competence as a system of generative processes" (1965, p. 4). Where competence represents particular linguistic knowledge derived from a general human mental capacity for language acquisition, *langue* represents the systematic elements of a language's grammar within a linguistic system. We may learn the elements of *langue* in a classroom but when we are able to use a language creatively we have acquired linguistic competence. Competence in or knowledge of French is what allows us to perform French by using it as a language or *langage* (i.e. a system of grammar or *langue* plus representative speech acts or *parole*).

References

Aronoff, M. (1980). Contextuals. *Language* **56**, 744–758.

Banton, M. (1981). The direction and speed of ethnic change. In *Ethnic Change* (Ed. C. F. Keyes). University of Washington Press, Seattle.

Bentley, G. (1981). Migration, ethnic identity, and state building in the Philippines: The Sulu Case. In *Ethnic Change* (Ed. C. F. Keyes). University of Washington Press, Seattle.

Bynon, T. (1977). *Historical Linguistics*. Cambridge University Press, Cambridge.

Chomsky, N. (1965). *Aspects of the Theory of Syntax*. MIT Press, Cambridge, Massachusetts.

Clark, E. V. and Clark, H. H. (1979). When nouns surface as verbs. *Language* **55**, 767–811.

De Saussure, F. (1916). *Course in General Linguistics* (Translated, 1966, W. Baskin). McGraw Hill, New York.

DeVos, G. (1975). Ethnic pluralism: Conflict and accommodation. In *Ethnic Identity: Cultural Continuities and Change* (Eds G. DeVos and L. Romanucci-Ross). Mayfield, Palo Alto, California.

Eastman, C. M. (1979). Language resurrection: A language plan for ethnic interaction. In *Language and Ethnic Relations* (Eds H. Giles and B. Saint-Jacques). Pergamon, Oxford.

Eastman, C. M. (1981a). The American Indian's language and culture in U.S. education. In *World Yearbook of education* (Eds J. Megarry, S. Nisbet and E. Hoyle). Kogan Page, London.

Eastman, C. M. (1981b). Language planning, identity planning and world view. *International Journal of the Sociology of Language* **32**, 45–53.

Eastman, C. M. (1982). *Language Planning: An Introduction*. Chandler and Sharp, San Francisco.

Eastman, C. M. and Reese, T. C. (1981). Associated language: How language and ethnic identity are related. *General Linguistics* **21**, 109–116.

Edwards, J. R. (1981). The context of bilingual education. *Journal of Multilingual and Multicultural Development* **2**, 25–44.

Fishman, J. (1972). Varieties of ethnicity and varieties of language consciousness. In *Language in Sociocultural Change* (Ed. J. Fishman). Stanford University Press, Stanford.

Giles, H., Bourhis, R. and Taylor, D. (1977). Towards a theory of language in ethnic group relations. In *Language, Ethnicity and Intergroup Relations* (Ed. H. Giles). Academic Press, London, Orlando and New York.

Keyes, C. F. (1981). The dialectics of ethnic change. In *Ethnic Change* (Ed. C. F. Keyes). University of Washington Press, Seattle.

Labov, W. (1972). *Sociolinguistic Patterns*. University of Pennsylvania Press, Philadelphia.

Mullings, L. (1978). Ethnicity and stratification in the urban United States. *Annals of the New York Academy of Sciences* **318**, 18–22.

Orvik, J. (1981). Cross-cultural education in Alaska. In *World Yearbook of Education* (Eds J. Megarry, S. Nisbet and E. Hoyle). Kogan Page, London.

Pool, J. (1979). Language planning and identity planning. *International Journal of the Sociology of Language* **20**, 5–22.

Selipsky, E. (1982). Changing patterns of speech across space and time. Mimeo, Department of Anthropology, University of Washington.

Tabouret-Keller, A. (1968). Sociological factors of language maintenance and language shift. In *Language Problems of Developing Nations* (Eds J. Fishman, C. Ferguson and J. Das Gupta). Wiley, New York.

10
Language, diversity and identity

John Edwards

In this chapter, I want to summarize the main aspects of the topics treated by the book as a whole, and to attempt to impose some order upon them. This is to be seen as an introductory effort, and I have no doubt that much of what I have to say will prove to be oversimplified, or inaccurate, or both. Nevertheless, I feel it is important to try and establish some base points, and I am encouraged to do so by the admirable contributions which precede me here. As I have argued elsewhere, the topic of linguistic minorities is, unsurprisingly but regrettably, one in which objective assessment is rare. However, in the present collection, some very useful ground-clearing and description has been accomplished, and this warrants some kind of summary statement. This is not to say, of course, that all of my comments here will necessarily be endorsed by all the contributors. In short, I present a brief outline, which I shall be enlarging upon later (Edwards, in preparation) and which I hope will be both immediately useful and heuristic.

Ethnic diversity

In a literal sense, countries like the United States, West Germany, Britain, Sweden, Australia and Canada *are* multicultural. That is, they contain populations of immigrant and/or indigenous origin which differ, culturally and linguistically, from the mainstream culture which has evolved in the course of history. Differences make themselves felt at points of contact and,

LINGUISTIC MINORITIES
ISBN 0-12-232760-8

in all modern instances, contact between majority and minority is inevitable. It is true, of course, that immigrant groups may exist for a time in self-sustaining concentrations—the "little Italy" in America, and the area within a city which is segregated along class lines (and hence very often along ethnic lines, too)—but these are usually temporary and, in all cases, do not present impermeable barriers to the larger society. Furthermore, points of contact give rise to social comparison and this, in turn, leads to evaluations, stereotypes and prejudices. The phenomenon of the disadvantaged child at school, for example, is a reflection of the importance of a contact point which makes social comparison possible.

Social comparison in heterogeneous societies is, I believe, inevitable. And, given what we know of social orders, comparisons lead inexorably to ratings in which different-but-equal judgements often give way to different-and-somehow-deficient ones. This is the problem faced by societies and, especially, by minority-group members within them. Although the social dynamics to which this may lead are obviously very varied, it is perhaps not unfair to label the two extremes on the continuum of possibilities as *submersion* and *segregation*. Group contact, after all, becomes impossible if group boundaries disappear, on the one hand, or if groups rigorously abstain from contact, on the other.

If we turn first to the latter extreme, we can note that imposed segregation is morally indefensible and self-imposed segregation is, for most minority groups, a temporary way-station on the road towards greater and greater contact with the mainstream. Not only is such contact necessary—its absence would make the act of emigration pointless for most people—it is often welcomed, and attempts are often made to expedite it. Analysis of immigrant populations in North America, for example, shows that, in the absence of coercive legislation to assimilate, the first generation's job is usually one of entrenchment, the second generation is characterized by bilingualism and an ever-increasing passage across group boundaries, and the third generation is essentially anglophone and culturally assimilated. Thus, O'Bryan, Reitz and Kuplowska (1976) have remarked that, for this third generation in Canada, the issue is no longer one of retaining the original language, but of acquiring it. The third-generation "return to ethnicity" (Hansen, 1952) does not usually, in fact, indicate a desire to re-embrace an original way of life, but is rather a romanticized longing for certain aspects of it—aspects which will not, incidentally, interfere with those elements which now make for success in the new context. It is also worth noting that the renewed interest in group origins and in ethnic language and customs is most often expressed by group members who are themselves secure, successful and (can one say it?) well-assimilated (see below).[1] Higham (1975) and Weinreich (1974) have both noted here that some form of pluralism has its greatest appeal for those who are strongly positioned in the new society (see also Weinfeld, 1978). Even Greeley (1978), a well-known proponent of the American "new ethnicity" has admitted that the movement is more élitist than popular.

Segregation, then, is not an option preferred by most minority group members, and the evidence for this is all around us. It might be argued, of course, that groups would like more segregation, as well as participating in the positive features of the larger society, if they could have both. Although official pressures may be absent, unofficial ones may have the same assimilating effect; and this, it could be supposed, is also a type of coercion. This is a nonsensical position, however. All societies which are at all stratified, and where there is the slightest possibility of social mobility, must necessarily contain such "pressures". Every avenue taken means another one denied, and it is for each individual to assess the relative merits of potential pathways. I do not mean to deny that some have access to more routes than others; however, this fact itself argues for more, and not fewer, interconnections within society. I believe that most ethnic minority group members are interested in gaining access to more and more of these pathways, a belief which makes the following quotation (Fishman, 1980a, p. 171) a curious one:

> Stable bilingualism and biculturism cannot be maintained on the basis of open and unlimited interaction between minorities and majorities. Open economic access and unrestricted intergroup interaction may be fine for various practical and philosophical purposes. Indeed, they strike most of us as highly desirable legal and social principles; but they are destructive of minority ethnolinguistic continuity.

As I have noted elsewhere (Edwards, 1981a), this seems to suggest that the price of stable cultural diversity is higher than most—"ethnics" included—would be willing to pay. It also indicates the possibility that ethnolinguistic continuity depends upon a static, compartmentalized pluralism which does not accord with real-life observation of group movements in any historical sense. It also suggests that Van den Berghe (1967) may well have been right in saying that cultural pluralism and democratic order do not always go hand-in-hand, and that fragmentation along ethnic lines may lead to imbalances of power which, in the long term, may have serious consequences.

To summarize here, we may consider that cultural pluralism, to some at least, has a separatist tone which may work against the best interests of ethnic group members. Part of the difficulty here is that (within the present context) an overemphasis upon *language* may blind writers to other aspects of ethnic identity; with regard to language itself, there is often an ignorance of the useful distinction between *communicative* and *symbolic* aspects (see below). Another difficulty associated with wearing a particular set of glasses has been that, in the resurgence of interest in *ethnicity,* the notion of *class* has been downplayed (see Darroch, 1979; Williams, 1981). Again, this is a point to which I shall return, but I can note in passing here Steinberg's (1981) observation that "throughout American history ethnic groups have espoused the pluralist doctrine in order to protect their class interests, but have been all too willing to trample over ethnic boundaries—their own as well as others—in the pursuit of economic and social advantage" (p. 256). I think Steinberg's argument deserves more consideration, although his use of the word "trample" indicates a certain mindlessness which is not an accurate description of what must be, in most cases, reasonable decisions to alter courses. Militant segregation (or "separatist pluralism"; see Chapter 8) is neither an accurate description of ethnic group desires, nor an adequate assessment of current and (likely) future trends.

What of *submersion,* the other pole in the ethnic diversity continuum? There is little doubt that this assimilation *has* characterized much of past minority-group behaviour. Societies which were once pluralist and which are now homogeneous testify to this. It is just this melting-pot process which so exercises modern proponents of cultural pluralism who argue, therefore, that (a) it should be stopped and (b) where it has occurred, it should be reversed. What are the grounds for this Orwellian formula of *cultural pluralism good* and *assimilation bad?*

First, we may note that assimilation may have many connotations, two of which are conformity to the dominant culture, and complete homogenization. The first, in the English-speaking context, is often referred to as "anglo-conformity". Here, ethnic minorities are expected to adapt themselves to the prevalent culture which is, itself, to remain generally stable. This is not a melting pot in the true sense, but it is what the melting pot has meant to many. The second major connotation of assimilation is a truer reflection of the action of a melting pot—*all* elements, indigenous and immigrant, minority and majority, intermingle, fuse, melt, and a new identity is produced to which all have contributed. This has been seen as superior to the first variant and Zangwill himself (whose play, *The Melting Pot,* introduced the phrase, and reinforced the theme, in modern times) was in favour of this process (Gleason, 1979). But this variety, as well as anglo-conformity, has been criticized by those seeing it as a surrender of individual identities before some new-world juggernaut.

The plot (or pot) is further thickened by the assertion of cultural pluralists that, awful as it is, the melting pot has not worked. In the American context, they quote Glazer and Moynihan's statement (1963) that the melting pot did not happen, that the "ethnics" have, in fact, bravely resisted assimilation, and that now is the time to actively encourage and support this enduring diversity. We have Gleason (and others) to thank for making it clear that Glazer and Moynihan did *not* mean that no assimilation had taken place. In fact, these writers felt that assimilation had indeed eroded certain aspects of ethnicity (language among them, at least in its communicative sense), although others aspects had remained.

This suggests to me that an examination of those facets of ethnicity which apparently disappear over time, and those which remain, would be enlightening. It would enable us to describe groups' positions on the submersion–segregation continuum and, as well, it might allow us to speculate on the desirability of such positions. I am assuming, obviously, that neither extreme is an accurate or desirable description of minority-group positions within a larger society. Outright segregation is clearly not the case for most groups—even when we consider the position of some, largely religiously defined, sub-groups who separate themselves extensively from the mainstream, we see some elements at least of symbiosis. But, on the other hand, it is not easy to deny the claim that complete submersion or homogenization is a bad thing—bad in the sense of erasing diversity of world perspectives, of eradicating realities which enrich us all.

I will suggest, generally, that public or observable aspects of ethnicity are gradually discarded, and that private ones remain. Thus, communicative language, distinctive dress and ornamentation, and other public manifestations of group identity tend to disappear; aspects of domestic life, the symbolic significance of language and religious observances may remain. As this has been documented by many writers (see, e.g. Edwards, 1977; Dinnerstein *et al.*, 1979), and as it accords with informal observation, I shall not discuss the elements of the public–private distinction further. What is necessary, however, is to consider why the distinction emerges and, more importantly, what implications it has for ethnic diversity in general and ethnolinguistic diversity in particular.

That some elements of ethnicity decline and others linger is obviously a reflection of social adjustment. That is, it indicates a desire to move away from segregation without undergoing complete submersion. Therefore, those aspects which would continue to "mark" the ethnic-group member, and possibly interfere with intra-society movement and upward mobility, are expendable (see Pienkos, 1977). Is this the blind turning away from true origins, under pressure from an overarching majority, which some have construed it to be? I think not. There is every indication that ethnic groups desire this change. Their patterns of adjustment, from the very time they become minorities, demonstrate a willingness to assimilate along these lines. Indeed, groups often demand greater expedition here than their spokesmen might like. Thus we see a decline in affiliation with group societies, schools.

churches and media as these become increasingly unwanted markers of distinctiveness. Lemaire (1966) has documented the growing gap between Franco-American societies and Franco-Americans themselves; Rumilly (1958) showed how French-speaking parishioners and parents asked for more English at church and at school. Fishman's (1966) work demonstrates that these trends are not unique to French-Americans, but also apply to other immigrant groups.

The general implication here is that "de-ethnicization" occurs because of the formidable attractions of mainstream life. The corollary is that any "re-ethnicization" will occur, if at all, in some similar fashion rather than through the naïve, if well-meaning, efforts of cultural pluralists. Thus, we can agree with Ravitch (1976) who notes that the process of Americanization (read also "Canadianization", "Australianization", "Anglicization", etc.) is one sponsored by ethnic groups themselves. To assume that they have been indoctrinated by some mass conspiracy is to credit them with little intelligence or self-interest; here, the words and actions of cultural pluralists often have a very condescending and paternalistic tone. The fact that the melting pot does not entirely render ethnicity, and that some (private and personal) elements remain for a long period, is evidence that a selection takes place in which some aspects of the former life are retired from active service. This is not a traitorous repudiation of the past, but good sense. It may be noted (in passing; see below) that the role of outside intervention in supporting private rather than public ethnicity may not resemble the sort advocated by many proponents of diversity.

On the basis of what has been discussed so far, it would seem that the sort of "participationist" pluralism mentioned by Gleason (Chapter 8; see also "liberal pluralism" (Gordon, 1981); "pluralistic integration" (Higham, 1975); and Higham (1982) on "soft" and "hard" pluralism) is a useful concept at both the policy and the real-life level. It prescribes a reasonable course for societies to follow and, as well, describes what most ethnic groups do anyway. It is the sort of model which allows Bullivant's (1981) reconiciliation of "civism" with pluralism within educational systems (see also Chapter 4). In general, it is a model which sees government paying particular attention to overall social issues, to aspects of life in which all participate (and/or wish to), while creating a tolerant milieu in which groups are free to maintain and develop private aspects of ethnicity.

An argument against this notion is that it means a trade-off between public and private ethnicity in which the retention of the latter, and the loss of the former, is a bad exchange, detrimental to group survival. However, if the case I have been making has any relevance at all, it will be seen that retention of public, visible markers of ethnicity is unlikely, with or without government support, except in cases where segregation is involved and maintained. It is clear that such segregation is not an attractive long-term option for most groups.[2] Also, participationist pluralism would seem to reflect group desires more fully than "spokesmen" would have us believe—thus, ethnic group members are "more main-stream and assimilationist than generally believed by language planners" (Drake, 1979, p. 226; see also Sowell, 1978). There is a further point here, which is raised by cultural pluralists, and which is important: Doesn't a participationist pluralism simply represent a way-station on the path to complete assimilation? Two answers suggest themselves. The first is that, even if submersion awaits at the end of the road, it is difficult to see how it could be avoided. Second, and more positively, there is the likelihood that private aspects of ethnicity will remain for a long time— exactly as long, in fact, as groups (and, more importantly, individuals) wish them to. In responding to the question of how post-third-generation groups can maintain a sense of ethnic identity, Glazer (1980) has recently stated that it is, rather, hard to see how it will disappear. Perhaps it never will. But, if it does, then it is useless for militant pluralists to bewail its passing.

Before closing this general section, I should point out that I have (a) borrowed heavily from the American experience, and (b) not dealt directly with indigenous minorities. As to the first point, I am aware that contexts differ but, in many ways (and especially for the contexts treated in this book) the American scene—varied and extensive—is a good exemplar (Fishman, 1966). And, with regard to (b), although the sources of minority and majority relations where indigenous groups are involved are obviously different from those involving immigrant populations, much of the argument is, *mutatis mutandis,* applicable (see Edwards, 1977). The case study of Irish, reported below, indicates that this view is reasonable. As well, in his introduction to a recent book on minority languages in Europe, Aitken (1981) shows that the studies therein—largely of indigenous language groups—do indeed deal with themes familiar in an immigrant-group context.

Language

While my comments above deal generally with diversity, they also relate to language. However, language must be singled out for further attention because it is a highly visible marker of group identity; indeed, for many it is the essential marker. This is an old idea, and I refer the reader to the quotations of linguistic nationalists including Herder, Humboldt, Fichte, Davis and others (see Introduction). It is also, however, a view held by more contemporary writers. Thus, Anderson and Frideres (1981) cite the ideas of Freeman, Shibutani and Kwan, Bram, Park and Handlin—for all of whom language was central, if not indispensable, to group identity (see also Reitz,

1980). However, it has also been acknowledged that language is *not* always essential for continued identity (see Borrie, 1959). Anderson (1979) discusses the loss of the mother tongue without the loss of ethnic identity; this implies that other markers—religion, group customs, etc.—may be important too, and it reminds us of the dangers of overemphasizing any single aspect.

Having said this, it is nevertheless clear enough why language can be readily seized upon as a symbol of identity, especially where a rekindling of group-ness is desired. In nationalist movements, for example, a language which has become dormant, or even extinct for most of the group, can reappear as a rallying point. As well, the very existence of a group language can serve as a constant reminder of group membership (see Edwards, 1977). However, the relationship of language to identity often remains murky, deliberately obscured by linguistic nationalists and selectively dealt with by academic apologists for group causes. It may be instructive, before proceeding further, to present a brief case study. This is intended to show something of language growth, maintenance, decline and attempted revival over the long term, and to consider what the process reveals of identity. I choose the Irish case here because the language has a history in which most of the chapters have already been written, because it is one which has attracted a good deal of revivalist interest, and because it illustrates points of widespread concern.

The course of Irish[3]

Before the Norman invasions of the twelfth century, Irish was secure. And, afterwards, speakers of French, English and other languages were largely Gaelicized (except within the Pale). In 1366, the Statutes of Kilkenny were enacted, prohibiting English settlers from adopting Irish ways and enforcing the use of English; the passage of these laws reflects the power of Irish (see Curtis and McDowell, 1968).

Beginning with the Tudors, however, real changes in the fortunes of Irish were set in motion. The proclamations of Henry VIII discouraged Irish, to say the least. In 1536, for example, a note to the people of Galway included the following: "Every inhabitaunt within the saide towne indevor theym selfe to speke Englyshe, and to use theym selffe after the Englyshe facion; and specyally that you, and every of you, do put forth your child to scole, to lerne to speke Englyshe." (Corcoran, 1916, p. 41; see also Corcoran, 1982.) The plantation schemes, with their inevitable disruptions, and the defeat of the Irish chiefs were also important factors in the decline of Irish. By the end of the sixteenth century, the Gaelic order had largely passed. Between 1600 and 1800, English grew in influence and became the language of regular communication for about half the population; increasingly, it became the language of status and power. In the nineteenth century Irish faced further difficulties. The received notion here was a simplified one: O'Connell, the Catholic clergy and the National School system killed Irish (Wall, 1969). O'Connell was utilitarian in his approach to language matters (although an Irish speaker himself), the Church had increasingly turned to English (especially since Irish was being used by Protestant proselytists) and the schools ignored Irish. As well, one must not omit the violent consequences of the mid-century famine.

By the middle of the nineteenth century, then, the number of *monolingual* Irish speakers was small and, in the context, bilingualism was usually an unstable condition. However, none of the factors noted above are sufficient to explain the very rapid language shift which occurred. De Fréine (1977) cites here the willingness of the population to abandon Irish—"most of the reasons adduced for the suppression of the Irish language are not so much reasons as consequences of the decision to give up the language" (p. 84; see also de Fréine, 1978). The mass of the Irish people were more or less active contributors to the spread of English. Binchy (1945) notes, for example, that the "persecution" theory does not fully explain the dramatic Irish decline; Brooks (1907) states that, although the English were far from blameless, "it is impossible to stamp out a language which the people are determined to keep alive" (p. 22). Irish, he feels, committed suicide rather than having been murdered (see also Ó Conaire, 1973, citing the views of Flann O'Brien, the well-known Irish writer, on this matter).[4] To simply fall back on clichés like "700 years of English oppression" or "the stifling of the will of a nation" is to see history in black and white only.

The rise of the Irish revival movement in the late nineteenth century was part of a larger European trend, especially in Celtic areas. Building upon the linguistic nationalism of Fichte, Herder and others, efforts were made to transform the "Celtic twilight" into the "Celtic renaissance". The Society for the Preservation of the Irish Language was established in 1876, followed by the Gaelic Union (1880). It was with the founding of the Gaelic League in 1893, however, that the revival effort really began in earnest. Douglas Hyde, the first president, had called for the de-anglicization of Ireland (1894) and, in the first instance, the League's aim was to maintain spoken Irish. Soon, however, it became an organization associated with actual revival and language shift. It had considerable success in placing Irish in schools and university, it commanded a widespread (if somewhat evanescent) public support, and it played an important role in the revolutionary movement. It did not, however, succeed in resuscitating spoken Irish among the population at large, nor did it make any lasting impact upon the maintenance and development of the Gaeltacht (Irish-speaking district). It was essentially a movement of Dublin-based upper-middle-class individuals, rather romantic in outlook, for most of whom Irish was an acquired competence.

The Gaeltacht itself, the shrinking home of native Irish speakers, has been a continuing source of difficulty, embarrassment and realism. There are perhaps 50 000 regular Irish speakers left now, almost all concentrated on the western littoral (Ó Danachair, 1969; but see also Fennell, 1981). The Gaelic League paid lip service to the Gaeltacht, its people and its way of life but, as Brown (1981) and Kiberd (1979) have suggested, did little for it. In fact, the whole Irish question can be seen to hinge on the Gaeltacht. Early associations of the area with poverty and backwardness did nothing for the cause of Irish, and recent efforts are plagued by a paradox. If nothing is done, the Gaeltacht will continue to shrink, encroached upon as it is by influences associated with English. When things are done—to sustain economic development, for example, in order to provide a practical foundation for an Irish-language lifestyle—there is a danger of creating an enclave, insulated to some extent from the full force of normal economic and other pressures, which is seen as artificial by insiders and outsiders alike. The most important factor for the Gaeltacht and for Irish is the attitudes and usage of the people. And here, Fennell (1981) notes that enthusiasm has not been strong for the revival effort. He claims that outside agencies failed to kindle this vital element and, while this is true, it perhaps neglects the views and attitudes of the people themselves, and their implicit linguistic choices. Now, most parents in the Gaeltacht have decided to bring up their children in English, a process reminiscent of the nation-wide shift a century and more ago. It goes without saying that this poses the gravest possible risk for the maintenance of Irish in its naturally spoken forms.

The government has, from the first, considered the Gaeltacht of great significance, yet it has been unable (or unwilling, or both) to stop the erosion. Indeed, the government has essentially entrusted the major thrust of the revival effort to the primary school. Here, the view that the English-run National School system of the nineteenth century had killed Irish seemed to lead to the idea that an Irish-run system could revive it—a specious argument, but one with powerful proponents. Infants' classes, for example, were to be conducted entirely through Irish, even though this would be an unknown language for the overwhelming majority. The teachers, naturally enough, bore the brunt of the effort, and the finding of sufficient numbers of competent Irish speakers proved difficult. As well, the teachers began to become uneasy with their role which they saw as more and more divorced from larger social trends and interests (see the Irish National Teachers' Organization (INTO) reports of 1942 and 1947). In any event while the schools have succeeded in producing a widespread, if thin competence among the general population they clearly have not accomplished that revival so wished for by the linguistic nationalists. Nor, indeed, do I think it at all possible for them to have done so. Nevertheless, the continuing dynamics of the Irish scene have created what has been termed a "crisis in Irish" in education (Murphy, 1981). Standards of Irish are allegedly low, there is a disjunction between primary and secondary level Irish, and teachers remain bitter about being the scapegoats for revival failure. Thus, the outgoing president of the INTO stated (in Murphy, 1981) that Irish must be taken outside the school, that the community must play its part, and that the burden of revival should not be placed upon teachers and children (the latter termed "digits in the Irish revival statistics" by Akenson, 1975).

Considering the Irish situation in general, we should see that the reasons for the decline of the language are many, and more complicated than some would have us believe. The interaction between Irish and English is not to be seen only along an oppressor–oppressed continuum. The evidence of linguistic contact elsewhere in Europe, and the historical rapidity of the shift from Irish to English make the Irish case an instructive one. Perhaps the most neglected element is the acquiescence of the population in the shift. The reasons for this cannot be explored further here but, as a first step, the reader might profitably consider some of de Fréine's ideas (1977, 1978). The historical and sociological forces bearing upon Irish, combined with (and often disputing) the emotionally charged views of many revivalists, have meant that there have been few careful sociolinguistic investigations. The most important of these, the Committee on Irish Language Attitudes Research report (1975) can itself be seen to have done little to create clarity. This is not completely due to the inadequacies of the report, nor is it particularly surprising in the context. The report does, however, point to the need for distinguishing between tolerance and action in language matters, and between communicative and non-communicative aspects of language (see below). The report (and earlier work; see Macnamara, 1971) demonstrates the symbolic value of Irish for many people; however, this does not equate with a desire to use the language.

Implications from the Irish scene

What generalities might we extract from the Irish language situation? First, it shows the progress of a language over time and the influences affecting its power and scope. For about 400 years, Irish remained strong in the face of linguistic competition, Gaelicized the new settlers and forced the passage of legislation intended to bolster English. This changed with new political and social conditions, but it took more than 200 years for English to gain a firm foothold. And then, in the last century, we note that the large-scale shift to

English occurred because of a complex of circumstances which cannot be easily ascribed to something as simple as English oppression. Of course it is true that if English had not arrived in Ireland it could hardly have displaced Irish; in that simplistic sense, it is the culprit. But was *Irish* then an oppressive force between Norman and Tudor times?[5] It is surely clear that language shift reflects sociopolitical change and this, given the historical perspective, absolutely dwarfs efforts made on behalf of language alone. This is not to say (see above) that language cannot serve a vital rallying purpose in nationalistic political movements, but it only does so when it retains some realistic degree of communicative function. This was not the case for Irish by the time the revivalists appeared, nor is it true for many immigrant languages in America and elsewhere today.

The second, and related, point is that language revival efforts can be seen as artificial when they operate in the face of historical realities; this is true in two senses. They are artificial, first of all, in that they are divorced from the forces of day-to-day reality for the mass of the population. It is simply not possible to bring about widespread language shift when the appeal is made on the basis of abstractions like culture, heritage or tradition; these are not, of course, trivial or ignoble aspects of life but they are not conscious priorities for most people. In Ireland we see that those people who might have been expected to respond best to revival rhetoric—the Irish-speaking Gaeltacht residents—did not do so in any united way (Fennell, 1981). Revivalism is often artificial, as well, in the type of language form it attempts to resuscitate. From a desire to standardize, to upgrade, to give fair play to a number of dialects, an academic variety may be produced which is some way removed from the maternal speech patterns of any native speaker (see Toynbee, 1956).

A third feature of the Irish situation which is generally applicable is the importance of a living heartland for a language, a place where the language is used regularly across a broad range of domains. If this has shrunk to such an extent that it is seen to require special support, then what I have described here as the "paradox of the Gaeltacht" occurs. If nothing is done, there is every likelihood of continued erosion. If things *are* done, then a real danger exists of creating a fishbowl in which language matters (and others) are treated with the same self-conscious attention which characterizes the half-an-hour-a-week German class. It is my view that, although there is nothing wrong with this attention *per se,* it hardly contributes to that unselfconscious usage of language which we associate with regular interpersonal interaction. And, the process of out-migration (or in-migration, for that matter: see Williams on the Basque heartland, Chapter 7) documents the desires of heartland residents which interfere with the hopes of revivalists.

Fourthly, it seems clear that there is, today, a strong Irish identity which does not involve the Irish language in a communicative sense. As will be seen below, the report of the Committee on Irish Language Attitudes Research (1975) revealed that Irish serves a symbolic function for most people and is, in Eastman's sense (Chapter 9), an "associated" language. Rodriguez (1983) has commented upon the fallacy of viewing the continuation of the ancestral language, for regular communication, as essential for the continuation of group identity, and the Irish case would seem to bear him out. The revivalist error was to single out communicative language as the most important marker of identity, and to ignore the evidence of daily life. For if we accept that (a) there is an Irish national identity, and (b) the vast majority neither speak Irish nor seem particularly interested in doing so, then it follows that identity does *not* depend upon language alone. Some would argue, I know, that the existing Irish identity is less than it might be because of the loss of the language, but this is a condescending line to take, and an historically naïve one.

The Irish experience also holds useful lessons on the role of the education system in language matters, and on the communicative–symbolic distinction; I shall consider each of these in further detail below. Generally, an examination of Irish demonstrates (as Fennell, 1981, concluded in his study of the Gaeltacht) that attempts to stop the erosion of shrinking minority languages are not likely to be successful. This is because the shrinking itself is a marker of larger trends which cannot be affected by linguistic action alone. Thus, language support is of dubious worth and, indeed, it may do some harm. Action taken may convince some that broader social change is going to occur; if this does not happen, minority-group solidarity may be damaged (see also below).

The communicative–symbolic distinction

I have referred already to this distinction and must now outline it more clearly, for continued confusion here has serious consequences. Language has both communicative and symbolic value and, for most majority populations, these two coexist. English speakers in Britain, for example, use the language in all regular domains; as well, it is the language of their past in which tradition and culture are expressed. However, the two aspects of language are separable, and it is possible for the symbolic to remain in the absence of the communicative (see Kelman, 1971; Edwards, 1977; Eastman, Chapter 9). This describes the linguistic situation of many minority groups. It will be noted, furthermore, that the symbolic value of language is essentially a private ethnic marker, while ordinary usage is a visible one. We should thus expect, on the basis of previous discussion, that communicative language shift would be a relatively early phenomenon in minority-group adaptation to a larger society. This expectation is confirmed in North America and elsewhere, but insufficient attention has been given to the continuing symbolic function of a language no longer spoken. Glazer (1980), for example, has stated that language maintenance inevitably declines in the United States, but that other aspects of ethnicity remain. This is too categorical, for it ignores the fact that symbolic language is, in fact, one of the "other aspects".

If we turn again to the Irish case, we see a clear example of this phenomenon. The most exhaustive research study of Irish attitudes, ability and usage (Committee on Irish Language Attitudes Research, 1975) sampled some 3000 respondents.[6] Most endorsed the value of Irish as a part of identity while, at the same time, felt pessimistic about its future as a medium of communication. As well, there was revealed a widespread lack of interest in promotion or restoration of Irish. These feelings would seem to be reflected in the minor ways in which Irish is actually used in day-to-day life; these are essentially ceremonial, trivial or in conjunction with English.

Ignorance of the communicative–symbolic distinction can lead to lack of clarity and misdirected effort. If language revivalists or restorationists conceive of language in communicative terms alone, and if their appeals are directed towards groups in which communicative shift has occurred, then they may (a) be unsuccessful in their attempts to promote language use; (b) reintroduce, under the mantle of pluralism, a sort of *anomie* which group members are likely to have resolved for themselves some time before (see Riesman, 1965); (c) promote a cynical view of any and all efforts on behalf of group identity. In 1976, for example, I described a bilingual education programme for French children in Vermont. As part of the study of the effects of this programme, parents (who spoke French) were asked to rate themselves along linguistic lines. About 55% saw themselves as mainly English, and another 13% felt they were in some transitional state between French and English. Also, there were other families in the programme who did not meet the criterion of speaking French at all. Yet, the project had been put in place, by well-meaning outsiders, precisely to bolster communicative French usage. The most cursory survey of the area showed that most families were well settled (originally from Quebec, they were not new immigrants), thought of themselves as Americans and retained French for essentially private functions—and this despite the fact that, unlike most other American immigrant groups, they were easily able to visit "home", keep up ties with relatives, etc. The programme, in its ignorance, attempted to sustain identity through public language use, via the children. When it terminated, because of local unwillingness to pick up the financial reins from the federal funding agency, it left in its wake a cynicism which extended to all forms of active intervention in defence of of identity. More importantly, however, the failure to affect a public marker of ethnicity actually weakened the desire for private elements—especially among the children, whose increasing lack of interest in public French transferred itself to other facets of their French background.

Language and identity

From what I have said so far, it will be seen that questions relating to a permanent cultural pluralism and, specifically, to the role of language in that state are complex. The pluralism/assimilation relationship is more involved than some think or wish to acknowledge. The relationship of language to identity is also not a simple one; it involves consideration of language functions and of the varying nature of different elements of identity. I believe that further useful information can now be added if we look at the viewpoints held by different groups on these matters. We can also look briefly at mediums for ethnic assertion (or reassertion), of which the most important has usually been the school.

Views of language and identity

In 1977, Fishman noted, concerning bilingual education, that parent and student attitudes and interests had been poorly researched—and this after about ten years of wide-ranging implementation of bilingual education programmes. While this may be, as Abramson (1983) has suggested in a more general context, evidence of a particularly American passion for immediate and apparently practical action, lack of adequate grounding is surely not confined to the American scene. It is always regrettable. Any programme or policy which is intended to have real social consequences would obviously do well to build upon the firmest possible foundations if it wishes to avoid becoming merely a matter of fashion, or the latest band-wagon. On the basis of the contributions to this volume alone, we can see that gaps in our understanding of wide-ranging public sentiment and opinion apply not only to bilingual education but also to the larger issues to which it is often related. Perhaps the current interest in cultural pluralism and the "new ethnicity" is bound to disappear. Perhaps, as Dinnerstein and Reimers (1982) have suggested, ethnicity is now chic. One way of looking at this is to pay attention to a diversity of views on pluralism, language and identity, and to search for similarities and differences.

In giving some attention to this matter here, I shall deal with five relevant groups, not all mutually exclusive. These are: (a) ethnic group members;

(b) ethnic group spokesmen; (c) the mainstream population; (d) the academic constituency; (e) the official, or governmental policy-makers.

a. Ethnic group members. Although the lives and views of ordinary group members are obviously of the greatest relevance for considerations of *their* language, identity and societal relationships, we do not have much formal information here. Nevertheless, the informal record is useful. In the United States, for example, we note the gradual lessening of the influence of specifically ethnic institutions and societies (Fishman, 1966; Lemaire, 1966). The assimilative tendency has not generally been expedited because of some abdication of responsibility by ethnic schools, churches and societies; rather, these institutions have declined in importance as group need for them decreased (Edwards, 1977). As regards ethnic language itself, there has not been much legal or official pressure on ethnic-group speakers to abandon their mother tongue. The important factor here has typically been the perceived advantage of life in the mainstream. The few moves to suppress immigrant languages in the last century were unpopular and soon revoked (see Dinnerstein *et al.,* 1979; Mann, 1979; Ornstein, 1979; Teitelbaum and Hiller, 1977). This is not to say, of course, that minorities might not have preferred a utopian society with mainstream accessibility *and* complete linguistic retention. Choices had to be made, and these were not easy ones. Steinberg (1981) notes that these choices—forced upon people by circumstances—undermined cultural maintenance. This is perhaps phrasing things too strongly (see above), but it is nonetheless clear that communicative language was a casualty for most ethnic groups. However regrettable this may be, we should remember that, in areas generally untouched by legal strictures, immigrants Americanized of their own volition and to the extent desired or made necessary by attractive options (Ravitch, 1976). Therefore, providing we acknowledge a distinction between public and private ethnicity, between communicative and symbolic language, we can observe the real-life laboratory of the United States and agree with Drake (1979) that most groups are assimilationist in their attitudes.

So far as indigenous minorities are concerned, perceptions of ordinary group members confirm what is mentioned above. It is true that, in many cases, group languages have suffered persecution or, at least, ignorance by majority populations. But even here we should not neglect the elements of choice and group volition. A public language may be suppressed so that it comes to play only a very reduced communicative role, or only a symbolic one. But there is at least some truth in Brooks' observation (1907) that a language cannot be murdered and that, where one seems to disappear, there are often grounds for thinking of suicide. If we compare the suppression of Irish with that of Czech, Estonian, Hungarian and even English, we see, of course, different historical circumstances—but the most important aspect of the difference has to do with group resistance or acquiescence. In either case, we see attitude and volition at work. Fennell (1981), in describing the decline of Irish and other "small" languages, observed that, in the final analysis, it is only group members themselves who can save communicative usage (see also Price, 1979).

This implies that any linguistic revival also depends upon group will. If we see a reticence here it may be because, despite the claims of spokesmen, group members have made the necessary adjustments, and have retained identity in the form desired, given changing circumstances which affect all. From this position, they are unlikely to be swayed by abstract appeals based upon ill-conceived ideas of some (impossible) static culture. In any event, if language loss several generations previously entailed change in lifestyle, it is simplistic to assume that reviving language will revive that earlier way of life.

Most minority groups are, above all, pragmatic—and this usually implies some degree of assimilation. Gaarder (1981) observes the almost complete lack of meaningful resistance to assimilation in the United States, and surely this is a reasonably general comment. A recent book provides some first-hand accounts which support the view. Morrison and Zabusky (1980) interviewed 140 first-generation immigrants to the United States, and one is struck by the great pains taken to acquire English. Sonia Walinsky (from Russia) asks passengers on an immigrant train to speak only English to her, as she is now an American. After a long day washing dishes, and a long walk, Demetrius Paleologas (Greece) studies English at night school. Elise Radell (Germany), determined not to be "left out", learns English. Wojtek Pobog (Poland) and Serge Nicholas (Manchuria) feel that army service and the English it required pushed them from the ghetto, and they are glad. Ricardo Massoni (Italy) pays a quarter to watch English films four or five times, to get "the ear accustomed". Colette Montgomery (France) struggles through English books four or five times. Karim Mohammed (Egypt), discussing cultural retention, mentions religion, Arabic name and family—but not language. All these reports confirm grosser observations about language shift. It is important to realize that most of these people had regrets connected with emigration, and not all preferred to describe themselves as American (though many did so). But the pragmatism and the desire to make the painful act of emigration worthwhile have led inexorably to language shift.

A lengthier description of adaptation to life in the larger society is given in an autobiography by Rodriguez (1983).[7] He discusses the public–private dimension I have noted above; home was Spanish and outside was English. Rodriguez considers that having to learn English at school, although painful, established his right to speak the language of *los gringos*. This, as he makes quite clear, created a loosening of ties with parents and relatives who were Spanish-speaking, for as his English increased his Spanish declined. For Rodriguez at least, "public individuality" (via English) caused a diminished "private individuality" (Spanish). Whether this need be so for all ethnic group members is doubtful, and Rodriguez's case might be taken as an example of the need for bilingual education. If so, however, it would be of the transitional variety (see below), for he is critical of those who reject assimilation; they are "filled with decadent self-pity . . . they romanticize public separateness" (p. 27). Besides, Rodriguez was to find that family life and intimacy could indeed be expressed through English—"intimacy is not created by a particular language; it is created by intimates" (p. 32). Rodriguez's journey was not an easy one, and his linguistic cost-benefit analysis will not be to everyone's taste. But, his is an honest account and his story—"the life of a middle-class man"—can be generalized.[8]

b. Ethnic group spokesmen. I have already discussed the gradually increasing gap between the lives of ethnic group members and the societies, churches and schools which were once so important to them. The fact that these institutions remain means that there exist persons who feel themselves to be group spokesmen and leaders, but who may also be some way removed from grassroots sentiments (see Vallee, 1981). These individuals, furthermore, are often ones who have prospered in the larger society. Indeed, their role as group spokesmen often reflects an admired ability to straddle two cultures. Relatively secure, these activists endorse cultural pluralism because they feel that "permanent minority status might be advantageous" (Higham, 1975, p. 211). We find Linton (cited in Weinreich, 1974, p. 101) noting that "nativistic tendencies will be stronger in those classes of individuals who occupy a favored position" (see also Riley, 1975; Edwards, 1977). The reader will also recall here the results of the Irish language survey (Committee on Irish Language Attitudes Research, 1975) which found markedly different viewpoints held by ordinary people and those involved in pro-Irish activities.

All of this is not to deny that spokesmen may well reflect the wishes of less visible group members and may galvanize latent desires—leaders are always a minority, after all. But it is surely worth noting that, in an area as sensitive as language and identity, care should be taken to see how far enthusiasm extends. The example of the French–English bilingual programme discussed above is a graphic illustration of the possible gap between the attitudes of spokesmen and advocates and those of the intended beneficiaries of social action.

Mann (1979) has outlined in some detail the distance between group spokesmen and the masses. Noting that rank-and-file "ethnics" in the

United States were not swept into the cultural renaissance, he cites the view of Myrdal that, far from a people's movement, the "new ethnicity" is supported by well-established intellectuals and writers. While they may be sincere, they are hardly typical, and Mann suggests that they are too ready to see mass support for their ideas in public ethnic activities and festivals— celebrations which have in most cases become thoroughly Americanized. The fact that intellectuals and others present an articulate, powerful and visible source of influence should not confuse us into thinking that they reflect large-scale opinion. They are a minority within a minority.

c. The mainstream population. What do majority-group members think of cultural pluralism and of the retention of minority language and identity? Historically, the evidence shows little tolerance or concern for minority matters at all and, as we should expect, such a stance is still prevalent in many quarters. While firm data are lacking here, reactions in the popular press to issues relating to ethnic diversity show a continuing fear of social fragmentation (see Edwards, 1980b). The title of one of Greeley's books, *Why Can't They Be Like Us?* (1971), summarizes the views of many. Bethell's provocative article (1979) pointed to the fragmentation that over-emphasis on ethnic language (and corresponding de-emphasis of English) might produce. Similar sentiments may be found in many newspaper accounts.[9]

There is, however, a more recent tolerance for ethnic diversity which seems to be emerging. The surveys of O'Bryan *et al.* (1976) and Berry *et al.* (1977) on unofficial languages and multiculturalism in Canada indicated a growing awareness that diversity can be a strength. A similar interpretation can be placed upon the findings of the report of the Committee on Irish Language Attitudes Research (1975). In fact, we might say that in many parts of the world a liberalism which is, at least in part, the product of relative affluence and security is now ready to embrace ethnic diversity, folkways and customs. This is not always based upon a great deal of knowledge, however—many people surveyed in the Canadian work knew very little about multiculturalism *per se* (see also Chisholm, 1983). And, where enthusiasm does exist it is often in the form of discovering an untapped commercial resource; ethnicity can be good for tourism. It would be unfair, though, to claim that awareness of the cash value of ethnicity is the major factor behind current tolerance.

When we reflect further on the meaning and implications of tolerance for diversity, we should consider at least three important questions: (a) is current tolerance necessarily a stable quantity; (b) does tolerance extend equally across all majority–minority and minority–minority relationships; (c) can we equate tolerance with active support for diversity, especially in linguistic matters?

Tolerance for diversity has not been, historically, something which ethnic groups could always count upon. The finding of scapegoats when times are bad has been a regrettably common occurrence, and it surely needs no documentation here. As well, the sort of "tolerance" which Skutnabb-Kangas (Chapter 1) discusses in the case of European guestworkers—where, when industrial productivity slows, workers are retained to serve as a cushion for economic shocks at the lowest end of the social hierarchy—operates from a base of self-interest and not from one of altruism. We should be careful, therefore, if we attempt to erect an enduring social policy upon public attitudes which may shift quite rapidly. At the very least, we should be concerned not to build false hopes, and not to dash minority-group expectations which have been encouraged to rise on unstable foundations.

We should also understand that, while there may be a greater degree of tolerance by majorities of minorities in general, this does not imply equal tolerance for all groups. Nor does it imply uniformity of goodwill within and across minority groups themselves. Kopan (1974) notes that antipathy to new immigrants in the United States came from those who had been new immigrants themselves only a little earlier. Kolack (1980), in studying ethnic communities in Massachusetts, refers to the often violent feelings between minority groups (see also Dinnerstein et al., 1979). Again, inter-minority hatred does not require extensive documentation here.

It is worthy of note that much special pleading is done for particular groups under the guise of a general cultural pluralism (Gleason, 1979). Arguments for Spanish-Americans, for example, often make reference to general diversity, and to general immigrant problems, but the focus is clearly on the one group (Edwards, 1980a). It has been found, in Canada, that French-Canadians are less supportive of multiculturalism than are English-Canadians, and this relates to fears of being relegated to the status of the "other" minority groups. French speakers comprise one of the two "charter" groups in Canada but they are also a minority; they are thus equal but unequal partners. Consequently, they are less tolerant of multicultural diversity and government support for other languages, etc. The official Canadian multicultural policy as originally outlined called for the encouragement of diversity "within a bilingual framework" and while this was an attempt to reassure French-Canadians it is not surprising that the agitations of other minority groups within elastically defined guidelines could be seen as eroding the French-Canadian status of *primus inter pares.*

Finally here, we should not equate tolerance for diversity with a desire to see *active* promotion of ethnic-group interests (especially where support derives from government sources). Thus, Seelye (1977) notes that where there is general support for bilingual education, it is for a remedial or transitional variety (see below)—that is, one which does not retard assimilation and may even expedite it. Drake (1979) feels that there has *not* been a shift towards active support for pluralism (see also Sowell, 1978; Mann, 1979). The implications of accepting the equation are obvious, and the current unease over bilingual education and pluralism might be seen as an attempt to force the distinction between tolerance and active support upon those who have been ignorant of it, or unwilling to recognize it (Edwards, 1982).

d. The academic constituency. Some of what I would otherwise have to say here is covered in section (b) above, for there are many academics who are also ethnic-group spokesmen. This is, of course, a quite reasonable combination of roles, providing that the academic stance is not confounded with more subjective advocacy. I have suggested elsewhere (Edwards, 1980b, 1981b, 1982) that, unfortunately, this confounding does occur; in some areas it is now almost to be expected. And, as the reader will gather from my earlier remarks here (and in the Introduction), it was a desire to combat this which gave impetus to the present collection. Drake (1979), Sowell (1978), Van den Berghe (1967) and others have also drawn attention to the colouring of arguments by "moralistic–ideological imperatives". To avoid mere repetition, I refer the reader to the articles noted above for examples of pluralist rhetoric under the guise of social scientific objectivity.

As well, however, we do have access to more disinterested academic approaches to language, identity, diversity and pluralism. To do justice to these would involve summarizing a great deal of material, mostly sociological and historical, and I do not mean to do this here (see Edwards, in preparation). Useful treatments will be found in Glazer and Moynihan (1963), Gordon (1964), Higham (1975), Mann (1979), Parrillo (1980) and Steinberg (1981); see also Gleason's discussion in Chapter 8. What I shall do here is mention two important features of the academic approach. The first has to do with an attempt to understand, describe and assess the realities and implications of majority–minority relations for all segments of society and for society as a whole. This is, of course, not a value-free exercise. The changing notions of pluralism, and the changing society within which these ideas were formulated are interrelated. But, given these limits, there have been many admirable efforts to document important current issues and to place them in historical perspective. The most successful of these have, above all, pointed to the relative nature of group interactions and have emphasized their dynamic qualities (as opposed to the static absolutism of many apologists for communicative language retention and cultural pluralism).

The second important facet of the academic approach is related to the first inasmuch as it involves the contribution of a balanced perspective to an area

rife with imbalances. That is, there has been a laudable effort in recent years
to counter the increasing deluge of polemical material on pluralism. This
second aspect, then, can be seen as the application of the first. Mann (1979)
notes that academics, having studied the matter for years, "did not have to
be reminded of the persistence of ethnicity in American life" (p. 44). They
became increasingly concerned with the oversimplifications and the distor-
tions of the "new ethnicity", which over-emphasized, as Gleason might say,
the *pluribus* and trivialized the *unum* of the American motto. This desire to
restore balance has led to works re-examining the pluralism–assimilation
relationship (Higham, 1975; Mann, 1979), re-emphasizing the explanatory
value of social class (Steinberg, 1981), considering the relationship between
the retention of ethnicity and social inequality (Porter, 1965, 1972, 1975),
and associating pluralism with caste (Stein and Hill, 1977). While we need
not agree with any or all of these treatments, they do try to respond to more
advocatory publications (e.g. Greeley, 1974; Henk *et al.,* 1972; Novak,
1971; Schrag, 1971). They supply the other side of the coin, as it were, and it
is only when we examine both sides that we know the value of what we hold.

e. Official policy-makers. Official views of pluralism, and especially of the
support of language, have followed a predictable pattern in many areas of
the world. As the general aim of government is to ensure society's survival
and prosperity (we may associate this primarily with democratic governments, but it is also true of undemocratic ones, although their reasons may
be different), it is not surprising to observe a concern for homogenization
and standardization, and a corresponding fear of particularism or social
fragmentation; it is easy to assemble illustrative relevant quotations from
world leaders of the past and present. In the name of unity, however, many
misdeeds have been done, and discrimination and persecution blot the
histories of all societies. An increasing tendency to tolerance and even
support for diversity is, therefore, a welcome appearance. It should come as
no shock, however, to see that government action on behalf of enduring
diversity does not generally extend as far as some proponents of pluralism
would like. The present stance of many governments reflects a continuing
concern for social integrity, along with a newer acknowledgement of the
value of diversity. This combination is not static, or uniform across contexts,
or insensitive to currents of opinion; this is as it should be. However, if we
acknowledge that some currents of opinion present themselves more forcibly
and more vocally to elected officials than do others, we can see that
government action may be swayed inappropriately.

Two examples from the American scene suggest themselves here. The
first is the passage of the 1968 Bilingual Education Act in which, *pace*
Fishman (1977), there are grounds for thinking that the legislation was a

response to "spokesmen" and not to a widespread movement (see Edwards, 1981b). Even so, the government can be seen to have responded in a way reflecting the combination of attitudes I mentioned above, for it essentially sanctioned bilingual education as a transitional device for assisting children of limited English-speaking ability into mainstream classrooms. We now see, therefore, further moves on the part of cultural pluralists to promote a metamorphosis of current bilingual education into a type more conducive to permanent diversity (or so it is imagined). These moves have run into severe counter-pressure from officials who no doubt view them as attempts to alter a workable balance between unity and diversity.

The second example relates to the Ethnic Heritage Studies Act (1972). This, to my mind, is a milder piece of legislation than the first, for its emphasis is more towards private than public manifestations of ethnicity. Yet Mann (1979) is right when he remarks that it was a response to "ethnic ideologues" and that it sanctioned their claim "that their own intense feelings of ethnicity applied to Americans as a whole" (p. 167). Mann is of the opinion that the best governmental response here would have been none at all, on the grounds that matters of ethnicity are best left to those directly concerned; this is a position with which I agree.

It is important to note, though, that many see lack of government legislation as ignorance or discrimination. They fail to understand that, as Mann implies, lack of response (in legislative terms) is itself a government action. My contention is that a refusal to legislate on matters of ethnicity is a reasonable response which can be supported by the sorts of evidence I have assembled here. This presupposes, of course, a real tolerance (*this* may well be backed up in law) for groups to define themselves as they see fit.

Bilingual education

In this section I want to look briefly at one of the most important mediums for the assertion of ethnic identity—the school. There are, of course, other avenues through which identity can be expressed (home, church, ethnic society, etc.) but they are not as contentious, mainly because they reflect private-domain ethnicity. School, on the other hand, is perhaps the single most important point of contact between minority and majority groups (see Edwards, 1979, 1981c) and can be seen as an arena in which many larger social issues are displayed and examined. In particular, the relationship of education to policies of cultural pluralism has, traditionally and currently, been a close if uneasy one. Because I have dealt with this relationship elsewhere in some detail, I will not repeat myself here; indeed, much relevant material will be found throughout the preceding discussion. Nevertheless, I must outline the argument in skeletal form at least.

Bilingual education is not merely a linguistic issue. The area, rather, is one in which social policies affecting minority–majority relations are argued and tested. Many of the purely pedagogical features of bilingual education have assumed a larger-than-life centrality, and statistical significance is often allowed to overshadow psychological meaningfulness (see Edwards, 1981a). While many would advocate an education which allows early instruction in the (minority) language of the child, a controversy has raged over when (and if) transition to the mainstream language should occur. Those who claim that transition to the majority language is unnecessary also propose permanent or semi-permanent minority language instruction. This poses practical problems—of scale, if of nothing else. As well, since the most that can be said is that transition may not be *necessary*, it hardly follows that it would be harmful and that some non-transitional (or, maintenance) variety is pedagogically required.

It is the distinction between transitional and maintenance bilingual education which animates cultural pluralists. The former variety can be seen to actually promote a smoother assimilation into the mainstream, while the latter can act as a servant to the cause of an enduring diversity. Most programmes, as I have noted above, are transitional (in the United States) and so there is an ongoing concern among proponents of pluralism. As linguistic nationalists, they view schools as "wholly political . . . instruments of state [or group] policy" (Kedourie, 1961, p. 84). Ravitch (1981) has questioned the use of the school in this way—it becomes, as she puts it, a "sociological cookie cutter"—because she fears the purely educational role becoming subservient to a political one. Of course, *all* education can be seen as political, but Ravitch's point is one of degree rather than absolute principle. Bullivant (1981) has recognized the importance of this matter and, in a study of six plural societies, discusses the dilemma of retaining the unifying function of education which abets cross-group mobility ("civism") while at the same time not restricting ethnic diversity. Bullivant essentially endorses the private–public distinction which I have outlined above, and decries attempts by public institutions to promote private ethnicity.

Given confusion in the area of pluralism and assimilation, it is easy to see that educational programmes can exacerbate minority–majority relations instead of ameliorating them, and can damage ingroup solidarity. I have already mentioned how an ill-considered French–English bilingual programme was destructive of private elements of ethnicity, and how the attempted revival of Irish at school turned children into revival statistics. Commenting on the latter situation, O'Doherty (1958) noted that "children's minds must not be made the battleground of a political wrangle" (p. 268). As well, however, Bullivant demonstrates how attention to educational programmes can distract attention from the solution of real sociopolitical problems suffered by minority groups. We can imagine how this is carried out by unthinking but well-meaning supporters of diversity; it is also possible to conceive of a more sinister version, in which government may adopt a multicultural or pluralistic stance as a way of keeping minorities in their place, while *appearing* to attend to their needs. This may sound paranoid or unlikely but it has, in fact, been seriously discussed (see, e.g. Breton *et al.*, 1980). If governments pay groups to retain aspects of public ethnicity, may they not also be ensuring the continuation of ethnic boundaries which unfairly contain group members?

One view relating to education is the simplistic notion (see above) that if schools have in the past trampled on minority languages, they must now work to rebuild them. If only it were so simple. This is a view which reduces ethnicity, for it neglects all the changes which have accompanied communicative language shift. It is true, as Steinberg (1981) observes, that schools traditionally ignored immigrant languages and that the ethnic groups' own parochial schools were limited to a small part of the potential constituency. Yet, we must ask why more forceful demands were not made on public school systems for minority-language instruction, especially in contexts like the United States where there were few legislative obstacles. We must also ask why the parochial efforts were not more expansive initially and why they typically declined from the base of importance which they did have. Furthermore, we can extend the argument and ask why current transitional programmes are not more widely criticized. The answers here are found in the preceding sections of this chapter. I might just add here a remark made by one of Morrison and Zabusky's (1980) interviewees. This man, a Chinese immigrant active in social and cultural affairs, represents an ethnic group which has typically been more zealous than most in preserving and promoting communicative language across the generations. Referring to a community school in the San Francisco Chinatown, he notes: "the trouble is the majority of the children don't want to go. We got the school going up to twelfth grade, but the most of them [sic] only go just through sixth grade. Even my own three kids, they don't like to go to the Chinese school" (pp. 81–82).

It seems to me that, while transitional bilingual education is a reasonable activity, deserving of public support (although there are many practical difficulties relating to resources, number of languages to be catered for, etc.), the maintenance variety is not so easy to defend from an all-society point of view. It involves direct administrative involvement in identity retention; that is, it reflects the idea that diversity is not only to be approved of, it is to be promoted to the level of official policy. There is no evidence to suggest that any meaningful aspects of ethnicity can be held in place by outside intervention, much less ones which are visible markers (like communicative language). There is, also, no evidence that this policy—misguided though it is—is supported in any active sense by large segments of the population, minority or majority. There is the real danger that such a policy can contribute, albeit in a minor way, to an artificial extension of the life of ethnic group boundaries and, in this way, promote particularism.

All of this may be taken to indicate that the only language maintenance programmes which make sense are those which are restricted to a small and particularly group-conscious minority within a minority (see Pannu and Young, 1980); such programmes have existed, and continue to exist, both within public education systems and on a parochial basis. Their longevity is always in doubt and they cannot reasonably be viewed as any sort of basis on which to build a generally pluralistic society. It is interesting, in this connection, to note the desire to have *both* majority and minority children in maintenance bilingual programmes. This is an understandable wish, from a base-broadening perspective, but it makes the fatal error of thinking that schools can act as agents of social change in the absence of extra-educational commitment (see Smolicz, 1979, 1981).[10] If we compare the linguistic facility of European children with that of their North American counterparts, we are observing the effects of quite different social realities, and not of different school treatments. Even the products of the much-vaunted immersion programmes—in which majority children learn through a second language—may not justify the efforts. Mackey (1981) and Genesee (1981) have both suggested that the *use* made of the second-language competence is disappointing. And, after all, the implementation of what has been learned is surely an important aspect of the whole exercise.

Concluding remarks

I have spent some time here discussing the course of ethnic diversity and language shift. As well, I have considered perspectives on this process, mainly under the headings of cultural pluralism and assimilation. It is clear, I think, that all of this converges on the question of group and individual identity, and it is equally clear that this is a contentious area, peculiarly resistant to disinterested assessment. In a recent response to criticism, I noted that the emotion-laden context in which issues like pluralism, assimilation and identity are usually treated tends to produce an inability or an unwillingness to distinguish between critical and hostile stances (Edwards, 1982; see also 1980a). That is, the advocatory nature of much of the literature casts things in black and white, with-us or against-us terms. While I understand why this exists, I find it a source of continuing regret that subjective analysis so often cloaks itself in apparent objectivity.

Identity—for *all* groups—is essentially a personal matter in which people define themselves as they see fit within their circumstances. It is only firm when it has been established by those who are to hold it; efforts to influence identity which derive from outside intervention, suggestion or policy only have value when they illuminate something which already exists, but which is latent, poorly understood or badly articulated. This suggests that we must look very closely indeed when we encounter official or semi-official attempts to create social policies of identity. We are right to be sceptical from the start, since the personal elements which are the bedrock of identity are unlikely to be captured in what are usually formal, public and rather self-conscious articulations. There is, as well, the real possibility that when private elements are examined publicly they undergo substantive change. Ethnic festivals today may say more about commercial aspirations than they do about continuing and deep-seated values; attempted revival or promotion of communicative language skills cannot recapture a way of life where these were used regularly; romanticized longings after elements of the past which were willingly foregone reflect the misplaced desires of well-assimilated and successful "ethnics".

Kelman (1972) argues against "deliberate attempts by central political authorities to create a sense of national identity" (p. 200), and this seems to me a reasonable position. The import of what I have said here suggests, in fact, that his view can be extended so that for "central political authorities" we could also read "well-intentioned outsiders", "group spokesmen", "cultural ideologues", etc. The attitudes from such sources are unlikely to mesh with those of the supposed beneficiaries of identity-formation and, because of this, are unlikely to have any enduring significance. In the shorter term, of course, this can disrupt and damage that identity which *has* been forged on the basis of pragmatic judgements relating to social advantage and disadvantage. Thus, to return to Kelman, "a sense of identity ideally ought to—and, in fact, is most likely to—emerge out of a well-functioning national system that meets the needs and interests of the entire population, rather than out of deliberate attempts to create it directly" (p. 201). Perhaps some pluralists might argue that, for some groups at least, the system is *not* well functioning and that this provides the motivation for their actions. If so, it is curious that the resolution of difficulty is seen to lie in the pluralization of power (see Van den Berghe, 1967).

Put simply, attempting to ensure national well functioning by attending to particular interests is retrogressive. Given sufficient time and sufficient attention to all groups, the approach might work in theory; however, this is rather utopian and, in any event, there is no indication of any sense of such long-term planning in the writings of those who promote cultural pluralism. Blindness to the implications of pluralism, to the private–public (and communicative–symbolic) distinctions in ethnic identity, to historical precedent and practice, to the heterogeneity of attitudes and desires, and to the limitations of education—all of this means that the views of many cultural pluralists demonstrate, in Dr. Johnson's words, the triumph of hope over experience.

Point summary

It may be useful to conclude by stating the major aspects of the argument in very simple point form:

1. Ethnic diversity reflects a combination of assimilative *and* pluralistic forces. Given some degree of latitude, people engage in personal self-definition in the course of which some elements of ethnicity are retired and others retained.
2. Shifts in communicative language use reflect powerful social changes, most of them economic. Appeals for revival or restoration will not be successful if they are based essentially upon cultural grounds.
3 Evidence suggests that the majority of ethnic-group minority populations are essentially assimilationist. Only a minority within the minority are ardently pluralistic.
4. Official policies should support overall social aims and unity; this acts for the "ethnics" as much as it does for others. Within such policies, however, there should exist a wide-ranging *tolerance* for diversity.
5. Areas where social science and public policy intersect provide dangers to objectivity, and should be examined carefully for outbreaks of special pleading.
6. Education, especially of a bilingual variety, cannot be the major agent in language restoration for particular groups, nor can it promote society-wide multiculturalism or pluralism in the absence of powerful extra-educational pressures or policies.
7. In considering policies of pluralism and linguistic revival, we would do well to take a wide historical perspective. The course of social change is slow, and today's programmes may be quite insignificant in the long term; this should encourage modesty, if nothing else.
8. Identity is personal. While we can create atmospheres in which desired elements can flourish, active promotion of these elements is dubious and possibly counter-productive.
9. Continuity of identity is not necessarily dependent upon communicative language retention.

Notes

1. We see here, incidentally, how cultural pluralism and assimilation are related, and not dichotomous, notions.
2. Special cases here may be thought to include groups living in large and concentrated numbers, where the concept of "minority–majority" takes on a different aspect. Even here, though, a longer historical perspective might indicate future breakdown of segregation, and increasing assimilation—repeating (on a larger scale, perhaps, and therefore over a longer time) the experience of other groups.
3. See also Edwards (1983, in press).
4. On language suicide see Denison (1977); but also Dorian (1981).
5. Since English is often singled out, in many contexts, as the oppressive force, it is worth remembering that it too had its subordinate days. From the Norman conquest to the fifteenth century, French effectively displaced English as the "official" language, and the latter was suppressed in religion, society, school and university.
6. Fishman (*Irish Times*, 15 August 1975) called it the best national language study he had seen.
7. This includes material he published earlier (1980a, 1980b).
8. An insightful review of Rodriguez's book is that of Adler (1982).
9. For example, the *New York Times* of 3 November 1974, 28 October 1975 and 22 November 1976. See also Cummins, Chapter 3.
10. Smolicz, a proponent of cultural pluralism and an advocate of social change through education, makes quite clear his own preferences (1979, p. xix). In this, he is more open than most cultural pluralists.

References

Abramson, H. J. (1983). On the passionate study of ethnicity (Review of A. D. Smith's *The Ethnic Revival*). *Contemporary Sociology* **12**, 134–136.

Adler, S. (1982). Review of R. Rodriguez' *Hunger of Memory*. *Commentary* **74**(1), 82–84.

Aitken, A. J. (1981). Foreword. In *Minority Languages Today* (Eds E. Haugen, J. D. McClure and D. Thomson). University Press, Edinburgh.

Akenson, D. H. (1975). *A Mirror to Kathleen's Face*. McGill-Queen's University Press, Montreal.

Anderson, A. B. (1979). The survival of ethnolinguistic minorities: Canadian and comparative research. In *Language and Ethnic Relations* (Eds H. Giles and B. Saint-Jacques). Pergamon, Oxford.

Anderson, A. B. and Frideres, J. S. (1981). *Ethnicity in Canada: Theoretical Perspectives*. Butterworths, Toronto.

Berry, J., Kalin, R. and Taylor, D. (1977). *Multiculturalism and Ethnic Attitudes in Canada*. Supply & Services Canada, Ottawa.

Bethell, T. (1979). Against bilingual education. *Modern Language Journal* **63**, 276–280.

Binchy, D. A. (1945). Review of J. L. Campbell's *Gaelic and Scottish Education and Life*. *The Bell* **10**, 362–366.

Borrie, W. D. (1959). *The Cultural Integration of Immigrants*. UNESCO, Paris.

Breton, R., Reitz, J. G. and Valentine, V. (1980). *Cultural Boundaries and the Cohesion of Canada*. Institute for Research on Public Policy, Montreal.

Brooks, S. (1907). *The New Ireland*. Maunsell, Dublin.

Brown, T. (1981). *Ireland: A Social and Cultural History, 1922–79*. Collins/Fontana, Glasgow.

Bullivant, B. (1981). *The Pluralist Dilemma in Education*. George Allen & Unwin, Sydney.

Chisholm, J. M. (1983). Language and group identity. B.Sc. Thesis, St. Francis Xavier University, Antigonish, Nova Scotia.

Committee on Irish Language Attitudes Research (1975). *Report*. Government Stationery Office, Dublin.

Corcoran, T. (1916). *State Policy in Irish Education A.D. 1536 to 1816*. Fallon, Dublin.

Corcoran, T. (1928). *Education Systems in Ireland from the Close of the Middle Age: Selected Texts with Introduction*. University College, Dublin.

Curtis, E. and McDowell, R. (1968). *Irish Historical Documents 1172–1922*. Methuen, London.

Darroch, A. G. (1979). Another look at ethnicity, stratification and social mobility in Canada. *Canadian Journal of Sociology* **4**, 1–25.

de Fréine, S. (1977). The dominance of the English language in the nineteenth century. In *The English Language in Ireland* (Ed. D. Ó Muirithe). Mercier, Cork.

de Fréine, S. (1978). *The Great Silence*. Mercier, Cork.

Denison, N. (1977). Language death or language suicide? *International Journal of the Sociology of Language* **12**, 13–22.

Dinnerstein, L., Nichols, R. and Reimers, D. (1979). *Natives and Strangers*. Oxford University Press, New York.

Dinnerstein, L. and Reimers, D. (1982). *Ethnic Americans*. Harper & Row, New York.

Dorian, N. C. (1981). *Language Death*. University of Pennsylvania Press, Philadelphia.

Drake, G. (1979). Ethnicity, values and language policy in the United States. In *Language and Ethnic Relations* (Eds H. Giles and B. Saint-Jacques). Pergamon, Oxford.

Edwards, J. (1976). Current issues in bilingual education. *Ethnicity* **3**, 70–81.

Edwards, J. (1977). Ethnic identity and bilingual education. In *Language, Ethnicity and Intergroup Relations* (Ed. H. Giles). Academic Press, London, Orlando and New York.

Edwards, J. (1979). *Language and Disadvantage*. Edward Arnold, London.

Edwards, J. (1980a). Bilingual education: Facts and values. *Canadian Modern Language Review* **37**, 123–127.

Edwards, J. (1980b). Critics and criticisms of bilingual education. *Modern Language Journal* **64**, 409–415.

Edwards, J. (1981a). The social and political context of bilingual education. Paper presented to the Invitational Symposium on Multiculturalism in Education, Queen's University (Kingston).

Edwards, J. (1981b). The context of bilingual education. *Journal of Multilingual and Multicultural Development* **2**, 25–44.

Edwards, J. (1981c). Psychological and linguistic aspects of minority education. In *The Education of Minorities* (World Yearbook of Education 1981) (Eds J. Megarry, S. Nisbet and E. Hoyle). Kogan Page, London.

Edwards, J. (1982). Bilingual education revisited: A reply to Donahue. *Journal of Multilingual and Multicultural Development* **3**, 89–101.

Edwards, J. (1983). *The Irish Language: An Annotated Bibliography of Sociolinguistic Publications, 1772–1982*. Garland, New York.

Edwards, J. (in press). Irish and English in Ireland. In *Language in the British Isles* (Ed. P. Trudgill). University Press, Cambridge.

Edwards, J. (in preparation). *Language and Identity*. André Deutsch, London.

Fennell, D. (1981). Can a shrinking linguistic minority be saved? Lessons from the Irish experience. In *Minority Languages Today* (Eds E. Haugen, J. McClure and D. Thomson). University Press, Edinburgh.

Fishman, J. A. (1966). *Language Loyalty in the United States*. Mouton, The Hague.

Fishman, J. A. (1977). The social science perspective. In *Bilingual Education: Current Perspectives* (Ed. Center for Applied Linguistics). C.A.L., Arlington, Virginia.

Fishman, J. A. (1980a). Minority language maintenance and the ethnic mother tongue school. *Modern Language Journal* **64**, 167–172.

Fishman, J. A. (1980b). Bilingualism and biculturism as individual and as societal phenomena. *Journal of Multilingual and Multicultural Development* **1**, 3–15.

Gaarder, A. (1981). Review of C. Paulston's *Bilingual Education: Theories and Issues*. *Modern Language Journal* **65**, 205–206.

Genesee, F. (1981). Bilingualism and biliteracy: A study of cross-cultural contact in a bilingual community. In *The Social Psychology of Reading* (Ed. J. Edwards). Institute of Modern Languages, Silver Spring, Maryland.

Glazer, N. (1980). Toward a sociology of small ethnic groups, a discourse and discussion. *Canadian Ethnic Studies* **12**, 1–16.

Glazer, N. and Moynihan, D. (1963). *Beyond the Melting Pot*. M.I.T. Press and Harvard University Press, Cambridge, Massachusetts.

Gleason, P. (1979). Confusion compounded: The melting pot in the 1960s and 1970s. *Ethnicity* **6**, 10–20.

Gordon, M. M. (1964). *Assimilation in American Life*. Oxford University Press, New York.

Gordon, M. M. (1981). Models of pluralism: The new American dilemma. *Annals of the American Academy of Political and Social Science* **454**, 178–188.

Greeley, A. (1971). *Why Can't They Be Like Us?* Dutton, New York.

Greeley, A. (1974). *Ethnicity in the United States*. Wiley, New York.

Greeley, A. (1978). After Ellis Island. *Harper's* **257**(1542), 27–30.

Hansen, M. L. (1952). The third generation in America. *Commentary* **14**, 492–500.

Henk, M., Tomasi, S. and Baroni, G. (1972). *Pieces of a Dream*. Center for Migration Studies, New York.

Higham, J. (1975). *Send These to Me*. Atheneum, New York.

Higham, J. (1982). Current trends in the study of ethnicity in the United States. *Journal of American Ethnic History* **2**, 5–15.

Hyde, D. (1984). The necessity for de-anglicising Ireland. In *The Revival of Irish Literature* (Eds C. Duffy, G. Sigerson and D. Hyde). T. Fisher Unwin, London.

Irish National Teachers' Organization (1942). *Report of Committee of Inquiry into the Use of Irish as a Teaching Medium to Children whose Home Language is English*. I.N.T.O., Dublin.

Irish National Teachers' Organization (1947). *A Plan for Education*. I.N.T.O., Dublin.

Kedourie, E. (1961). *Nationalism*. Praeger, New York.

Kelman, H. C. (1972). Language as aid and barrier to involvement in the national system. In *Advances in the Sociology of Language* (Ed. J. A. Fishman). Mouton, The Hague.

Kiberd, D. (1979). *Synge and the Irish Language*. Macmillan, London.

Kolack, S. (1980). Lowell, an immigrant city: The old and the new. In *Sourcebook on the New Immigration* (Ed. R. S. Bryce-Laporte). Transaction Books, New Brunswick, New Jersey.

Kopan, A. T. (1974). Melting pot: Myth or reality? In *Cultural Pluralism* (Ed. E. Epps). McCutchan, Berkeley.

Lemaire, H. (1966). Franco-American efforts on behalf of the French language in New England. In *Language Loyalty in the United States* (Ed. J. A. Fishman). Mouton, The Hague.

Mackey, W. F. (1981). Safeguarding language in schools. *Language and Society* **4**, 10–14.

Macnamara, J. (1971). Successes and failures in the movement for the restoration of Irish. In *Can Language be Planned?* (Eds J. Rubin and B. Jernudd). East-West Center Press, Honolulu.

Mann, A. (1979). *The One and the Many*. University Press, Chicago.

Morrison, J. and Zabusky, C. F. (1980). *American Mosaic*. Meridian, New York.

Murphy, C. (1981). The crisis in Irish. *Irish Times*, 25 May.

Novak, M. (1971). *The Rise of the Unmeltable Ethnics*. Macmillan, New York.

O'Bryan, K. G., Reitz, J. G. and Kuplowska, O. M. (1976). *Non-official Languages: A Study in Canadian Multiculturalism*. Supply & Services Canada, Ottawa.

Ó Conaire, B. (1973). Flann O'Brien, "An Béal Bocht" and other Irish matters. *Irish University Review* **3**, 121–140.

Ó Danachair, C. (1969). The Gaeltacht. In *A View of the Irish Language* (Ed. B. Ó Cuív). Government Stationery Office, Dublin.

O'Doherty, E. F. (1958). Bilingual school policy. *Studies* **47**, 259–268.

Ornstein, J. (1979). Bilingual education—boon or boondoggle? *New Jersey Education Association Review* **53**(2), 16–18.

Pannu, R. and Young, J. (1980). Ethnic schools in three Canadian cities: A study in multiculturalism. *Alberta Journal of Educational Research* **26**, 247–261.

Parrillo, V. N. (1980). *Strangers to These Shores*. Houghton Mifflin, Boston.

Pienkos, D. (1977). Ethnic orientations among Polish Americans. *International Migration Review* **11**, 350–362.

Porter, J. (1965). *The Vertical Mosaic*. University Press, Toronto.

Porter, J. (1972). Dilemmas and contradictions of a multi-ethnic society. *Transactions of the Royal Society of Canada* **10**(Series 4), 193–205.

Porter, J. (1975). Ethnic pluralism in Canadian perspective. In *Ethnicity: Theory and Experience* (Eds N. Glazer and D. Moynihan). Harvard University Press, Cambridge, Massachusetts.

Price, G. (1979). The present position and viability of minority languages. In *The Future of Cultural Minorities* (Eds A. E. Alcock, B. K. Taylor and J. M. Welton). Macmillan, London.

Ravitch, D. (1976). On the history of minority group education in the United States. *Teachers College Record* **78**, 213–228.

Ravitch, D. (1981). Forgetting the questions: The problem of educational reform. *American Scholar* **50**, 329–340.

Reitz, J. G. (1980). *The Survival of Ethnic Groups*. McGraw-Hill Ryerson, Toronto.

Riesman, D. (1965). *Individualism Reconsidered*. Free Press, New York.

Riley, G. A. (1975). Language loyalty and ethnocentrism in the Guamanian speech community. *Anthropological Linguistics* **17**, 286–292.

Rodriguez, R. (1980a). Aria: A memoir of a bilingual childhood. *American Scholar* **50**, 25–42.

Rodriguez, R. (1980b). An education in language. In *The State of the Language* (Eds L. Michaels and C. Ricks). University of California Press, Berkeley.

Rodriguez, R. (1983). *Hunger of Memory*. Bantam, New York.

Rumilly, R. (1958). *Histoire des Franco-Américains*. L'Union Saint-Jean-Baptiste d'Amérique, Montreal.

Schrag, P. (1971). *The Decline of the WASP*. Simon & Schuster, New York.

Seelye, H. (1977). Sociology and education. In *Bilingual Education: Current Perspectives* (Ed. Center for Applied Linguistics). C.A.L., Arlington, Virginia.

Smolicz, J. J. (1979). *Culture and Education in a Plural Society*. Curriculum Development Centre, Canberra.

Smolicz, J. J. (1981). Culture, ethnicity and education: Multiculturalism in a plural society. In *The Education of Minorities* (World Yearbook of Education 1981) (Eds J. Megarry, S. Nisbet and E. Hoyle). Kogan Page, London.

Sowell, T. (1978). Ethnicity in a changing America. *Daedalus* **107**, 213–237.

Stein, H. and Hill, R. (1977). *The Ethnic Imperative*. Pennsylvania State University Press, University Park, Pennsylvania.

Steinberg, S. (1981). *The Ethnic Myth*. Atheneum, New York.

Teitelbaum, H. and Hiller, R. (1977). The legal perspective. In *Bilingual Education: Current Perspectives* (Ed. Center for Applied Linguistics). C.A.L., Arlington, Virginia.

Toynbee, A. (1956). *A Study of History* (Abridgement by D. C. Somervell). Oxford University Press, London.

Vallee, F. G. (1981). The sociology of John Porter: Ethnicity as anachronism. *Canadian Review of Sociology and Anthropology* **18**, 639–650.

Van den Berghe, P. (1967). *Race and Racism*. Wiley, New York.

Wall, M. (1969). The decline of the Irish language. In *A View of the Irish Language* (Ed. B. Ó Cuív). Government Stationery Office, Dublin.

Weinfeld, M. (1978). Myth and reality in the Canadian mosaic. *McGill University Papers in Migration and Ethnicity* **78**(3).

Weinreich, U. (1974). *Languages in Contact*. Mouton, The Hague.

Williams, G. (1981). The problematic in the sociology of language (Review of *International Journal of the Sociology of Language*, 1980, **26**). *Journal of Multilingual and Multicultural Development* **2**, 219–225.

Name Index

Subject Index